*Financial Mail
on Sunday*

Complete Guide to Personal Finance

JEFF Prestridge has been personal finance editor of *Financial Mail on Sunday* since 1994. Before that, he was personal finance editor of the *Sunday Telegraph* (1990–1994) and deputy personal finance editor of monthly financial magazine *Money Management* (1987–1990). In his 20-year career, Jeff has also starred as an audit clerk, a stocktaker, a self-employed businessman typing up manuscripts for students and an economist with Bristol & West building society. He has also been a fork-lift truck driver, a dustman and a barman.

During his 15 years in journalism, Jeff has won a series of awards for his personal finance journalism, ranging from awards for campaigning journalism, business scoops, all-round personal finance knowledge and his ability to explain personal finance in simple plain English. In a nutshell, Jeff puts the consumer, not the personal finance industry, first.

Unlike many other personal finance journalists, Jeff has completed the Financial Planning Certificate – a series of three exams which independent financial advisers must pass if they want to provide financial advice to the public.

MONEY

'A commodity that's better than poverty,
if only for financial reasons.'

Woody Allen

*Financial Mail
on Sunday*

Complete Guide to Personal Finance

Jeff Prestridge

RANDOM HOUSE

BUSINESS BOOKS

First published in 2001 by Random House Business Books,
Random House, 20 Vauxhall Bridge Road, London SW1V 2SA

Random House Australia (Pty) Limited
20 Alfred Street, Milsons Point,
Sydney, New South Wales 2061, Australia

Random House New Zealand Limited
18 Poland Road, Glenfield,
Auckland 10, New Zealand

Random House (Pty) Limited
Endulini, 5a Jubilee Road, Parktown 2193, South Africa

The Random House Group Limited Reg. No. 954009

Papers used by Random House are natural, recyclable
products made from wood grown in sustainable forests.
The manufacturing processes conform to the environmental
regulations of the country of origin.

ISBN 0 7126 8002 0

Companies, institutions and other organisations wishing to make
bulk purchases of books published by Random House should
contact their local bookstore or Random House direct:

Special Sales Director
Random House, 20 Vauxhall Bridge Road, London SW1V 2SA
Tel 020 7840 8470   Fax 020 7828 6681

www.randomhouse.co.uk
businessbooks@randomhouse.co.uk

Typeset in Sabon by MATS, Southend-on-Sea, Essex
Printed and bound in Great Britain by
Mackays of Chatham PLC, Chatham, Kent

Dedication

THIS book is dedicated to the most important people in my life – Stan the Man, the Brandy Man; the ageless Helen of Sutton Coldfield; the wonderful Susan (my long-suffering wife), Matthew (the next Bob Taylor), Mark (Baldrick) and James (Buster); Plop (the dancing queen), Michael, Chris and Hannah; Si Pie (Marathon Man), Joy, Ossie and Sonia; David, Lisa and Tilly; Oma, Opa and the flying fell runner Stephen; and the three 'J's – Josh, Jason and Johnny. Finally, but not least, Joaney Baby, the much-missed Den and Julie.

Boing! Boing!

Contents

Acknowledgements

I HAVE to be honest with you and say that this book has been a painful undertaking. Personal finance is an intimidating subject and to attempt to write the 'definitive' book is a Herculean task.

The fact that I have managed to complete it is down to a number of key people. Firstly, I have to thank David Sinclair, ex-editor of *Financial Mail*, for coming up with the idea of a personal finance book. Without him, there would simply be no book.

Secondly, I would like to thank Jo Bowlby and Scott Gormley for encouraging me throughout the many months I have been putting this book together. Jo, my agent, has been a brick and has gently cajoled me into delivering when others would have simply given up the ghost. As for Scott, ex-assistant editor of *Financial Mail*, he is simply a maestro.

Thirdly, I would like to thank Clare Smith at Random House for her perseverance. And of course the personal finance team at *Financial Mail* who have coped marvellously while I have struggled to put words onto paper. Sally Hamilton, Neil Simpson, Stephen Womack, Clare Hall, Toby Walne and Cathy Simmonds (now enjoying life at KPMG) are all personal finance superstars in their own right. Ben Laurance, editor of *Financial Mail* has also been a brick. Thanks to Alicia Williams for checking all the phone numbers.

Finally, I would like to thank all those people who proof-read individual chapters. But a big special thanks goes to Alan Mudd of Savills Private Finance Ltd in Manchester who has read every single word of this book and given me great advice. Muddy, you are a top drawer adviser – long may you thrive.

Foreword

JOURNALISM

'The only thinkable alternative to working.'

Jeffrey Barnard

PERSONAL finance is an integral part of our lives. However, it can intimidate us. I see it for myself every week when reading through the letters I receive as personal finance editor of *Financial Mail on Sunday*. Educated people, professional people, are often the authors of these letters – dentists, doctors and policemen. They have managed to come to grips with dentistry, the workings of the body or the law of the land but when it comes to tackling the policy documents of an insurance plan, they are totally bewildered.

I am not surprised. For far too many years the financial services industry has smothered itself in jargon, essentially to bewilder the consumer and conceal poor value for money. Successive governments have not helped, making some areas of personal finance such as tax and pensions impenetrable, even to some of the finest brains in Britain. Indeed, on occasion they have been instrumental in causing some of the biggest problems to impact upon the personal finance world. A good example is pensions misselling.

It is against this backdrop that I have written this book on personal finance. Wherever possible, I have tried to cut through the personal finance verbiage and describe complex areas in simple, good old plain English. It hasn't been an easy task. Indeed, I have spent many a night burning the midnight oil and banging my head against the study wall in an attempt to penetrate the deepest bowels of the personal finance world.

This book will not solve your personal finance worries – that is completely down to you. But if it helps to expand your knowledge and understanding of the personal finance world, or if it provides you with just one tip to go out and improve your personal finance lot, the book's aim will have been fulfilled.

Please let me know what you think about the book. I plan to update it on a regular basis and make it the *Encyclopaedia Britannica* of the personal finance world. Do drop me a line.

Good personal finance hunting.

Introduction

MONEY

> 'The only likeable thing about rich people.'
>
> *Lady Astor*

THIS book is designed to arm you with enough information to go out with confidence and make key financial decisions that will shape your financial livelihood throughout your life.

It is split into key sections – banking, tax, borrowing, insurance, pensions and savings. These are the cornerstones of the personal finance world. Get these right and you will be well on the way to a secure financial future.

These key personal finance foundations are then accompanied by a whole host of good personal finance advice – from top tips through to useful addresses and top providers. No stone is left unturned which means everything, from cycle insurance through to spread betting, is given an airing.

I defy anyone to dip into this book and not come out with something which will enable them to be more financially astute.

1

Choosing a Bank Account

BANK

'A place that will lend you money if you can prove that you don't need it.'

Bob Hope

BANKS may not be everybody's cup of tea but you will not get far in the financial world without a bank account – or more accurately a current account. A bank account is a key personal finance building block, not only providing you with a straightforward and secure way of looking after your financial affairs but also enabling you to obtain access to other key financial products such as a mortgage or a credit card.

Unfortunately, millions of people still do not have a bank account. If you are one of these people, you should seriously consider opening an account. If you don't have an account because you have been rejected by banks in the past, try applying again, maybe through another provider or one of the new bank players.

Alternatively, it may well be worth applying for a bank account operated by the Post Office. This account, in the process of being launched, is targeted primarily at people who have previously been excluded from banking facilities in the past. It is commonly known as the Universal Bank.

Although bank accounts are primarily offered by the big high street banks, don't get caught into the trap of thinking that the likes of Barclays, HSBC, Lloyds TSB and Royal Bank of Scotland should be your first port of call. Current accounts are now offered by a number of former building societies such as Halifax and Woolwich (now part of Barclays bank). They are also provided by many of the country's leading building societies such as Nationwide and Norwich & Peterborough.

Indeed, many of these newish entrants provide a far better banking deal than the high street banks.

Some key questions and answers

Q What is a bank account?

A In a nutshell, it is a current account with a financial institution that provides banking services. It will enable you to make payments to other people or institutions as well as provide you with somewhere to deposit your earnings or income. There are also bank accounts for small businesses offering similar services.

Q Why bother? Can't I just keep my money under the bed at home and pay for everything by cash?

A Some people still prefer the bed to the bank but it is a fact of life that a bank account is a must for people who want to go on and own a home and have access to important personal finance tools such as a credit card. Bank accounts are also a more secure way to conduct your financial affairs than keeping large amounts of cash at home. And if these points haven't convinced you, it is a fact that many bank accounts are now far more user-friendly than before, furnishing account holders with interest on credit balances (unheard of a few years ago) and a whole array of payment facilities.

Q When I open a bank account, what will the bank provide me with?

A Most accounts should provide you with the following banking services:

1. A CHEQUE BOOK. Although banks are increasingly discouraging the use of cheques, they remain an essential payment tool. They provide you with a safe way of making payments, especially through the post.

2. PAYING-IN SLIPS. These allow you to make deposits into your account. Some banks provide you with a personalised paying-in book. Others incorporate paying-in slips – again personalised – into the back of your cheque book.

3. A CHEQUE GUARANTEE CARD. This bit of plastic will ensure that any cheque you write will be honoured by your bank – up to the agreed limit stated on the card which should be £50, £100 or even £250. It will also allow you to pay for goods by cheque when out shopping. These cards give you payment power and some banks do not make them available until after a short probationary period during which you must demonstrate an ability to keep your account in good order.

4. A CASH CARD. This will enable you to withdraw cash from a cash machine (an automated teller machine or ATM) which will then be debited from your account. When you are issued with the card, your bank will furnish you with a PIN number. It is this PIN number you then use to withdraw cash from the ATM. Cash withdrawals can usually be made from any cash machine – and many cash machines abroad – although you may be charged for the privilege. As a general rule, if you use your own bank's cash machine, you will not incur a withdrawal charge. However, if you use a competitor's cash machine, you may end up paying a fixed charge though this is less likely than a year ago.

5. A PAYMENT OR DEBIT CARD. These cards are in many ways a cheque guarantee card and a cash card rolled into one. Provided

you have enough money in your account, you can make payments of any amount via a debit card. You can also use the card to obtain cash, usually at a supermarket, via a process called 'cashback'. There will usually be a limit on the amount of money you can withdraw in this way.

6. THE ALL IN ONE MULTI-FUNCTION CARD. Many banks now provide all-singing, all-dancing cards which serve as a debit card, cheque guarantee card and cash card all in one.

7. STANDING ORDER. All bank accounts offer standing order facilities – these allow you to make regular payments to an organisation simply by filling in one form. The form is provided by the recipient of your funds and completed and signed by yourself. Your bank then takes an agreed sum from your account on a set date, typically every month, quarter or year. Many people set up standing orders so that a regular amount can be taken from their account to pay regular premiums on home insurance or a savings scheme. A standing order can be cancelled simply by writing to your bank and instructing them to stop further payments.

8. A DIRECT DEBIT. This is another way of making regular payments from your account with the minimum of paperwork. Unlike standing orders, however, direct debits enable you to pay regular bills of both a fixed or variable amount. Also, you instruct the organisation to take payments from your account rather than tell your bank to make payments on your behalf as with a standing order. Direct debits are often used to pay utility bills such as gas and electricity bills or to meet the minimum payment on a credit card bill. A direct debit can be cancelled by writing to the company taking your payments.

9. BANK STATEMENTS. Banks are obliged to furnish you with regular monthly statements showing all the transactions on your account and the amount of funds you have in it. As well as enabling you to keep on top of your finances, a bank statement will allow you to identify any mistakes – yes, banks do make mistakes from time to time – and get them rectified straight away.

10. OVERDRAFT FACILITIES. As well as providing you with a convenient home for your money, most current accounts offer so-called overdraft facilities. This means you can use your account to borrow money from the bank. There are two types of overdraft – the 'authorised' overdraft where you agree with the bank a set limit on any borrowings and the 'unauthorised' overdraft where you slip into the red without first telling your bank or you exceed your authorised overdraft limit. Charges on both types of overdraft are high but especially so on unauthorised overdrafts – they are best avoided.

Q OK, I am now convinced about the merits of a bank account. How do I open one?

A First, you will have to obtain an application form from your intended bank. At the same time, the bank will provide you with a written outline of the account's key features including charges. It is imperative you go through this with a fine-tooth comb. If you don't understand any of the details, ask.

The bank will also ask you for identification – such as a current and valid passport, a national identity card or a full UK driving licence. It will also ask you to prove that you live at the address you have given on your application form. Usually, a bank will ask for two separate forms of address proof, provided by a gas or electricity bill, a council tax statement or an income tax statement.

Q Is it possible to open a joint account?

A Yes, although you will both have to fill in the application form and provide relevant personal details. You will also be asked to sign an additional declaration confirming that you agree to be joint owners of the money in the account and jointly responsible for any debts. This means your bank can recover money to pay off debts from either of you irrespective of who actually caused the debt in the first place.

Q Can I run my bank account via the Internet or by telephone?

A Yes. Most big banks now offer current accounts which can be run exclusively by the internet or by telephone. Indeed, many of the big banks have set up separate brands to handle customers who want to run their current accounts via the Net or by telephone. They include Abbey National (Cahoot), Co-operative (Smile) and Halifax (Intelligent Finance). The pioneer in telephone banking was First Direct, part of HSBC. Now, most current accounts can be telephone operated.

One must also not overlook 'PC' banking and digital TV banking. With PC banking, your bank provides you with software which you install on your PC and you then use in conjunction with a modem and a secure phone line to do your banking. In this way you can do most of your banking from the comfort of your home. Royal Bank of Scotland has led the field in this area although PC banking is being overtaken by Internet banking which is seen as more flexible.

Digital TV banking is still in its infancy but customers can use the usual sound and picture TV format to check their bank balance and monitor transactions. They can also go on-line to do transactions. HSBC is a pioneer in this area.

Q Why bother with the Net or telephone?

A Bank branches are fast disappearing, which means it is becoming increasingly difficult for many people, especially those in rural communities, to do all their banking via a local branch. The big plus factor of telephone and Internet banking is that most are 24-hour based. That means you can do your banking when you want to rather than be dictated to by bank branch opening hours. Over the phone, or via the Net, you can easily carry out simple banking tasks such as checking your account balance, checking the most recent transactions on your account, ordering holiday money and ordering a new cheque book or paying-in book. If banking over the Internet, seek assurances from your bank that the service is safe, secure and confidential – there have been a number of problems.

Q It is great news about the number of current accounts on offer. But what is a current bank account going to cost me?

A As a general rule, you will not incur charges on your bank account provided you stay in credit. The only exceptions to this rule are if your bank charges you for cash withdrawals at cash machines outside its own network (a rarity). Also, most banks levy charges if you ask for non-standard services such as a duplicate bank statement (needed, for example, if you've mislaid a statement) or request that a cheque you have written be stopped.

Where the banks make their big money is if you go into overdraft territory – dipping into the red. If you have spoken to your bank beforehand and requested an overdraft, which has then been granted, you will pay interest (usually double-digit interest) on any borrowings. You may also incur a flat charge – typically levied per month or per quarter – as well as an initial arrangement fee for the granting of the overdraft.

However, dip into the red without telling the bank and the charges mount up even more. As well as interest charges (higher than those levied on authorised overdrafts), the bank may well insist that you pay a fee every time you use your account as well as pay a fee for the sending out of the overdraft letter. It is also possible that the bank may put a stop on you making cash withdrawals. It may also 'bounce' i.e. refuse to honour any cheques you make out which are not backed by a cheque guarantee card as well as refuse to make payments set up on direct debit or via standing order. Go down this route and charges really do rack up. Some banks, for example, may charge you in the region of £25 for returning a cheque to you. Don't get yourself into this situation.

There are a few bank accounts now available where customers pay a regular service charge – usually monthly – irrespective of whether the account is in credit or debit. Barclays and its Additions current account has led the way in this field with copycat versions being launched by rivals. The idea is that in return for this service charge, customers get a package of account perks. These perks vary but typically include preferential overdraft rates, legal helplines and free insurance. Such accounts are often referred to as 'packaged' accounts.

Q In choosing a bank current account, what key factors should I consider?

A Convenience and cost are the two major issues. In terms of convenience, you need to find an account that will give you ready access to your money. For some people this may mean an account offering a large number of cash machines near to home or work or access to a nearby branch. For others, it may mean 24-hour telephone banking. In terms of cost, you need to compare the cost of operating various bank accounts, both in the black and the red. Moneyfacts, based in Norwich, Norfolk, provides full details on all current accounts offered. This information provides an excellent starting point for anyone looking to open or change bank accounts. Of course, asking friends is also a good way of finding out about banks which offer a good current account backed by satisfactory service.

Q What happens if a bank turns me down after applying for an account?

A Don't despair. Banks are within their rights to reject your custom – and in most instances don't have to tell you why they have given you the proverbial two fingers. Some banks will turn you down simply because you have failed to agree to pay a regular amount of money, such as a salary, into the account. Others may turn you down because they used a credit reference agency to check up on your credit worthiness and found you lacking. If a bank turns you down in this way, it has to tell you it has done so.

Q Once my bank account is up and running, can I expect a certain level of service from my provider?

A Yes. All leading providers of current accounts now adhere to the so-called 'banking code'. This voluntary code lays down minimum standards of good banking practice and outlines your responsibilities as a customer and the bank's as a provider. In a nutshell, the code ensures your bank will treat you in a fair way – although the code will not stop it clobbering you financially if you start going into the red without telling them first. Your bank should furnish you with a copy of the banking code. Alternatively, you can get one from the Banking Codes Standards Board, 33 St James Square, London SW1Y 4JS (020 7661 9691: website: www.bankingcode.org.uk).

Q What if I have a complaint against my bank? What should I do?

A You need to put your complaint in writing. Your bank is then duty bound to consider your complaint and to provide an answer. If the answer proves unsatisfactory, you then have the right to take your case to the Banking Ombudsman or the Building Societies Ombudsman dependent upon who is the supplier of your account. When dealing with your complaint, your bank or building society must inform you of your right to take your complaint to an ombudsman. Both the bank and building societies ombudsman schemes have the right to make awards up to £100,000 which are binding on banks but not so on building societies. However, it is extremely rare for building societies to reject the ombudsman's decision. These two ombudsman schemes are being replaced by the Financial Ombudsman Service.

Q Once I have set up an account, can I then switch if I am unhappy?

A Yes, and more people are now switching banks because of new players in the market. Switching accounts is not difficult although it can prove more laborious than you imagine. Your best approach is to open your new account before closing your existing one. By doing this, you will not find yourself in an embarrassing situation where you have no banking facilities for a while, thereby not being able to get hold of cash or have access to a cheque book.

In moving accounts, remember that you will have to contact companies with whom you have direct debit arrangements and ask them for a new mandate, thereby ensuring payments are taken from the new account. You will also have to ensure that your employer is given details of your new account so that your salary can be directed into it. New standing orders will have to be set up with your new current account provider and the old ones cancelled with your previous bank.

You will also have to return any cash cards and cheque guarantee cards to your old bank account provider.

Some banks, following pressure from the regulators, have now quickened up their transfer procedures for people wishing to move their accounts away.

Dos and Don'ts

- **DO** complain if you think you have been unfairly charged by your bank or the level of service offered is unsatisfactory. Complain in writing and complain promptly – don't sit on your hands. Banks are prepared to listen and will waive charges if you put up a convincing case. If your bank provides you with an unconvincing response, you then have the right to take your case before the Banking or Building Societies Ombudsman. These schemes are being amalgamated into the Financial Ombudsman Service.

- **DO** remember that some bank accounts now pay interest on credit balances. It is worth checking them out – don't accept that a current account always pays you 0.1% interest on credit balances. A postal-based current account is likely to pay more than a branch-based current account.

- **DO** contact your bank straight away if you think you may be running into difficulties with your account. Most banks are flexible and understanding and will provide temporary or long-term overdraft facilities. However, if you don't talk to your bank, you do run the risk of incurring heavy penalties such as sky-high interest charges and daily account handling charges. In some instances banks will freeze your account. So speak to them before they write to you. Remember, don't expect your bank manager to read your mind or know about your change in financial circumstances.

- **DO** remember that any interest you earn on your current account could be subject to tax. Interest will be credited to your account net of 20% tax. If you are a basic rate taxpayer, there is no further tax to pay. If you are a higher rate taxpayer, you will be liable for a further 20% tax. Starting rate taxpayers (those paying 10% tax) can reclaim 10% of tax already deducted while non-taxpayers can claim back all the tax or apply to have their interest credited gross. Your bank should provide you with an annual interest summary detailing how much interest you have received. You can use this to fill in your tax return detailing the income received from savings and the tax already paid.

- **DO** keep details of any correspondence you have with your bank. This includes the names of bank staff you talk to and the dates of contact. This will prove invaluable in following up problems.

- **DO** get to grips with the bank charges levied on your account before you become a victim of them. Providers of bank accounts are not in business as charities and therefore are looking for every opportunity to apply charges. As already stated, the general rule you should observe is: keep your account in credit and the bank will find it difficult to apply charges. Break this rule, by going into overdraft, and you will soon experience a whole phalanx of charges, some of them hefty. You will also incur bank charges if you ask for non-standard services such as a duplicate bank statement, stopping a cheque or requesting a banker's draft. The bank should supply you with a list detailing all these charges – don't bin it, file it.

- **DO** remember that overdraft rates are variable and can increase if interest rates in the general economy are rising.

- **DO** remember that overdrafts are different to bank loans. With an overdraft, there is no set repayment programme – your bank simply allows you to borrow up to an agreed limit but it can ask for the money back at will. With a bank loan, you obtain the loan proceeds and then agree to repay a fixed monthly amount over an agreed time period.

- **DO** double-check your bank's stance on cash machine charges before you start using your cash card willy-nilly in order to get cash. Some banks and building societies (notably Nationwide and the Co-operative) allow customers to take cash from anyone's cash machine without charging for the service. Other banks may charge customers a fee for using a competitor's cash machine although such fees are now a rarity. Your bank should tell you which cash machines are fee-free.

- **DO** double-check your bank's stance on so-called 'clearing'. Many banks will not allow you to withdraw money against a cheque paid into your account until the cheque has cleared – in other words, until your bank has received funds from the bank which issued the cheque. This process can take up to three days. Withdrawing money against an uncleared cheque may result in you incurring account charges or even worse having your own cheques bounced.

- **DO** take care in running your bank account. Do not keep your cheque book and cheque guarantee card together and do not allow anyone else to use your personal identification number (PIN). Also, inform your bank straight away if you discover or suspect that your cheque book, cheque guarantee card or cash card has been stolen.

- **DO** always write your cheques in ink. Writing cheques in pencil means you lay yourself open to people altering your cheques to suit themselves. Also, try to remember to fill in your cheque stub – it will enable you to check your bank statement when you receive it.

- **DO** ensure that cheques made out to you will be paid into your account by your bank. If the amount in words and figures differ, the bank will not accept it. Nor will it accept dated cheques (those made out more than six months ago) or those made out to you but with your name misspelt.

- **DO** provide your full account details when you write to your bank with a query. You should furnish them with the full account name and the account number. This will ensure your query is handled promptly.

- **DO** try to keep a record of money going in and out of your account. Although this can prove tedious, it will ensure you do not end up going overdrawn without authorisation.

- **DO** scrutinise your bank statements. Banks do make mistakes but unless you point them out, they will usually not be rectified. Common errors arise with regard to standing orders and direct debits where the wrong amount is taken from your account. Your bank will correct errors – but you have to tell them.

- **DON'T** have lots of money sitting in your current account. If you have surplus funds, you are far better off putting them in a savings account where you will get a half-decent rate of interest. Although some current accounts now pay interest on credit balances, the interest rates available are not as competitive as on many savings accounts offered by banks, building societies and new savings players such as insurance companies and leading retailers such as Tesco and Sainsbury.

- **DON'T** sit on your hands if you think you are getting a poor deal from your bank account. If you are unhappy with the way your account is being managed, shop around. Current account providers are far more bountiful than they were five years ago – and many of the new players are offering a superior service to traditional players.

- **DON'T** feel obliged to buy other financial products from your bank. High street banks may be masters at running bank accounts but when it comes to other products such as unit trusts or credit cards, they invariably provide mediocre value for money. Indeed, when it comes to insurance, value for money flies out of the bank window. You are better off looking elsewhere.

- **DON'T** sign a cheque until you have filled in the name of the payee and the amount. Incomplete signed cheques are a tempting acquisition for the unscrupulous.

- **DON'T** go Internet banking simply because it is the height of banking fashion and many banks want you to go down such a route. Internet banking is fine for those people who like to do their banking via a computer and from the comfort of their home. But it is not for everybody. If you go down the Internet route, ensure the bank account will not be too restrictive. Ask, for example, whether it will provide you with a cash card, thereby enabling you to withdraw cash with ease. For many people, 'bricks and mortar' Internet banking is the best option. This is where high street banks allow you to do your banking over the Net as well as use their branch network or the telephone.

Did you know?

- **DID** you know that some banks now provide so-called fee-free, interest-free overdraft buffer zones? These allow customers to go overdrawn without incurring any charges. It is well worth asking your bank if they provide such a facility. Although the zone is typically no more than £100 (occasionally as high as £500), it is a welcome comfort factor.

- **DID** you know that many high street banks have now linked up with the Post Office, enabling bank customers to conduct basic banking services?

- **DID** you know that your bank has to give you 14 days' warning of any charges to be taken from your account? Such pre-notification of charges is part of the banking code.

- **DID** you know that most bank accounts offer a range of extra services? These may include the provision of foreign currency for your holidays, automated same-day transfer, which enables you to put money into another person's account straight away without going through the clearing system, and eurocheques, enabling you to write your own cheques abroad. Although most of these services will cost you extra, they are worth finding out about.

- **DID** you know that banks now allow you to select your own personal identification number? This should help you to remember your PIN when withdrawing cash from a cash machine.

- **DID** you know that if your card is fraudulently misused before you have informed your bank of its loss or theft, you will not have to pay more than £50 of any loss?

- **DID** you know that most cheques are pre-printed with the words 'account payee' or 'A/C payee'? This means the cheque can only be paid into the account written on the cheque, thereby making it extremely difficult for someone else to bank it.

- **DID** you know that you are more likely to get divorced than change your bank account? If you are unhappy with your bank, don't sit on your hands. Do something about it.

- **DID** you know that you cannot stop a cheque you have written if it is backed by a cheque guarantee card?

- **DID** you know that if you set up a direct debit with a specific company, the company is obliged to meet certain conditions designed to give you a level of assurance? If the amount to be taken from your account is due to change, the company is obliged to give you advance warning – usually 10 days – of the increase. So, for example, if the premiums on your term assurance are designed to increase each year in line with inflation, and you pay for them by direct debit, the insurance company should write to you once a year informing you of the new premiums to be taken from your bank account.

Also, if an error is made, either by your bank or the company taking the debit, you are guaranteed a full and immediate refund from your bank of the amount paid.

Finally, you can cancel a direct debit by writing to the provider of your current account. If you do this, it also makes sense to write to the company whose direct debit you wish to cancel.

So what now?

- **FOR** anyone choosing a bank account, either for the first time or because of a wish to switch, *Moneyfacts* magazine (01603 476476) is the best starting point. It lists details on all the current bank accounts available and enables you to make comparisons on key features.

  For more general information on banks, the British Bankers' Association has produced a series of informative fact sheets on banking – everything from banks and credit reference agencies through to switching accounts. Contact the BBA at Pinners Hall, 105–108 Old Broad Street, London EC2N 1EX (020 7216 8801), website: http:/www.bba.org.uk.

2
Homes and Mortgages

HOME

'The place where, when you have to
go there, they have to take you in.'

Robert Frost

Choosing a mortgage

BUYING a home is the biggest commitment you will ever make in your life. Get this decision right and you are well on the way to laying down solid financial foundations.

Most people buy their home with a mortgage. A mortgage is the longest financial commitment you will make, typically extending over 25 years of your life. However, the mortgage maze has never been more complicated. Over the past five years, the market has undergone a massive transformation – new players have taken their place on the financial scene and new types of mortgage present an increasing choice for home loan-seekers.

Thankfully, the days when hopeful borrowers had to queue outside a local building society for a loan have long gone. But in place of the queues there is now almost a mortgage glut. Banks, insurance companies, so-called centralised lenders and other personal finance players are all vying for your business and offering a wide range of loan schemes. Add a thriving remortgage market – where a borrower changes lender to arrange a better deal – and it is no surprise that many people find the mortgage maze a daunting process.

Yet do not despair – obtaining the right mortgage is possible provided that you follow a few basic steps.

Q I want a loan to buy the home of my dreams. Where do I start?

A The key area to sort out first of all is affordability. There is absolutely no point borrowing more than you can afford. If you do, you may end up with the home of your dreams, but also with recurring financial nightmares while you scramble together enough money every month to meet your mortgage commitment.

Q So how do I make sure I do not end up with a mortgage that will cripple me financially?

A Most lenders will help by making sure you do not overburden yourself financially. When assessing your borrowing ability, a lender will take five key factors into account – your income, existing debts such as credit cards or other loans, the amount of deposit you have available, your past credit record and your employment status.

1. Income

Most lenders use a method known as an income multiplier to calculate how much they are prepared to lend. A 'three-plus-one' multiplier basis allows a lender to advance an amount equivalent to three times the main salary plus one times the secondary income.

So if a couple have respective salaries of £40,000 and £26,000, the lender would be prepared to advance a maximum £146,000. However, an alternative lender might use a 'two-and-a-half-times-joint' multiplier, which means that the couple will be allowed to borrow £165,000.

The income a lender is prepared to take into account varies. But as a general rule, income that is guaranteed or has been received regularly in the past will be considered. In contrast, income that is not guaranteed, such as occasional overtime, will probably be ignored.

The lender will also need proof of your income and will probably ask for recent pay slips or previous P60s – forms from your employers detailing your pay in past tax years. It may also write to your employer in order to gauge how secure your employment is. If you are self-employed you will probably have to produce at least three years' audited accounts to prove your income, though some lenders are more flexible and will simply write to your accountant requesting confirmation of your income and your ability to repay the mortgage.

2. Existing financial commitments

If you have outstanding loans or credit card bills, a lender will reduce the sum it is prepared to lend you based on your income. This is because there is already a financial strain on your household budget and the lender does not want you to be overstretched. How much it reduces the loan amount depends on the size of your existing debts. Lenders tend to adopt one of two approaches – they will either reduce the advance by the size of the outstanding debt or they will recalculate the permitted maximum loan taking into account the monthly cost of a borrower's existing credit.

For example, take our couple with respective salaries of £40,000 and £26,000 and a lender prepared to lend on a 'three-plus-one' basis. If they have an existing loan of £3,600 that costs £80 per month, the lender could reduce its maximum loan of £146,000 by £3,600 and allow the couple to borrow £142,400. Alternatively, the lender would calculate the monthly cost of the couple's maximum loan (£146,000) and deduct from it the monthly cost of the credit – £80. This reduced amount would be the monthly mortgage repayment that the lender would allow and the maximum mortgage would be based on this.

3. Size of deposit

Though some lenders will allow you to borrow a sum equivalent to 100% of the value of your dream home, deals such as these are the exception rather than the norm. Most lenders require a deposit of between 5% and 10% of the value of the home. The bigger the deposit, the more favourably a lender will look upon you and a wider range of mortgage deals will be available to you.

4. Credit history

If you have a chequered financial history you will find it difficult to obtain a loan from a mainstream lender. When considering your mortgage application a lender will check whether you have previous mortgage arrears, have had a county court judgement recorded against you or have a bad credit record. Some lenders will tolerate past financial indiscretions provided that you declare them openly – in other words, they don't find out first – and your explanations are satisfactory.

5. Employment status

Though lenders are more aware of the increasingly flexible jobs market, they prefer to lend to people who have displayed job stability in the past or who can show a defined career path. They are less partial to people who constantly change jobs or who have big gaps in their employment history.

Q Fine, I'm eligible for a mortgage. Which one do I choose?

A There are two key decisions you have to make. First, you need to determine what type of mortgage you require. Once you have decided that, you need to choose an interest rate option with which you feel comfortable. Obviously, these decisions need to be made in the context of your financial situation – that is, the amount you can truly afford to earmark for a home loan.

Q What types of mortgage are there?

A Essentially, there are two – a repayment mortgage and an interest-only mortgage.

Q What is the safest?

A A repayment mortgage. These loans, also known as capital and interest mortgages, usually involve borrowing a sum over 25 years. Borrowers make a monthly payment to the lender, which is made up of interest charged on the amount borrowed and a capital repayment. As the capital is gradually repaid each month the outstanding debt is reduced. In the early years most of each payment will be the interest while the majority of the capital will be paid off during the later years of the loan. At the end of the mortgage term the loan is repaid in full and you have no further mortgage commitment.

Q What are the main attractions of a repayment mortgage?

A They are simple, easy to understand and offer security. You have a cast-iron guarantee that provided you make your monthly payments on time your mortgage will be cleared by a set date. Most providers of such loans also adopt a flexible approach and allow you temporarily to reschedule your payments if you encounter financial problems.

Q What about the drawbacks?

A Repayment mortgages are not portable, which means that if you move home you will need to repay the loan and start a new mortgage. You must also arrange separate insurance to ensure your loan is repaid if you die before the end of its term. Mortgage protection insurance is the answer. This decreasing term assurance offers an initial sum assured equal to the loan but then falls during the loan's term to match the outstanding debt. Premiums are not expensive and policies are offered by all major insurance companies.

Q How does an interest-only mortgage work?

A You agree to pay the monthly interest on the loan you have taken out and to repay the capital borrowed at the end of the term as a lump sum. The repayment of the capital is usually funded by the maturity proceeds from an investment plan such as an endowment policy, the tax-free cash sum available from a pension or the value of an Individual Savings Account.

Q Don't endowment mortgages belong in the past?

A They are certainly no longer sold by the bucketload as they were in the Eighties and early Nineties – and for good reason. They are inflexible, often provide poor value if surrendered early and have left many homeowners wondering whether their policies will clear their outstanding mortgages.

Q How does an endowment mortgage work?

A In effect you make two separate monthly payments during the agreed mortgage term – you pay the interest on your loan plus a premium on an endowment policy with an insurance company. The objective of the endowment, through prudent investment management by the insurance company, is to generate a lump sum that will be large enough to clear your mortgage at the end of its term and leave you with a little tax-free surplus to use as you wish.

Q Are all endowment policies the same?

A No. They fall into three main categories. First, there are expensive full endowments that guarantee that your loan will be met, come what may. Secondly, there are low-cost endowments. These cheaper policies ensure that your mortgage will be repaid if you die before the end of the mortgage term, but they do not guarantee that their value will be sufficient to meet your outstanding loan at the end of its term. Thirdly, there are low-start endowments where premiums, usually in the first five years, are kept low. But thereafter, premiums rise. The idea behind such endowments is that they help first-time homebuyers at a time when money is tight. However, such endowments are rarely sold these days, have a bad reputation and can provide a nasty payment shock when the low-start premiums are replaced by full-blown premiums. Avoid like the plague.

The most popular type of low-cost endowment has been the with-profits policy which attracts annual (or reversionary) bonuses depending on the insurance company's investment performance. Falling bonus rates in recent years mean that many homeowners face a worrying potential shortfall in the value of their with-profits endowment. Some have increased their premiums to ensure that such a situation does not occur.

Q Do I need to sell my endowment if I move house?

A No. You may keep the premiums going and use it as the repayment vehicle for your new loan. Indeed, surrendering an endowment policy before the end of its term seldom makes good financial sense because the value you receive will be meagre. It is the poor value offered by endowments other than at maturity that makes them dangerous. Unless you are certain you will keep an endowment going until it matures, such plans are best avoided – they are too inflexible.

Q Are pension mortgages a better bet?

A Not really. Like an endowment, you pay two monthly amounts – one to pay the interest on your interest-only loan and one to pay the premium into a pension policy. When you take your pension, the tax-free lump sum that you are eligible to receive in addition to your lifetime income will be sufficient to clear your mortgage.

In theory such a choice looks attractive. Your pension premiums enjoy tax relief, your pension fund grows primarily free of tax and the tax-free cash available at retirement can be used to repay your loan. All that is missing is term assurance to repay your loan in the event of your death before the end of the mortgage term. That is something that can be arranged easily, costs little in terms of monthly premiums and may be bought through your pension provider, enabling your premiums to enjoy tax relief in the same way that your pension contributions do. It is also a flexible arrangement if you decide to move house because you simply take your pension with you.

But in practice such a mortgage strategy is fraught with danger. Like a low-cost endowment, there is no guarantee that the tax-free lump sum you may generate from your pension will be sufficient to repay your loan, especially if your pension has not performed well.

There is also no guarantee that you will remain eligible to make pension contributions, maybe for example, as a result of a spell out of work, or be eligible to increase contributions as a result of Inland Revenue rules. In addition, you cannot access your pension until you are 50 – not ideal if you want to clear your mortgage early. But, more fundamentally, a pension exists to provide you with an income in retirement, not with the means to clear a mortgage debt. By muddying the waters between the two you risk the danger of leaving yourself impoverished in retirement.

Q So what about an Isa-backed mortgage?

A As with endowments and pensions it involves considerable risk, so treat it with caution. You pay interest on a loan that does not decrease while simultaneously paying premiums into an Individual Savings Account (Isa). This may be invested in a mix of cash and investments such as unit trusts and investment trusts and the idea is that the Isa will repay your loan at the end of the agreed term. Separate term assurance is required to repay your loan if you die before end of the mortgage term.

In theory, such an arrangement seems fine. The value of your

Isa grows tax-free. It is also a more flexible set-up than an endowment, which discriminates against those who are unable to last the full savings course. If your Isa's investment performance is strong, you can repay your loan early. But in practice, like pension and endowment mortgages, your ability to repay your loan depends ultimately upon the ability of your Isa to deliver satisfactory investment performance. And that is not guaranteed. If the final value of your Isa is not enough to clear your loan, you will have to make up the shortfall from elsewhere.

One final important point on Isas. There is no guarantee that Isas will be around in the long term as has happened with Peps where new contributions have not been permitted since April 1999. If you take out an Isa-backed mortgage, be aware that future changes in government could change the tax status and rules that go with Isas. These changes could make Isas unsuitable for repaying your mortgage.

Q We've looked at the main repayment options. How about interest rate options? Isn't it best simply to opt for a standard variable rate mortgage?

A No. Just because standard variable rate mortgages have been available for years does not mean that they offer the best value – far from it. By taking out a standard rate deal your mortgage payments will rise and fall in line with the lender's mortgage rate. While that may be fine when rates are falling, it may lead to financial heartache if rates rise and you suddenly have to find extra money from an already tight household budget. The unpredictability of standard mortgage rates is their biggest problem.

Q If standard variable rate mortgages are unpredictable, what is the answer?

A One solution is the fixed-rate mortgage. You lock into a fixed monthly repayment cost for a predetermined period – typically anything from one to five years. By taking this option you are buying certainty and you know that whatever happens to interest rates your monthly mortgage outgoing will not change.

Q Are there any catches with it?

A A fixed-rate mortgage may look an expensive option when interest rates fall. And once you take out such a deal it is difficult to break away from it. Lenders tend to charge hefty redemption penalties if you decide to repay or change your loan before the fixed-rate period ends. But if payment certainty is crucial to you such disadvantages should not deter you from taking out a fixed-rate mortgage.

Q What happens once the fixed-rate deal comes to an end?

A You will probably be offered a new fixed-rate loan based on prevailing interest rates at the time. Alternatively your payments will be linked to the lender's standard variable rate which could lead to a nasty payment shock. Your lender should explain the options available to you before you take out your original deal and should also remind you of them once the fixed-rate term draws to a close.

Q What about capped-rate deals. Don't they offer the same attractions as a fixed-rate deal?

A Not quite. With a capped-rate mortgage, the lender sets an upper rate limit – the cap – above which your mortgage interest rate cannot go for a set period. But it may fluctuate below this level, according to the standard variable rate.

Some lenders offer so-called capped and collared mortgages where the mortgage rate will fluctuate between a collar – the minimum interest rate – and a cap – the maximum. Such deals are attractive because you know in advance what your minimum and maximum mortgage payments will be. But if payment certainty is crucial, a fixed-rate deal is better. Like a fixed-rate offer, your capped-rate lender will offer you either an alternative deal once the capped-rate period ends or link your payments to its standard variable rate.

Q Are there any other mortgage rate options I should consider?

A In recent years, cashback mortgages have become increasingly popular. These provide you with a cashback, usually a percentage of the loan you have taken out, once all the mortgage formalities have been completed. The cash may be used to meet any linked mortgage costs, buy new furnishings or as you please.

Such deals usually mean that your payments are linked to the lender's standard variable rate for a predetermined period, which means you have no payment security. Occasionally, however, lenders offer cashbacks with fixed-rate mortgages and some discounted rate deals may also offer the facility.

With a discounted deal, the initial interest rate you pay is reduced for a set period. The discount usually takes the form of a limited period reduction in the lender's normal standard variable interest rate. At the end of the discounted period, payments are linked to the lender's standard variable rate. Discounted deals, popular in the past few years, are ideal for first-time buyers who may have extra household expenses in the early years of home ownership and who appreciate the reduced early payments. But remember that your mortgage payments are not guaranteed and may increase during the discounted rate period if interest rates rise. You will also have to pay hefty redemption penalties if you decide to switch mortgages before the discounted rate period draws to an end.

Q Are discounted rate mortgages the same as deferred interest mortgages?

A No. With a deferred interest mortgage you pay reduced interest payments for an agreed period – the same as with a discounted rate mortgage. But unlike a discounted rate scheme, you are obliged to make good the underpayments made in the early years. The interest you defer is added to your loan, increasing the capital you owe. Such schemes are fraught with danger and can lead to your mortgage debt spiralling out of control. They are best avoided.

Q What about the new-style flexible mortgages we are hearing more about?

A They represent an exciting development in the mortgage market. These schemes have been introduced by innovative lenders such as Bank of Scotland, Woolwich and Virgin and provide borrowers with greater flexibility over mortgage repayments. Though they are all different, they allow you to increase or reduce repayments in line with your financial affairs. Look upon them almost as a giant money pot – you can pay your salary into it, draw cash and even pay bills from it. The key point to remember is that, as with an interest-only mortgage, you will have to clear the mortgage pot at some stage so you need to be disciplined.

Q Fine, I now know all there is to know about the different types of mortgage and the various rate options. What will it cost me to arrange a mortgage?

A Costs tend to fall into five areas. Most lenders demand an arrangement fee when you apply for a mortgage. This can be anything between £50 and £250 and is usually non-refundable. However, most lenders will add this fee to your loan. You will also need a solicitor or licensed conveyancer to handle the legal issues. He or she will incur costs in carrying out a local search on the property of your choice as well as land registry fees when transferring ownership of the home to you. It is not unusual for a solicitor to charge fees equivalent to 1% of the purchase price of your home.

You will also have to pay stamp duty which is charged on the sale of homes costing more than £60,000. The amount and percentage rate you pay will depend upon the house price. Between £60,001 and £250,000 stamp duty is 1%. Between £250,001 and £500,000 it is 3% and above £500,000 it is 4%.

The fourth cost is the mortgage indemnity guarantee premium. This is typically charged when you are borrowing a sum worth more than 90% of the value of your home. The insurance your money buys covers the lender if you get into a mess with your mortgage. The cost of such insurance varies widely and it may be added to the loan if you do not want to pay it up front.

Finally, there are the survey fees. These vary depending upon the extent of survey you require. This is a cost you should not skimp on – it is imperative that you pay a fair price for a property and you need to know in advance if the home of your dreams has any major defects.

Q What about tax?

A Miras (mortgage interest relief at source) has disappeared. As a result, there are no tax breaks for homeowners anymore.

Q Where should I go to get a mortgage?

A The choice is yours. You may visit your local building society or bank branch and arrange a mortgage interview. Alternatively you may consult a mortgage adviser who will shop around for the most appropriate loan deal, but check whether he or she is independent and free to choose any loan from the marketplace. Nowadays, many lenders will arrange loans over the telephone, especially new players such as insurance companies.

Q What assurances do I have when dealing with someone who offers me a loan?

A A good question. Until recently the mortgage market resembled a cattle market and almost anyone could advise the public on mortgages. Now a semblance of order has been introduced with the setting up of the Code of Mortgage Lending Practice. This is a voluntary code followed by lenders and mortgage advisers and sets standards of good mortgage practice to which members are expected to adhere. If you are taking out a loan, a lender or adviser should inform you of the code's existence and the assurances it gives you – if not, alarm bells should start to ring. Recent evidence suggests that the code's rules are being ignored by some advisers, so proceed with caution.

Q Is it possible to obtain a copy of the Mortgage Code?

A Yes. Contact the Council of Mortgage Lenders, 3 Savile Row, London W1S 3PB, tel 020 7437 0075, www.cml.org.uk.

Dos and Don'ts

- **DO** consider the remortgage option if you are currently repaying a standard variable rate mortgage. By changing loans you could save yourself a lot of money.

- **DON'T** extend the term of your debt if you have a repayment mortgage and you wish to remortgage. So, if you are five years into a 25-year repayment mortgage, make sure your new repayment mortgage is for 20 years.

- **DON'T** take out a mortgage without first checking what redemption charges you may face if you relinquish your loan early. Many lenders offer what appear to be exciting loan deals but add a nasty sting in the tail with their redemption penalties. Be wary of any mortgage where the redemption penalties extend beyond the special mortgage offer period – the end of the fixed-rate term, for example, or the expiry of the discounted period.

- **DO** shop around. It pays to look and compare deals before applying for a loan. An independent mortgage adviser should help you in this process. Good financial newspapers also include details of attractive mortgage deals in the personal finance pages. Also, don't be frightened of using the Internet.

- **DON'T** land yourself with a mortgage whose repayments will be a struggle to meet. It makes far better sense to opt for a smaller loan even if it precludes you from buying the home of your dreams.

- **DO** check the flexibility of your loan before signing on the dotted line. Many lenders allow you to make early capital repayments. Check this is the case beforehand.

- **DON'T** forget insurance. It is vital if you become unable to meet your mortgage repayments because of illness or redundancy. Though premiums may be expensive, some policies provide valuable cover. See the following section on mortgage payment protection.

- **DO** remember that if you are borrowing a sum worth more than 90% of the value of your home you will probably be asked to pay a mortgage indemnity guarantee premium. This payment will provide you with no cover whatsoever – it merely covers the lender if you get into difficulties with your repayments. If you are required to pay MIG, the cost will be based on the amount of loan above 75% of the value of your home – not 90%. To quantify this, let's take the example of a house valued at £75,000 and your wish to borrow 95%. MIG could cost more than £1,200.

- **DO** be wary of loans that require you to buy buildings and contents insurance or a sickness protection policy from or through the lender. While the loan rate may look attractive, the lender is probably making up for his generosity by charging you high premiums for insurance. You are free to shop around for the best insurance deals and lenders cannot insist that you buy cover from them as a condition of the mortgage.

- **DO** remember that some lenders, especially building societies, have introduced loyalty schemes for long-standing borrowers. Though these vary, they usually mean a reduced mortgage rate – a 0.5% reduction off the standard variable rate is typical – once you have had your loan with the lender for a set time.

- **DON'T** forget that low-cost endowments, pension and Isa mortgages do not guarantee that the funds available at the end of the mortgage term will be sufficient to repay the mortgage.

Did you know?

- **DID** you know that in 1990, 75% of new mortgages were

backed by endowment policies? By 1996 the percentage had fallen to 37%.

- **DID** you know that you do not have to go to a bank or building society for a mortgage? Insurance companies such as Standard Life, Scottish Widows and Prudential, even retailer Virgin, are all players in the mortgage market.

- **DID** you know that research shows that about 25% of endowment policyholders are likely to surrender their policy within two years? Unless you are sure that you will stay the 25-year term, avoid endowment mortgages.

- **DID** you know that buying insurance with a mortgage – a so-called conditional loan – is the equivalent of adding between 0.25% and 0.5% on the mortgage rate you pay? Don't be mugged into buying it.

So what now?

- **CHOOSING** a mortgage is probably the most important financial decision you will take. It is imperative that you get it right – choose the right type of loan for your financial circumstances and the right interest rate option. Take your time, seek help and advice, and don't be afraid to question anything you do not understand. Negotiate the mortgage maze successfully and not only could you become the proud owner of the house of your dreams, but you could save thousands of pounds in the process.

Mortgage payment protection

MOST people who take out a mortgage to buy a home for the first time understand the need to protect such a major asset. Usually they buy buildings and contents insurance to protect their home and possessions against the consequences of fire or burglary.

Similarly, they buy life insurance that will pay off their loan should they die before it has been repaid. Yet when it comes to insuring against the inability to meet their mortgage payments because of illness or redundancy they seldom bother, mainly because they believe that those evils will never disrupt their lives. At present only about 30% of homebuyers take out mortgage payment protection insurance.

This section looks at why you should consider such cover.

Mortgage payment protection insurance: key questions and answers

Q Doesn't the state come to the rescue to help you meet your mortgage payments if you become unemployed or ill?

A Not any more. Help with mortgage payments through the benefits system is restricted to people receiving income support or income-based Jobseeker's Allowance. If you have savings of more than £8,000 you will not be eligible for income support and that means you will get no help with mortgage payments. If you become too ill to work but your partner works 24 hours or more a week, you will not receive income support or help with mortgage payments.

Q What state help is available?

A Provided you are eligible for benefit, assistance will depend on when you took out your present mortgage. If you took it out before October 2, 1995, you will receive no state help for the first eight weeks. For the next 18 weeks, the state will pay half your mortgage interest payments. After that it will pay all of your interest payments.

If you took out your mortgage after October 2, 1995, less help is available. You will receive no assistance with mortgage payments for the first 39 weeks. After that, the state will meet all your mortgage interest payments. Benefit is limited to the first £100,000 of your mortgage and will not cover any capital part of your mortgage payments or pay premiums on a life policy or savings plan (such as an endowment) linked to your mortgage. Nor will it cover any mortgage arrears.

Q OK, the state will not rush to my rescue if I become ill or lose my job. How do I ensure that my mortgage payments are met if personal disaster strikes?

A You can rely upon your own personal savings but these can soon dwindle away, especially if your illness lasts a long time or you don't find a new job as quickly as you expected. An alternative approach is to buy mortgage payment protection insurance. It is commonly referred to as accident, sickness and unemployment insurance and it provides financial protection for homebuyers who become unemployed or ill and are unable to work.

Q How does this insurance work?

A You pay a monthly premium based on the cover you require. The level of cover depends on the size of your mortgage payments. If you become unemployed or are unable to work because of accident or illness, the policy will pay your mortgage, usually by making direct payments to your lender. Benefit will normally be paid for a maximum of 12 months though some insurers will pay for longer. Payments stop as soon as you return to work.

Q Can the insurance cover the payment of premiums for savings plans or insurance linked to my mortgage?

A Yes. It can cover monthly premiums on an endowment policy, an Individual Savings Account or a buildings and contents insurance policy.

Q Are any age limits imposed on the cover?

A Most insurers will cover you only between 18 and 65.

Q Are policies available to the self-employed?

A Yes, but if you are self-employed you need to check the policy's small print thoroughly because exclusions can make claiming difficult. Most insurers will accept a claim only if you have involuntarily ceased trading and declared this to the Inland Revenue. Furthermore, you must have registered for Jobseeker's Allowance even though you may not qualify for benefit.

Contract workers need to tread carefully. Most insurers will accept a claim only if the worker is either on an annual contract that has been renewed at least once or has been under contract to the same employer for at least two years. For workers on different contract arrangements a claim will be accepted only if they have spent at least six months with the same employer and the contract has been renewed at least twice. In this case an insurer will pay only if the contract has been terminated early, and the benefit will be paid only until the date the contract would have expired.

Q Do these policies cover part-time workers?

A Yes. Most insurers will cover part-time workers provided they work at least 16 hours a week.

Q Are benefits from my policy paid as soon as I become ill or I am made redundant?

A No. Most insurers apply three delaying tactics. Firstly, they will not pay unemployment claims during the first two months of a policy. This is to prevent claims from people who were aware of impending unemployment when they took out the insurance.

Secondly, most insurers apply a 60-day excess on each claim and no benefit is paid during this period. If you are still out of work after this initial period the policy will pay your mortgage payments for up to a year.

Finally, benefit is usually paid monthly in arrears. Add this proviso to the 60-day excess period and it means that the first full monthly benefit from a mortgage payment protection policy will not be paid until 91 days after you claim. If you claim partway through a month the first payment will be calculated on the basis of 1/30th of the monthly benefit for each day of the claim.

Q How does this insurance work if the mortgage is on a joint basis?

A You can arrange the insurance to cover a predetermined proportion – for example 50/50 or 60/40. If you become ill or lose your job the policy will pay the cover allocated to you. The policy may be set up so that 100% of the mortgage payment is covered if either partner claims, but premiums may be expensive.

Q What about policy exclusions?

A There are many – so tread carefully. Most policies will not cover sickness claims if they relate to a medical condition that you suffered in the year before taking out insurance. Cover for self-inflicted illness such as alcohol or drug abuse is also excluded. Under the unemployment element of the insurance, claims will not be allowed if you lose your job as a casual, temporary or seasonal worker or if you are made redundant as a result of your own misconduct.

Q Can I buy the separate insurance elements of accident, sickness and unemployment?

A Yes, some insurers will provide cover against unemployment only or accident and sickness cover on its own. Obviously, these policies are cheaper.

Q How do I buy mortgage payment protection insurance?

A Most lenders will offer cover when you take out a new loan. Alternatively, you can buy it direct from an insurance company or through an insurance broker. It pays to shop around because plans differ in the cover they provide, the exclusions they contain and the premiums they charge. You will probably not be asked to have a medical, but you will be asked to give details of your medical history. Don't be economical with the truth – a subsequent claim could be turned down.

Q Can I buy cover after I have bought a new home or moved house?

A Yes, though it may be a more expensive option than buying it when you take out a loan. Most policies are portable – if you change lender, you can keep the plan going.

Q Can an insurer change the cover it offers once the policy is in force?

A Yes. Insurance companies may change the level of cover, alter premiums or even cancel your policy, but they should give you advance warning.

Q What happens if my employer offers generous sick pay arrangements or if I have already bought permanent health insurance or critical illness cover? Do I still need to obtain cover?

A You probably don't need mortgage payment protection insurance, but you should consult an independent financial adviser over whether your present financial protection is adequate.

Q Is there any difference between permanent health insurance and mortgage payment protection insurance?

A Yes. Though both policies will pay benefits if you suffer illness, the latter will pay until you recover or your chosen retirement date. With mortgage payment protection, payments are usually restricted to a maximum of one year. Accordingly, permanent health policy premiums are higher, but this insurance does not offer cover against the financial consequences of unemployment.

Q What happens if I need to claim?

A The policy document explains what you need to do. Usually you fill in a claim form and support it with evidence of the validity of your claim – for example, a redundancy notice or a doctor's report. To claim on the unemployment section, you will have to provide proof that you have signed on as being unemployed.

Q What if I am unhappy about the protection I have bought?

A Complain to the insurer immediately in writing. If you receive no satisfaction, contact the independent Insurance Ombudsman Bureau which will assess the merits of your complaint. If your insurer is not a member of the ombudsman scheme contact the Personal Insurance Arbitration Service. Both these schemes are being integrated into the Financial Ombudsman Service.

Dos and Don'ts

- **DON'T** think that just because you didn't arrange mortgage payment protection when you took out your loan you can no longer buy insurance. Many companies sell it to existing home owners.

- **DON'T** opt for a policy that offers the lowest premiums. Premiums usually reflect three factors – the number of exclusions in a policy, the level of cover required and the pricing policy of specific insurers. There is little point opting for a dirt-cheap plan if it later becomes impossible to make a valid claim.

- **DO** shop around. While most lenders will offer cover when you take out a loan, it may not be the cover you want or represent the best value. Shop around and talk to an independent financial adviser or insurance broker.

- **DON'T** buy a mortgage payment protection insurance policy if you have existing financial protection. If you have alternative cover such as permanent health insurance or critical illness cover, further protection may not be needed.

- **DON'T** confuse mortgage payment protection with mortgage indemnity guarantee insurance – they are totally different. Mortgage payment protection insurance protects YOU if you become unable to meet your monthly mortgage payments because of unemployment or illness. But mortgage indemnity guarantee insurance protects your LENDER from your inability to meet your mortgage payments.

- **DON'T** be confused by the different names applied to mortgage payment protection insurance. It is also described as accident, sickness and unemployment insurance, or given such titles as Paymentcare or Paymentcover. The policies all protect you in the event of illness or losing your job.

- **DO** be aware some mortgage lenders insist that you take out protection cover as a condition of the loan. Make sure that the policy you are being sold is worth the paper it is written on. If it is riddled with exclusions, look elsewhere for your loan and protection cover for it.

- **DO** remember that payment protection insurance may be used to cover premiums for home insurance, mortgage-related savings vehicles and life assurance as well as your mortgage repayments.

- **DON'T** think that long-term illness will never happen to you. An accident or unexpected illness could force you to stay off work for months during your working lifetime.

- **DON'T** buy a mortgage payment protection insurance policy without getting to grips with the terms and conditions. Ask questions, find out what it covers and more importantly what it doesn't cover.

Did you know?

- **DID** you know that providers of mortgage payment protection insurance have agreed to offer a basic minimum level of cover for policies sold after July 1999? Anyone who buys a policy now can be assured that:

- The plan will pay benefits after a maximum of 60 days;
- It will pay benefit for a minimum of 12 months;
- There will be a minimum of six months between any policy changes;
- Contract workers will be able to claim for unemployment provided they have worked for the same employer for at least a year;
- Self-employed people will be able to claim provided they have told the Inland Revenue that they have involuntarily ceased trading and have registered for Jobseeker's Allowance.

- **DID** you know that before October 1995 homeowners unable to work through accident, sickness or unemployment were entitled to have 50% of their mortgage payments paid immediately by the state, rising to 100% after 16 weeks? However, state help is now much reduced and anyone who has bought, remortgaged or moved house since October 1995 must wait nine months for state help. Even then, they may not be eligible.

- **DID** you know that four out of five homeowners will receive no income support if they become ill or are made redundant? This makes the need for payment protection insurance essential.

So what now?

- **IF** you are buying a home or are an existing homeowner it is essential to consider the merits of mortgage payment protection in the same light as life insurance. But don't buy cover without shopping around and without reviewing your existing financial protection. Adequate cover through your employer or other insurance such as critical illness or permanent health policies may already be in place.

Home insurance

PEOPLE have been insuring their homes for almost 300 years. The first household insurance policy was issued by the Sun Insurance Office in 1710, during the reign of Queen Anne.

Not surprisingly it was pretty basic and simply covered fire and fire damage. But since Sun Insurance's pioneering move, household insurance has changed beyond recognition. Today, policies are offered by financial companies such as banks, building societies and insurance companies. They may be bought over the telephone, direct from the insurer or through a financial adviser.

As a homeowner, you need two types of home insurance to enjoy peace of mind. Contents cover protects your household possessions, and buildings cover pays for damage to your home caused, for example, by fire or subsidence. These two types of cover may be bought separately, but it is often more convenient – and usually more cost-effective – to buy them under one policy.

Choosing the most appropriate deal from the wide range on offer can be a nightmare. Though many companies have added extras of all kinds to their policies, the number of conditions, caveats and exclusions has also expanded, creating what could be an expensive pitfall for the unwary. Let the buyer beware!

Home insurance: key questions and answers

Section 1 – buildings insurance

Q What is buildings insurance?

A Your home is probably the biggest financial commitment of your life, so it makes sense to ensure you have adequate insurance cover in case anything goes wrong with it. Buildings insurance provides cover against problems with the structure of your home as well as permanent fixtures and fittings such as baths, toilets and fitted kitchens.

Policies usually – but not always – include garages, garden sheds and greenhouses as well as boundary walls, fences, gates, paths, drives and, if you are fortunate enough to have one, an outdoor swimming pool.

Your house is usually covered against a stated list of risks, ranging from damage caused by flood, fire or subsidence to damage caused maliciously, storms or as a result of theft. Most policies pay for accidental damage to underground pipes and cables, glass in doors, windows, baths, basins and toilets. Cover may be extended to include damage caused by DIY mishaps, but the insurer may charge extra for this.

Q Do I need to arrange buildings insurance myself?

A Yes. If you own your home your mortgage lender will usually insist that you have insurance. If you own a flat, your freeholder will probably arrange the buildings insurance for you. And if you rent a home, either from a council or privately, buildings cover will be arranged by the owner.

Q How much buildings insurance cover do I need?

A The sum insured is the amount of money for which your home is covered and is the most an insurer will pay even if your home is burnt to the ground. It is also the amount it would cost to rebuild your home though that is not the same as your home's market value, which could be greater or less.

Q How do I know the cover I have is adequate?

A Adequate buildings insurance is a condition of a loan being granted by a bank, building society or other mortgage lender. A chartered surveyor, who is a member of the Royal Institution of Chartered Surveyors, will prepare a professional rebuilding cost assessment for buildings insurance purposes. You may work out your own sum assured though the calculations are rather complicated. The Association of British Insurers has a useful leaflet that includes tables to help you. Write to ABI, 51 Gresham Street, London EC2V 7HQ.

Some insurance companies offer unlimited cover. This means you do not have to worry about how much cover you need or whether it is adequate. Other insurers offer premiums based on a simple assessment of where you live and the type, age and size of your property.

Q Do buildings insurance policies contain exclusions?

A Yes. It is essential you find out what these are before you buy your policy. Common exclusions are storm damage to gates or fences, frost damage, and structural damage caused by sonic bangs from aircraft. Buildings insurance does not cover wear and tear so if your property is not in a good state of repair a claim may not be paid in full. Your insurer may apply restrictions if your home is not lived in for more than 30 days.

Q What about excesses? Do these apply to buildings insurance?

A Yes. Most insurers insist you meet the first part of any claim. The level of excess depends on under which section of the policy you are claiming, but it is typically between £50 and £100. However, in the case of subsidence claims the excess can be as much as £1,500.

Q Will I still be able to obtain buildings insurance if my home is in an area prone to subsidence?

A Yes, but the increased level of risk means that your premiums or excesses will be higher. Even if your property has been affected by subsidence you should still be able to insure it as long as repair work has been carried out successfully.

Q Will I need to cut down any trees in my garden in case they cause subsidence?

A Not unless you have been asked to do so by a surveyor. However, you can take a number of steps to minimise the risks of subsidence:

- Contact your buildings insurer at the first sign of any structural damage to your home – for example, if cracks wider than the edge of a 10p piece appear in a wall. The quicker a problem is identified the more easily it can be remedied. Most cracks turn out not to be evidence of subsidence problems and can be dealt with by using grout or sealant.
- Plant trees the same distance as their expected mature height away from buildings. A young Scots pine may be only one metre high in the local garden centre but in your garden it could grow to a lofty 30 metres.
- Don't remove established trees without consulting a specialist, especially in clay soil areas. The clay could swell and destabilise your home's foundations.
- Clear blocked drains immediately – they may cause subsidence.
- Prune trees and shrubs to a sensible height. This reduces the risk of soil drying out and subsidence developing.
- Clear gutters regularly of leaves, dirt or rubbish.
- Check pipes for leaks, especially during winter.
- Always have a full structural survey carried out when you buy a home. It will identify potential problems.

Q What should I ask an insurer before I buy a buildings insurance policy?

A There are seven key questions:

1. Does the policy offer a discount on premiums? Some insurance companies offer initial discounts to new customers, a reflection of today's fierce competition for your business. Others discount premiums for elderly customers and some offer age-related discounts to people as young as 45. If you change insurer, ask the new company if it will pay any transfer fee charged by the old one.

2. Does the policy provide cover if I accidentally injure another person or damage their property? Most policies pay damages for which you are legally liable – usually up to £1 million plus costs. Check this before proceeding.

3. Is an excess payable if I claim? Many insurers apply an excess to any claim so find out how much it is and if it varies with the type of claim. Excesses for subsidence claims can be substantial.

4. Does the policy provide temporary alternative accommodation if my home is badly damaged and I cannot live in it? Most policies usually pay a predetermined sum towards the cost of a temporary home.

5. Does the policy offer help in an emergency? A good buildings insurer offers legal and emergency assistance in a crisis, normally over 24-hour telephone helplines.

6. Are there any exclusions or restrictions in the policy? All buildings insurance policies have exclusions. Find out what they are before buying the policy – there is nothing worse than making a claim only to discover it is invalid because of an exclusion of which you were unaware.

7. How do I complain if there is a problem with the insurance? Ask the insurer to provide full details of its complaints procedure.

Q How do I pay my buildings insurance premiums?

A Premiums may be paid monthly or annually. If you are offered a monthly payment option, check whether the insurer charges extra for the privilege of spreading your premium payments.

Q If I claim against my policy, will my premiums go up the following year?

A Not necessarily. Your premiums are affected by the level of all claims made, not just by you. If claims are high across the country, then your premiums could rise.

Q Can I rest on my laurels once I have bought a satisfactory buildings insurance policy?

A No. It is essential to ensure that your cover remains up-to-date and adequate. Most insurers automatically index-link your sum assured to take into account changes in rebuilding costs, but check that yours does. If you improve your home, perhaps by installing central heating or building an extension, tell your insurer. The sum assured will probably need to be adjusted upwards.

Shop around for alternative quotes when your policy is due for renewal. You could find a better deal elsewhere.

Section 2 – contents insurance

Q What is contents insurance?

A A contents insurance policy covers everything you would take with you if you moved home. That usually includes furniture, household goods, food and drink, televisions, videos, computers, stereo equipment, clothing and valuables, usually up to a stated limit. Boats, caravans and motors are usually insured separately.

A policy pays if any of your home contents are lost or damaged. Typically, claims result from a burglary or fire, but a policy should also pay if your possessions are damaged or lost as a result of an explosion, water leaks or if your home is vandalised.

Most policies pay for accidental damage, but the extent of cover varies. Many pay to replace accidentally broken mirrors and glass in furniture while some policies cover accidental damage only to TVs, videos, computers and stereo equipment. Policies that cover accidental damage to all contents may be bought, but this cover is usually offered as an optional extra and costs more.

Most policies may be extended to cover accidental damage or

loss of valuable items that you frequently take out of your home. This option, known as an all-risks extension, may be used to cover jewellery, cameras and sports equipment.

Q Do I need to arrange contents insurance myself?

A Yes. The onus is entirely on you. No mortgage lender can insist that you take out contents cover.

Q How much contents insurance cover do I need?

A The sum insured is the total amount of money for which your contents are covered. It is the most your insurer will pay even if your possessions are totally destroyed. It determines the premiums you pay so it is vital you calculate the amount correctly otherwise you could lose out when claiming.

To get an idea of the sum insured go through every room in your house, including the loft, garage, cellar and garden shed. Write down what it would cost to replace every item at today's prices – don't forget carpets, rugs and expensive wallpaper! The only exception is clothing and household linen where the value should be adjusted downwards to reflect wear and tear. A man's suit, for example, has a life-span for insurance purposes of five years, so for each year you have had the suit, its present new value should be reduced by a fifth.

The total will probably surprise you – most people under-insure themselves – but your contents insurance should be based on it. Some insurers offer a maximum amount of cover which, if sufficient to cover all your possessions, removes the need for you to calculate an accurate sum insured. If it is insufficient, most companies offer extra blocks of cover.

Q Are contents policies all written on the same basis?

A No. Most insurance companies offer two types of policy. New-for-old policies, sometimes referred to as replacement as new cover, meet the full cost of replacing items if they are stolen or destroyed. Alternatively, the cost of repair will be met if the items are damaged. Most household items apart from clothing and household linen may be insured on a new-for-old basis, but you should check the policy for exclusions. Insurers usually apply an excess to every claim on a new-for-old policy.

Wear-and-tear policies, also known as indemnity policies, pay to replace or repair your possessions, but with an appropriate reduction for wear, tear and depreciation. Because claims are smaller, premiums are lower than for equivalent new-for-old policies. Many insurers apply an excess to claims.

Q Do contents insurance policies contain exclusions?

A Yes. Most policies contain a range of exclusions and limits on individual claims and it is vital that you know what these are before buying a policy. Commonly, there are limits on the value of works of art, ornaments, jewellery or other expensive items. The insurer may agree to raise these though it may be wiser to insure high-value items separately.

Most contents policies will not meet a theft or damage claim if you let or sub-let your house and there is no evidence of forced entry.

Q What should I ask an insurer before I buy a contents insurance policy?

A There are 10 key questions:

1. Does the policy cover accidental damage? Most policies offer cover against accidental damage such as spilling red wine over an expensive carpet, but you will probably have to pay extra for it. It can prove invaluable.

2. Does the policy offer a discount on premiums? Some insurers cut contents premiums for people over 45, security-conscious home owners, non-smokers and people with a claims-free history.

Discounts are available to those who combine their contents and buildings insurance or who use the same insurer for their car and home.

3. Is the policy flexible? Some insurance companies automatically increase the level of contents cover at Christmas to account for the gifts you are likely to have around the home. Some increase cover for couples about to marry and who may have wedding presents stored at home. Others automatically provide cover for possessions lost away from home – on holiday, for example. Check what your policy will and will not do under such circumstances.

4. Does the policy cover children who go to college? Some policies provide free student cover for household goods and personal effects. The amount may be up to 15% of the sum insured under your policy.

5. Does the policy cover the cost of replacing locks in my home if my keys are stolen? Most insurers – but not all – automatically cover the cost of replacement locks.

6. Does the policy provide cover if I accidentally injure another person or damage their property? Most policies pay damages for which you are legally liable up to a maximum of £1 million.

7. Is there an excess on claims? Most insurers apply an excess to claims.

8. Does the policy provide alternative temporary accommodation if my home is badly damaged and I cannot live in it? Most policies help towards the cost of a temporary home. The payment may be as much as 20% of the sum insured.

9. Does the contents insurance cover high-value items? Most insurers impose a maximum limit on the level of cover for any single household item. If the value of some of your possessions exceeds this

limit you should obtain separate cover from a specialist high-value insurer.

10. Does the policy offer legal help in an emergency? Some insurers offer legal expenses cover and though this will increase your premium, it could prove useful if you need help to settle a claim with a third party. Typically, protection includes cover for personal injury claims, employment disputes and litigation involving the home. Claims for libel, divorce or criminal litigation are usually excluded.

Q Will my contents insurance cover me if I work from home?

A Most policies will not cover losses arising from business activities at home. Your insurer may extend your policy to provide such cover or you may need to buy a specific policy to cover business activities.

Q How do I pay my contents insurance premiums?

A Premiums may be paid monthly or annually. If you are offered a monthly payment option check whether you will pay extra for the privilege.

Q Once I have bought my policy, are there any golden rules to follow?

A Yes. There are seven:

1. Do not let or sub-let your house without first telling your contents insurer – your policy could be declared null and void. Letting increases the risk of a claim so an insurer will probably impose conditions on your policy and increase your premiums.

2. Do not buy travel insurance that offers personal possessions cover without first checking what is covered under your existing contents policy. Many contents insurers automatically include cover for

personal possessions away from home, so buying similar cover under a travel policy is a waste of money. You should ask for a discount on travel insurance premiums if you do not require personal possessions cover.

3. Do not embark upon DIY without checking that your policy's accidental damage section covers the consequences of mishaps.

4. Keep your policy up to date. Most insurers automatically link the sum assured under your policy to the Retail Prices Index so that it increases in line with inflation, but check that yours does. If you add to your possessions, ask your insurer to increase the sum assured to reflect the increased value of your contents.

5. Most insurers offer premium discounts to people whose homes meet certain minimum standards. These include having deadlocks fitted to front doors and fitting key-operated window locks on all ground-floor and other accessible windows. Make every effort to prevent theft from your home. There are a number of simple and easy ways to do this.

- Fit proper security locks on all points of entry – back doors and windows as well as your front door.
- Ask a neighbour or friend to keep an eye on your home while you are away. Ask them to move the post from the front door so it cannot be seen, put out your dustbin and cut the lawn. If you do not have time switches, ask them to turn lights on at night so that no one can guess your home is unoccupied.
- Join the neighbourhood watch scheme.
- Have an alarm system fitted. An alarm is a great deterrent, so use it even if you go out for only a few minutes.
- Do not leave ladders or tools around outside the house – it encourages thieves.
- Do not leave valuable goods in full view – they may prove an irresistible temptation.

6. Be careful with high-value items. Keep receipts and take photographs if possible, especially of antique items. Articles worth more than £1,000 should be listed and insured individually.

7. Keep an eye on the competition. When your policy comes up for renewal, shop around for alternative quotes.

Q How do I claim on a buildings or contents policy?

A Making a claim is straightforward provided you follow a few simple steps:

- Check whether the claim you want to make is covered by your insurance. Your policy documents should explain this, but if in doubt contact the insurer or the insurance broker who arranged the policy in the first instance. If your claim involves burglary, theft, malicious damage or vandalism contact the police immediately.

- Ask your insurer for a claim form as soon as loss or damage occurs. Complete it as soon as possible and return it to the insurer with estimates for the cost of repairs or replacement. If you cannot obtain estimates immediately, send the claim form first and send the estimates later.

- Keep all damaged items – the insurance company may want to see them. Keep bills for immediate emergency repairs – they may form part of your claim.

- Your insurance company should pay your claim or arrange for a claims inspector or loss adjuster to assess damage.

- If you are unhappy with the payment, contact the insurance company. Explain your dissatisfaction and follow its complaints procedure if necessary. If you are still unhappy, take your complaint to the Insurance Ombudsman or the Personal Insurance Arbitration Scheme – schemes being embraced within the Financial Ombudsman Service.

Q How do I buy home insurance – contents or buildings?

A Home insurance may be bought from a number of sources, but you should shop around if you want best value for money. An independent financial intermediary will scour the market on your behalf for the best home insurance deal. Do not confuse these intermediaries with company agents who can recommend the insurance policies of only a limited number of companies.

Home insurance may be bought direct from insurance companies, usually over the telephone. You can save money buying this way because the insurance company does not pay commission to an agent such as a bank or building society for arranging the sale. But take your time and don't be afraid to ring several direct insurers for quotes.

Finally, read the policy details thoroughly to make sure there are no hidden huge excesses and long lists of exclusions.

Dos and Don'ts

- **DON'T** panic if you discover subsidence just after you have switched home insurer. If a claim is made less than eight weeks after a new policy has been taken out, the original insurer should accept the claim. After that, the new insurer will deal with it.

- **DON'T** under-insure when it comes to buying home insurance, either contents or buildings. If you do, any claim is likely to be scaled down.

- **DON'T** be afraid to ask questions when buying buildings insurance. No two policies are alike and many contracts are full of confusing terms and conditions. Before handing over any premiums it is vital that you fully understand what your policy covers and what exclusions it makes. It is far better to discover the exclusions beforehand than when submitting a claim that is later turned down.

- **DO** keep your home insurance documents to hand. Most insurers operate a telephone claims system whose staff will guide you through the process. If you have to claim, contact the company as quickly as possible and have all the details ready.

- **DO** check your insurer's stance on prolonged absences from home. Your buildings insurance will usually be void if your home is left empty for more than 30 consecutive days.

- **DO** check out the free extras offered by some contents insurers as standard policy features. They include £250 for freezer contents, automatic cover for tools and equipment in garden sheds, garages and other outbuildings, £5,000 worth of cover for computers, printers and faxes used for business purposes in the home, and cover for loss or damage caused by removal men.

- **DO** realise that you must change your home insurance policy – buildings or contents – if you move house. This is because the risk has changed. You may be able to remain with your existing insurer, but you will have to take out a new policy or have your existing policy amended.

Did you know?

- **DID** you know that you can cut hundreds of pounds from your home insurance costs by shopping around for the most appropriate policy? At present many home owners take out loans from lenders who insist that home insurance must be bought at the same time. But the only reason their mortgage deals look so attractive is because you are paying over the odds for home insurance.

- **DID** you know that one household in four has no cover?

- **DID** you know that fire damage is the second most common reason after flooding for building insurance claims? Most insurers offer a discount if you install smoke detectors in your home.

- **DID** you know that some plants may deter burglars? They include berberis, colletia (a spiny shrub), ilex (prickly holly trees), maclura (an impenetrable hedge) and ulex.

- **DID** you know that many banks and building societies charge a fixed fee if you move your home insurance elsewhere? Did you also know that many insurers will pay this transfer fee on your behalf if you buy a policy from them?

- **DID** you know that if you buy a property which has had structural problems, it will be difficult to get buildings insurance? One way round this is to take over the existing buildings insurance from the vendor of the property.

So what now?

- **THE** home insurance market is fiercely competitive and that is great news for anyone looking for insurance or in search of a better deal. But the complex and confusing exclusions and excesses can make it difficult to buy the right policy. Take your time when buying, do not accept the first insurance package offered to you, and ask questions if you don't understand any part of the policy. That way, you will obtain value-for-money home insurance.

CHAPTER **3**

Life and Health Insurance

INSURANCE

'A guarantee that no matter how many necessities a person has to forego all through life, death is something to which he can still look forward.'

Fred Allen

Life insurance

THE first principle of good financial planning is to make sure that your dependants will not be left short of money if you die or you become too ill for work.

Each year about 3,000 people celebrate their 100th birthday, but not many of us will live to such a ripe old age. Sadly, some will die prematurely either in an accident at work, on the roads or from a sudden illness. For many families hit by the death of the bread-winner, bereavement may soon be followed by financial turmoil as the household income dries up. And while state benefits provide some help, their impact is marginal, if not woefully inadequate.

For families who wish to avoid such financial traumas the

answer lies in the purchase of life insurance – in simple terms, a policy that pays out when the insured person dies. It is an essential buy for anyone with dependants, particularly partners and children.

But buying life insurance is not as simple and straightforward as it should be. There is a wide range of policies on the market, some of which are poor value for money. This section is aimed at sorting the life insurance wheat from the chaff.

Life insurance: key questions and answers

Q Who needs life insurance?

A Anyone who has dependants. Most people's largest financial protection needs occur when they marry and have children, usually between their mid-twenties and early forties. It is at this time that the death of a parent can have the most serious financial repercussions on a family. It is vital that financial protection should be in place to replace an earner's income or to pay for carer services until the youngest child reaches 18.

When children become independent, the need for parents to maintain high life insurance cover becomes less of an issue and they can begin to address other key financial affairs such as saving for the future. However, insurance protection should remain in place to cushion the impact of their partner's death on their standard of living.

Q How much life insurance should I have?

A That will depend upon four factors – your age, the number of dependants you have, your income and your outstanding debts.

People with young families need life insurance more than people in their forties and fifties whose children have left the family home. For a young family, the loss of a parent could mean that the surviving partner must try to maintain the family's standard of living for 18 years or until the youngest child becomes independent. So a realistic level of life insurance cover is a must. For parents in their forties and fifties protection is still important, though cover does not have to be so extensive.

The more dependants you have, the more cover you need. However, insurance bought to cover the cost of bringing up your children should be timed to end when they become self-supporting, usually at 18.

The level of replacement income your partner will need if you die will be an important factor when determining the amount of cover required.

If you die, it is imperative that your surviving partner is not left with a financial millstone such as a large mortgage. Life insurance should clear such debts in the event of your death.

Q OK, I'm convinced about the merits of life insurance. What type should I buy?

A You should first look at term insurance. This temporary form of life insurance is offered by most insurance companies, a number of friendly societies and newcomers to the financial marketplace such as Marks & Spencer and Virgin. It is based on a simple concept – the insurer guarantees to pay the policy benefits if you, the life assured, die within a given time. If you survive to the end of the policy's term, no benefit will be paid.

The term of the policy depends upon you. It may be anything from a few years to several decades, but it should coincide with your need for protection. Policies may be written on your life or on the life of yourself and your partner. Term insurance is the least expensive form of life cover and for most people it is the best option.

Q But aren't there different types of term insurance?

A Yes, so you need to buy the one most appropriate for your needs. They fall into the following categories:
- Level term. The benefit payable on death remains the same throughout the policy's term. At the end of the term the

policy has no value and simply expires. Level term insurance is often bought to cover the repayment of a fixed loan – an interest-only mortgage, for example – in the event of death.

- Decreasing term. The benefit payable on death decreases in stages each year until it is zero by the end of the policy's term. Such insurance is often used in tandem with the purchase of a repayment mortgage whose capital value falls over the mortgage term. Decreasing term insurance, or mortgage protection insurance as it is more commonly known, ensures that a mortgage is repaid in full if the borrower dies early.

- Convertible term. Term insurance may be converted into permanent cover when your original policy's term comes to an end, usually by buying a whole-of-life insurance or an endowment policy.

  Its main attraction is that you cannot be refused the right to take out the new policy no matter what the state of your health.

  However, there are a number of rules governing conversion. Firstly, you cannot increase the sum assured when you convert – it is restricted to the sum assured on the original policy.

  Secondly, you must convert before your term insurance ends.

  Thirdly, though you cannot be refused conversion, the new premiums you pay will be determined by your age and sex – but not your state of health – which means they will inevitably rise.

  Lastly, conversion comes at a price and it tends to be on average 10% more expensive than basic level term insurance.

- Renewable term. This type of insurance allows you to exchange your term insurance for another policy at the end of the term. The big attraction of this option is that you have guaranteed insurability – you will be insured irrespective of your state of health when you come to renew. Renewable term insurance is often offered as an option on convertible term policies and vice versa.

- Increasing term. The sum assured increases during the policy's life, typically by 5% or 10% a year. Such insurance costs more than level term insurance, but your benefits are protected against the ravages of inflation. The right to increase the sum assured usually ends when you reach 65 although some providers may continue to increase it until later.

- Family income benefit. Benefit is paid on a regular basis from the death of the policyholder to the expiry of the policy's term. Policies are usually written on a joint basis, which means income payments are made as soon as one partner dies. They are also usually written to coincide with the expected period of dependency of the youngest child in the family. Policies may be arranged that will pay a level income or an income that rises by a predetermined amount each year.

Q Can term insurance be bought through a pension?

A Yes. If you have a personal pension you may usually buy term insurance through the plan. By doing this your premiums will benefit from tax relief in the same way as your pension premiums do. But buying term insurance in such a way does not always make best sense. Even after tax relief, pension term insurance premiums may be more expensive than buying the equivalent cover direct from an insurance company.

Furthermore, if you buy term assurance with a pension, the life assurance premiums reduce the amount you can put into a pension, thereby eating up valuable allowances.

Q Are term insurance benefits taxable?

A Proceeds from most term insurance policies are free of income tax and capital gains tax. This is because they contain no investment element and are classed as 'qualifying' policies.

Q What is a 'qualifying' policy?

A Before a term insurance policy may be classed as qualifying and its proceeds paid free of tax, it has to pass certain tests. If the term is less than 10 years:

- the policy must be valid for at least a year,
- it must provide benefit only as a result of your death or disability, and
- any surrender value payable must not exceed the premiums paid.

If the term is more than 10 years:

- the policy must provide benefit only as a result of your death or disability,
- premiums must be paid annually or more frequently for at least 10 years or three-quarters of the term, whichever is the shorter,
- the total premiums payable in a year must not exceed twice the total payable in any other year and one-eighth of the total payable over the whole term,
- the sum assured must not be less than 75% of the premiums payable up to your 75th birthday or the policy's expiry date, whichever is the earlier.

The proceeds of some term insurance policies are tax-free irrespective of these qualifying rules. They include decreasing term insurance policies used exclusively for mortgage protection and term insurance that is part of a tax-exempt friendly society savings plan.

Q Apart from term insurance, what other life cover can I obtain?

A Most insurance companies also offer 'whole-of-life' policies. In simple terms, such policies guarantee to pay the sum assured on the death of the insured person, whenever it occurs. Because whole-of-life insurance is not limited to a specific period in the way that term insurance is, premiums are more expensive because it is certain that the insurance company will eventually pay the sum assured. When you reach a specified age, say 70 or 80, you may not have to pay further premiums, but your cover will continue.

Whole-of-life policies are investment-based. Typically, policyholders pay a monthly premium that buys units in an investment fund. Some of these units are then encashed by the insurance company every month to pay for your guaranteed life cover. How many of your units are encashed will depend upon the level of cover you require.

Most insurance companies offer a range of cover options, ranging from minimum to maximum cover depending on your needs. If you opt for minimum cover, the deduction made to pay for your life cover will be low, and more of your premiums will be used to build an investment fund.

If you choose maximum cover the deduction to pay for it will be much larger, leaving little of your premium to be invested. It is likely that after five or 10 years, either your premiums will rise for the cover to be maintained, or the cover will be reduced so that your premiums will not have to rise.

With standard cover you should not have to pay higher premiums in the future provided that the underlying investment fund performs satisfactorily. Furthermore, these policies allow you to change between maximum cover and minimum cover during your lifetime to coincide with your changing needs and circumstances.

Q So it's a straight choice between term insurance and unit-linked whole-of-life policies?

A If only! You may also buy with-profits whole-of-life policies. These guarantee to pay a minimum amount of life cover if you die, but this sum is increased each year by the addition of annual or reversionary bonuses. Once added, these bonuses permanently increase the sum assured. When you die a further terminal bonus will usually be paid and this increases the life insurance payout further. Like unit-linked whole-of-life policies, these policies have an investment value though it tends to be low in the early years.

So-called universal policies are also available and these work in the same way as a unit-linked whole-of-life policy. Units are encashed every month to pay for the life cover, but these policies offer a wider range of benefits.

These can include waiver of premium, which ensures that your policy premiums will be paid if you are unable to work. Disability benefit allows for the sum assured to be paid if you become permanently disabled. Other benefits may include critical illness cover and fatal accident benefit. This pays an amount over and above the sum assured if you die an accidental death.

Such a jack-of-all-trades policy provides an array of all-important protection insurance needs – which means premiums may be high. It is a non-starter as a savings vehicle.

Q What about the tax treatment of benefits from a whole-of-life policy?

A It is similar to that for term insurance. The first thing to determine is whether the policy is qualifying. A whole-of-life policy is deemed to be qualifying if:

- it pays a capital sum only on death or disability,
- premiums are paid for at least 10 years or until death, and paid at least on a monthly basis,
- the total premiums payable in a year must not exceed twice the total premiums payable in any other year and one-eighth of the total premiums payable over the whole term (or over the first 10 years where premiums are payable throughout life),
- the sum assured is not less than 75% of the premiums payable before the life assured's 75th birthday.

If your policy meets these conditions – your insurer should confirm whether it is qualifying – no income tax will be payable on any investment gain provided that you do not surrender your policy or make it paid up (stop paying the premiums) within 10 years. If you do, your policy is deemed to be non-qualifying and you may have to pay tax of up to 18% on the investment proceeds.

Q What's best – straightforward term insurance or whole-of-life cover?

A Term insurance. Though the idea of permanent cover for life sounds appealing, whole-of-life policies present too many complexities. Policies tend to be swamped with charges and many people buy plans in the expectation of building up a juicy investment fund. Such expectations, often fuelled by commission-hungry salesmen, are rarely fulfilled and many policyholders surrender their policies early. Some experts believe that you should never mix savings and insurance within the same plan – which is exactly what a whole-of-life policy does.

In comparison, term insurance is simplicity itself. You pay your premiums and if you die before your policy expires, it pays benefit. If you survive, you receive nothing.

Q If I take out life insurance, will I need to have a medical?

A Not necessarily. You may be asked a few medical questions when you complete the insurer's application form. If the insurer needs further details, it may consult your doctor or ask you to have a medical. If you have suffered from illness in the past or are excessively overweight, your premiums may be increased to reflect the greater risk you represent to the insurance company. In some cases an insurer may refuse cover altogether.

Q Do term insurance rates differ for men and women?

A Yes. Premiums for men tend to be higher because on average they do not live as long as women. Premiums for smokers are more expensive.

Dos and Don'ts

- **DO** pause before jumping into the life insurance jungle. Check how much cover you already have – for example, through an employer's pension fund, existing investment policies and your mortgage. Only then should you consider buying cover.

- **DO** keep savings and insurance separate. It is one of the golden rules of personal finance. If you want life cover, choose term insurance.

- **DO** consider a family income benefit policy if you have a young family. Such policies, which pay out a regular tax-free income, may be set up to run for as long as your children remain at home. Major providers include Norwich Union, Standard Life and Scottish Widows.

- **DO** seek independent financial advice. While buying life insurance is relatively straightforward, making sure that you are buying adequate cover is a different matter. A good adviser will help you determine how much cover you require, taking into account your existing insurance, age, number of dependants, your income and financial liabilities. He or she should review your cover on a regular basis to make sure it meets your financial needs. It is also a fact that the competitiveness of products varies from year to year, necessitating a regular review – say every three or four years.

- **DON'T** be afraid to shop around for alternative term insurance even if you already have cover. Term insurance premiums have fallen over the past few years through increased competition and reduced concerns over the possible impact of AIDS on claims. Many people could save money by cancelling their present policies and shopping around for alternative cover.

- **DO** write your term insurance policy in trust. By doing this, the proceeds from the policy will not form part of your estate when you die and will be excluded from any inheritance tax assessment. Payment of a death claim under a policy written in trust is usually faster because probate is not required.

- **DON'T** think that a whole-of-life policy represents a sound savings vehicle – it doesn't. The investment value of a whole-of-life policy remains meagre for many years. If it is a savings scheme you want, look elsewhere.

- **DON'T** buy life insurance if you have no dependants – you are pouring money down the drain.

- **DO** remember that if you stop paying premiums on your term insurance policy, your cover will expire with no cash value.

- **DON'T** surrender a life insurance policy without first taking financial advice.

- **DON'T** be enticed by mailshots or newspaper adverts offering free gifts or free initial cover if you take out a specific policy. You are much better off consulting a financial adviser.

- **DON'T** forget that life insurance is equally important for a non-working partner. If you are the breadwinner and your non-working partner dies, a life insurance policy would pay for home help while you continue to work.

Did you know?

- **DID** you know that 32% of British adults have no life cover? And a further 27% believe they are making inadequate provision?

- **DID** you know that life insurance can play an important role in protecting a business from disaster? Known as key person or key man insurance, cover may be bought to protect your business from the disruption caused by the death of a key employee.

  Cover that will protect a business partnership if a partner dies is also available. The insurance allows surviving partner(s) to buy the deceased partner's share from the estate to which it would otherwise automatically pass. Similar insurance may be bought by directors of a business to protect their interests in the event of a death of a fellow director.

- **DID** you know that some companies monitor term insurance rates on a regular basis and can provide you with quotes over the telephone? A leading player is Term Direct, call 020 7684 8000.

- **DID** you know that the Association of British Insurers produces useful leaflets on life insurance? Write to ABI, 51 Gresham Street, London EC2V 7HQ.

So what now?

- **LIFE** insurance is a vital weapon in your personal finance armoury. You owe it to yourself and your family to have the right type and level of cover in place. Check your policies now.

Permanent health insurance

LONG-term illness is something that we pray will pass us by. But sadly, it strikes more people than we care to imagine. Government figures reveal that more than 670,000 men between 40 and 64 are absent from work for more than six months in any one year because of injury or illness. Many of these people and their families suffer financial hardship as a result, and the state offers only minimal help.

Permanent health insurance, or income replacement insurance, is the answer for people worried about long-term loss of income. In theory such insurance, which has been around for more than 100 years, should be high on any family's financial shopping list, but in practice it is rarely bought – primarily because of high premiums and a long list of policy exclusions.

This chapter looks at how permanent health insurance works, warns of the potential pitfalls awaiting the unsuspecting and advises how best to buy a policy.

Permanent health insurance: key questions and answers

Q What is permanent health insurance?

A It is a policy that will pay a regular income if you suffer long-term sickness or injury. Benefit usually starts after an initial waiting period that may be four, 13, 26 or 52 weeks. It is payable until you return to work, die, or the policy term expires, whichever is the earlier. Insurance of this type is also referred to as income protection insurance, long-term disability insurance, income replacement insurance, disability income insurance or personal disability insurance. Do not be put off by the different names – they all mean the same.

Q Doesn't the state come to the rescue when you are ill?

A It does, but help is minimal. If you are an employee, your employer is required to pay statutory sick pay (SSP) – £57.70 a week at present – for the first 28 weeks of your illness. At the end of that period you have to claim for state incapacity benefit for which you must undergo a test for eligibility. Self-employed people are not entitled to SSP and have no choice but to apply for incapacity benefit. Permanent health insurance, unlike state handouts, is designed to protect your standard of living during a period of long-term illness.

Q What is meant by long-term sickness or injury?

A Insurance companies have different definitions of what constitutes long-term illness. To trigger the policy's benefits you must typically demonstrate that you are unable to follow your usual occupation as a result of sickness or accident. But some policies insist that you must not be able to do any occupation before benefits are paid – and you should avoid these like the plague. They are a licence for insurance companies to make huge profits from your misery because making a valid claim is virtually impossible.

If you suffer a disability or illness that enables you to return to work but only on reduced earnings, maybe as a result of going part-time or taking a less well-paid job, your insurance company will probably pay you a reduced benefit. This will be enough to make you financially better off working than by staying off sick, but less well off than working full-time at your normal job.

Q Do these policies offer cover for redundancy?

A No. If you require such cover, you should consider accident, sickness and redundancy protection (see section on mortgage payment protection insurance).

Q How much benefit will the policy pay?

A The aim of a permanent health insurance policy is to replace earnings lost through sickness or injury without reducing your financial incentive to return to work. As a result, all policies set a maximum income benefit limit. This used to be 75% of average monthly earnings in the year before disablement, minus state benefits and benefits from any other disability insurance. But now permanent health insurance benefits are tax-free the usual maximum benefit is between 50% and 60% of a claimant's gross salary, plus state benefits.

Q Why is it called permanent?

A It is permanent in that the insurer may not cancel the policy no matter how often you claim for benefit. It is not permanent in the sense that once you have bought it, you have cover for your entire lifetime. Policies usually expire when the policyholder reaches 60 or 65. Insurance companies will not normally write new policies for applicants within five years of these age limits.

Q Is the benefit tax-free?

A Yes.

Q What is the difference between critical illness and permanent health insurance? Don't they both provide cover in the event of illness?

A Yes, but critical illness cover provides a lump-sum payment on the diagnosis of one of a number of diseases. Permanent health insurance provides a regular monthly income if you are unable to work as a result of sickness. The range of illnesses covered by permanent health insurance tends to be wider than those covered by a critical illness policy, which lapses once you have made a claim. With permanent health insurance, cover continues if you make a claim and later return to work.

Q If I opt for a long initial waiting period before benefits become due, will that mean lower premiums?

A Yes. A policy with a 13-week waiting period will typically charge lower premiums than one with a four-week one. This is because the insurance company will not have to pay benefit as quickly, and its costs will be lower. But there is no point opting for a long waiting period if this creates great financial hardship. The waiting period chosen should tie in with the end of sick pay from your employer, usually 28 weeks.

Q Can benefits increase each year or do they remain the same?

A You may opt for cover that provides an income which increases at a predetermined rate each year. But this costs more than a policy that offers a level rate of income.

Q What about premiums? Do they increase each year or do they remain the same?

A Some insurance companies guarantee that the premium you pay when you take out the policy will never change unless you decide to increase the level of cover it provides. Others guarantee not to increase premiums for an initial period, typically five years, after which they may adjust – increase – them after reviewing the claims position across all their permanent health insurance policies. If your premium is to be increased, you will be offered the option of reducing your cover rather than paying more.

If you have chosen to have your benefits increased each year, your premiums will increase to cover the new levels.

Q Do premiums differ for men and women?

A Yes. Statistics show that on average women are more likely to suffer ill health than men during their working lives. Consequently, premiums are higher for a woman than for a man of the same age and occupation.

Q What other factors determine the size of premium I pay?

A One is your occupation. Most insurance companies classify you into one of four occupation grades. Class 1 embraces people in administrative or professional occupations and represents the lowest insurance risk. Such people pay the lowest premiums. In contrast, Class 4 comprises people whose work involves heavy manual labour and they are seen as riskier policyholders. They pay higher premiums. Insurance companies refuse to insure people in high-risk occupations such as steeplejacks.

Other factors include whether you smoke and how long you wish the policy to pay benefits. The shorter the payment period, the cheaper the premium.

Q What happens if I change my job to one that is in a different class occupation?

A It depends upon your insurance company. Some offices will continue to provide cover while others may cancel it. It is vital to tell your insurance company if you change jobs – failure to do so could invalidate a future claim for benefit.

Q Are there illnesses that a permanent health insurance policy will not cover?

A Yes. Most insurers exclude AIDS, self-inflicted injury, illness caused by drug or alcohol abuse, an act of war or criminal activity, pregnancy, childbirth or associated complications.

Q If I do not claim from my permanent health insurance policy, do I get anything back?

A In most cases the answer is no. A conventional policy has no investment element built into the premium. If the policy expires and you have not made a claim you will receive nothing – there is no surrender value. However, though some insurers sell unit-linked permanent health insurance policies that do have a surrender value, these tend to be more expensive. No one should buy such a policy on the strength of its expected future investment value – it is the quality of protection that is paramount.

Q Do employers offer permanent health insurance to workers?

A Some do and if your company offers it, make sure you are covered by the scheme. Many employers offer group cover to their workers free of charge, but even where cover is not free, premiums will usually be much cheaper than if you bought the identical cover yourself.

Q For whom is permanent health insurance suitable?

A It should be a priority for anyone for whom loss of earnings will cause great financial hardship. The self-employed often stand to lose the most if they are unable to carry on a business because of long-term illness. For employed people, who should initially receive sick pay from their employer, permanent health insurance benefits should be timed to start when sick pay ceases. Cover should also be considered by people who look after the family home – it can enable you to pay for home help if you become ill.

Q When my policy is paying benefit, must I continue to pay the monthly premiums for the cover to remain in force?

A No. Premiums are normally waived. You will only start paying them again once you return to work.

Q Will I have to undergo a medical to obtain cover?

A Not necessarily. As with private medical insurance (see next section) insurance companies normally offer cover in two ways:

1. Medical history declaration. A medical examination may be required after you have provided details of your medical history. If you have a complaint that is likely to recur, the insurer will either exclude that condition from your cover, charge you an extra premium to include it, or refuse cover absolutely. It is vital that you provide the insurer with all your medical details – if you fail to declare key information a claim for benefit could be refused.

2. Moratoria. Under this format, cover is offered immediately and you are not required to fill in any declaration form or undergo a medical. But the policy will automatically not cover any medical condition that existed before you took out the insurance until you remain free of treatment, advice or medication for that condition for a minimum period, usually two years. Though policies of this kind are easy to arrange, they can cause problems later when a claim is turned down.

Q How do I make a claim on a permanent health insurance policy?

A Contact the insurance company as soon as possible – don't wait for any deferred period to lapse before claiming. Once you have completed the claim form, the company will check your eligibility for benefit. It may wish to obtain a medical report from your doctor or carry out an independent medical examination. It will also assess the maximum benefit to which you are entitled and may ask you for proof of your income.

Q What happens when I am well enough to return to work?

A Contact your insurer who will stop benefit payments. If you go back to work on a part-time basis or take a lower-paid job, your insurer may pay you reduced benefit. If you return to your normal occupation this is called a rehabilitation or partial benefit. If you find work in an alternative occupation, it is called a proportionate benefit.

Q Who offers permanent health insurance?

A Most insurance companies such as Legal & General, Norwich Union and Standard Life sell these plans.

Q How do I buy a policy?

A Speak to an independent financial adviser. No two permanent health insurance policies are alike because exclusions vary and cover differs widely. An adviser should find you a policy to suit your job and your financial circumstances. Otherwise shop around and trawl through the policy details carefully.

Q What if I am unhappy with the policy once I have bought it?

A Don't sit on your hands. Complain in the first instance to the insurance company or the financial adviser who sold you the insurance. If you have no joy, then it should tell you of the independent disputes settlement body to whom you may refer your complaint. Most insurers belong to the Insurance Ombudsman, the Personal Insurance Arbitration Service or the Personal Investment Authority Ombudsman Bureau. These schemes are being embraced within the Financial Ombudsman Service.

Dos and Don'ts

- **DON'T** buy a permanent health insurance policy without first understanding when your policy will pay benefits. Policies vary greatly – some will pay if you are unable to do your own job while others will pay out only if you are unable to do any job.

- **DO** make sure you understand the exclusions in your policy. Nothing can be more upsetting than to discover that your illness is one of them.

- **DON'T** expect the state to rush to your rescue if you suffer long-term illness. Eligibility for incapacity benefit is strict. After 28 weeks of illness claimants must undergo a test that checks their ability to carry out a range of work-related activities such as walking, sitting and going up and down stairs. Even if you qualify, benefits are minimal and taxable.

- **DO** remember to tell the insurer if you change jobs. Failure to do so could invalidate a future claim.

- **DON'T** forget to ask your employer if it offers a group-sponsored permanent health insurance policy. Membership of such a scheme will cost less than if you obtain cover individually.

- **DO** take independent financial advice when buying a policy. The permanent health insurance market is extremely complicated and you could buy a wholly inappropriate policy.

Did you know?

- **DID** you know that Department of Social Security statistics reveal that you are 16 times more likely to be unable to work for more than six months than you are to die before 65? Protecting your income in the event of such a long-term illness makes sense.

- **DID** you know that at any time more than 1.7 million people have been off work for six months or longer due to sickness, accident or disability?

- **DID** you know that there are three types of permanent health insurance? The first is an 'own occupation policy' and pays benefits if you cannot continue to work in your present job. The second is an 'any suitable occupation policy' that pays when you cannot do any work suitable to your level of experience and training. The final category is the 'any occupation' policy that covers you if you are unable to do work of any kind. The first category is best – avoid the others, especially the third, at all costs. You have as much chance of making a valid claim as winning the National Lottery jackpot.

- **DID** you know that some insurance companies offer limited-benefit permanent health insurance plans? These restrict the payment of benefit to a maximum number of years – two-, three- and five-year periods are typical. Such cover requires lower premiums, but once the benefit period has expired you will receive no further payments.

- **DID** you know that only 15% of the working population has any form of insurance against the financial consequences of becoming disabled?

So what now?

- **IT** is vital that you take action to protect yourself and your family in the event of long-term illness – state help is inadequate and difficult to obtain. Permanent health insurance is one of a number of solutions to consider, but do not buy a policy without taking independent financial advice. Your financial adviser should have a handle on key issues such as claims records, speed of payments and the appropriateness of cover offered by individual providers. Don't forget – cheapest is seldom the best.

Private medical insurance

WHATEVER government is in power, it seems that the National Health Service is a financial thorn in its side. When Tony Blair's New Labour swept into office, one of its priorities was to address the chronic underfunding of the NHS and usher in a new bright era for those who worked in the service and those who used it.

Unfortunately, it has had limited success. Long hospital waiting lists remain as big a problem as ever while stories of patients waiting on trolleys in corridors for treatment because no beds are available are commonplace. In light of such events sales of private medical insurance should be booming as people seek to jump the long queues and receive medical care in more comfortable surroundings than the average Health Service hospital ward.

Yet this is not the case. After the boom of the Eighties, sales of private medical insurance have remained stagnant since the early Nineties. In theory, private medical insurance makes good sense, providing a cast-iron guarantee that you will receive medical treatment where and when you want it.

But in practice the companies that dominate the market have not made the product user-friendly. Many policies have more holes, or exclusions, than a Swiss cheese and premiums are not cheap. Indeed, the sector has consistently incurred the wrath of the Office of Fair Trading which believes that too many of its products are too complex. The path to private medical insurance should be trodden with care.

Private medical insurance: key questions and answers

Q What is private medical insurance?

A It is a form of insurance intended to cover the costs of private medical treatment for curable, short-term medical conditions – often referred to as acute conditions. Such insurance will usually cover the costs of medical specialists, surgery, accommodation and nursing, drugs and X-rays. Private medical insurance does not tend to cover the cost of treatment of incurable long-term illnesses such as asthma, diabetes or multiple sclerosis. Such ailments are referred to as chronic illnesses.

Q What types of treatment are covered by private medical insurance?

A It depends upon the policy. Hospital treatment falls into three broad areas:

1. In-patient treatment. Patients are required to stay overnight for private treatment. Most policies cover this.

2. Day-patient treatment. Patients are admitted to hospital for private treatment that requires occupation of a bed, but are not required to stay overnight. Such treatment is often referred to as day-care or day-case. Most policies cover this.

3. Out-patient treatment. Patients receive treatment at a hospital that does not require occupation of a bed. Many policies do not cover this.

Q Do these policies, like other forms of insurance, have exclusions?

A Yes. Though the range of exclusions varies from insurer to insurer, common conditions that policies will not cover include alcoholism, drug abuse, dental treatment, general practitioner services, HIV/AIDS, infertility, normal pregnancy, sterilisation and cosmetic surgery.

Q How long do such policies run?

A They are annual contracts, but most insurers will automatically renew cover each year provided you have paid all the premiums. However, your premium may jump in price from year to year. In the past, increases have been above the rate of inflation as a result of soaring healthcare costs.

Q Does that mean I have to pay premiums annually?

A No. Most insurance companies allow you to pay premiums on a monthly basis, enabling you to spread the cost of cover throughout the year.

Q Are there policies that cover the whole family?

A Yes. There are policies for single people, single parents, married couples, couples and family. Some insurance companies provide children with free cover.

Q Is there an upper age limit above which I cannot take out private medical insurance?

A Most insurance companies will not issue new policies to people above 75.

Q What determines the size of my premium?

A The major influence will be the level of cover and benefits you require. Policies that cover a wide range of medical conditions and offer a choice of hospitals will demand higher premiums than those where the treatments covered are restricted or where the choice of hospitals is limited. Your age will also be taken into account in determining premiums – the older you are, the higher your premiums. Many insurers have introduced policies under which private medical treatment will be granted only if there is a NHS waiting list longer than six weeks for the operation you require. These policies tend to have lower premiums. You may cut the cost of monthly premiums by agreeing to pay an excess every time you make a claim.

Q Is it possible to categorise policies?

A It is not easy. Broadly speaking, policies fall into three categories – comprehensive, standard and budget. Comprehensive plans tend to cover the full cost of basic medical services such as hospital accommodation, surgeons' and anaesthetists' fees, drugs and dressings and out-patient services. They also cover such things as the use of alternative medicines and osteopathy. In contrast, budget plans generally provide full refunds for basic services, but offer limited out-patient services and few extras. Standard plans fall between the two and offer more restricted out-patient services and fewer frills than comprehensive plans. Unfortunately, one company's standard plan is another's comprehensive policy so you need to exercise great care when choosing cover.

Q How do I apply for private medical insurance?

A All insurers will ask you to complete an application form. This will form the basis of the contract you make with the insurer so it is imperative you provide all the information required. If any details turn out to be inaccurate, your insurer may invalidate a claim.

Q Will I need to provide details of my current health when I apply for a policy?

A It depends. Insurance companies issue policies in two different ways. The first method requires full details of your medical history. Depending upon the information you supply, you may be required to undergo a medical examination. If you have suffered from specific illnesses in the past, the insurer will exclude these from your medical cover – either for good or for a limited period – or it will charge an extra premium.

The second method is for the insurance company to issue a policy immediately. However, this will not cover you for the subsequent treatment of illnesses that you have suffered in your immediate past – usually the past five years. Such pre-existing conditions will be covered only when you have remained free of symptoms, treatment, medication, tests and advice for about two years after your policy has started. These policies are issued on a moratorium basis.

Q What policies are best?

A While cover from a moratorium policy is easier and quicker to get, such policies can cause heartbreak when you discover that a claim will not be met. A policy that requires you to make a medical declaration before cover is granted offers the assurance of knowing where you stand – provided that you fill in the form correctly. Failure to disclose key details could jeopardise future claims.

Q Can I take out a policy if I am disabled?

A Yes. You should disclose your disability. Most insurers will exclude from your cover treatment of any medical conditions arising from your disability, but will allow you to claim for treatment that is unconnected with it.

Q What happens if I am asked to work abroad? Will my cover still be valid?

A Most schemes do not provide cover for policyholders who are working abroad permanently. Cover for temporary overseas workers is more common though the trip must not exceed a fixed period, usually 30 days. Some plans provide cover for treatment needed while on holiday abroad.

Q Can I switch insurers?

A Yes, though you should tread with caution. By taking out cover with another provider you may lose cover for existing medical conditions that your previous insurer provided. The promise of lower premiums elsewhere does not always mean a better deal for you – and it probably means less cover.

Q How do I make a claim?

A Your insurer should provide the details when you take out a policy. Always contact your insurance company before receiving any private medical treatment. By doing this you will avoid incurring bills that your insurer will not meet. Your insurer will confirm cover of your treatment, advise you of any limits on specialists or hospitals you may use and how the medical bills will be paid. Most good insurance companies provide telephone helplines to assist you in making a claim.

Q When I claim on a private medical insurance policy, can I go to the hospital of my choice for treatment?

A It depends upon the policy. Some restrict hospital choice so it makes sense to check first. Some also restrict the type of accommodation for which you are eligible while in hospital. Check out this information before buying a policy.

Q What happens if I buy a private medical insurance policy but later decide it is not for me?

A Most policies include a cooling-off period – usually two weeks – to cancel your policy from the time you receive the documents. If you cancel within this period, any premiums already paid will be refunded. After that the insurer is not obliged to refund your premiums.

Q What happens if I take out a policy with which I am subsequently unhappy?

A As with any form of insurance, you have the right to complain. You should first contact the person or company which sold you the policy, preferably putting your complaint in writing. If it is not resolved, the company should refer you to and provide details of an independent complaints body. In most cases, this will be the Insurance Ombudsman at South Quay Plaza, 183 Marsh Wall, London E14 9SR, tel. 0845 600 6666, or the Personal Insurance Arbitration Service at 12 Bloomsbury Square, London WC1A 2LP, tel. 020 7421 7444. These schemes are being embraced within the Financial Ombudsman Service.

Q Can I get tax relief on premiums?

A No. Tax relief used to be available to the elderly but this has been stopped. Benefits are tax-free.

Q Who offers such policies?

A The two biggest insurers are BUPA (British United Provident Association) and PPP (Private Patients Plan). Other players include Abbey Life (part of Lloyds TSB), Allied Dunbar (part of Zurich), Clinicare, Exeter Friendly, Prime Health (part of Standard Life), Norwich Union, OHRA, Royal & SunAlliance and WPA (Western Provident Association).

Q How do I buy a policy?

A Though private medical insurance may be bought over the telephone, it makes sense to seek financial advice before choosing a particular policy. Individual plans vary greatly and simply opting for the policy with the lowest premium may prove a big mistake; there is no point buying a low-cost policy that contains so many exclusions that making a claim becomes extremely difficult.

An independent financial adviser will examine individual policies and tell you which offers the best value for money. He or she should also explain the baffling jargon used by private medical insurers – usually to mislead you.

For a list of Association of British Insurers members who sell private medical insurance write to the ABI, 51 Gresham Street, London EC2V 7HQ.

Q If my employer offers private medical insurance cover should I take it?

A The answer is invariably yes. Because your company obtains cover at group rates from the insurer, the deal it offers you will probably represent great value for money.

Q Are there alternatives to private medical insurance?

A Yes. Some private-sector hospitals offer interest-free credit schemes that allow you to spread payment of your medical bills over a fixed period, typically a year. Such schemes do not address the financial problems that a long stay in a private hospital may bring – they simply spread the financial pain over a longer period.

Hospital cash plans are a further option. These pay a tax-free sum for every day you are treated as an in-patient or day-patient in either an NHS or a private hospital. Other cash benefits may be payable for treatments such as dental work. But such plans are no match for private medical costs insurance because of the low benefits on offer. At the other extreme, major medical expenses cover can be bought that will provide a tax-free cash sum if you undergo surgery. But this offers no guarantee that the cost of private treatment will be met and fails to provide cover for non-acute operations.

Q How much does private medical insurance actually cost?

A A very good question. A survey in the July 1998 edition of *Money Management* magazine tried to quantify the monthly cost of specific plans – and it made uncomfortable reading. Individual companies demand different premiums according to different hospital bands – hospitals categorised according to the level of charges they impose – and different contracts.

For example, Norwich Union's Trust Care policy is a so-called comprehensive plan that covers the costs of hospital accommodation, surgeons' and anaesthetists' fees, in-patient drugs and dressings, out-patient services, home nursing and a private ambulance.

For a 30-year-old single person, the monthly premium works

out at between £22.71 and £46.34 depending upon the choice of hospital band. For a couple where the man is 50 and the woman 46, premiums are higher – between £61.33 and £125.13. For a family where the man is aged 40, the woman 36 and there are two children under 18, premiums range between £72.04 and £146.98.

Norwich Union's Personal Care policy, a budget plan, has limits on the use of out-patient services and home nursing and does not refund the cost of a private ambulance. Naturally, its premiums are cheaper – for the three examples illustrated, monthly premiums are £21.40, £59.20 and £70.50 respectively – and only one hospital band is available.

Dos and Don'ts

- **DO** remember that private medical insurance premiums have traditionally risen above inflation. What may appear affordable insurance now may become an expensive luxury in the years ahead.

- **DON'T** take out the first policy you are offered. Shopping around for private medical insurance is an absolute must. No two policies are the same – it will pay you to take your time, seek advice and find a plan that fits your requirements.

- **DO** find out from your insurer whether there is a cap on the maximum benefit payable in any one year. Some insurers impose a ceiling on benefits and that means there is no guarantee that your private medical bills will be met.

- **DO** ask your insurer whether your policy has a waiver of premium option. This benefit means an insurer will meet the cost of paying for your premiums if you are unable to work after making a claim for in-patient treatment. It is an attractive policy feature, but it adds to the overall cost.

- **DO** check whether your policy has a no-claims discount. Some private medical insurers will reduce premiums for policyholders who make no claims for years.

- **DON'T** be afraid to ask questions. Private medical insurance is rife with impenetrable jargon and policy exclusions. If you don't understand a company's marketing literature, ask your independent financial adviser or the company for an explanation. Jargon is often used to hide important facts.

- **DON'T** take out private medical insurance without considering other types of protection – they may be more appropriate. It may make better sense for you to increase the amount of life cover you have, especially if you have young children. Alternatively, it may be more appropriate for you to arrange financial protection to cover a period of long-term illness.

- **DO** opt for a joint policy rather than two individual policies if you are married. It should work out cheaper.

- **DON'T** be persuaded into taking out cover because the company offers a free alarm clock, free Air Miles or some other gimmick. What you need is proper medical cover at an affordable price.

- **DON'T** be persuaded into switching policies. Switching may be in the interests of the salesman but it will invariably not be in yours – you will lose a host of benefits.

Did you know?

- **DID** you know that about 14% of the UK population has access to some form of private health insurance either through an employer or by arranging their own cover?

- **DID** you know that about 3.5% of the £40 billion we spend every year on healthcare is funded by some form of private medical insurance?

- **DID** you know that more than 50% of private medical insurance policies are employers' schemes with contributions paid either by the employer or jointly by the individual and the employer? If your employer offers such a scheme, join it. The alternative is to take out an individual plan where you pay all the premiums.

- **DID** you know that private medical insurance sales total about £1.7 billion a year?

- **DID** you know that private medical insurance can be bought in three main ways? It can be bought over the telephone in much the same way as many people arrange their household or car insurance. It can also be bought through an independent financial adviser who will search for the best deal for you. Finally, it may be obtained from a company salesman who will sell you his company's insurance, irrespective of how good the policy is. Independent financial advice is the best way.

- **DID** you know that sales of private medical insurance are not covered by the Financial Services Act? This means that salesmen do not have to disclose how much commission they are paid for selling individual plans.

So what now?

- **WHILE** private medical insurance is a welcome solution to NHS queues, no one should venture into this financial arena with their eyes closed. The private medical insurance market offers little protection available for the unprepared. Do not tangle with it unless you are able to separate the policies designed to sting you from those that will provide you with sound, value-for-money cover.

Long-term care insurance

UNTIL recently, meeting the cost of long-term care in later life has not been a personal finance issue that most people, especially the elderly, have had to worry about. The state has invariably come to their rescue.

Unfortunately this is no longer the case. The welfare state has withdrawn its helping hand from all but the needy although under a Labour government, this withdrawal has been reversed with the National Health Service paying for 'nursing care by a registered nurse' – not living and accommodation expenses. As a result, making sure that we have the financial resources to meet the onerous costs of long-term care, or that we have insurance in place that will cover those costs, is now an essential part of sound financial planning.

There is no doubt that long-term care will become one of the key personal finance issues of the new millennium. For those about to retire, or who have elderly parents, this section is essential. It is in your long-term interests to know as much about long-term care as possible.

Long-term care insurance: key questions and answers

Q It's not a problem. Only a minority of elderly people need care, don't they?

A No. As people live longer, more elderly people need long-term care. The Department of Health says that 41% of the population aged 65 or over suffer from long-standing illnesses that limit their daily activities. Such people need some form of care on a daily basis, whether it is the provision of meals or round-the-clock assistance. It is estimated that 25% of us will require long-term care before we die.

Q It's not a problem. Isn't that what families are for?

A Yes, immediate families remain a major provider of informal long-term care, with adult children often looking after aged parents. However, such bonds are weakening as families become more geographically diverse because of increasing job mobility. Working adults often live miles from their parents and are prevented from providing care by work commitments. For those who can provide it, the pressures can be tremendous and exhausting.

Q It's not a problem. The state will come to the rescue, won't it?

A No. Changes introduced by the Community Care Act 1990 mean that only those people with assets worth less than £18,000 (effective from April 2001) may apply for assistance with care fees. Assets include everything from bank or building society savings to National Savings, shares and investment funds such as endowments, Peps and Isas. They also include the value of your home if you cease to live in it as a result of requiring care unless there are special circumstances where it can be disregarded – for example, if a loved one or elderly relative still lives there.

Q What if I have more than £18,000 in capital?

A Quite simply, you will have to pay all your care costs. And these are expensive, often more than £20,000 a year.

Q What happens if I need long-term care?

A Your local authority will first assess you to see what care you require. It has a legal obligation to provide you with this though it will assess your financial situation to determine how it will be paid for. If you own your own home, the authority has the power to levy a charge against it for the costs it incurs in looking after you. If you require residential or nursing-home care, you do not have to accept the offer of local authority care. You may opt for a private care home or one run by a voluntary body. The local authority will provide financial support if you are eligible, though you will have to pay any fees above the level it sets.

Q So long-term care provision is no longer free and anyone with assets of more than £18,000 will probably have to pay for its costs. That simply means that we will all have to save a little harder for our retirement, doesn't it?

A Setting aside money in a bank or building society to meet the costs of future long-term care seems like a sensible exercise. But remember, individuals with assets of more than £18,000 are required to pay all their care costs. And it requires a huge pile of savings to meet full-time care costs that may spiral beyond £20,000 a year.

For example, a person may put £25,000 into a bank or building society account on retirement to help fund care costs should the need ever arise. Assuming this earns gross interest of 5.75% per annum – 4.6% net – for the next 20 years, the investment would yield more than £61,000. In theory this looks like a tidy sum, but if annual care costs based on present levels of £20,000 per year were to rise at 6% a year, it would not meet one year's care fees.

Q So what is the answer to the long-term care funding dilemma?

A It is called long-term care insurance. It works in the same way as insuring your car against the cost of accident damage or insuring your home against fire. You insure yourself against the possibility of requiring long-term care. You may never need to claim on it, but it is there to provide reassurance and to protect your assets from the clutches of the local authority.

Q Are all long-term care insurance policies the same?

A No, there are pre-funded schemes and there are immediate care plans.

Q What is a pre-funded long-term care plan?

A You pay a monthly or annual premium before needing long-term care. If you become unable to perform a set number of tasks

– the so-called activities of daily living that include washing, eating, dressing and going to the toilet unaided – you will receive a regular income from the plan that can be used to pay for long-term care costs. These could be to pay someone to provide home care or they may represent the charges levied by a nursing or residential home.

Typically, you need to fail at least two or three activities of daily living before the plan starts to pay benefits though some plans will pay earlier. Pre-funded policy benefits will usually be paid for as long as long-term care is needed though some plans limit payouts to a predetermined period.

Q Are all pre-funded long-term care plans the same?

A Not at all. Seemingly comparable plans can be as different as chalk and cheese so you need to tread through the long-term care insurance market with great care, preferably guided by a good independent financial adviser. As described above, pre-funded plans may differ in the period over which benefits will be paid. They may also differ in terms of the number of daily activities you need to fail to trigger benefit payments. Some insurers will pay if you fail only two activities, others will pay once you fail three. Others pay reduced benefit if you fail two, rising to full benefit once you are unable to carry out three tasks. It is vital to check these terms before buying a particular plan.

Q Are there other differences?

A Yes. A big problem with insurance of this kind is that premiums could be wasted – you may not need long-term care. To overcome this, investment-backed pre-funded plans have been devised. These not only provide insurance to meet the costs of long-term care should it be required, but they also provide investment benefits if the need for long-term care does not arise. In simple terms, you invest a lump sum in the plan and every month an amount is deducted to pay for long-term care insurance. When you make a claim, your cover kicks in.

At the same time, you will receive the value of the investment fund. If you don't claim, your plan has an investment value that you can either draw upon or leave for somebody else when you die. Non-investment-backed plans, in contrast, have no investment value. If the policy is surrendered, it has no value. Futhermore, if you don't claim on the policy, you get nothing from it other than the reassurance it has provided. Had you needed long-term care, benefits would have been payable.

Q How do pre-funded schemes differ from immediate care plans?

A Immediate care plans provide cover for people who need care straight away. In return for a lump-sum payment, a fixed income is paid for the rest of your life. The income depends primarily upon life expectancy so those in the poorest of health usually receive the largest level of income. The payments cease when you die.

Q Fine, there are insurance solutions available to the long-term care time bomb. But how much does it all cost?

A Premiums vary depending upon the type of plan you require, the age at which you start the plan, the number of activities of daily living required for benefit to begin and whether you are female or male – premiums for women tend to be higher because they live longer.

A recent survey in *Money Management* magazine showed that a man of 55 could pay anything between £32 and £70 in monthly premiums for £1,000 of monthly benefit from a so-called non-investment-backed pre-funded plan. A woman of the same age could pay anything between £39 and £91. At 65, the premiums are higher. A man could pay between £51 and £136 while a woman could pay between £63 and £136.

For an investment-backed pre-funded plan, a man of 55 could make a single payment of between £5,679 and £46,139 for £1,000 of monthly benefit. A woman of the same age could pay between £7,365 and £60,041.

Q Which companies are big in the long-term care insurance market?

A Not surprisingly, in view of their healthcare specialisation, BUPA, Prime Health (owned by Standard Life) and PPP Healthcare all offer plans. Other players include Abbey Life, Commercial Union, Irish Life, Norwich Union, Royal Skandia and Scottish Amicable. The best way to approach these companies is through an independent financial adviser.

Dos and Don'ts

- **DO** take independent financial advice before choosing a particular long-term care insurance plan. Insuring against the costs of future long-term care makes great sense, but it is not easy to choose the most appropriate plan.

- **DON'T** delay. The cost of insuring against long-term care rises with age. The sooner you start to think about making provision – preferably no later than your retirement – the easier will be the cost of such cover on your purse.

- **DON'T** rely upon the state to come to the rescue over the problem of funding long-term care costs – you will be disappointed. The state now helps only the needy.

- **DO** take advice from your family. Before making a commitment to long-term care, whether buying insurance cover or choosing a home, discuss your plans with your immediate family. Any plans you make are likely to impact upon them, whether from an inheritance point of view or the financial or physical input they will have to make in providing assistance with your long-term care needs.

- **DO** consult a solicitor before making a long-term care commitment. Before entering a care home, update a will to ensure your eventual estate is distributed according to your wishes. Preparing a power of attorney in the event of becoming unable to look after your finances is good advice. It means your financial affairs will be looked after by someone you have appointed rather than by a stranger.

- **DON'T** take out a policy you feel uncomfortable with. Buying long-term care insurance can mean a big financial commitment. Ensure you understand the policy you are buying. Check when the cover will begin, whether premiums will rise every year and whether counselling is available when you make a claim. If in doubt, don't proceed.

- **DO** be aware of recent changes to long-term care. This means that 'nursing care by a registered nurse' is now free. However, this will not alter the fact that people requiring long-term care in a nursing or residential home will still have big bills to pay.

- **DO** be aware that the government has taken steps to stop the elderly selling their homes to meet nursing fees. Local authority loans are now available with no interest paid until the loan is due to be repaid.

Did you know?

- **DID** you know that there is an 18% chance that a 65-year-old man will need long-term care? There is a 36% chance that a 65-year-old woman will need long-term care? This rises to 42% at 75.

- **DID** you know that 92% of pensioners estimate their home to be worth more than £25,000? They are unlikely to receive state support if they require nursing-home care.

- **DID** you know that more than 40,000 homes are sold each year in the UK to fund long-term care costs? Long-term care insurance would prevent the need for such drastic action. The government has taken steps to stop homes being sold via the offer of local authority loans.

- **DID** you know that the possibility of needing long-term care in the future for those who are already 65 is greater than the risk of a 30-year-old dying before age 65?

- **DID** you know that the average weekly fee for a residential care home is £300? For nursing homes, where 24-hour professional nursing care is available, it rises to £400.

- **DID** you know that rules for state help with regard to long-term care are different in England, Scotland, Wales and Northern Ireland?

- **DID** you know that the government has indicated its intention to introduce so-called 'CAT' standards for long-term care insurance products? This will give buyers of cover assurances on cover, terms used in literature and access to key information.

So what now?

- **THE** possibility of requiring long-term care in our later lives is something few of us are brave enough to address before the need is upon us. But more of us will have to make future financial provision against the costs – the state will simply be unable or unwilling to bail us out. The message is loud and clear – the earlier the issue of long-term care planning is addressed, the easier it will be on your wallet. Take action now.

Critical illness insurance

IT is a chilling thought that 95% of adults in the UK have no financial protection to help them cope were they to suffer a serious illness. But having to take time off to recover can wreak havoc on the family budget.

Some employers offer insurance cover for workers who suffer

from long-term illness, but they are the exception rather than the rule. And the welfare state is no longer as kind as it used to be. Benefits payable to those who fall ill and cannot work are under constant review and in some cases have been reduced.

Critical illness insurance is a possible solution. Since policies were first offered in this country in the mid-Eighties by Abbey Life, now part of the Lloyds TSB financial services combine, sales have rocketed – from 132,000 in 1991 to 626,000 in 1997.

Yet the sad fact remains that too few people have seen the critical light. Have you? If not, read on – but ignore this section at your peril.

Some key questions and answers

Q What is critical illness insurance?

A Also known as dread disease cover, this insurance pays benefits on the diagnosis of certain specified critical illnesses. Over the years the range of diseases covered has increased to more than 30, though contracts differ from one company to another. However, most policies will pay after heart disease, strokes, renal failure, some cancer, paralysis, major organ transplants and coronary artery bypass surgery.

They will also pay if a policyholder becomes permanently totally disabled as a result of injury or illness.

Q How does a policy pay out?

A Typically, the benefit is paid as a one-off lump sum and is tax-free. The maximum payable varies between providers, but usually ranges between £100,000 and £250,000. Payment is generally made within 28 days of a serious illness being diagnosed though in the event of permanent disability it will take longer – usually six months to a year.

Q How may the benefits be used?

A It is entirely up to you. They may be used to pay off a mortgage or clear outstanding debts. They may also be used to pay for childcare or home help as well as adaptations necessary to a home or car. Crucially, benefits from a critical illness policy give you time to come to terms with your condition and decide what changes you want or need to make to your life.

Q Does a critical illness policy pay if I die?

A No. Benefits are payable only to survivors. Obviously, the shorter the required survival time, the better. Some insurance companies will pay as long as you survive a critical illness for a minimum 15 days. However, policies that combine critical illness and life cover may be bought.

Q Is critical illness cover the same as permanent health insurance?

A No. They cover different needs. A permanent health insurance policy – or income protection plan as it is often known – pays a regular income in the event of long-term sickness or injury. The payments cease if the policyholder recovers from the illness. In contrast, a critical illness policy will make a one-off payment after diagnosis of a serious illness, providing the policyholder with the opportunity to protect his or her quality of life by allowing repayment of a loan, funding a holiday for convalescence or paying for care.

There are a number of instances where payments under one plan would not be allowed under the other. If, for example, you suffer from severe back pain, you will not be covered under a critical illness policy, but will probably qualify for payment under the terms of an income protection plan. In contrast, a minor stroke would probably qualify for a critical illness payment, but it would not necessarily be eligible under an income protection scheme.

Q Why should I buy such insurance?

A For some people, surviving a major illness or accident followed by years of failing health is a fate worse than death. And as medical science advances, the chances of surviving a major illness are greater than ever.

The financial consequences of serious illness can be massive, leading to a loss or drop in income for the sufferer as well as limiting the earnings potential of any carer. A critical insurance policy can provide a welcome financial boost at a time of great emotional stress and financial hardship.

Q But surely I will never suffer a serious illness?

A Don't be so sure. The armada of statistics supporting the need for insurance cover against serious illness is overwhelming. Let me give you a few frightening statistics:

■ The Imperial Cancer Research Fund says one in three people in Britain will be diagnosed with cancer at some point in their life. More than 750 new cases are discovered every day, with two in five of them surviving the disease for at least five years.

■ According to the British Heart Foundation, 800 people will have suffered a heart attack today. More than 50% survive.

■ Research carried out by insurance giant Hanover Re reveals that one in four men and one in five women will contract one of the conditions covered by a standard critical illness product before they reach 65.

■ The same company also says that 100,000 men under 65 will die this year, but five times that number will suffer a critical illness.

■ The average age of claimants under insurer Allied Dunbar's critical illness cover is 44 for men and 41 for women. Serious illness is not confined to the elderly – it may strike at any time.

■ In the Fifties, almost nine in 10 people who suffered a stroke died almost immediately. Today, while one-third die straight away, one-third remain handicapped and the rest make a full recovery. The chances of surviving a critical illness are far greater now.

Q Who should buy critical illness cover?

A There are few people who would not benefit from taking out such cover. Single people usually have no need for life cover because they have no dependants, but critical illness cover is a must.

Without it, a serious illness could turn them from being independent to reliant on friends, family or the state. Similarly, a couple dependent on two incomes could be hit hard financially if one income stopped because of illness. A payment from a critical illness policy would provide a financial buffer.

Q Are there any age limits?

A Most providers allow people to take cover between the ages of 17 and 70. It can be for a limited time – a specified number of years – or for life.

Q Can a policy cover a partner?

A Yes, but benefits will be paid only when the first one suffers a serious illness. Children may also be covered, though normally only from the age of two.

Q What happens if I have suffered a serious illness in the past?

A You will probably have problems obaining cover, though some insurers may offer you a policy that excludes cover for the illness you have previously suffered.

Q How much does it cost?

A Critical illness insurance is not cheap. Allied Dunbar, for example, charges a 29-year-old, non-smoking male £15.72 a month for a stand-alone policy that provides £100,000 of benefit for life. But these premiums will be subject to upward review. Policyholders who want their premiums fixed throughout will pay £42.72 a month. Equivalent premiums for a 29-year-old female are £18.02 and £39.02. Premiums for smokers are higher.

Criticial illness cover may also be bought as an additional benefit to an endowment taken out with a mortgage. This ensures that the mortgage is paid off if the borrower dies or becomes seriously ill. Buying cover in this way can be cost-effective. For example, Allied Dunbar demands an additional £7.90 in monthly premiums if critical illness cover is required by a 29-year-old man as part of a £100,000 endowment.

Q How do I buy a sound policy?

A Choosing the right critical illness policy is tricky – there are more than 60 providers offering 200 versions of such insurance. Policies vary widely in the illnesses they cover so don't simply opt for the cheapest plan because it will probably offer limited cover.

Similarly, do not opt for a policy that covers the longest list of diseases – it may not be the most appropriate. Policies that appear to cover every serious illness imaginable are sometimes merely an excuse for the insurer to charge higher premiums.

A critical illness policy should cover heart attack, cancer, stroke, kidney failure, major organ transplant, coronary artery bypass surgery and total permanent disability.

If you are in any doubt, speak to an independent financial adviser. He or she should have a finger on the pulse of the critical illness policy market.

Q Who offers critical illness cover?

A Most leading insurance companies including Allied Dunbar, Legal & General, Skandia, Swiss Life and Zurich Life offer plans. But many banks and building societies have now joined the act. They include Alliance & Leicester, Barclays, Halifax, Midland, Nationwide and Woolwich. Even Virgin and Marks & Spencer offer policies.

Q How do I take out such insurance?

A As with most insurance policies, you will need to complete a proposal form. You will be asked if members of your family have suffered major illnesses in the past. If they have, your policy may be rated, which means you will pay higher premiums. You may need a medical before being accepted for cover, but this does not necessarily mean you will have to pay higher premiums. Remember that when you take out a policy, there will be a waiting period – typically three months – before you can make a claim.

Q What if I have to make a claim?

A When you take out a policy, let your partner or family know where the documents are kept. Then if you suffer a serious illness they can contact the insurer for a claim form. Once this is signed, the insurer can obtain medical details that will determine if a payment should be made.

Q What happens once I have made a claim?

A The policy lapses. You may make only one claim under a critical illness insurance policy. The only exception is if you have a family policy that covers your children. In some cases where your child suffers a critical illness a payment may be made without affecting your benefit.

Q What happens if I take out a policy only to decide I don't want the plan after all?

A Most insurance companies allow a breathing space of two weeks during which you may cancel if you change your mind. This is often referred to as the cooling-off period.

Q And finally, what happens if I want to complain, maybe because my claim is not being met?

A Complain in writing to the company. If you have no joy, you will probably be able to refer your complaint to the ombudsman scheme to which your insurance company belongs.

Dos and Don'ts

- **DON'T** buy a critical illness policy purely on the basis of the cost of the premiums. You could end up with an unsatisfactory policy that offers limited cover.

- **DO** ensure that the company supplying your policy is financially secure and stable – in other words, that it will still be there to pay benefit in the future.

- **DO** check to see if permanent total disability is covered by your plan. If not, you could suffer an illness or injury that left you unable to work again in the future, but one for which you could not make a critical illness claim because it was not specifically listed.

- **DO** check whether the insurance company offers a counselling service in the event of a claim. Some insurers offer help to enable you to cope more easily with the life-changing event you have just undergone.

- **DO** ensure that the company you are dealing with is a member of an ombudsman scheme. This could avoid the need for legal action if your insurer refuses to honour your claim.

- **DO** go through the policy carefully before you sign on the dotted line. Look out for exclusions. Many policies will not pay out if serious illness is caused by drug or alcohol abuse.

- **DO** take independent financial advice before buying a critical illness policy. A good adviser will guide you through the critical illness maze and ensure that you buy a policy that is within your financial budget and provides the cover you need. He or she should also check the insurer's claims record to ensure that the company you choose has a good reputation for meeting valid claims promptly.

Did you know?

- **DID** you know that many famous people have survived major illnesses? Singer and film star Olivia Newton-John and *EastEnders* actress Wendy Richards have survived cancer. Politician Michael Heseltine and film star and singer Adam Faith have survived heart attacks.

- **DID** you know that one in eight healthy women will contract cancer before reaching 65? Of these, 70% will survive the cancer for more than a year while 50% will survive for more than five years.

- **DID** you know that in a typical year, for each person who dies, 16 suffer long-term illness or disability?

So what now?

- **IF** you think a critical illness policy is for you, your first step should be to consult an independent financial adviser. If you don't already use one, ask friends to recommend one. An adviser will be able to recommend the policy most suitable to your specific needs and financial resources and will obtain quotes for you. If you are happy with them, complete the selected insurer's application form. Cover will usually begin immediately, or you may be asked for further medical information.

CHAPTER **4**

Borrowing

CREDIT

'A system whereby a person who can't pay a debt gets another person who can't pay it either to say he can.'

W. C. Fields

AT some stage in our lives, we all need to borrow money. Such borrowing may result from a short-term cash flow problem or it may result from a desire to fund a major purchase such as the acquisition of a new car or a new piece of furniture for the home. And of course, the vast majority of wannabe homeowners have no choice but to borrow via means of a mortgage in order to fund the purchase of a home (a process discussed in chapter 2).

It is fair to say that it has never been easier to borrow money. However, the temptation of easy credit can be the downfall of many people's personal finance affairs. To be blunt, you need to be mighty careful when entering the borrowing minefield because traps, nasty interest penalties and financial woe await the unsuspecting.

Q I have a short-term cash flow problem. Should I take out a loan?

A The answer is definitely no. It is far better to consider other options first of all. For a kick-off, you should see whether you have funds available from other savings to cover any temporary shortfall. You should also speak to your bank. Most banks will now grant customers temporary overdraft facilities almost as a matter of course. Admittedly, as explained in the chapter on bank accounts, such facilities do not come cheaply with banks eager to levy a menagerie of charges – arrangement fees, interest and monthly usuage fees. However, provided you are sure that your financial difficulties are temporary only, such a flexible borrowing arrangement makes sense for most people.

Two further points. Some banks provide free temporary overdraft facilities as part of their banking package – it is worth finding out whether your account offers such a service. Secondly, ensure the overdraft you have with your bank is authorised – in other words, it has been approved by the bank. Failure to get authorisation will lead to a whole raft of charges descending upon you.

Q What if I need to borrow money to make a major purchase?

A You then move into formal loan territory. However, before you do this, you should ask yourself a number of questions:

1. Do I really need to make the purchase now or can I wait a few months until I have built up sufficient savings?

2. Do I already have any savings I can draw upon to meet the cost of the purchase? While having savings to draw upon in case of a financial emergency can be a comforting factor, remember that the interest rate you will earn from your savings will pale into insignificance compared to the interest charged on any loan. Also, interest on savings is taxable. As a result, it can often make sense to fund major purchases out of savings rather than getting locked into a formal agreement with a loan company.

3. Can I borrow from relatives, a friend or parents? Borrowing in such a way can ensure you get a fair deal when it comes to

interest charges. However, you must be sure that you will honour the loan agreement – otherwise a friendship could be ruined for life. Indeed, if you borrow in this way, it is best to do so in as formal a way as possible – putting any arrangements down in writing and setting up a standing order to meet monthly repayments.

4. How much can I afford to repay each month if I borrow? There is no point borrowing money which then means your finances are plunged into chaos because of the steep repayment schedule. Only borrow sums where you can comfortably afford the monthly repayments. You must be aware that if you take out a loan and then you are unable to meet the payments – in other words, default – you can land yourself in serious financial difficulty.

Q OK, I've answered those four questions. Do I simply get a loan from my bank or respond to the first loan mailshot which comes winging its way through my letterbox?

A An emphatic 'No' to both questions. You should explore all possible loan avenues available to you in search of the most competitive loan deal around. Remember, most loans carry with them expensive interest payments. It is in your interests to keep these to a bare minimum.

Q Fine. So what routes should I explore?

A There are various.

ROUTE 1: YOUR EMPLOYER. Some employers are prepared to offer staff free or cheap loan arrangements, especially if the loan's purpose is work related – for the purchase of a travel season ticket for example. Although such loan arrangements are convenient and usually cost-effective, don't enter into such an agreement lightly. Do bear in mind that if you move jobs before the loan comes to an end, you will be required to clear the outstanding debt by way of making a lump-sum payment. Also, your loan may be treated by the taxman as a benefit in kind.

ROUTE 2: NIL PER CENT DEALS. Some retailers, in order to drum up business, offer 0% loan arrangements on the purchase of some goods. Provided the goods are what you really want and are not simply overpriced in order to fund the 0% loan deal, such loan arrangements can be a cost-effective way forward. However, you must be aware that these deals come in different guises and are not without their hidden nasty traps.

The most straightforward 0% deal is where you put down a small deposit – typically between 10% and 20% of the purchase price – and then you repay the balance in monthly instalments over an agreed period paying no interest whatsoever. Provided you can afford the deposit, this arrangement is the most straightforward.

Then there is the limited period interest-free credit. Here, you pay a deposit and then pay monthly interest-free payments for an agreed period. At the end of this period you are given two options. You can clear the remaining balance by way of a lump-sum payment thereby escaping any interest charges. Or you can clear the out-standing balance by way of continued monthly payments but this time with interest payments on top. If you are certain that you will have funds available to make the lump-sum payment, such a loan deal can make sense but if not, it can prove expensive. Interest payments, once they kick in, can be high. Also, you need to remind yourself that the outstanding balance needs to be cleared in time in order to escape interest charges – don't expect the company to do so. After all, it is in their interests for you to pay interest charges.

Finally, there is the buy now, pay later 0% deal. Here you are not required to pay anything for an agreed period of time but then you must pay the full purchase price. Failure to do this will result in you being obliged to pay for the goods by means of monthly payments which include interest charges. Like the limited interest-free credit arrangement, buy now, pay later schemes require you to be financially disciplined. If you don't think you will have the funds available to pay for the goods at the end of the agreed period, it will probably pay you to go elsewhere.

ROUTE 3: PERSONAL LOANS. This is the route chosen by most people who want to borrow money to fund a major purchase. Offered by most banks and building societies, personal loans work as follows. You borrow an agreed sum over an agreed time period and you then make monthly fixed payments, part capital and part interest. Loan rates, which are fixed, do vary widely so it will pay you to shop around. *Moneyfacts* (01603 476476) publishes a regular table of personal loan deals including details of the minimum and maximum advances available, interest rates payable and the length of loan terms. Companies that provide personal loans include: Abbey National, HSBC, Lloyds TSB, Nationwide building society, Sainsbury's Bank and Tesco. Personal loans are offered with and without insurance. The insurance will usually cover payments if you are the victim of an accident, sickness or unemployment. However, this insurance can bump up monthly payments considerably so check the policy details thoroughly before signing up for it. Often, these policies are not worth the paper they are written on and making a claim is nigh impossible.

Q Are there any other sources of borrowing?

A Yes. You shouldn't rule out the following.

ROUTE 4: A CREDIT UNION. If you are a member of a credit union, it is possible to borrow money at attractive interest rates, presently 1% per month. You can only borrow from a credit union if you are first a member and you already save on a regular basis with the union. See JIGSAW piece 18 for further details on credit unions.

ROUTE 5: BORROWING AGAINST AN ENDOWMENT POLICY. It is often possible to borrow money against the value of an endowment policy. This can prove an attractive way of borrowing because loan rates are usually attractive. However, the policy must not be assigned to a lender – linked to a mortgage – and you must still be paying the policy's premiums. Nor must the policy be unit-linked – it must be with-profits-based. Insurance companies are often flexible concerning how such loans are repaid. Provided you intend to clear your loan with the proceeds from your endowment on maturity, most insurers will only demand that you make interest payments. If you have an endowment and are considering a loan, speak to your endowment provider to see whether such an option is open to you.

ROUTE 6: BORROWING AGAINST THE VALUE OF YOUR HOME. Some lenders will allow you to take out a further loan against the value of your home provided you have sufficient equity left in the home. This can prove an attractive way of borrowing because interest charges tend to be more in line with mortgage rates than with those for personal loans. Most lenders will insist that you pay a fee for having the house valued.

ROUTE 7: CREDIT CARDS. There is nothing to stop you funding big purchases by means of a credit card provided the card issuer will extend you a big enough borrowing limit. However, this can prove a costly option unless the interest rates on your card are extremely attractive – most, unfortunately, are not. Also, borrowing via a credit card requires great financial discipline. You are under no obligation to make regular payments to clear the debt, other than the minimum payment required by your credit card company. Indeed, credit card companies don't want you to clear the debt quickly because they can then make lots of money at your expense.

Q Is it possible to compare the costs of different forms of borrowing?

A It is not easy. APRs (annual percentage rates) can help. An APR, which represents the total annual charge for credit expressed as a percentage, takes into account all charges involved in obtaining a loan – including arrangement fees, any compulsory insurance or maintenance contracts that must be taken out, the amount and frequency of the loan repayments and the length of the loan. So if you are looking at two competing personal loan deals, the APRs quoted should give you a very good indication of the best deal available. However, different assumptions are made when calculating APRs for different forms of credit. This can result in different forms of credit looking more expensive than others – even though they are not.

As well as an APR, it is a good idea to find out the 'total cost of credit' or the 'total amount payable'. This will tell you the total amount you will have paid out by the time you have finished the loan. It can provide for frightening reading.

Dos and Don'ts

- **DO** be wary of mailshots promoting loan deals, especially from companies you have never heard of before. Better deals elsewhere are likely to be on offer.

- **DO** be wary of adverts in local and national newspapers for loan deals. Many offer a terrible interest deal.

- **DO** bear in mind that if you borrow from another person, as opposed to a loan organisation, your friend or relative will have to declare the interest received on their tax return.

- **DO** check out the procedures for early repayment if you take out a personal loan. Most lenders will charge you at least two months' interest as an early redemption penalty. Find out this information before you take out a loan.

- **DO** bear in mind that if you borrow funds against the value of your house, you are offering your home as security for the loan. This means that if you do not keep up your repayments, your lender can repossess your home and sell it off to pay off the loan. If you take out a personal loan from a bank and building society, these are unsecured loans which means your home is

not at risk if you default on the loan although you will blemish
your credit record.

- **DO** bear in mind that if you are looking to buy a car, the
  borrowing options available to you are often much wider than
  for conventional borrowing. These can include hire purchase,
  personal contract hire and personal contract purchase. See
  JIGSAW 20 for a full explanation of these additional options.

- **DON'T** take out a personal loan from your bank simply
  because you feel obliged to do so through some sense of loyalty.
  You owe your bank or building society nothing. But you do
  owe yourself a duty to ensure you get the best possible loan
  terms, which often means going elsewhere.

- **DON'T** just sit on your hands if you are turned down for a
  loan. Find out why. It may be because the company has given
  you a bad credit score or because you have an adverse credit
  reference. It should tell you which method it has used to turn
  you down. If it is because you have a poor credit reference, then
  you should check out your reference to see whether it is correct.
  If it is not, you have the right to request corrections. Experian
  (0115 941 0888) and Equifax (08705 783783) are the
  country's main credit reference agencies. See GOLDEN
  NUGGET 43 for further details.

- **DON'T** sit on your hands if you start to run into difficulties in
  making loan repayments. Contact the lender straight away.
  Don't bury your head in the proverbial sand because it will just
  make your life more difficult. Also, consider enlisting the help
  of a debt adviser. The local Citizens Advice Bureau should be
  able to help. Other helpful organisations include your local
  Money Advice Centre, the Consumer Credit Counselling
  Service (020 7211 8608) and the National Debtline (0845
  9500511).

Did you know?

- **DID** you know that if you borrow more than £5,000 in total from your employer, you will have to pay tax on the difference between the interest you would have paid if you had been charged interest at the so-called 'official rate of interest' and the interest you actually paid? The official rate is determined by the Inland Revenue. However, even if you have to pay this tax, a loan from your employer will probably work out to be a better deal than a loan from an alternative provider.

- **DID** you know that if you are a member of a certain profession or a member of a trades union, you can often obtain competitively priced loan deals? It is worth asking the question.

- **DID** you know that new-style flexible mortgages now allow homeowners to borrow money to fund major purchases? These new-style mortgages enable you to make repayments whenever you want to as well as draw funds from the mortgage pot to fund purchases. Provided the borrowing keeps you within the overall borrowing limit set by your lender, you will pay interest on the extra borrowings at mortgage rate levels. Major players include Bank of Scotland, Virgin and Woolwich.

So what now?

- **OBTAINING** finance to make a major purchase is easy. But you owe it to yourself to ensure you get a deal which suits you and not just the lender. So be prepared to do your homework, shop around, be patient, ask questions (however embarrassed they may make you feel) and don't take the first loan deal you see or which is offered you. If you have doubts about a certain finance deal, trust your gut instinct and go elsewhere. Even if you agree to the loan, you usually do have 14 days – a so-called cooling off period – to change your mind. Just remember: get yourself locked into a rotten loan deal and you will end up regretting it for a long, long time to come.

Credit cards

OVER the past five years the UK credit card industry has undergone a dramatic transformation. Though it was once dominated by mighty banks such as Barclays (Barclaycard) and Lloyds TSB who believed they could charge customers what they pleased, the credit card market has become fiercely competitive as new players have entered. These firms, mainly from the United States, have changed the credit card scene by introducing cards that charge much lower interest rates than the big banks. The traditional companies have been forced to respond and offer customers a better deal.

In this section, we look at how credit cards can work to your financial advantage – provided you are prepared to do a little homework.

Credit cards: key questions and answers

Q What is a credit card?

A It is simply a form of borrowing. The card issuer sets a maximum credit limit and you can spend as much as you like up to that limit provided you repay a minimum amount each month.

Q How does it differ from other plastic such as debit and charge cards?

A A debit card is linked to your bank account. The cost of anything bought with this card, or any money withdrawn with it will be taken from your account almost immediately. It is effectively a plastic cheque.

With a charge card, you charge your purchases to the card. But when you receive your monthly statement you are required to repay the outstanding balance in full. You are not allowed to roll over debt into the next month as you can with a credit card.

A more recent development is the electronic purse, which you 'load' with money before you go shopping.

Q What charges do credit cards levy?

A Interest is the main charge. You will be charged interest each month on the outstanding balance on your credit card account. Typically, this will be between 1% and 2% irrespective of underlying bank base rates. This is equivalent to an annual interest rate of between 12% and 24%.

Q Is interest charged from the day I make a purchase?

A It depends. With most cards, provided you repay your bill in full each month, you will pay no interest. This means that you benefit from up to 56 days of interest-free credit from the day you make a purchase to the day payment is due. If you do not repay the debt you will be charged interest on new purchases either from the purchase date or the date the transaction is put through your account.

Some cards do not offer an interest-free period. This means that transactions attract interest charges immediately irrespective of whether you clear the balance. If you prefer to clear your debts each month these cards are not for you – you are better off with one that offers an interest-free period.

Q Do interest rates move up and down in line with bank base rates?

A In theory yes, but in practice no. Many card issuers are quick to push up their rates if bank base rates rise, but are reluctant to cut them when bank rates fall. Credit card interest rates seldom fall below double digits unless a company offers special short-term teaser rates to tempt people to apply for its card.

Q Are there additional charges?

A Yes. Many companies charge an annual management fee of between £10 and £12 irrespective of how often you use the card, though some will waive it once you have spent a certain amount. Cards that do not apply an annual fee include Alliance & Leicester, Capital One, People's Bank Connecticut and RBS Advanta.

Many companies levy a range of charges if you break the terms and conditions of your card or if you require additional services. Exceeding your agreed borrowing limit or being late with a monthly payment usually incurs a fixed penalty fee. The card issuer will apply a charge if you request an additional monthly statement or a second card for a partner, if your cheque or direct debit to clear any of your outstanding balance returns unpaid or if you use your card overseas.

Companies cannot simply apply extra charges willy-nilly. When you obtain your card, the issuer will send you a booklet setting out the card's terms and conditions and details of any extra charges will be included. It is vital that you read the booklet thoroughly and keep it in a safe place. Some card issuers detail the charges they can levy on the reverse of your monthly statement.

Q How much do I have to repay each month?

A Most credit card issuers stipulate a minimum payment of £5 or 5% of the outstanding balance on the card account. But remember that any uncleared balance will attract interest charges. Every month, your card issuer will send you a statement detailing transactions on your account and the outstanding debt. It will also include details of the minimum payment required and the date by which this should be paid. You can make the payment by post or at your local bank, though the bank may charge for this service.

Q How much can I spend on my card?

A The card issuer will set a limit when it assesses your initial application. Usually, after six months it will review the limit and may increase it. It will usually inform you of a new spending limit by writing to you or by a note on your regular monthly card statement. But do not simply regard an increase in your limit as a licence to spend – you still have to repay the money eventually and pay interest on the debt in the meantime.

Q Can I have any credit card I choose?

A Yes, you may apply to any card issuer. Some recent players on the UK credit card scene, such as US companies Capital One Bank and People's Bank Connecticut, offer more attractive rates than traditional card providers such as Barclaycard. Today there are about 1,300 brands of credit card in the UK, offered through more than 30 card issuers.

When you apply for a card, the issuer will first carry out a credit check on you. Your application may be turned down, especially if you have a poor credit record (see below). Amazingly, some issuers have even turned down customers because they have never previously held a credit card.

Q Can I transfer my balance to a card that offers cheaper interest rates?

A Many card issuers actively seek customers willing to transfer credit card debts from another provider by offering enticing introductory interest rates. These are significantly lower than the company's standard rates and tend to apply only to the amount of debt you transfer rather than any new balances you incur. They usually last for a predetermined period, typically six months. When you transfer, your old card company should not levy any exit charges – indeed, it might tempt you to stay by offering to cut its interest rates or waive its annual fee.

Q Can I get my card issuer to reduce its interest charges?

A Some issuers levy reduced charges on customers who agree to have the minimum monthly payment paid from their bank account by direct debit. Others charge lower rates if you use your card a lot.

Q Can I withdraw cash on my credit card?

A Yes, though you need to tread carefully. Most card issuers charge higher interest on cash withdrawals than on purchases while some levy a fixed transaction fee of up to £5. They also charge interest immediately – there is no interest-free period. When you receive your credit card you will also be sent a personal identification number (PIN) under separate cover. By using this number you will be able to obtain cash via an ATM (automated teller machine) or cash machine.

Q What about card incentive schemes?

A Many cards offer incentive schemes to encourage you to use your card more. Barclaycard, for example, offers Profile Points that may be redeemed against goods bought through the Profile Points catalogue. Cashback credit cards are also increasingly popular. With these you earn 'cash' every time you use your card. However, you should not choose a credit card simply because it offers an attractive incentive scheme especially if you are using it to borrow. The competitiveness of its interest rates and charges should be the most important determining factor.

Companies that offer incentive schemes as part of their credit card package include Alliance & Leicester, American Express, First Direct, Goldfish, Liverpool Victoria, Midland Bank, NatWest, Sainsbury's Bank, Tesco and TSB.

Q What about gold cards?

A Gold cards were once the preserve of the rich, but these days you do not necessarily have to be wealthy to qualify for one. However, remember that its interest rate may be higher than a normal credit card and that you will be paying for a range of benefits, such as travel insurance, that you may not require. Platinum cards are even available.

Q What about store cards? Are they a better deal than a traditional credit card?

A No. The only reason to apply for a store card, which is simply a credit card issued by one particular retailer, is if the store does not accept other credit cards. But beware – most store cards levy high interest charges. Major stores that offer credit cards include John Lewis, Bhs and Marks & Spencer.

Some stores operate so-called budget cards. With these, cardholders agree to pay a monthly sum and are given a credit limit that is a multiple of that payment. For example, a monthly payment of at least £10 and a multiple of 30 would give you a credit limit of £300. Interest rates on these cards may be high.

Q What about affinity credit cards? Are they worthwhile?

A Affinity cards may be linked to a leading charity or even your favourite football team. The charity or affinity group benefits in two ways – it receives a payment when you first take out the card, plus a sum linked to the level of your card spending. Interest rates tend to be in line with those levied on traditional cards, but do not expect a more benevolent attitude just because your card is linked to a charity. If you fail to repay the minimum monthly payment on time you will still be hit with a penalty charge.

Q How do I compare the competitiveness of individual credit cards?

A All credit card issuers are required to tell you the annual percentage rate (APR) levied on transactions. In theory, this is a measurement of the cost of credit and takes into account the monthly interest charge levied by the card issuer and any annual fee it may charge. But this calculation is flawed because it fails to consider any interest-free period offered by the issuer. Some issuers have manipulated the APR by using assumptions that reduce the impact of their annual fees on the rate they quote. A better competitive test for potential card buyers is to compare the monthly interest rate and the annual fee charged by different providers.

The way you intend to use your card should also influence your choice. If you simply want to use a credit card to obtain interest-free credit, then find one that levies no annual fee and offers the maximum 56-day interest-free period. The interest rate that the card levies will not concern you if you do not intend to borrow. However, if you intend to use your card for short-term borrowing the monthly interest rate is all important.

Q Who offers credit cards?

A All the major UK banks – Barclays (Barclaycard), Lloyds TSB, HBSC and NatWest – offer credit cards. But these tend not to offer the best deals around and cards are now available from leading building societies (Nationwide), newly converted banks (Alliance & Leicester), friendly societies (Liverpool Victoria), American banks (People's Bank Connecticut, Capital One) and even leading supermarkets such Sainsbury and Tesco.

Q Where can I obtain further details on credit cards?

A Contact the Credit Card Research Group at 2 Ridgmount Street, London WC1E 7AA, call 020 7436 9937. For details of credit card interest rates, Moneyfacts Publications provides comparative information. Write to Moneyfacts House, 66–70 Thorpe Road, Norwich NR1 1BJ, or call 01603 476476.

Dos and Don'ts

- **DON'T** regard credit cards as an easy way to borrow. With interest rates more than three times the present bank rate they can be expensive.

- **DON'T** take out a card simply because it offers an enticingly low introductory interest rate. Assess the card's true competitiveness by comparing the issuer's standard interest charges with those of other providers. If they appear expensive, take your business elsewhere.

- **DON'T** opt for a gold card simply because the provider says it represents an important status symbol. Though a gold card will allow you a higher credit limit, enable you to draw more cash out on a daily basis and provide free insurance, you will pay for all this through higher interest rates.

- **DO** remember that when you buy with a credit card the card issuer is jointly liable, together with the supplier of the goods or services you buy, if anything is wrong with the goods. This means that you can claim from the credit card company if the supplier cannot or will not compensate you.

- **DO** remember that not all credit cards offer interest-free credit. If this is what you want, apply for a card that charges interest only from the statement date and that imposes this interest only if you do not settle the statement in full.

- **DON'T** fall into the inertia trap. Check the interest rate you pay on your card on a regular basis. If it is uncompetitive consider transferring your business to another card issuer.

- **DO** report the loss of your credit card immediately. Most card issuers operate a 24-hour emergency telephone service to which you can report the loss. Typically, you will have to pay £50 towards the cost of any fraudulent transactions made before you notified the issuer of the loss. Most card issuers offer cheap insurance that protects your card and any others you may hold against loss or fraudulent use.

- **DO** take care of your credit card, especially overseas. NEVER disclose your card personal identification number (PIN) to anyone, NEVER discard transaction slips that display your card number and NEVER give your card details over the telephone to a caller you have never spoken to or dealt with before.

- **DO** find out what comes with your credit card. It might include useful add-ons such as travel insurance and life cover.

- **DON'T** use a credit card to pay for expensive items such as a new car or furniture when you want to spread payments over a long period. A personal loan is probably better and cheaper.

- **DON'T** be enticed by smooth credit card advertising or attractive mailshots that come through your letterbox. Before signing up for a card, check out its competitiveness.

Did you know?

- **DID** you know that Barclays was the first British bank to introduce credit cards in the UK? Barclaycard was launched in 1966.

- **DID** you know that there are more than 500,000 UK outlets where credit cards and debit cards may be used?

- **DID** you know that you may use your credit card overseas, either to pay for goods or to draw cash (in local currency, of course!) from a cash machine?

- **DID** you know that some credit card issuers offer up to 100 days' free insurance against theft, loss or damage on most goods bought on their cards? Other benefits include discounts on holidays, membership of car rescue services and free assistance with legal, travel and medical matters.

- **DID** you know that a credit card issuer must provide certain information if it turns you down for a card? It must tell you the name and address of the credit reference agency it used to obtain details of your credit record. The two main credit reference agencies in the UK are Experian Ltd, PO Box 8000, Nottingham NG1 5GX, call 01159 410888, and Equifax Europe, Dept IE, PO Box 3001, Glasgow G81 2DT, call 08705 783783.

- **DID** you know that all credit cards, apart from store cards, are linked to an international card scheme such as American Express, MasterCard or Visa which allows them to be used in millions of outlets worldwide?

- **DID** you know that your card payments can be protected if you become ill, suffer an accident, lose your job or die? Protection policies are offered by most card issuers and are not expensive, but check the terms and conditions carefully – the policies may contain exclusions that could make a valid claim almost impossible.

- **DID** you know that if you buy faulty goods with a credit card, the card issuer will refund your money as a last resort?

So what now?

- **THERE** is no doubt that the credit card arena is now a buyer's market. Provided you are prepared to do a little homework, cards may be found to meet all financial needs – whether you want to borrow or simply obtain interest-free credit. But once you have the card in your wallet, ensure it continues to offer value for money. If it becomes uncompetitive, take your business elsewhere.

CHAPTER

5
Savings

MONEY

'What you'd get on beautifully
without if only other people weren't
so crazy about it.'

Margaret Herriman

Deposit savings

AT the heart of everybody's savings portfolio should be money left
on deposit – with a bank, building society or one of the new deposit
takers. Deposit savings should be the first home you look for when
you decide to start saving – maybe so you can amass a deposit for a
new home or simply save for the future.

However, choosing a savings account is no longer as simple as
it used to be. Choice, as in most spheres of personal finance, is
greater than ever before with more providers vying for your money.
This in turn has led to the development of a whole range of different
savings accounts with different terms and conditions. Unless you
tread carefully, you can end up with an account which will cause
you more misery than joy.

Deposit savings: key questions and answers

Q What is a deposit account?

A It is simply a vehicle operated by a bank or building society which allows you to save without worry that your capital is at risk. Your money grows in value by attracting interest.

Q Can the capital I invest in a deposit savings account grow in value?

A Your capital cannot grow by capital gain, nor for that matter can it fall as a result of capital loss. Your money grows in value by the fact that it earns interest. The key, therefore, is to ensure you are getting an attractive rate of interest.

Q So are all savings accounts the same?

A No way. Accounts can be broadly classified into the following categories:

CATEGORY ONE: INSTANT ACCESS ACCOUNTS. As their names implies, these accounts allow you instantaneous access to your money and are ideal as a home for your emergency money – funds that you can get hold of in a hurry to meet unexpected bills or pay for the repair of a household crisis (breakdown of the central heating or the pipes freezing). Interest rates usually improve the more money you have in your account although it must be said that instant access accounts do not tend to pay attractive interest rates. So only have as much money in an instant access account as you feel you need to have immediate access to – any surplus should be saved elsewhere.

CATEGORY TWO: NOTICE ACCOUNTS. Often referred to as high-interest accounts, these savings vehicles provide higher interest rates to depositors who are prepared to give notice of their intentions to make withdrawals. Periods of notice vary but are typically 30, 60 or 90 days. So, for example, a 30-day-notice account will usually give you two options when it comes to making a withdrawal – you can either give notice and then wait the 30 days for your money. Alternatively, you can obtain your money straight away but lose 30 days' interest on the amount being withdrawn. In theory, the longer the notice period, the better the interest rate you should earn on your money but it doesn't always work out like that because of the competitiveness of the savings market. Like instant-access accounts, savings rates on notice accounts are usually tiered, which means that the more you save, the better the deal you should get.

CATEGORY THREE: TIME DEPOSITS OR BONDS. These accounts typically offer you a fixed-interest rate for a fixed period – anything from one to five years. Usually, because the interest rates are fixed, the terms and conditions of these deals are strict – no additional investments can be made and early access to your savings cannot be obtained or only after paying a heavy penalty. Again, the more money you invest initially, the more attractive the fixed-rate deal you will lock into. Given you are in effect locking your money away for a fixed period, these accounts should only be used if you can afford to be without the money for the term of the offering. A recent version of a fixed-term bond is the stepped or escalator bond. Here the annual interest rate you earn increases every year throughout the bond's life. Obviously, in assessing the merits of such bonds, it is essential to calculate the average rate of interest you will be earning over its term and then to compare it against alternative savings accounts. Don't be mesmerised by the high interest rate on offer in the bond's final year.

CATEGORY FOUR: REGULAR INCOME ACCOUNTS. Most savings accounts pay interest on an annual basis. But a number are available which pay monthly or quarterly income. These accounts are usually notice accounts with a monthly income option and are ideal for retired people who require a regular income from their savings.

CATEGORY FIVE: REGULAR SAVINGS ACCOUNTS. A number of savings institutions now offer savings accounts which encourage you to make deposits on a regular monthly basis. Usually, monthly deposits are made by standing order or direct debit from your bank. And usually the account provider will pay an interest bonus if you manage to invest on a regular basis for a set period. A number of building societies have established a good reputation for offering these accounts. They include: Britannia, Market Harborough, Nationwide and Yorkshire.

CATEGORY SIX: OTHER. Most deposit takers offer specific children's savings accounts. Some also target the elderly with accounts for people over a set age. With children's accounts, the key is to look at the competitiveness of the interest rate being paid – don't be mesmerised by any free gifts on offer. With accounts designed for the elderly, it is essential to assess their competitiveness against accounts available to all and sundry. There is absolutely no point taking out an over-55s savings account, for example, if the interest rate on offer is much lower than available on ordinary savings accounts. Many deposit takers now also offer affinity savings accounts. One of the biggest affinity links is with football clubs where you open an account operated by a bank or building society. The institution then pays over an amount to the club on an annual basis dependent upon how much money supporters have saved with it. Football clubs that offer such savings accounts include Darlington (through Darlington building society) Stoke, Ipswich, Manchester United, Port Vale (all Britannia building society). Coventry (Market Harborough building society), Charlton (Woolwich bank), Huddersfield (Yorkshire building society) and West Bromwich Albion (West Bromwich building society). While these accounts are a good way of supporting your club (and can offer club discounts), they can offer you a poor savings deal.

Q How are savings accounts operated?

A Most accounts are still branch-based. That is, you can go into the local branch of the institution you save with and make deposits and withdrawals. Many people find such a way of saving to be most convenient. But many institutions are now offering postal alternatives which allow you to conduct your savings affairs from your armchair at home. The rates on these accounts are usually superior to those available from branch-based accounts because the costs involved in offering them are less for the provider. The savings institution will provide you with prepaid envelopes for making withdrawals or receipts. A number of accounts are now telephone-based – again, like postal accounts, rates on these tend to be attractive. Internet-based savings accounts have also arrived.

Q How are savings accounts taxed?

A Interest generated from a savings account is usually paid net of 20% tax. If you are a lower or basic rate taxpayer, you will not have to pay any additional tax. If, however, you are a higher rate taxpayer, you will have a further 20% tax to pay. So if you are a higher rate taxpayer, and your savings account has earned gross interest of £200, the building society will credit your account with net interest of £160. But because you are a 40% taxpayer, you will have a further £40 tax to pay – via your tax return.

Q What if I am a non-taxpayer? Do I have to pay 20% tax?

A No. Non-taxpayers can register to receive interest without tax being taken off. This is done by completing a form R85 which can be obtained from your bank or building society or failing that from your local tax office.

Q What if the savings account is in joint names?

A Interest paid on a joint savings account is normally divided equally for tax purposes between the joint investors. If both the account holders do not expect to be liable for tax, they should each complete a separate registration form R85.

Q What about children and tax on savings?

A A parent or guardian can register a child's savings account for interest to be paid gross through completion of form R85. However, you must remember that children under the age of 18 are potentially liable to income tax in their own right subject to utilisation of their personal allowance – £4,535 for the tax year ending April 5, 2002. You must also be aware that where money in a savings account has come from gifts from one or both parents, and where the annual interest before tax on the money from either parent is more than £100, then the whole of the interest on such gifts is treated for income tax purposes as that of the parent or parents and not of the child.

Q Can I hold deposits inside an Isa?

A Yes. You can currently invest £3,000 in a cash Isa. Your cash can be held inside a mini Isa or as part of a maxi Isa. By doing this, the interest you generate on your deposits will be tax-free. Most banks and building societies are currently offering cash Isas. If you hold a Tessa, remember that once it matures, you will be able to transfer the capital – not the interest generated – into the cash component of an Isa, thereby ensuring your savings remain tax-free. Cash Isas can now be taken by anyone aged 16 or over.

Q How do I open a deposit account?

A You will have to complete an application form. You will also have to provide a variety of personal identification such as a recent household bill with your name on it, your passport, driver's licence and birth certificate.

Q So where do I go to open a deposit account?

A Most banks and national building societies offer a comprehensive range of savings accounts to suit all tastes. You should also not ignore your local building society. Small building societies tend to offer competitive rates of interest because they do not have the massive centralised overheads of larger competitors, nor do they spend millions of pounds in national advertising campaigns. The new players into the savings arena should also not be ignored. These include Direct Line, First Direct, Virgin, Standard Life, Legal & General, Scottish Widows, Prudential's Egg, Tesco and Sainsbury. All these players offer attractive savings rates.

Q And how much will I have to invest?

A It depends. Minimum savings levels vary widely between deposit takers. But as a general rule, the more you invest initially, the better the interest rate you will get.

Dos and Don'ts

- **DON'T** blindly chase best savings rates. Many banks and building societies have a reputation for offering attractive interest rates on new savings deals, only to cut rates once you are safely on board. Northern Rock is a past master at this. If you take out a best savings buy, it is up to you to keep an eye on the interest rate you are enjoying and its competitiveness against the rest of the competition.

- **DON'T** take out a savings account and then stuff the passbook in a drawer and forget about it. It is up to you to check whether the savings account you have taken out is giving you value for money. If it isn't, it is up to you to take action.

- **DO** read the account's terms and conditions before signing up for it. Many accounts offer attractive interest rates only because they impose restrictions on the way you can operate the account. Some institutions, for example, will restrict the number of withdrawals you can make in any one year – exceeding a predetermined limit will result in a lower rate of interest being earned. Others will ask you to make an agreed number of deposits – failure to do this will again result in a loss of interest.

- **DON'T** sit on your hands if you have a fixed-term savings bond which comes to the end of its term. If you do this, your money will probably start earning a paltry rate of interest – take action by moving the proceeds into a competitive account.

- **DO** register to receive savings interest free of tax if you are a non-taxpayer. It is a simple process – just ask for a form R85 from your account provider. It just does not make financial sense to pay tax on your savings and then go through the process of claiming it back.

- **DON'T** assume that longer notice savings accounts will necessarily pay you the best savings rates. The savings market is now so competitive that new entrants are paying better rates on instant-access accounts than more traditional players are paying on long-term notice accounts.

- **DON'T** ignore your local building society. Most local building societies, convenient to use, offer some of the best savings deals around because they do not carry the bureaucracy of larger savings organisations. Many local building societies now restrict their business to local people so as to deter carpetbaggers (people after building society windfalls) – so use them.

- **DON'T** take out a savings account with a building society simply in the hope of earning yourself a conversion windfall – you will probably disappoint yourself. Most building societies now ask new savers to sign away any windfall rights to a charity or only offer accounts which do not entitle you to any future conversion bonus. It is much better to ensure you are earning an attractive rate of interest than to play the conversion hunt.

- **DO** check when interest is credited to your account. An account which credits your interest on a regular basis is better than one which pays the same interest rate but only credits interest on an annual basis. In the former case you are benefiting from the compounding effect – that is, interest being paid on interest.

- **DON'T** forget that the major disadvantage of deposit accounts is that the capital can only grow through the reinvestment of income. Such accounts are therefore vulnerable to the ravages of inflation. The key is to ensure the interest rate you are earning is above the rate of inflation. If so, your savings are benefiting from real growth.

- **DO** take your time in choosing the right account for your own personal circumstances. If, for example, you are looking for an account to use to save up for a holiday, then you are probably better off in a notice account. But if you want to put money away in case of a financial emergency, then an instant-access account is a better bet.

- **DON'T** be bullied into moving your money out of a savings account. Many financial salesmen and advisers will attempt to persuade you to do so by offering seemingly more attractive offerings such as unit trusts and investment bonds. But remember, these vehicles also involve more risk. If capital security is sacrosanct stay put.

- **DO** check as to whether you still have any savings accounts opened from a long time ago. If you do, the chances are that you are receiving a poor savings deal. Dig out your old savings passbooks and transfer the proceeds into better paying accounts.

Did you know?

- **DID** you know that most financial sections of national newspapers now include best-buy savings tables? These tables enable you to ascertain which companies are offering the best deals as well as gauge what kind of deal you are currently getting from the savings institution looking after your money.

- **DID** you know that *Moneyfacts*, a monthly publication, includes comprehensive details on savings rates available from most savings institutions? Further details from: Moneyfacts Publications, Moneyfacts House, 66–70 Thorpe Road, Norwich NR1 lBJ (01603 476476).

- **DID** you know that the Inland Revenue has published a useful booklet (IR110) on the taxation of interest from savings accounts? Copies are available free of charge from your local tax office.

- **DID** you know that your savings are protected if your bank or building society runs into financial trouble – up to a maximum of 90% of the first £20,000 invested?

- **DID** you know that many banks offer offshore savings accounts? These accounts allow you to earn interest gross although it is still taxable. Building societies that offer offshore accounts include Bradford & Bingley, Britannia, Cheshire, Derbyshire, Nationwide, Newcastle, Norwich & Peterborough, Portman, Skipton and Yorkshire. These accounts are based in places such as Guernsey, the Isle of Man and Gibraltar.

So what now?

- **THE** nearest thing to a fundamental investment truth is that no one should buy risk investments until they have an adequate emergency fund on deposit. Failure to do so is akin to trying to run before you can walk. But as has just been highlighted, it is not simply a question of going out and buying the first deposit account you can get hold of – you need to ensure the account you buy meets with your financial needs and crucially will give you a solid savings deal.

National Savings

THERE can be few safer choices than National Savings for investors searching for a savings home. The government-backed National Savings was set up more than 130 years ago and remains a key player in the keenly competitive savings market. It offers a range of products to suit most savers' tastes – from premium bonds to pensioner savings bonds.

But do not think that because National Savings have a rock-solid reputation they will provide the solution to all your savings needs.

National Savings has two roles: to provide products that are totally secure and backed by the government, and to bring in cash to help the government pay its bills.

Product competitiveness is not a key role or objective. How keenly National Savings products are priced depends primarily on borrowing targets set for it by the government and the interest the government is prepared for it to pay in raising that money.

As with any area of personal finance, tread the National Savings maze with caution. And under no circumstances buy a product simply because it is National Savings. You could end up disappointed.

Q What is National Savings?

A It represents the savings arm of the government and provides a means for people to save safely and without worrying whether their money is at risk. When you invest in a National Savings product you are, in effect, lending your money to the government.

Q What kind of products does it offer?

A All National Savings products are capital-secure – investors will get their money back whatever happens. Products fall into four main areas: tax-free investments, investments that pay a regular income, guaranteed fixed-rate investments and savings accounts. Many of these products are especially suitable for children.

Q Capital security is fine, but what about the competitiveness of the interest rates on offer?

A Every year, the National Savings managers agree with the government how much money they should raise from the public through product sales and at what cost – in other words, the interest rates they are prepared to pay. It is this agreement that determines the competitiveness of National Savings products. They are rarely top of the pops when it comes to great savings schemes. When you buy a National Savings plan, you will get a fair deal but not necessarily the best one around.

The individual products on offer are:

Capital bond

This is a fixed-rate investment that provides a guaranteed rate of interest as long as it is held for five years.

Q For whom is it most suitable?

A It is for savers who want to know exactly how much their investment will return and who can afford to tie their money away for five years without drawing an income on it. Capital bonds come into their own when interest rates are falling.

Q Who can hold one and what are the minimum and maximum amounts you can invest?

A Anyone. The minimum holding is £100 and the maximum is £250,000.

Q Can I take an income from a capital bond?

A No. Interest is automatically reinvested in the bond every year to increase its capital value. At the end of five years, savers receive a return of initial capital plus the accrued interest which is paid gross.

Q Can I get my money back early?

A Yes, but there are penalties. If you sell your bond within the first year, you will receive no interest. Thereafter you will receive a reduced interest depending on how long you have held the bond. Money is normally repaid within two weeks. Getting your money back early may be a sensible option if interest rates are rising and the capital bond's guaranteed interest rate starts to look unattractive.

Q What is the bond's tax treatment?

A Interest is paid gross, but not tax-free. Taxpayers must pay income tax on the interest – 20% for basic rate and 40% for higher rate taxpayers. Income from a capital bond should be declared on your tax return. Further details on capital bonds can be obtained by asking for booklet NSA 768 at your local post office.

Children's bonus bond

This is a tax-free investment though in many ways it represents a children's version of a capital bond. It provides guaranteed rates of interest for each of a series of five-year periods until the age of 21.

Q For whom is it most suitable?

A It is primarily for taxpaying parents and grandparents who want to put money aside for their children. The sum amassed will provide the young person with a tax-free lump sum to help them on their way through adulthood.

Q Who can hold one and what are the minimum and maximum amounts you can invest?

A It can be bought by anyone over 16 for anyone under 16. The minimum purchase is £25 and the maximum holding per issue is a meagre £1,000. All bonds mature on the holder's 21st birthday.

Q Can income be taken from a children's bonus bond?

A No. Interest is automatically reinvested in the bond every year to increase its capital value. At the end of five years, the holder receives details of the guaranteed interest rate for the next five years.

Q Can I get my money back early?

A Yes, but there are penalties. If you sell your bond within the first year, you will receive no interest. Thereafter you will receive a reduced interest.

Q What is the bond's tax treatment?

A Interest is tax-free. Normally, if a parent gives a child money to invest the parent is liable for tax on all the interest if it exceeds £100 in any tax year. But interest on children's bonus bonds is exempt from this rule. Further details on children' bonus bonds can be obtained by asking for booklet NSA 769 at your local post office.

Fixed-rate bond

This is a guaranteed fixed-rate investment, though it differs markedly from a capital bond. Interest is guaranteed for a set period – 6 months to 18 months – and is paid net of 20% tax. An enhanced interest rate is available if a large sum is invested.

Q For whom is it most suitable?

A It is primarily for taxpayers who do not want to tie up their money for too long but who want the assurance of a guaranteed rate of interest.

Q Who can hold one and what are the minimum and maximum amounts you can invest?

A They can be bought by anyone over 16. The minimum purchase is £500 and the maximum holding is £1 million.

Q Can income be taken from a fixed-rate savings bond?

A Interest can be paid monthly, annually or reinvested in the bond.

Q Can I get my money back early?

A Yes, but there are penalties. Withdrawals may be made at a few days' notice.

Q What is the bond's tax treatment?

A Interest is paid net of 20% tax. This means basic rate or lower rate taxpayers have no further tax to pay. A basic rate taxpayer will have a further 20% tax to pay.

Income bond

This is an investment that pays a regular income. Interest is paid gross though it is taxable. The interest rate is also variable and holders are notified in advance of any change.

Q For whom is it most suitable?

A It is for people who want to generate a monthly income from their savings while knowing that their capital is secure. Because income is paid gross, it is ideal for non-taxpayers.

Q Who can hold one and what are the minimum and maximum amounts you can invest?

A It can be bought by anyone over seven. The minimum purchase is £500 and the maximum holding is £1 million.

Q Can income be taken from an income bond?

A Yes. Interest is paid on the 5th of every month into a bank or building society account of your choice. Monthly payments start once the bond has been held for six weeks. If the interest rate changes six weeks' notice will be given.

Q Can I get my money back early?

A Yes, but you may incur penalties. If you want to withdraw capital you have a choice – give 90 days' notice and suffer no loss of interest or withdraw immediately subject to a penalty equivalent to 90 days' loss of interest.

Q What is the bond's tax treatment?

A Interest is paid gross but it is taxable. Taxpayers must declare it to the Inland Revenue. Further details on income bonds can be obtained by getting booklet DNS 767 from your local post office.

Premium bond

This is a tax-free investment that offers holders the chance to win £1 million or one of more than 500,000 other prizes ranging from £50 to £100,000 in a monthly draw.

Q For whom is it most suitable?

A For people with small amounts to invest, it represents no more than a gamble that will return your 'stake' whenever you want it. For wealthier people who can afford to buy large blocks of bonds, the possibility of winning a tax-free prize is enhanced.

Q Who can hold one and what are the minimum and maximum amounts you can invest?

A Anyone over 16. Below this age, you may hold bonds bought for you by your parents, grandparents, great-grandparents or guardians. The minimum purchase is £100 and the maximum holding is £20,000 per person.

Q Can income be taken from a premium bond?

A No. Premium bonds do not earn interest. Instead, each bond bought has an equal chance of winning a prize in the monthly draw. Bonds are eligible for the prize draw one month after purchase.

Q Can I get my money back early?

A You can sell your premium bond at any time. Repayment usually takes about two weeks.

Q What is the bond's tax treatment?

A Prizes are free of all tax and premium bond holdings do not have to be declared on your tax return.

Pensioner's bond

This is a guaranteed fixed-rate investment. It offers a secure monthly interest fixed for either two or five years. At the end of that time, you have the option to lock into fixed rates for a further two or five years though the deal on offer may differ from the previous one.

Q For whom is it most suitable?

A It is aimed exclusively at people over 60 who require a regular monthly income and who do not want to put their capital at risk.

Q Who can hold one and what are the minimum and maximum amounts you can invest?

A Bonds may be held by individuals aged 60 or over. The minimum holding is £500 and the maximum is £1 million.

Q Can income be taken from a pensioner's bond?

A Yes. A monthly payment is made on the 19th of every month into a bank or building society account of your choice.

Q Can I get my money back early?

A You can make withdrawals within the two or five years subject to either 60 days' notice with no interest paid on the amount withdrawn or immediate access on 90 days' loss of interest. At the end of two or five years, a bond may be cashed without notice and without penalty.

Q What is the bond's tax treatment?

A Interest is paid gross and non-taxpayers do not have to complete an Inland Revenue registration form to enjoy tax-free income. But taxpayers will have to pay tax on any income payments they receive.

Index-linked savings certificate

This is a tax-free investment. It provides a hedge against inflation by offering savers a guaranteed rate of interest above the Retail Prices Index over either two or five years, in addition to indexation of the capital sum invested. For example, if the guaranteed rate of interest is 2% and the annual rate of increase in the RPI over the two or five years was 5%, the certificate would return 7% per annum.

Q For whom is it most suitable?

A It is ideal for higher rate taxpayers who want to protect their savings from tax and inflation. The linking of returns to inflation protects savings from inflation while its tax-free status makes it an ideal home for savings.

Q Who can hold one and what are the minimum and maximum amounts you can invest?

A Anyone. It can also be held by trustees, registered friendly societies, charities, clubs and voluntary bodies. The minimum purchase is £100 and the maximum holding is £10,000 per issue.

Q Can income be taken from an index-linked certificate?

A No. The certificate matures on the second or fifth anniversary of purchase dependent on which issue you have bought, but no income is paid in the meantime.

Q Can I get my money back early?

A Yes, but you will be penalised. If your certificate is repaid in the first year, you will receive no interest and no index-linking. After that, you will receive a reduced rate of interest. It rarely pays to hold a bond beyond its maturity date because you will suffer a reduced rate of interest or none at all. Normally, you are offered the opportunity to invest the proceeds from matured index-linked certificates in the current issue of certificates.

Q What is the certificate's tax treatment?

A All returns are free of tax even if a certificate is repaid within its first five years.

Fixed-interest savings certificate

This is a tax-free investment that provides a guaranteed rate of return at the end of either two or five years dependent on the term selected. After that time you may take the returns tax-free, keep the matured certificate in force (though it rarely pays to do so) or reinvest the proceeds in the current issue.

Q For whom is it most suitable?

A It is ideal for higher rate taxpayers who want to protect their savings from taxation and who want to know in advance how much they will receive from their money. Obviously, these certificates may start to look unattractive if interest rates rise during the term chosen but, conversely, they may look good value if rates fall. You should buy a fixed-interest savings certificate only if you are prepared to last the course.

Q Who can hold one and what are the minimum and maximum amounts you can invest?

A Anyone. They may also be held by trustees, registered friendly societies, charities, clubs and voluntary bodies. The minimum purchase is £100 and the maximum holding is £10,000 per issue.

Q Can income be taken from a fixed-interest savings certificate?

A No. The certificate matures on the second or fifth anniversary of purchase dependent on which term you have chosen, but no income is paid in the meantime.

Q Can I get my money back early?

A Yes, but you will be penalised. If your certificate is repaid in the first year, you will receive no interest unless you bought the certificate with the maturity proceeds from an earlier one. After that, you will receive a reduced rate of interest on your savings. It rarely pays to hold a bond beyond its maturity date because you will suffer a reduced rate of interest. Normally, you are offered the opportunity to invest the proceeds from fixed-interest certificates in the current issue.

Q What is the certificate's tax treatment?

A All returns are free of tax even if a certificate is repaid within its first five years.

Investment account

This is a 30-day savings account that pays variable interest rates. Interest rates are higher for larger deposits.

Q For whom is it most suitable?

A It is for people who need a flexible deposit account. A passbook is issued with which deposits and withdrawals may be made at any post office. Interest is paid gross, but it is taxable. Interest rates are not always attractive and can be bettered by shopping around.

Q Who can hold one and what are the minimum and maximum amounts you can invest?

A Anyone aged seven or over. Minimum deposit is £20 and the maximum holding is £100,000.

Q Can income be taken from an investment account?

A Interest is credited to the account annually on December 31. It is therefore not suitable as an income generator – income bonds and pensioner bonds are better value.

Q Can I get my money back early?

A You can make withdrawals by giving a month's notice, or immediately subject to 30 days' loss of interest.

Q What is the account's tax treatment?

A Interest is paid gross but taxpayers must declare it to the Inland Revenue. Unlike an ordinary account (below) there is no tax-free element.

Ordinary account

This is a savings account that pays a variable interest rate and allows holders instant access to their cash through most post offices.

Q For whom is it most suitable?

A It is for savers who need an instant-access account, but interest rates are rarely competitive. A redeeming feature is that the first £70 of interest each year is tax-free – an attraction for non-taxpayers. A passbook allows holders to make deposits and withdrawals at any post office.

Q Who can hold one and what are the minimum and maximum amounts you can invest?

A Anyone aged seven and over. Children may make their own deposits and withdrawals. Minimum deposit is £10 and the maximum holding is £10,000.

Q Can income be taken from an ordinary account?

A Interest is credited to the account annually on December 31. It is therefore not suitable as an income generator – income bonds and pensioner bonds are better value. No interest is earned in the month you make a withdrawal or deposit.

Q Can I get my money back early?

A You may withdraw up to £100 at post offices – more if you are a regular account user. For larger withdrawals you must send your passbook to National Savings.

Q What is the account's tax treatment?

A Interest is paid gross and the first £70 of interest is tax-free. Taxpayers must declare interest over that amount to the Inland Revenue.

Cash Isas

Q What is the minimum investment?

A £1. Interest which accumulates is tax-free.

Q What is the maximum investment?

A £3,000.

Q Can I make additional deposits into my plan?

A Yes. The minimum addition is £10.

Q Is that all the accounts that National Savings operates?

A There is just one more – the treasurer's account. That is designed for people who manage the finances of a non-profit-making organisation such as a charity, club or society. The account accepts deposits from £10,000 and withdrawals may be made subject to a 30-day interest penalty.

Q How do I buy a National Savings product?

A The starting point for most people is the local post office where booklets on National Savings' full range of products are available. These all contain application forms. Certain products, including savings certificates, premium bonds, children's bonus bonds, capital bonds may be bought and investment and ordinary accounts may be opened over the post office counter. All others may be bought by post. National Savings also sells selected products such as premium bonds over the telephone.

Q Where can I get further information?

A National Savings operates a telephone-based sales information unit that sends out product details on request. Its Internet site, www.nationalsavings.co.uk, provides users with full product details plus application forms that users may print out.

Q Do independent financial advisers recommend National Savings?

A Some do because of the security the products offer. But National Savings does not pay advisers commission for recommending their plans and many advisers ignore them. However, if your financial adviser fails to include National Savings products in your savings portfolio, you should ask why.

Dos and Don'ts

- **DO** check the terms and conditions of any National Savings product before parting with your money. Many deals come with strings attached and you may be penalised if you want early access to your money.

- **DON'T** think that just because National Savings products are backed by the government they necessarily represent good value for money. If there is little pressure on National Savings to raise money for the government, it will not go out of its way to pay attractive savings rates. Comparable deals from building societies and banks can often provide better value.

- **DON'T** hold on to a National Savings product after it has matured without first checking what savings deal you will continue to receive. Many products offer extremely poor returns once they have been held for the required period. It often pays to look elsewhere for an alternative home for your savings.

- **DON'T** buy a National Savings product unless you are totally comfortable with it. If in doubt, seek independent financial advice.

Did you know?

- **DID** you know that the Post Office Savings Bank, the forerunner of National Savings, was set up in 1861 by the Palmerston government to encourage ordinary wage earners 'to provide for themselves against adversity and ill health'?

- **DID** you know that National Savings has two prime goals: to provide a totally secure and government-backed means for people to save, and to provide the government with funding?

- **DID** you know that National Savings is the country's second-largest savings institution? It has more than 30 million customers who between them have a massive £63 billion invested.

- **DID** you know that National Savings has a product that may be held within a tax-free Individual Savings Account?

- **DID** you know that National Savings is an executive agency of the Chancellor of the Exchequer? It has great freedom over its day-to-day management though its targets – and the competitiveness of its products – are still determined by government.

So what now?

- **ANYONE** putting together a savings portfolio should consider National Savings products as a key component. Safe and government-backed, they will never let you down. But remember – if you want a secure home for your money, National Savings is the answer. If you want attractive savings rates, you are probably better off looking elsewhere.

Friendly society tax-free investment plans

FRIENDLY societies have been part of the fabric of Britain's financial services industry since the 16th century. They were first formed as local self-help groups that came to the aid of members who fell upon hard times. Today, though many of the 300-plus surviving societies offer an array of investment and financial protection schemes, most still operate on a local basis to sell tax-friendly investment schemes.

Their 10-year tax-exempt savings plans remain a popular investment vehicle for many people, especially parents who want to squirrel away long-term money for children. But because these plans are tax-free does not mean that they represent good value for money. As in any area of personal finance, the principle of caveat emptor – let the buyer beware – applies.

Friendly society tax-free investment plans: key questions and answers

Q What is a friendly society 10-year tax-exempt savings plan?

A It is an investment plan that allows savers to accumulate a tax-free nest egg after 10 years.

Q How do they work?

A Present limits laid down by the government allow you to save a maximum of £25 a month or £270 a year. Your money is invested in a fund of your choice which in turn will probably be invested in a mix of equities and bonds. Provided you hold the fund until the plan matures at the end of 10 years, the proceeds are free of all tax. Most friendly societies will accept lower premiums, usually from £10 per month. Some also allow a one-off lump-sum premium payment. This buys an annuity that meets your monthly premiums for the 10-year term.

Q Can I take an income from my plan?

A No, it is a capital investment plan only.

Q Who can take one out?

A Anyone aged between 18 and 70, but only one plan may be held at any given time. You may contribute to plans for your children and grandchildren as well as for yourself as long as they and you have only one plan each. If a plan is taken out for a child it is usual for it to be written to age 18 or 21. This means that you contribute for longer than 10 years, but the proceeds are tax-free. By writing a policy to this age, the payment of the plan's proceeds may be timed to coincide with a child's move into higher education thereby helping with university fees, or perhaps as a deposit on a first home.

Q Is all my money invested?

A No. When the plan is first set up, charges consume a large part of the monthly premiums (see below). The plan also includes life cover and if you die during its term your estate will receive a tax-free cash sum equal to the value of the plan or the amount of life cover, whichever is the greater. Some of your premiums are used to buy this life cover.

Q I can't see how I can fail to go wrong with such a plan. Am I being naive?

A Unfortunately, yes. There is no point taking out a plan unless you are prepared to last the 10-year course. If you cash in the plan before it matures you could get back less than you put in or be stung by heavy surrender penalties. Furthermore, the proceeds from a plan cashed in before the 10 years are up may be liable to tax.

Q Are there any other disadvantages?

A Yes. Charges can chisel away at the tax-free status of these 10-year bonds. Most friendly society savings plans levy a myriad of charges that eat into the premiums you give them. They levy a policy set-up charge as well as taking a percentage of your premiums in initial charges. Most also levy a fixed monthly policy fee to cover the cost of collecting premiums. This hits hardest at those who are saving less.

Friendly societies are obliged to reveal the impact of charges on potential returns from a policy before investors sign on the dotted line. Comparing charges with those of other friendly society plans – something an independent financial adviser will do for you – will show which plans offer value for money.

Q Can I circumvent some of these charges by buying direct from the company rather than through an adviser or salesman?

A No. The same charges will be levied irrespective of which way you enter the friendly society door. The company makes more money out of you if you buy direct rather than through an adviser because it does not have to share the charges or commissions with a third party.

Q But what about the likely investment performance of the friendly society savings plan? Isn't that as important an issue as charges?

A Yes. When selecting a friendly society plan you must take care about how and where your money will be invested. Most societies will offer conservatively managed with-profits funds where the value of your plan will attract bonuses every year in line with the society's investment performance. These plans will seldom let you down because of their exposure to a wide range of financial assets such as property, bonds, gilts and equities. For example, Tunbridge Wells Equitable Friendly Society is renowned for its strong with-profits record.

Alternatively, you may opt for a unit-linked fund that tends to be invested primarily in equities. Some friendly societies offer unit-linked funds that invest in specific stock markets such as the UK or specific themes such as ethical investments. Funds that track the performance of the UK stock market are also available.

Before opting for a particular plan, check its investment record either by asking the society concerned for past performance figures or by referring to the tables in one of the personal finance magazines. *Money Management* magazine provides details of the past performance of some friendly society tax-exempt plans in its Insurance Funds section.

Q What happens when the 10-year savings period ends?

A Most societies will offer you a number of choices. You may cash in the policy and enjoy a tax-free sum or you may make the policy 'paid up'. This means that you pay no further premiums but leave the plan to benefit from further investment growth. You may also keep the policy going and save for a further 10 years, or simply take out a new tax-free plan.

Q I'm interested. How do I obtain further details?

A Many friendly societies advertise in national newspapers. The biggest players include Family Assurance, Homeowners, Holloway, Liverpool Victoria, Royal Liver, Scottish Friendly and Tunbridge Wells Equitable Friendly Society.

Q Can I get anything else from a friendly society?

A Many friendly societies sell protection products such as permanent health and critical illness insurance policies. A number offer pensions, Individual Savings Accounts and single-premium investment bonds. All are worthy of consideration, but you must check the charges before making a commitment.

Q Is there anything else I should know about friendly societies?

A Yes. The friendly society industry has had its fair share of scandal over the past 10 years. Lancashire & Yorkshire friendly society made some disastrous investment decisions that adversely affected investors' tax-free savings plans and was taken over by Family Assurance in the early Nineties. In 1999 financial regulators imposed a massive fine on Liverpool Victoria for mis-selling products to the public. Investors should tread carefully and not be mesmerised by the magic words 'tax-free'.

Dos and Don'ts

- **DO** remember that friendly society investment plans may be taken out on behalf of children. This contrasts with Individual

Savings Accounts where plan holders must be 16 or over.

- **DO** check the charges before taking out a plan. In particular, watch for fixed monthly fees that can hit your premiums hard, especially if you have decided not to save the maximum amount.

- **DON'T** be put off by the strange names of some friendly societies. Scottish Legal, for example, does not restrict sales to members of the Scottish legal profession – it sells tax-exempt savings plans nationwide and is Scotland's largest friendly society.

- **DON'T** be tempted into buying a tax-exempt savings plan simply because the friendly society is offering a free alarm clock, pen or Marks & Spencer voucher. Buy one only if it fits into your long-term financial objectives.

- **DON'T** buy a plan unless you intend to stay the course. Otherwise you are better off opting for a more flexible tax-free savings vehicle such as an Isa, which will allow you to access your savings without penalty and without compromising its tax-free status.

- **DON'T** buy a policy if you don't understand the charges. If they don't make sense, there is a good chance the friendly society doesn't want you to understand them. In other words, it is trying to pull the wool over your eyes.

Did you know?

- **DID** you know that one in 10 people hold a friendly society investment plan?

- **DID** you know that some friendly societies will reduce their charges if plans are bought for several family members? Ask whether such an option exists if you intend to buy policies in bulk.

- **DID** you know that if you bought a plan before 1994 when the maximum monthly savings limit was raised to £25, you may increase your premiums to the new limit? If you do this, check whether the maturity date of your plan will be altered. Some companies will extend the term of your bond for a further 10 years from the date when increased payments began.

- **DID** you know that friendly societies are mutual organisations like building societies? They belong to their members and are not answerable to shareholders.

- **DID** you know that there are various types of friendly society? There are sickness societies that pay benefits during ill health, accident societies that pay benefits to members' families after accidents and burial societies that pay on the death of a member or spouse?

- **DID** you know that you can obtain further details about friendly societies from the Association of Friendly Societies, 10–13 Lovat Lane, London EC3R 8DN (call 020 7397 9550)?

So what now?

- **TAX-EXEMPT** savings plans from friendly societies represent a painless way of long-term saving, especially if you want to put aside money for young children. But tax-free does not mean risk-free, and heavy charges can sharply reduce a plan's benefits. Once you have decided to buy a friendly society tax-exempt savings plan, choose one with reasonable charges otherwise it may turn out to be less than friendly in future years.

Peps and Tessas

PERSONAL Equity Plans (Peps) and Tax Exempt Special Savings Accounts (Tessas) have revolutionised the savings market in this country.

Since Peps were launched at the beginning of 1987 and Tessas were introduced three years later, millions of people have been encouraged to save for the first time. The figures speak for themselves – more than 4.7 million people hold tax-free deposit-based Tessas, while more than three million have bought equity-based Peps.

Despite their success, the present government has overhauled the tax-free savings market. From April 1999, Tessas or Peps have no longer been available. In their place is the Individual Savings Account (Isa), a vehicle that combines many of the benefits provided previously by Tessas and Peps.

Not that Peps and Tessas should be forgotten or cast aside. If you still hold these – and many people have a lot of money tied up in them, especially Peps – it is imperative that you look after them.

Peps and Tessas: key questions and answers

Q If I hold a Pep at present, can I make any further contributions?

A No. New contributions into Peps have not been permitted since April 5, 1999.

Q With Isas now available, do I have to transfer my existing Peps into an Isa?

A No. Peps are 'ring-fenced' – they remain a totally separate investment vehicle. You cannot transfer your Pep investments into an Isa.

Q Are Peps still tax-free?

A Yes. There is no capital gains tax to pay on any investment growth and income continues to roll up tax-free. However, the income advantages of a Pep are not as attractive as they used to be. From April 1999, dividends from UK equities have been paid net of 20% tax, but the tax credit that Pep managers may reclaim on behalf of investors is only 10%. Before April 1999, the credit was 20%. This means that the income benefits of a Pep are not as substantial as before. The reduction in the amount of tax credit also applies to Isas.

Q So, if I have a Pep, what can I do with my money other than simply leave it to the vagaries of stock markets?
A You have three options. One, you may leave your money where it is. This makes sense if you are happy with the way your investment is being managed and you have no need to access your savings.

Two, you may change the underlying investments. Most Pep managers offer a range, from low-risk bond-based funds at one end of the risk spectrum to international funds at the other. If your existing Peps are heavily invested in one particular area – the UK stock market for example – it may pay to switch some of that money into other funds run by your Pep manager – a corporate bond-based fund, for example, or maybe a European fund.

By doing this, you will diversify your investment portfolio. There may be fees involved so don't make changes for change's sake. Check the costs first.

Three, you may transfer your Pep to another provider. If you believe your Pep has failed to come up to expectations you should consider transferring the plan to another manager. The tax-free status of your money will not be impaired and it is easy to arrange – the company you select to look after your money will carry out all the administration on your behalf. There will probably be costs involved – the original Pep manager may levy exit charges and the new manager will invariably levy initial charges on the sum transferred.

Q Transferring a Pep seems a good option, but how do I know in the first place whether or not my Pep is performing well?

A Your Pep manager should send you a statement at least twice a year detailing the value of your holdings. You should monitor the performance of individual holdings, especially unit trusts and investment trusts, against their peer groups to see how they are performing on a relative basis. If your money is invested in consistently underperforming investment funds, then a transfer to another Pep provider with a better all-round investment performance record makes great sense.

Q Can I take an income from my Pep, maybe to help me in retirement?

A Yes, you are allowed to draw an income from your Pep without impairing its tax-free status. Most providers offer this facility.

Q What about Tessas? Are the rules the same as for Peps? Are contributions into Tessas no longer allowed?

A No, the rules are slightly different. Since April 6, 1999, it has not been possible to buy a new Tessa. But if you took one out before April 5, 1999, you may continue to fund it until it matures in five years.

Q What are the funding limits?

A You may invest £9,000 in a Tessa taken out before April 5, 1999. Maximum investment in the first year is £3,000, you may invest £1,800 in each of years two to four and £600 in the final year. Provided the Tessa is held for five years, all returns are tax-free.

Q Are these funding limits in addition to, or part of, the Isa investment limits?

A They are separate. There is nothing to stop you funding both a Tessa and an Isa provided your finances can stand the cost.

Q Why should I continue with my Tessa if I may now use an Isa?

A If you have started a Tessa, there is little point surrendering it simply because Isas are now available. For some people, especially risk-averse savers, Tessas may be a better option than Isas because they pay a better rate of interest although this is a rarity. Most savings institutions now pay comparable rates of interest on Isas and Tessas.

The big advantage that Isas have over Tessas is that the Isa savings pot may be accessed without destroying its tax-free status. Withdrawal of capital from a Tessa voids the account's tax-free status immediately. If you already have a Tessa and are prepared to save long-term, keep it.

Q What happens when my Tessa matures at the end of five years?

A You have two options. You may use the money as you please or you may transfer the capital element of your Tessa – in effect, the contributions you have made – into the cash component of an Isa. If you opt for the latter course, the transfer will preserve the tax-free status of your money. It will not count against existing Isa contribution limits.

Q Does this rule apply to follow-on Tessas?

A Yes. Before April 5, 1999, many savers will have rolled over the capital from a first Tessa into a follow-on, or roll-over, Tessa, maintaining the tax-free status of the money in the process. When follow-on Tessas mature after five years, you may either take the cash, or pocket the interest and transfer the capital element into the cash component of an Isa.

Q What if I took out a roll-over Tessa before April 5, 1999? Am I allowed to top it up if I didn't invest the maximum £9,000?

A Yes. If you took out a roll-over Tessa, you are allowed to fund any shortfall. For example, if you transferred £6,000 into a follow-on Tessa before April 5, 1999, that will be deemed to be your first year's contribution. You may invest a further £3,000 over the next four years, subject to the annual savings limits of £1,800 in years two to four and £600 in year five.

Q What is to stop me taking out a follow-on Tessa instead of an Isa when my first Tessa matures?

A You can no longer take out a follow-on Tessa – they ceased to be available after April 5, 1999.

Q The great thing about Peps is that the plan may be transferred to another company if it is not delivering satisfactory returns. Does the same apply to Tessas?

A Yes. You have the right to transfer a Tessa to another provider if the interest rate you are receiving becomes uncompetitive. In doing so, you will not endanger the tax-free status of your savings. Like Peps, an exit charge may be levied, plus a set-up fee charged by the new provider. But these will pale into insignificance if you benefit subsequently from improved interest rates.

Dos and Don'ts

- **DON'T** sit on your hands and expect your Tessas and Peps to deliver what you expected when you first bought them. It is up to you to check their progress and assess whether they are still giving value for money.

- **DO** seek independent financial advice. If you are not sure whether your Peps and Tessas are performing satisfactorily, speak to an independent financial adviser. He or she will tell you whether you should be taking appropriate action – such as transferring to another provider or switching the underlying investments – and take a look at your investments in the context of your long-term financial objectives.

- **DO** continue to fund a Tessa if you have one. Though Isas have replaced Tessas and Peps, you may still fund a Tessa set up before April 5, 1999.

- **DO** consider the transfer option. When your Tessa or follow-on Tessa matures, don't simply run off with the money. Remember, you have the right to maintain the tax-free status of part of your money (the capital) by transferring it to the cash element of an Isa. If long-term saving is your goal, this could be a sensible route to follow.

- **DO** remember that a Tessa is a long-term savings vehicle. You cannot touch its capital element without removing the tax-free wrapper. You may, however, access the interest.

- **DO** remember that you may take an income from your Pep without impairing the tax-free wrapper. This may prove sensible in retirement where income generation is often a priority.

Did you know?

- **DID** you know that thousands of people have squirrelled away six-figure sums into Peps, building themselves a substantial investment pot? Such money should be looked after by a manager who will add to it either by improving its capital value or by generating a decent income from it, or both.

- **DID** you know that the tax treatment of Peps is identical to that of Isas?

- **DID** you know that you may transfer both your Pep and Tessa to another provider in order to benefit from better returns? Use this facility – it's your right.

- **DID** you know that you may continue to contribute to a Tessa or a follow-on Tessa until they mature? This is a great way of boosting the savings you have tucked away in a tax-free environment.

So what now?

- **IF** you hold a Tessa or Pep, keep a watching eye on how they are performing. It is simply not enough to ignore their progress and expect everything to turn out perfectly – it won't. If your savings are underperforming, then the quicker you take corrective action, the better. Remember, it's your money and your financial future – they deserve your keenest attention.

Individual Savings Accounts

WE all need to save money – whether for a rainy day, a financial emergency or, more importantly, our retirement. Most of us turn initially to the trusty building society, and quite rightly so – our capital is secure, we trust an institution that has been around since Adam was a lad and the interest we earn on our savings is a decent return.

Yet simply relying on a building society to take care of our financial future is not a sound strategy. Other financial assets need to be considered. These include equities, equity-related products such as unit trusts and investment trusts, bonds and, of course, pensions.

The government has recognised this by introducing the Individual Savings Account (Isa), a vehicle that replaced the Personal Equity Plan (Pep) and the Tax Exempt Special Savings Account (Tessa) in April 1999. It is an investment plan that allows savers to provide for their future in a range of investments including shares, bonds, investment funds and deposits. All dividends from the plan are totally free of tax and all capital gains are tax-free.

Isas: key questions and answers

Q What is an Isa?

A It is a tax-free savings wrapper. Any investments held within an Isa are free from income tax or capital gains tax. It is a personal tax-free savings haven and you don't need to declare its existence on any return you file to the taxman.

Q Who can take one out?

A Anyone over 18 who is ordinarily resident in the UK for tax purposes. Cash-only Isas can be taken out by anyone aged 16 or over.

Q So how does an Isa work?

A You are allowed to invest up to £7,000 in any tax year – April 6 to April 5 – in an Isa. This may be invested in one lump sum or through regular savings contributions.

Your contributions are then invested in a mix of financial assets – the choice is yours though there are restrictions. £3,000 may be invested in cash including bank or building society deposits, National Savings or money funds run by some unit trust groups. A further £1,000 may be used to buy life assurance. The £3,000 balance, or the entire maximum subscription of £7,000, may be invested in stocks and shares, including unit trusts, investment trusts and direct equities.

The pot of money you assemble within an Isa should grow over time as a result of rising stock markets or the accumulation of gross interest.

Q But what about Tessas and Peps? Aren't they exactly the same as Isas?

A Isas have replaced Tessas and Peps. From April 6, 1999, you have not been able to take out a new Tessa or Pep, though if you have an existing Tessa, you may continue to add to it until it matures at the end of five years. You may continue to hold Peps, though new contributions have not been possible since April 6, 1999.

An important difference between Isas and Peps is in the income benefit of holding UK equities. Before April 6, 1999, holders could claim back under the Pep wrapper tax credits on dividends from UK equities equivalent to 20%. This effectively boosted income payments under the tax-free wrapper by the same value. But from April 6, 1999, this tax credit has reduced to 10% and will disappear altogether in 2004.

Q What if I hold Peps and Tessas. Can I convert them to Isas?

A Peps are completely ring-fenced from Isas which means you can continue to hold them for as long as you wish. Like Isas, they will enjoy the 10% tax credit until 2004. Once your Tessa matures – whether it is a roll-over plan or a first Tessa – you have two choices. You may either take the proceeds and enjoy them as you please or you may re-invest the capital element of the Tessa (the contributions you have paid into your plan) into the cash component of an Isa. If you do this, the transfer will be deemed to be tax-free. Furthermore, it will not count against your Isa contribution limits – this means you are effectively giving your Isa a big contribution boost.

Q Who will manage my Isa money?

A A wide range of companies such as investment houses, banks, building societies and insurance companies, offer Isas. And more than one company can look after your annual Isa contribution – it is entirely up to you.

Option One is to choose a maxi Isa run by a single company. You may invest up to the maximum £7,000 per year through this Isa, though the operating company does not have to offer all three investment options – cash, equities and insurance. All it must offer is the equities option; it may choose whether to provide the others.

Option Two is a mini Isa. This allows three companies to manage each separate investment component of your money – for example, a building society to manage the cash element, a friendly society or insurance company to manage the insurance component, and an investment house to look after the equities. You don't need to take out each of the mini elements. You may only use one.

Mini and maxi Isas may not be mixed in a single tax year. However, you may take out a mini Isa in one tax year, followed by a maxi Isa the next.

Q Can I make withdrawals from my Isa?

A Yes. Unlike Tessas, where the tax breaks are removed if you touch the plan's capital before five years, Isas allow withdrawals without jeopardising the plan's tax-free status. But the withdrawals may not be 'netted off' against contributions to determine how much may be invested in an Isa. Once the maximum £7,000 has been contributed, for example, no further payments may be made, irrespective of the number of withdrawals made in the same tax year.

Q Is there a minimum holding period?

A No, but an Isa will obviously work best if viewed as a long-term investment vehicle.

Q How do I know I am not getting a poor deal when I buy an Isa?

A The government has introduced a system of approval called CAT marking. Anyone buying an Isa that has earned a CAT mark may be confident that it has fair Charges, is Accessible and does not offer investors onerous Terms and conditions.

The rules on CAT marking are specific. As far as an Isa's cash element is concerned, CAT means the following:

C – there should be no one-off or regular charges of any kind. There should be no other conditions imposed, such as limits on the number of withdrawals.

A – the minimum savings level should be no higher than £10.

T – the interest rate earned on cash held within the Isa should be no more than two percentage points below the prevailing base rate, in other words competitive. Interest rates should be adjusted upwards within one calendar month of a base-rate rise, so that savers enjoy higher interest rates as quickly as possible.

For the insurance component of an Isa, CAT stands for:

C – annual charges should be no more than 3% of the value of the fund. There should be no other charges such as initial fees, reduced allocation in the early years, or nasty capital units.

A – the minimum premium should be no higher than £250 per year or £25 per month. Withdrawals should be subject to no more than 7 days' notice.

T – the surrender value of the insurance plan (the value you receive if you sell) should fully reflect the value of the underlying assets and not be suppressed by onerous conditions imposed by the provider. It must also be at least equal to premiums paid after three years.

Finally, for the investment element of an Isa, CAT means:

C – annual charges should be no more than 1% of the plan's net asset value, in effect the investment plan's value. There should be no other charges such as initial (set-up) or exit fees.

A – the minimum investment should be no higher than £50 per month or £500 lump sum.

T – funds should have at least 50% of their assets invested in shares listed on European Union stock exchanges. This ensures that investors do not buy esoteric funds such as those investing in emerging markets or commodity shares where share prices can swing violently.

A single price should be offered for the buying and selling of unit trusts and investment trusts, thereby eliminating confusing and costly bid-to-offer spreads.

Certain sophisticated investment funds such as split-capital investment trusts and highly geared investment trusts (those that borrow money to increase their exposure to equity markets) are not eligible.

Providers of Isas whose plans meet the required CAT standards will be able to say so in their advertising. Operators whose plans do not meet them must declare the fact.

Q Does that mean I should buy only CAT-branded Isas?

A Not at all. Some non-CAT-backed Isas, especially those that are equity-based, offer investors the prospect of enhanced returns. Also, most CAT-backed Isas may be bought only directly from a provider.

Q Can I assume that a CAT-backed Isa is safe?

A Not at all. The CAT backing means only that the plan on offer has met certain conditions on charges, accessibility, terms and conditions. It offers no assurance that your plan, if it is primarily equity-based, will not fall in value if stock markets worldwide collapse.

Q How will I keep track of my Isa?

A You should receive a statement at least twice a year showing the value of your plan. You will be able to compare contributions against the plan's value.

Q What happens if my Isa fails to deliver the returns it promised?

A As with Peps, you have the right to transfer your plan to another provider from April 6, 2000. These transfers will not affect your permitted Isa contributions.

Q May I transfer building society windfall shares into my Isa as I used to be able to do with Peps?

A No. Isa rules do not permit this, though they allow the transfer of shares received from an approved profit-sharing or savings-related share option scheme run by an employer. Transfers must be made at the share's current market value and they count towards your permitted Isa contributions.

Q How long will Isas last?

A The government has said they will be available until at least 2009. However don't forget – governments do change and Isas could be impacted by such change.

Dos and Don'ts

- **DON'T** take out the first Isa you are offered. They come in all shapes and sizes so it pays to shop around and identify a plan you feel happy with and that meets your investment objectives.

- **DON'T** take out an Isa simply for the sake of it. Attractive though the tax breaks are, there is no point in taking out an account if you have bigger financial priorities such as paying off outstanding bills. Clear all debts before making savings, because interest charges on loans or credit cards will invariably be higher than any returns you may expect from investments.

- **DON'T** invest more than you can afford. There is little point in taking out a plan if you are forced to close it months later because you need cash quickly. You are better off investing your money elsewhere.

- **DO** think 'regular'. You don't have to put big sums into an Isa, you can squirrel away small amounts on a regular basis. It's easier on your wallet that way.

- **DO** take financial advice. If you have any doubt whether an Isa is for you, a professional adviser will be able to look at your financial objectives, analyse whether an Isa is in your best interests, and if so recommend the most appropriate plan.

- **DO** understand the risks involved. Most Isas invest some contributions in equities or investment funds such as unit trusts and investment trusts. These investments can be risky – so beware.

- **DO** read all the terms and conditions. While CAT-backed Isas give you assurances over charges, access to your money, and terms and conditions, you must read through all the terms and conditions before signing on the dotted line. Remember: caveat emptor – let the buyer beware.

- **DO** your homework. Before buying an Isa from a company, check its record in its area of investment expertise. If you are buying an equity Isa, for example, check the company's investment record. If it is no good, think again about buying from it. Also, check to see whether the manager responsible for delivering past performance is still at the helm. If they are not, beware.

- **DO** trust your instinct. If you see an Isa whose claims look too good to be true, they probably are. If a particular Isa makes you nervous, look elsewhere.

- **DON'T** wait until the end of the tax year before buying an Isa. It makes no sense to delay your purchase until then, as everyone used to do with Peps. The sooner your money is working for you within the Isa tax-free wrapper, the better.

Did you know?

- **DID** you know that Isas are available not only from banks and building society branches – but also at supermarkets? They are also available on the Internet.

- **DID** you know that anyone over 18 and ordinarily resident in the UK for tax purposes may take out an Isa? A married couple may take out separate plans and between them invest a maximum of £14,000 per tax year. Cash Isas can be taken out by anyone 16 or over.

- **DID** you know that once you have bought your Isa, you are not committed to its provider? You may take out a plan with another provider the following tax year.

- **DID** you know that you may boost your Isa by transferring capital from a maturing Tessa into the plan without affecting your Isa investment allowances?

- **DID** you know that you may make withdrawals from your Isa without affecting the account's tax-free status?

So what now?

- **ISAs** are an ideal vehicle through which to make a long-term savings commitment. Though the tax breaks are not as attractive as they are with pensions, Isas are far more flexible. They allow you to save with the assurance that you may access your money in a financial emergency. They should form an important component of a saver's investment portfolio. If you have yet to take out an Isa, start looking now.

Unit trusts

MOST people would acknowledge the prudence of keeping some money on deposit to pay for unexpected bills or to meet a financial emergency. But at some stage in our lives we need to think about the bigger financial issues such as saving for children, saving for a child's further education or saving for retirement. Because these may be considered well in advance, the range of savings options available involves more than simple deposit accounts.

One suitable long-term savings tool is the unit trust. Over the past 10 years, and helped by the popularity of Peps, unit trusts have become a commonplace investment vehicle for people prepared to expand their savings horizons beyond the building society. As long-term equity investments they cannot be beaten, though that does not mean that they are not without risks. Unit trusts come in all shapes and sizes and offer varying levels of risk and reward.

Unit trusts: key questions and answers

Q What is a unit trust?

A It is a vehicle that allows you to invest in world stock markets. Investors pool their money in a fund and the unit trust's manager invests that cash in a spread of company shares. Unit trusts are often described as collective investments because many people subscribe to the same investment.

Q Why not simply invest in a selection of shares?

A For some people, buying and selling their own shares makes great sense. It is a relatively easy process – cheap and cheerful share-dealing services, many of them telephone-based or Internet-based, are widely available. But it can be a dangerous game especially if you invest in only a narrow range of shares. You may invest in some leading UK companies but still be hit by sharp share price corrections or even company collapses.

Because unit trusts are pooled investments, your money obtains exposure to a broad spread of shares. This reduces your investment risk. Many trusts also invest internationally, which is difficult – though not impossible – to do yourself. But remember that while unit trusts dilute risk by investing across a range of companies, they are not immune from the effects of stock market fluctuations or crashes. Unit prices fall as well as rise.

Q How does a unit trust work?

A When you invest in a unit trust, you buy units in the fund. These rise and fall in value in line with the share price performance of the fund's underlying assets. When stock markets boom, your units will rise in value. Conversely, when markets fall, your units will fall too.

Q Where is my money invested?

A That depends upon the trust you choose. Each trust has a predetermined set of investment objectives to which it must keep. For example, this may be to obtain capital growth for investors by investing in UK companies or it may be to invest in the stock markets of the Far East. Usually, the fund's name will give you a good idea where your money will be invested.

At present there are some 2,000 unit trusts in existence. Most invest exclusively in a major world stock market such as the UK or North America or a geographically defined range of markets such as Europe or the Far East. Others invest in smaller companies or the world's emerging stock markets.

Q Where do I start?

A Before buying a unit trust, you must ensure that the fund meets your financial objectives. For example, there is little point buying a unit trust if you know that you will want your money back in three months. There is little chance that you will get all your money back – keeping your cash in a building society would be a better bet.

Equally, there is no point buying units in a trust that invests in emerging markets if you are not prepared for a rocky ride and the chance that your investment may fall in value. Unit trusts work only if investors are prepared to regard them as long-term investment vehicles.

For most people the sensible approach is to buy a UK-invested unit trust first of all. Only after they feel comfortable with this fund should they consider overseas trusts. A 'core and satellite' approach to unit trust investment can make sense – where the bulk of the money is invested in UK funds and the rest in overseas trusts.

However, in view of the wide range of trusts on offer it is probably best not to adopt a DIY approach. A good independent financial adviser will help you select from a range of trusts that meet your long-term financial objectives.

Q Can I receive an income from a unit trust?

A Yes. A number of unit trusts generate income. The favourite sector for income seekers is the 100-strong UK equity income fund sector. Many of these have a record of delivering consistent income and capital growth for investors. Top of the list are income trusts such as ABN Amro Equity Income, Jupiter Income, BWD UK Equity Income and Newton Higher Income. Corporate bond-based trusts are also increasingly popular with investors looking for income. These funds invest in bonds issued by some of the country's top companies.

Income from a unit trust is paid net of 20% tax so basic rate taxpayers have nothing further to pay. Higher rate taxpayers must pay an additional 20%, and non-taxpayers can reclaim the tax. However, if a unit trust is held inside an Individual Savings Account (Isa), income builds up tax-free.

Q Are there any other taxes I may have to pay?

A When you sell your units you may have to pay capital gains tax on any investment gains you have made from your holding. However, you may use your annual capital gains tax allowance – £7,500 for the tax year ending April 5, 2002 – to mitigate any bill. If your unit trust is held inside an Isa, there will be no capital gains tax charge.

Q Why are they called trusts?

A Each unit trust must be set up by a deed of trust approved by the Financial Services Authority. The deed sets out the trust's investment objectives, the range of securities in which it is authorised to invest and the trustees of the fund. The trustees' role is to act as an independent referee and to make sure that the manager runs the fund in accordance with the deed. But that role does not extend to protecting investors against falling stock markets or poor investment management.

Q Are unit trusts the same as investment trusts and new Open-Ended Investment Companies (OEICs)?

A All three are collective investment vehicles that allow you to invest in world stock markets through a broad spread of shares managed by an investment expert. As long as the fund you have bought meets your financial objectives, and you view the investment as long-term, it doesn't matter if it is a unit trust, investment trust or OEIC.

Unit trusts and OEICs are open-ended investment vehicles, which means that the fund's size expands and contracts according to investor demand. Your units (unit trusts) or shares (OEICs) always reflect the value of the fund's underlying assets. In contrast, investment trusts are close-ended, which means there are a fixed number of shares in issue. Such a structure may mean that the shares do not fully reflect the trust's underlying assets when investor demand is low.

Q Is there an insurance element to a unit trust?

A No. Unlike investment funds such as investment bonds, a unit trust is a pure investment fund. Apart from any charges that the fund manager might take, your money is used to accumulate units in an investment fund. This makes unit trusts one of the best ways to obtain exposure to equity markets.

Q What are the charges?

A You pay two main charges when investing in a unit trust. The initial, or set-up, charge will probably range between 5% and 6%, and an annual management charge – typically between 1% and

1.75% – will be made for running the trust.

Q It all seems transparent compared with the charges levied by competing products. Is that so?

A Yes and no. Though unit trusts do not apply surrender penalties and hefty policy charges, the traffic is not all one-way. A disadvantage of unit trusts is in their pricing. An investor buys units in a trust at the offer price and sells at the bid price. The difference between the bid and offer prices of a unit trust – called the spread – may range between 6% and 11%. If you bought units in a trust and sold them almost immediately, you would lose more than the money taken in initial charges. Many unit trusts are being converted to Open-Ended Investment Companies, a move that will result in single pricing and the removal of differential bid and offer prices.

Q How much do I need to invest in a unit trust?

A Most companies allow investment in either of two ways. You may invest a lump sum – anything between £500 and £1,000 – or set up a regular monthly savings scheme. Saving on a regular basis is less painful on the wallet and means you do not put all your money into the stock market at once. Most unit trust companies will let you save as little as £50 per month and if you save regularly you may increase, decrease, stop or suspend monthly payments.

Q Can I hold unit trusts in a tax-free Individual Savings Account?

A Yes. Most companies offer Isas and you may invest your entire allowance (£7,000) in unit trusts. If you are thinking of investing in a unit trust, it makes better sense to do it through an Isa simply because of the tax freedom it provides.

Q Who offers unit trusts?

A Most of the country's leading financial services companies now have a range of unit trusts. Leading players in the market include Fidelity, Jupiter, M&G, Invesco, Perpetual and Schroder. All the banks offer funds, but their investment records tend to be poor. Insurance companies, building societies and friendly societies offer funds and new players include Virgin and Marks & Spencer.

Q Who are the market leaders?

A Though companies such as Jupiter, Invesco Perpetual and Schroder have established a good track record of running unit trusts, no investment house is best at running all types of funds. Some groups display areas of investment excellence but are mediocre elsewhere. Some guidance is given in the chapter on top providers. A group's track record in specific investment areas may be obtained by reviewing its past performance.

Most personal finance magazines publish statistics on all unit trusts (see chapter on useful reading) and these allow an individual trust's short- and long-term investment record to be ascertained. The tables are presented in such a way that a trust's performance may be easily measured against that of its immediate peer group. For example, all American and Japanese trust performance figures are displayed together.

When assessing relative performance look for a fund that has consistently performed well compared with one that displays periods of good performance followed by patches of woeful returns.

Q How do I buy a unit trust?

A You may buy direct from the unit trust company – over the telephone or with an application form – or you may buy through a financial adviser. You can also use the Internet through so-called fund supermarkets. Before buying, ask the company to send details of the fund in which you are interested. It should include the fund's latest report and accounts and these will show where the fund is invested. It should also provide a key features document that will indicate the impact of charges on your intended investment. This information lets you check that the trust's objectives meet your own financial goals and that the minimum investment requirement, together with the frequency and timing of income payments, suit you.

Q Is it cheaper to buy direct from the unit trust provider?

A No. Most unit trust companies charge the same irrespective of whether you buy direct or through an adviser. If you buy direct they make more money out of you by not having to pay commission to an adviser. Some financial services companies offer discount dealing services which enable you to buy unit trust funds more cheaply than by going direct.

Q What happens once I have bought my units?

A When the unit trust company receives your order, it will buy units in the fund of your choice and send a contract note confirming the units bought and the cost. You may also receive a unit trust certificate, though most companies no longer issue them.

Q What information do I subsequently receive?

A Every six months you should receive a manager's report detailing the progress of your unit trust. It should tell you about the performance of the fund, comparing it against relevant stock market indices. It should also contain information about the investment manager's strategy and the trust's future prospects. Most companies issue six-monthly statements detailing the units you hold, transactions conducted since the last statement and the value of your holding.

If your trust pays an income you will be sent a tax voucher detailing income received and the tax paid on it. This voucher is an important document and should be kept in a safe place. It will be needed if you have to complete a tax return or if you are a non-taxpayer and wish to reclaim any tax paid.

Q Do I have to take income from a trust or can I reinvest it to buy more units?

A Most unit trust companies offer two types of unit for income-oriented funds – income units or accumulation units. If you wish to receive your income, opt for the income units. Otherwise opt for the accumulation units where the income remains within the fund and boosts the price of your units.

Q What about selling my units?

A You can sell easily. When you invested, your unit trust company should have provided details about how to sell. It will ask you to complete a special withdrawal form or the renunciation form on the reverse of your unit trust certificate. A written note telling the company you wish to sell or a telephone order to sell may be sufficient. You should receive your money within seven days together with a contract note detailing the terms of the sale.

Q Unit trusts seem an ideal way to obtain equity exposure. But what about their actual performance?

A Over the five years to February 2001 the average UK unit trust has delivered a total return of 73% – way above inflation (15%). Some unit trusts have lost money over the same period, especially those invested in the Far East and emerging markets. Generally, a typical unit trust has delivered an investment return above inflation.

Q Where can I obtain further information about unit trusts?

A The Association of Unit Trusts and Investment Funds (AUTIF) publishes a series of leaflets for investors. It covers saving for children, monthly savings, and unit trusts and tax. The association's directory of unit trusts provides key details on individual funds, including charges and minimum investment requirements. Details from the Unit Trust Information Service, 65 Kingsway, London WC2B 6TD, call 020 8207 1361.

Dos and Don'ts

- **DON'T** be mesmerised by adverts that extol the virtues of a particular unit trust. Unit trust groups are adept at enticing people to invest in a fund with a tremendous past investment performance. They are less skilful at warning you about the dangers of investing at the top of the stock market.

- **DO** squirrel away money in a unit trust savings scheme – it is one of the best ways to save for the long term. Most unit trust groups operate such schemes.

- **DO** consider an index-tracking unit trust – they have revolutionised the industry in recent years. Their objective is simply to match or track the performance of a leading stock market such as the FTSE All-Share or the FTSE 100. This is done through sophisticated computer techniques – there is no manager to decide which shares to buy and which to ignore.

  Though index-tracking unit trusts are not immune from stock market falls, investors at least know where they stand. If the market rises, their fund rises and if the market falls, their fund falls in price by the same amount. Many actively managed funds, which market themselves on the ability of a manager to outperform the stock market, often fail to deliver and consistently underperform the stock indices they are attempting to beat.

  Gartmore, Legal & General, HSBC, Royal & SunAlliance, Scottish Amicable and Virgin run index-tracking unit trusts that mirror the performance of the FTSE 100 or the FTSE All-Share indices.

- **DO** keep a close eye on your investment. Many people hold on to poorly performing unit trusts for too long. If your trust is not delivering the investment goods, then consider selling and switching your investment to a company that will take greater care of your money.

- **DON'T** select a unit trust purely on the strength of a creditable past performance record. Make sure the trust fits your long-term financial objectives and your risk profile.

- **DON'T** be overwhelmed by short-term performance numbers. Good consistent long-term performance is a far more compelling case for buying a unit trust.

- **DON'T** select a unit trust simply because it has low charges. Sharp charges count for nothing if the trust fails to deliver investment performance.

- **DON'T** be frightened of being boring. Many people lost money from unit trusts through the Nineties after choosing exotic funds such as those investing in emerging markets, the Far East and Japan. In contrast, people who chose lower-risk investments such as UK funds or international funds have fared much better.

- **DON'T** panic if your investment falls in value. A unit trust is a long-term investment and will deliver real value only if you hold out for the long term.

- **DO** avoid so-called broker unit trusts. These funds are managed by financial advisers and invest in a selection of unit trusts managed by the country's top investment houses. The theory is that the adviser adds value by choosing fund winners. But in practice this rarely happens, mainly because such funds levy high charges that suppress investment performance. There have been many scandals in this area. Avoid broker unit trusts like the plague.

- **DON'T** invest unless you are prepared to lose money. All unit trusts involve an element of risk unless you buy a cash-based unit trust. If you cannot live with the thought that your investment may fall in value, keep your money in a competitive building society savings account.

- **DO** remember that when you buy an overseas unit trust, you are taking a currency risk as well as a stock market risk. For most people it is far better to keep their money at home by buying a UK-invested unit trust.

- **DON'T** forget that unit trusts have not escaped their fair share of scandal. Do not be afraid to ask questions before parting with your money and if you still feel uncomfortable, don't proceed. Once you have made your investment, keep a close eye on it and be prepared to ask questions if the fund manager does not deliver good returns.

Did you know?

- **DID** you know that you can check the price of your unit trust holdings in the business pages of most leading national newspapers? You can also check the performance of your holding in the unit trust performance tables in most monthly personal finance magazines (see chapter on useful reading).

- **DID** you know that most unit trust companies allow you to split your monthly saving between various trusts, further diversifying your investment risk?

- **DID** you know that you may switch investments if you feel that better investment opportunities lie elsewhere or if your present holding is not delivering the performance you expected? Most groups let you switch trusts without having to pay the full initial sales charge. But remember that when you switch, you could be liable to capital gains tax.

- **DID** you know that some groups will let you invest as little as £20 per month through a regular saving scheme?

- **DID** you know that some unit trusts invest worldwide, providing exposure to world stock markets as opposed to merely a specific region? These are called international funds. Some unit trust groups also offer managed or fund of funds trusts which invest across their own range of trusts.

- **DID** you know that many unit trust companies offer cash funds? These trusts pay a decent rate of interest and are a useful place to park or shelter surplus money.

- **DID** you know that unit trusts may be bought for children? Adults buy units in their own name but may add a child's initials to show who owns them. This is known as a designated account. When the child is old enough – usually 18 – the units can be claimed by completing a stock transfer form.

- **DID** you know that citywire.co.uk now allows you to track the performance of top unit trust managers? This Internet site highlights investments managers who have delivered better returns than their competitors through thick and thin.

So what now?

- **UNIT** trusts are an ideal way to save for the long term. But not every trust is a sure-fire investment winner. Before buying a trust, do your homework – make sure it is the right one for you and be prepared to hold it for at least five years. Only patient investors truly enjoy the rich rewards that can come from holding unit trusts.

Investment trusts

INVESTMENT trusts are the hidden nuggets of the savings world. Though they have been around for 130 years, it is really only in the past 10 years that the management groups behind them have started promoting their wares. For anyone interested in saving for the future, whether for retirement, a dream holiday or a child's education, investment trusts should be at the top of their shopping list.

Investment trusts: key questions and answers

Q What is an investment trust?

A It is a collective investment fund similar to a unit trust (see section on unit trusts above) and an Open-Ended Investment Company (see section on OEICs below). It pools investors' money and uses it to invest in the shares of a broad spread of companies, diluting the risk to investors. The companies may be big blue-chip UK firms, international giants or little-known concerns and fledgling companies that have yet to obtain a stock market listing. Whatever the underlying investment, the aim is that your holding will grow in value and increase your personal wealth.

Q How do I know what individual trusts are investing in?

A Each trust has precise investment objectives to which the manager must adhere. This makes it easier when it comes to choosing a trust appropriate to your savings needs. The marketing literature will spell out its objectives and these, plus the fund's name, will give a good indication of where your money will be invested.

However, there are a number of trusts whose names give no clue to their investment objectives. Scottish Investment Trust, for example, does not invest in the fortunes of Scottish companies – its assets are invested worldwide.

Q Who manages investment trusts?

A They are primarily managed by some of the country's leading investment houses – the same fund management groups that manage unit trusts. Big players include Baillie Gifford, Edinburgh Fund Managers, JP Morgan Fleming, Foreign & Colonial, Gartmore, Henderson, Invesco Perpetual, Jupiter, M&G and Martin Currie. When you invest in a trust, you gain access to some of the best investment brains in the country. Fund managers, supported by first-class research, analyse where best to invest your cash, both on a country and company basis.

Q Is an investment trust the same as a unit trust?

A No, though they both fulfil the same role – to reward long-term investors with attractive returns by investing in equities. An investment trust, unlike a unit trust, is a company and it issues shares that are listed on the UK stock market. Though the price of these shares, like those for any listed company, will reflect demand from buyers and sellers it is the performance of the underlying assets that determine the trust's share value. Many investment trust houses have a long track record of delivering excellent returns to investors.

The company structure of an investment trust means that the investment manager is supervised by an independent board of directors. The board will ensure that the manager acts according to the objectives of the trust. It has the power to appoint a new manager if the trust does not perform satisfactorily – a reassuring factor for investors.

Q Because there are two factors which contribute to a trust's share price – demand for shares and the performance of the underlying assets – surely that makes investment trusts more risky than unit trusts?

A In a way, yes. An investor holding an investment trust that performs poorly, either because the sector it invests in is out of favour or because of indifferent investment management, can suffer a double whammy. Not only can the trust's shares be hit by the poor performance of the underlying assets, but they can also be affected because more people want to sell their holdings than buy more.

When this happens the shares fail to reflect the value of the underlying assets, commonly known as trading at a discount. Conversely, when a trust is performing well there may be more buyers than sellers and the shares may trade at a premium to the value of their underlying assets.

Anyone buying an investment trust should be aware that

investor sentiment affects the value of the shares they are buying. Astute – or just plain lucky – investors can benefit from a performance boost if a trust comes back into favour and its discount closes or narrows. Similarly, an investor may lose out by buying a trust's shares at a premium only for the trust to fall out of favour and its shares move to a discount. But if you buy an investment trust for the long term, discounts and premiums should not really affect you. If your shareholding increases in value over time, you should be happy.

Q Investment trusts are companies and I am buying shares in them, so do I become a shareholder when I buy into them?

A Yes. As a shareholder, you will usually be entitled to receive the annual report and accounts, a six-monthly update on the trust's performance, and be invited to the annual general meeting and to vote on certain proposals.

Q Why should I buy an investment trust?

A There are five key reasons:

1. Performance. Investment trusts have a good record of achieving superior long-term returns for investors. Though past performance is no guarantee of future performance, it is a reassuring guide. Research company Standard & Poor's Micropal says the average UK investment trust has returned 108% over the five years to February 2001.

Over the same period you would have obtained only 13% had you squirrelled your money away in a typical savings account.

2. Professionalism. Investment trusts are managed by some of the country's top investment houses and you can be reassured that your savings will be looked after professionally. The investment trust manager will assess which companies to buy for the trust as well as which to sell or ignore altogether. For trusts with broad

international exposure, the manager will also decide in which countries' stock markets to invest.

3. Price-conscious. Investment trusts are renowned for their low annual management charges – more of your savings work for your long-term benefit – and combined with strong investment per-formance, this makes investment trusts an attractive savings option. Though annual charges vary they rarely exceed 1% of the fund's value. Indeed, some long-established trusts have lower charges because of the considerable size of assets under management and the economies of scale this brings to their operations.

4. Proliferation. There are investment trusts for all tastes – from those investing exclusively in the UK to those investing in specific sectors (for example, technology or smaller companies) or geographic areas of the world. As a general rule, most investment trusts will aim to deliver a combination of long-term income and capital growth, long-term capital growth or a consistently high level of income. Whatever your investment objectives, there is a trust to meet your needs.

5. People-friendly. Investment trusts are flexible products that can be used in various ways. Many investors buy them simply as the foundation of a long-term savings portfolio, others invest in them to meet known future financial commitments such as school or university fees, or to fund a pension.

Q I'm convinced that investment trusts are for me. How do I buy them?

A Through a stockbroker or an independent financial adviser. However, one of the most user-friendly ways to buy an investment trust is through a savings and investment plan. These are run by trust management groups and allow you to buy shares either as a one-off investment or on a regular basis from as little as £20 a month. And the costs of buying are usually trimmed to the bone. Many groups that run savings and investment plans do not apply any purchase charges other than the mandatory stamp duty of 0.5%, though they will usually levy a charge if you subsequently sell your shares.

Savings and investment schemes are as flexible an investment vehicle as you will ever discover. If you start a savings scheme and later want to suspend contributions for a while, most groups will allow this without penalty, unlike many other competing products. Investors may also increase contributions or make one-off investments as they wish. Most investment houses will also allow contributions to be switched to another of their trusts.

Details of investment trust groups that operate low-cost savings and investment schemes are available from the Association of Investment Trust Companies, Durrant House, 8–13 Chiswell Street, London EC1Y 4YY. All the leading investment trust groups including Alliance, Baillie Gifford, Edinburgh Fund Managers, JP Morgan Fleming, Foreign & Colonial, Gartmore, Invesco Perpetual and Scottish Investment Trust offer such plans.

Q How do I set up a savings and investment scheme?

A Contributions may be paid by standing order or direct debit. Once your plan is established, most groups will keep you updated on how it is progressing, tell you how many shares you have acquired and its overall value.

Q What is the tax treatment of an investment trust?

A As a private investor, any income from your investment trust will be paid net of 20% tax. While basic rate taxpayers will have no further tax to pay, higher rate taxpayers will have an additional 20% tax charge. Non-taxpayers can claim back the tax. You may also be liable to pay capital gains tax on any gains you make from your investment trust holding when you sell, though you may use your annual capital gains tax allowance (£7,500 for the tax year ending April 5, 2002) to reduce the bill.

Q Can I hold an investment trust inside an Individual Savings Account?

A Yes. An investment trust makes a splendid underlying investment for an Isa because of the spread of risk it offers. All income and investment gains from it will be tax-free. The maximum annual Isa allowance of £7,000 can be put inside an investment trust-based Isa.

Dos and Don'ts

- **DON'T** overlook generalist investment trusts. These have been around for donkeys' years and have rarely let investors down. They invest in a broad spectrum of world stock markets and across a broad range of companies. By investing worldwide, as opposed to concentrating on any particular stock market, these trusts are usually of lower risk than specialist trusts that concentrate on a particular stock market or a single investment theme.

  Many generalist trusts have a long record of success and some have proved their worth over more than 100 years. A further point in their favour is that many are of considerable size and have more than £1 billion of assets under management – a reassuring factor for investors. Despite their unexciting name, generalist trusts should be a first port of call for investors who want to put money into investment trusts. Big players include Foreign & Colonial, Alliance, Monks, Second Alliance and Scottish Investment Trust.

- **DON'T** touch an investment trust unless you know exactly what you are getting into. Over the past five years the industry has been extremely innovative in creating new types of investment trust share. These have included capital shares (which offer the potential for geared returns and losses), income shares and zero dividend preference shares (low-risk shares which generate all their returns in capital form). Take professional advice before getting mixed up with these investments.

- **DON'T** touch a new investment trust launch unless you know exactly what you're doing. New investment trusts are only ever launched for marketing purposes and the investment rationale behind them may be weak. Put your money instead into a trust that has been around for some years and has established a creditable track record.

- **DO** be aware that investment trusts, like any stock market listed company, may be taken over by a competitor or predator. Your investment may not last as long as you thought or you may be offered the option to transfer your holdings into an alternative investment vehicle.

- **DON'T** tangle with investment trust warrants unless you know what you are doing. Warrants, which allow you to buy shares in the same trust at a set price on a fixed date in the future, are attractive for investors prepared to take higher risks to obtain higher capital growth. The majority of investors should give them a wide berth.

- **DON'T** put your money in an investment trust if capital security is sacrosanct. Investment trusts are equity vehicles and like all shares can rise and fall in value, sometimes sharply. If capital security is important, keep your money on deposit.

- **DO** check out a trust's investment objectives and its track record before parting with your cash. Do not buy an emerging markets investment trust if income generation is a priority – you are better off with a UK income fund. Similarly, do not opt for a UK investment trust if you are after excitement from your investment. Instead, look at an emerging markets or a Far Eastern investment trust where the investment risks and rewards are high.

  Most leading personal finance magazines carry statistics and tables that allow you to compare the relative performance of individual funds (see chapter on useful reading). If the trust you are thinking of buying has a poor track record when measured against funds with similar investment objectives, alarm bells should ring.

- **DO** continue to monitor your trust once you have bought it. While buying the right investment trust is important, it is up to you to see whether the fund delivers the returns you expected. Don't sit on your hands if you are the victim of poor performance – take your money elsewhere.

Did you know?

- **DID** you know that the first investment trust was formed 130 years ago and is still in existence today with assets of more than £2 billion? Foreign & Colonial is the country's largest investment trust and it invests worldwide.

- **DID** you know that an investment trust may be used as the basis for a pension, to repay a mortgage or to plan for future school fees? Some investment trust groups such as Edinburgh Fund Managers and Foreign & Colonial have launched pension plans based around their investment trusts.

- **DID** you know that more than 200 investment trusts run by about 50 management groups offer savings schemes that will accept lump sums and regular contributions?

- **DID** you know that you can hold an investment trust inside a tax-free Individual Savings Account?

- **DID** you know that you can invest as little as £20 a month in an investment trust through a savings and investment scheme?

- **DID** you know that many investment trust companies offer share exchange facilities that enable you to swap your existing shareholdings – for example, those from privatisations or building society conversions – for a holding in an investment trust? Such a service can leave people who have acquired a random selection of shares with a more balanced portfolio.

- **DID** you know that investment trusts may borrow money to increase their exposure to equities? This process, known as gearing, can enhance investor returns if equity exposure is increased in a rising stock market. Conversely, it may exaggerate losses if the money borrowed is invested in equities that later slump.

- **DID** you know that investment trusts come in all types and sizes? Some – the so-called generalist trusts – invest internationally, some concentrate on UK investments and some invest in specific regions of the world (for example, the Far East, Europe or North America). Others invest in specific sectors such as venture capital, smaller companies and property.

So what now?

- **INVESTMENT** trusts are one of the most cost-effective ways to obtain exposure to world stock markets. If you are looking for a long-term home for your money, they make an obvious choice. But like any investment, don't buy the first fund that catches your eye. Shop around and ask for details from a number of investment trust groups before choosing. And don't forget to ask for information on their savings and investment schemes – they are simply the best way to buy an investment trust.

Open-Ended Investment Companies (OEICs)

THERE is no doubt that packaged investment products are the best way to invest in the stock market. Though many people enjoyed handsome gains from privatisation shares in the Eighties or windfall shares from demutualising building societies and insurance companies in the Nineties, it is dangerous to base an investment portfolio around a number of individual shares – especially if your financial future depends upon their performance.

A far more sensible approach is to complement them with holdings in collective investment products such as unit trusts and investment trusts. These vehicles are managed by some of the country's leading investment houses and they diversify risk by investing in a broad range of shares in the UK and overseas.

Though not immune from the effects of stock market corrections, the funds usually benefit from a cool professional head at the helm and their spread of shareholdings. In the past couple of years, unit trusts and investment trusts have been joined by the Open-Ended Investment Company investment, or OEIC for short.

Do not be alarmed by the yobbish-sounding acronym. If the experts are to be believed, OEICs are set to become standard fare for investors in search of an equity home for their money. While unit trusts were highly popular in the Eighties and Nineties, OEICs are set to rule the investment roost in the years to come by providing investors looking for cost-effective equity exposure with an ideal first port of call.

In the past couple of years, some of the City's biggest investment houses have asked holders of their unit trust funds to vote on converting them into OEICs. For many people, the change from OEICs to unit trusts has led to much confusion, not helped by legal obligations heaped on the investment companies who have been quickest off the mark to make the transformation.

Literature accompanying proposals to convert unit trusts into OEICs is riddled with impenetrable legal jargon and many people do not fully understand what they are voting on. But do not despair – this chapter cuts through the legal verbosity with an essential question and answer guide to OEICs. Ignore it at your peril.

Q What is an OEIC?

A OEIC (pronounced oik), stands for Open-Ended Investment Company.

Q I'm still none the wiser. What does it do?

A An OEIC is simply a vehicle that allows people to band together and invest their money cost-effectively. Like a unit trust, money is pooled and invested in a spread of shares to reduce stock market investment risks. The only difference between a unit trust and an OEIC is that the latter is a limited company rather than a trust governed by trustees.

Q Who runs OEICs?

A The same companies that currently manage unit trusts and investment trusts – the investment houses and insurance companies. Because it is structured as a company, an OIEC must have a board of directors, including independent as well as internal directors. The fund operation is controlled by a designated corporate director and the investors' interests are safeguarded by a depository. Like the manager of a unit trust and its trustee, these two officers must be independent of each other and not be members of the same group of companies.

Q What is so special about an OEIC?

A It is merely an updated version of a unit trust. Investors in OEICs buy shares rather than units in a trust. New shares are created when someone wants to invest. Crucially, shares in an OEIC will trade at one price – unlike a unit trust which has separate prices for buying and selling. Pick up a copy of the *Financial Times*, for example, and turn to the companies and markets section. Under the heading 'authorised investment funds' you will see two prices quoted for unit trusts – a selling price (the bid price) and a buying price (the offer price).

Investors buy units in a unit trust at the offer price – always higher than the bid price – and offload them at the bid price. In contrast, look at the prices quoted for Threadneedle funds – all of which are OEICs – and you will see just one price quoted per fund. This is the price at which you buy and sell the shares.

Q Apart from a single price, what else sets OEICs apart from unit trusts?

A An OEIC may act as an umbrella for many different funds and a single OEIC can replace lots of unit trusts, cutting costs for investors. Standard Life, for example, has restructured its £1 billion range of unit trusts into an OEIC. As part of the change, the initial cost of investing in either the company's gilt fund or UK Equity High Income fund has halved to 3%, while that for the successful UK Equity Growth fund has dropped from 6% to 3.5%. The company says that reduced charges are a reflection of the cost-effectiveness of managing an OEIC compared with a range of unit trusts.

Q Can OEICs invest in the same assets as unit trusts?

A Like unit trusts, OIECs invest primarily in equities and fixed-interest stock. But unlike trusts, they do not have the power to invest in risky derivatives or property. At present cash fund OEICs and fund of funds OEICs – a fund investing in other funds – are not allowed.

Q Why are fund managers changing from unit trusts to OEICs? Unit trusts have allowed millions of people to experience exposure to world stock markets without paying over the odds, often through user-friendly regular savings schemes. Why change a winning formula?

A Fund managers believe that unit trusts are out of date. Despite strong stock markets over the past few years and the boom in tax-free Personal Equity Plans during the Nineties, fewer than one in 10 people own a unit trust. Managers say this is because they are too complicated and people do not understand them. They are right

– separate buying and selling prices are confusing and may be used to hide additional charges.

Q   So having one price for an OEIC gets rid of charges?

A   Not quite. It will still cost you to buy a stake in an OEIC, but charges will be clear and separately stated. Returning to our copy of the *Financial Times* and the prices quoted for Threadneedle OEICs, we see that there is a charge against each fund – this is the percentage of your initial money that the company will take for making an investment. An OEIC will also levy an annual management charge that will be clearly stated in advance.

Q   Isn't all this change simply an excuse for fund managers to make more money?

A   Yes and no. In the long term, they hope that OEICs will sell better than unit trusts and boost their profits. Many hope to sell OEICs into continental Europe. But they will lose revenue in the short term because they will not make profits by matching units from a seller to a buyer at a different price. This is what they do with unit trusts, making juicy profits in the process.

Q   Can I put an OEIC into a new-style Individual Savings Account?

A   Yes. You may put £7,000 into an OEIC-based Isa. With OEICs you have two investment options. You may take out a so-called maxi Isa which allows you to invest the whole of your annual Isa allowance (£7,000) in an OEIC or a range of OEICs. Maxi Isas are offered primarily by leading investment houses.

Alternatively, you may buy a mini-equity Isa that allows you to invest a maximum of £3,000 per tax year in OEICs. A further £3,000 may be invested in a separate mini-cash Isa, plus an additional £1,000 in a mini-insurance Isa.

Q   Is the tax treatment of OEICs different from that of unit trusts and investment trusts?

A No – both within the fund and on investors. Dividends are paid net of 20% tax while any capital gains made by investors are potentially liable for capital gains tax. But remember that fund switches within an OEIC umbrella do not attract capital gains tax charges. This contrasts with unit trusts where a switch from one fund to another triggers a potential capital gains tax liability.

Q How do I monitor my OEIC?

A OEIC prices are quoted daily in leading national newspapers so you may update the valuation of your investment portfolio as frequently as you like.

Q With the birth of OEICs, does it mean that unit trusts will cease to exist?

A Probably. But it will take a while for all fund managers to convert their holdings.

Q What about regulation and investor compensation? Do I have the same safeguards with an OEIC as I do with a unit trust?

A Yes. Like unit trusts, OEICs are closely regulated by government agencies including IMRO (Investment Management Regulatory Organisation), the Financial Services Authority and the Personal Investment Authority. Furthermore, OEICs are covered by the Investors Compensation Scheme if the fund manager hits financial problems.

Q So that's it? Game, set and match to OEICs?

A Not quite. Some financial experts believe that OEIC providers are pulling the wool over investors' eyes when they say they are cheaper. They point to the introduction of something called a dilution charge – payable by investors who wish to sell shares in a fund. OEIC providers insist that the charge is to guard against dilution of a fund's assets during times of active trading, thus protecting the interests of existing investors.

But if this dilution charge is added to an OEIC initial charge investors simply end up with a disguised bid-to-offer spread. Explaining a dilution charge to an investor could be said to be even more confusing than getting to grips with bid-to-offer spreads. A dilution charge is the equivalent of the penalties insurance companies can apply to investors who wish to withdraw money from their funds – the dreaded market value adjuster. A further potential problem with OEICs is contagion. If one of the funds under the OEIC umbrella defaults or has problems, the other funds may be called on to bail it out.

Q Are OEICs more risky than investment trusts?

A That is difficult to answer. Investment trusts have a wider remit than OEICs and may borrow heavily to increase exposure to equities if such a strategy would reap rich rewards. That makes them potentially more risky, but not all investment trusts put their money in risky investments and not all trusts borrow. Each individual OEIC and investment trust is essentially a different investment – it is up to you to choose a product that fits your attitude to risk and with which you feel comfortable, whether it is an OEIC or a trust.

Q I'm confused. What do I do? Invest in an OEIC or leave them well alone?

A As with any investment decision, do not put money into anything you don't understand or with which you feel uncomfortable. Before investing in an OEIC or voting to convert a unit trust into an OEIC, do your homework – ask questions and demand answers, either from your professional adviser or from the fund management group itself.

Q If I need further help on OEICs, where should I go?

A The Association of Unit Trusts and Investment Funds (AUTIF) has put together a useful and informative booklet on unit trusts, investment trusts and OEICs. Its title is 'Effective Investment

– a Guide to Investment Funds'. Copies are free and may be ordered by phoning 020 8207 1361 (24-hour service). Further information may be obtained by writing to the Unit Trust Information Service, 65 Kingsway, London WC2B 6TD.

Q And if I am convinced that I want to buy an OEIC, where should I go?

A Buying an OIEC is no different from buying a unit trust. You may buy an OEIC direct from the investment company, either over the telephone or through a salesman. You may also buy OEICs through a financial adviser or a stockbroker – the choice is yours. Or use the Internet or a discount broker.

Dos and Don'ts

- **DON'T** be frightened by the term OEIC. Simply treat it as another form of collective investment and an excellent way of investing in stocks and shares.

- **DON'T** be panicked if you hold a unit trust and the managers write to you saying that they intend to convert the fund into an OEIC. You should be no worse off than before and your investment will not be affected adversely by the transition.

- **DON'T** be put off by the impenetrable literature that your trust company will send you if it intends to convert its unit trusts into OEICs. This material is a legal requirement and is written for lawyers rather than laymen. If you have any doubts, speak to the company directly or contact a financial adviser who should be able to allay your fears.

- **DO** remember that OEICs provide essentially the same investment opportunities as unit trusts. OEICs may be used to invest in international stock markets as well as UK shares and fixed-interest stocks.

- **DO** keep a close eye on the performance of your OEIC investment. Like unit trusts, there are bad OEIC fund managers as well as good ones. If your savings are managed by one of the bad brigade, switch to an OEIC manager who will give your investment the opportunity to grow in value. If in doubt, take professional advice.

- **DON'T** forget that like unit trusts and investment trusts, most OEICs are equity-based. That means the value of your investment can fall as well as rise. Don't invest in an OEIC unless you fully understand the risks involved.

- **DON'T** forget that the best way to invest in an OEIC is through a tax-free Isa.

Did you know?

- **DID** you know that OEICs have been introduced under the European Communities Act 1972? As a result of qualifying as European collective investments under the UCITS (Undertakings for Collective Investment in Transferable Securities) Directive, British OEICs may be sold anywhere within the European Union.

- **DID** you know that British unit trusts do not qualify under UCITS and may not be sold outside the UK?

- **DID** you know that you may invest in an OEIC either by making a lump-sum payment or by investing a small amount per month in a regular savings scheme?

- **DID** you know that OEICs qualify as a suitable investment for a tax-free Individual Savings Account?

- **DID** you know that many of the country's leading investment companies have converted their unit trusts into OIECs? These include Edinburgh Fund Managers, Fidelity, JP Morgan Fleming, Standard Life, Henderson Global Investors and Threadneedle Asset Management.

- **DID** you know that the investment performance of individual

OIECs may be scrutinised in leading personal finance magazines such as *Money Management* and *Bloomberg Money*? (See chapter on useful reading.)

- **DID** you know that OIECs can provide a multi-class structure of shares? For example, it is possible to have one class of shares designated in sterling and others in different major currencies. It is also possible to have classes of shares available to retail investors and classes available to institutional investors.

- **DID** you know that OEICs are umbrella funds? This means you may switch from one type of fund to another without incurring a chargeable event for capital gains tax purposes.

- **DID** you know that research by investment house Fidelity revealed that 98% of independent financial advisers believed OEICs to be equally beneficial to or more beneficial than unit trusts?

- **DID** you know that as an OEIC investor you will receive an annual report and accounts? You will also be allowed to attend the annual general meeting and ask the board questions.

So what now?

- **VIEW** an OEIC simply as a cost-effective way to invest in equities. Don't be confused by the differences between unit trusts, investment trusts and OEICs. If you feel comfortable with the investment strategy pursued by the investment manager, are prepared to keep a close eye on your investment and you invest for the long term, an OEIC is as good a way to enjoy the thrills and spills of shares as any other form of collective investment.

Investment bonds

DIRECT investment in equities is only for those with nerves of steel or who have the financial resources to withstand substantial capital losses. For most people looking to increase their financial wealth by investing in shares, packaged investment products are a far sounder proposition.

They come in all shapes, sizes and in different forms – unit trusts, Open-Ended Investment Companies, maximum investment plans and investment trust companies to name just four. And they share a common feature – they all allow indirect investment in equities, UK and overseas-based, usually cost-effectively.

Investment bonds are a common form of packaged investment. Though somewhat overshadowed in recent years by the rise of unit trusts and the more retail-focused marketing approach adopted by investment trusts, they remain a valuable financial tool and can be a tax-efficient way of investing.

Investment bonds: key questions and answers

Q What is an investment bond?

A It is a product that allows you to make a single premium investment in an investment fund of your choice. Investment bonds are often called unit-linked bonds or single-premium bonds. Your money buys units in an investment fund and you are required to make a lump-sum investment rather than regular contributions.

Q Who offers them?

A Most life insurance companies. They issue investment bonds as single-premium whole-of-life policies. This means that though they are primarily investment vehicles, they provide limited life cover. Typically, this cover is 1% of the repurchase value of the units belonging to a policy at the time of death. In other words, a sum equivalent to 101% of the policy's value is returned by the insurance company when the holder dies.

Q How do they affect your tax situation?

A Investment bonds are subject to internal taxation – in other words, any tax due is paid on your behalf. Basic rate tax is paid on income generated by investments within the bond and capital gains tax is paid on profits made by the bond. This differs from the tax treatment of unit trusts, for example, where no capital gains tax is paid within the trust, but investors may be liable personally to pay such a tax when they take gains, subject to their capital gains tax allowance (£7,500 for the year ending April 5, 2002).

The internal taxes paid within an insurance bond cannot be reclaimed by investors. This makes investment bonds unsuitable for non-taxpayers. Though investors do not have to pay basic rate income tax or capital gains tax on the proceeds from an investment bond, they may have to pay an additional income tax charge. This depends on the taxable income they have earned in the year they encash their bond.

However, the taxation of investment bonds is not all bad news. The bonds may be tax-efficient for many investors, especially those who want to take a regular income from their investment and whose tax position is likely to change over the period the bond is held.

Q Investment bonds invest in unit-linked funds. But where are these funds invested?

A A great attraction of investment bonds is that they offer a wide choice. Most insurance companies offer a range of links – from low-risk deposit-based funds through to high-risk specialist funds investing in specific stock markets worldwide. The funds generally fall into the following categories:

1. Money funds. These invest in deposit-based vehicles. They do not offer the potential for capital growth, but the unit price of your money will rise as a result of accrued interest. The funds represent a

safe haven for your cash though they should not be seen as a long-term home – more as a parking place while you consider other funds that may provide better future returns.

2. Fixed-interest funds. These invest in a range of fixed-interest stocks such as UK gilts, foreign government stocks and corporate bonds issued by both British and international companies. They are relatively low-risk.

3. Managed funds. The most popular choice for investors. They invest in a wide spread of assets – from cash deposits to gilts, property and equities – and as a result their unit prices are not as prone to the market fluctuations of equity-based bonds. They are also usually the insurance company's flagship and they receive royal treatment. A well-run managed fund is a big marketing tool for an insurance company; a badly run fund is its worst nightmare.

4. Property funds. These invest primarily in UK commercial property such as warehouses, office blocks and retail developments. They are long-term investments and their unit prices may be adversely affected by a loss of confidence in the commercial property market. Sometimes investors may suffer long delays in getting their money out of a property fund as a result of the fund's illiquidity.

5. General funds. A broad spread of blue-chip companies based in the UK or overseas is the investment basis for these funds. Because of their wide exposure to international stock markets and individual shares, general funds are usually lower risk than UK equity funds and international equity funds that invest in specific regions of the world.

6. UK equity funds. As their name implies, these invest in the shares of UK quoted companies.

7. International or specialist funds. These offer you exposure to specific geographic areas such as Europe, individual stock markets

such as Japan's or specific investment themes such as commodities and smaller companies. Their focused investment approach usually makes these funds high-risk.

Q What about with-profits funds?

A Some investment bonds offer a unit-linked with-profits fund. But with-profits bonds are often marketed as separate investments – see the section on with-profits investment bonds below.

Q All these fund links are fine, but no one will need to use them all. Aren't they just a waste of time?

A For most investors the answer is yes. All they need to do is to use the managed fund and leave the rest to the investment manager. But some may want to spread their investment across a number of specific funds. Insurance companies usually allow you to invest your money in up to 10 funds, subject to meeting the required minimum investment level for each link.

Investment bonds also allow a change of investment links at any time – for example, to take advantage of better investment prospects elsewhere. The number of changes is unlimited though the insurance company will levy a charge for carrying out your wishes. Typically, this is equivalent to 0.5% of the value of the units you are switching, but most companies allow one free change in any single year.

When switching an investment, units in the new chosen fund are invariably bought at the lower 'bid' price rather than the 'offer' or normal sales price. This means investors effectively do not pay another initial charge for the privilege of switching. Quite rightly, the insurance company assumes that an initial charge was paid when setting up the investment bond, so you should not be double charged.

Q May I take an income from my investment bond?

A Yes. Most companies allow regular withdrawals from an investment though care needs to be taken that the capital value of your bond is not being reduced to furnish you with an income.

Q How much income may I take?

A It is up to you, but current tax rules allow an annual sum equivalent to up to 5% of your original investment to be withdrawn without immediate payment of income tax. Such a sum may be drawn for a maximum of 20 years. So if you make an investment of £10,000, you may withdraw £500 per year without immediate payment of tax. If you elect not to take this withdrawal in one tax year, you may take it in a following tax year. For example, if you do not withdraw the 5% in the first three years of a £10,000 bond, you could take £2,000 in year four – the £1,500 of unused allowances from the first three years plus the permitted £500 withdrawal for year four.

Q What if I want to take more than 5%?

A You may do this, but the excess may attract tax according to the income you have earned in the tax year you take it. So-called 'top-slicing' calculations are applied to see whether tax is paid. How these are applied is best shown by way of example.

For example, assume that you have bought a £10,000 bond. If you take no income in years one and two, but decide to take £2,000 in year three, then you will have taken £500 above your permitted £1,500 allowance (£500 per year). This is called the chargeable gain.

This is then top-sliced by the number of full years the policy has been in force. Assuming that the £2,000 was taken at the end of year three, the top slice would be £167 (£500 divided by three).

This sum is added to any other income earned in the same tax year you have taken the excess withdrawal and its tax treatment may fall into one of three categories. The calculations are based on the tax year ending April 5, 2002:

1. If the total is less than the higher rate income tax threshold (£29,400 in the tax year ended April 5, 2002), the top slice falls within the basic rate tax band. As a result, there is no tax charge to pay on the gain because the insurance company behind the investment bond has already paid basic rate tax on your money on your behalf.

2. If your income before the top slice was added was above the higher rate income tax threshold, the entire top slice would fall within the higher rate tax band. Since the insurance company has already paid 22% basic rate tax, you will become liable for income tax at 18% (40% minus 22%) on the entire gain of £500 – a further tax charge of £90.

3. If adding the top slice takes you above the higher rate income tax threshold, the further tax charge is determined by the amount of top slice above the threshold. Assuming that your income before the top slice was added was £29,300, £100 of the slice would fall within the basic rate tax band and £67 within the higher rate tax band. The further tax charge would be £67/£167 (the proportion of top slice attracting higher rate tax) multiplied by £500 (the chargeable gain) multiplied by 18% (40% minus 22% tax). This works out at £36.

Q I may have to pay tax on withdrawals above 5%. When else will I have to pay tax?

A Your investment bond will become potentially liable to tax when it is encashed – if you die, it is sold, or it matures. The chargeable gain has to be calculated, top-sliced and added to your taxable income to determine whether there is a further tax charge. How this works is best shown below:

Assume that you bought an investment bond for £10,000 and encashed it three years later for £11,800. The chargeable gain is £1,800 (£11,800 minus £10,000) and the top-slice gain is £600 (£1,800 divided by three). Whether further tax is payable depends on your taxable income and any charge would be calculated as follows. Again, assume the tax year ended April 5, 2002:

1. If your taxable income plus top-sliced gain is below £29,400 (the higher rate income tax threshold), there is no further tax to pay.

2. If your taxable income is more than £29,400, the full chargeable gain of £1,800 is subject to tax of 18% – a tax charge of £324.

3. If your taxable income is just below £29,400, then the charge is determined by the proportion of top slice above the higher rate income tax threshold. Assuming a taxable income of £29,100, this means that £300 (half) of the top slice is above the threshold. The further tax charge is £300/£600 (proportion of the top slice above the threshold) multiplied by 18% (additional tax rate) multiplied by £1,800 (chargeable gain). This works out at £162.

Q What if I have made regular annual withdrawals during the bond's life. Do these affect my tax bill when I surrender my with-profits bond?

A Yes, these have to be taken into account. Again, for example, let us assume that you bought an investment bond for £10,000 and encashed it after 10 years for £25,000. During that time you made regular 5% withdrawals.

The final gain is £30,000 – £25,000 plus £5,000 of withdrawals (£500 a year for 10 years).

Chargeable gain is £20,000 – the final gain (£30,000) minus the original outlay of £10,000.

Top-slice gain is £2,000 – the chargeable gain divided by the number of policy years. This is added to your taxable income to determine whether you have further tax to pay.

This calculation can become more complicated if you have made a withdrawal in excess of the 5% allowance. Here, any excess is treated in the year it is taken and has to be stripped out of any tax calculation made on a bond's surrender.

Secondly, let us assume the same example as above, but instead of annual withdrawals of 5%, imagine that withdrawals of £2,000 are made in year three and £3,000 in year seven.

The final gain is again £30,000 – £25,000 plus £5,000 of withdrawals.

In year three, the excess gain of £500 is sliced over three years to determine whether higher rate tax is due.

In year seven, £1,000 is sliced over four years – years four to seven – to determine whether higher rate tax is due. The sum is sliced back only as far as the last chargeable event.

The total of gains already dealt with from a tax point of view is £1,500.

Chargeable gain is £30,000 minus the original investment (£10,000) minus £1,500 (gains already dealt with) – a total of £18,500.

Top-slice gain is therefore £1,850 – the chargeable gain divided by the number of full years the policy has been in force. This is added to your taxable income in the year of the policy's surrender to determine if you must pay further tax.

Q That is all very complicated. In summary, what, if any, are the tax advantages of holding an investment bond?

A They are as follows:

1. The 5% tax deferred income facility may be used by basic rate taxpayers and higher rate taxpayers to provide a boost to their income. By making this withdrawal, there is no requirement to pay immediate income tax on it – it is not treated as current income for income tax purposes. Remember, an income of £1,000 not liable to tax deduction is the equivalent of £1,282 of taxable income to a basic rate taxpayer. To a 40% taxpayer, it is the equivalent of £1,667.

2. The 5% tax allowances accumulate if you do not use them in any year. They are not lost as is the case with allowances for other investments – individual savings accounts, for example.

3. Basic rate taxpayers have no tax to pay on gains from an

investment bond – capital gains tax or income tax – provided that the top-slicing rule does not push their taxable income above the threshold for higher rate tax.

4. Bond withdrawals of up to 5% per annum do not affect an elderly person's right to age allowance.

5. Further tax charges may be avoided if a bond is not encashed until the holder is a basic rate or lower rate taxpayer. A higher rate taxpayer, for example, could take 5% withdrawals every year and encash the bond when he or she becomes a basic rate or lower rate taxpayer. This avoids tax on any profits and is a tactic used by many bondholders who encash their policies after they have retired and suffered a drop in their taxable income.

Q And what are the tax disadvantages?

A They are as follows:

1. Capital gains tax and basic rate tax is paid automatically within the bond and cannot be reclaimed – this makes investment bonds unsuitable for non-taxpayers. It also makes investments such as unit trusts and investment trusts more attractive, especially to investors who do not normally pay capital gains tax.

2. Further tax charges may be triggered if annual withdrawals exceed 5% and when the bond is disposed of.

Q Finally, how much will an investment bond cost me?

A Typically, you will pay an initial management charge of between 5% and 6%. An annual charge is also levied, usually applied monthly at the rate of 1/16% or 1/12% of the bond's value.

Dos and Don'ts

- **DON'T** invest in the more speculative funds offered under an investment bond unless you can afford to lose your money and are prepared to endure a long rocky ride. A better approach is to invest the core of your money in a cautious fund such as the managed fund, and put smaller amounts in more risky unit-linked funds.

- **DON'T** withdraw more than 5% each year from your investment bond unless you are fully aware of the potential tax drawbacks and the risk to your capital.

- **DON'T** invest in an investment bond without fully understanding the tax implications. If in doubt, seek financial advice. You may be better served by other packaged investments such as unit trusts or investment trusts.

- **DON'T** consider an investment bond unless you are prepared to take a long-term view. Quite simply, they are long-term investments.

- **DON'T** forget that investment bonds offer a wider choice of investment funds than unit trusts and investment trusts.

- **DON'T** switch funds within an investment bond purely because the facility exists. Change funds only if it makes good investment sense. Seek professional advice if you are unsure.

- **DO** remember that managed funds are primarily available only through life insurance policies such as investment bonds. A good managed fund is ideal for people who are new to investment.

Did you know?

- **DID** you know that an investment bond is a non-qualifying life policy. This means the proceeds from an investment bond on encashment are not tax-free.

- **DID** you know that income from an investment bond is automatically invested without incurring a tax charge? This contrasts with income from a unit trust which, even if it is automatically reinvested to buy more units, is treated for tax purposes as if you have received it.

- **DID** you know that proceeds from an investment bond are not liable to capital gains tax? But they may be liable to higher rate tax, leading to a tax charge on any gains.

- **DID** you know that switching between funds within an investment bond is not treated as a disposal for capital gains tax purposes? For the active investor this can be a big advantage.

- **DID** you know that investment bonds are administratively convenient? All investment administration and tax accounting takes place within the fund. This keeps your own paperwork to a minimum.

So what now?

- **INVESTMENT** bonds are not everybody's cup of tea – and rightly so. While offering the opportunity to defer tax through the 5% annual withdrawal allowance, they presently provide a lower net return to most investors than a unit trust or Open-Ended Investment Company invested in the same assets. They are also not as tax-efficient as some competing investments such as Individual Savings Accounts.

   In addition, it is imperative to realise that withdrawals in the early years may seriously erode the value of your investment and compromise the bond's ability to turn itself into a successful long-term investment. You should therefore buy an investment bond only after consulting an independent financial adviser who will make sure that it meets your financial objectives and may be used to your tax advantage.

With-profits investment bonds

MOST investments fall into two distinct categories – deposit savings that are as solid as the Rock of the Gibraltar and equity-based investments that rise and fall in line with the fortunes of the world's stock markets.

In recent years a product has emerged that has bridged these two investment poles – the with-profits investment bond. In some ways its emergence is surprising because its rise in popularity has coincided with the demise of the with-profits endowment policy – a mortgage repayment vehicle now viewed by many homeowners as too inflexible. The with-profits investment bond offers investors a halfway house between the thrills and spills of equities and the security of deposits.

Sales of with-profits investment bonds support this view. In the late 1990s, sales boomed and there is little to suggest that the rise in sales will falter. Many insurance companies have established a solid track record in the bond market and more investors are latching on to the competitive returns and security available from these products.

There is no doubt that with-profits investment bonds should form part of any investor's balanced investment portfolio. But these products are not without flaws – as in other areas of the personal finance world, investors need to tread carefully.

A with-profits bond is a popular version of an investment bond. For more detailed information, especially on the tax treatment of these products, it is vital that you read the section on investment bonds.

With-profits investment bonds: key questions and answers

Q What is a with-profits investment bond?

A It is a product that allows you to invest a lump sum in the with-profits fund of an insurance company within the structure of an investment bond. The idea is that investors benefit from the best of both the with-profits and the investment bond worlds. With-profits funds are invested in a mixture of equities, fixed-interest securities and property, and provide holders with a broad spread of underlying investments. An investment bond is also called a 'non-qualifying' life policy – there is no basic rate income tax or capital gains tax to pay on any proceeds. These tax advantages may be utilised by investors in their personal finance planning.

Q How does my with-profits investment grow?

A It shares in the profits made by the insurance company's with-profits fund. Each year, your investment is credited with a reversionary or annual bonus determined by the insurer and to a large extent it reflects the investment success of the fund. Critically, once this bonus has been allocated, it may not be taken away except in exceptional circumstances. A further bonus may be payable when the bond is encashed; this is often referred to as the terminal bonus.

Q If the annual bonus is related to the investment track record of the insurance company, surely that means it can fluctuate widely from year to year, making with-profits an unpredictable investment.

A In theory yes, but in practice insurance companies try to smooth out bonus payments to give investors as comfortable a ride as possible. During periods of strong stock market gains, insurance companies will store up profits to compensate for years when returns are lean rather than pay bigger bonuses. As a result, with-profits bonds may lose some of their shine as equity investment vehicles power ahead. But during periods of market uncertainty, companies are able to protect bonus payments by drawing on profits made in the past.

Q Is my capital guaranteed, as with a deposit savings account?

A No. Insurance companies have the right to levy what is called a market value adjuster on your with-profits investment. This may reduce its value and it is applied if, for example, you encash your bond during adverse stock market conditions. Furthermore, most insurance companies levy an initial charge on your investment – anything up to 5% – which means that some of your capital is swallowed up immediately. And if that were not enough, some companies apply exit charges if the bond is encashed before five years. The highest charges are levied in the earliest years.

Q If my capital is not guaranteed, why should I bother with such an investment? I may as well plump for the safety of a high-interest savings account?

A The market value adjuster is applied sparingly by insurance companies. Indeed, there are specific periods – a bond's fifth anniversary, for example – when a company guarantees that it will not be used. Provided you view a with-profits investment bond as an investment to be held for at least five years, it should deliver higher returns than bank and building society savings accounts.

Q Fine words, but where's the proof?

A A survey in the October 1998 edition of *Money Management* magazine showed that a single premium investment of £10,000 in a with-profits bond in July 1993 by a 45-year-old man would have had a cash-in value five years later of between £14,272 (with National Provident Institution) and £16,035 (with Britannic Assurance). These overall returns of 43% and 60% respectively are in excess of inflation (up 16% over the same period), above the typical return from a deposit account (20%-plus) but below those from the average unit trust (up 81%).

Q May I take a regular income from my with-profits bond investment?

A Yes, though it is not strictly income. For tax purposes, it is treated as a return of a proportion of your original investment. Indeed, the withdrawal may involve a reduction in the capital value of your bond.

As with the rules for all investment bonds – see the section on investment bonds – you may make an annual withdrawal equivalent to 5% of your original with-profits bond investment without immediate payment of income tax. This may be taken for a maximum of 20 years. So if you buy a with-profits bond worth £10,000 you may draw an income of £500 for 20 years without paying tax.

For taxpayers, such a facility may prove invaluable. An income of £500, for example, that is not liable to tax deduction is the equivalent of £641 of taxable income to a basic rate taxpayer. To a 40% taxpayer, it is the equivalent of £833 of taxable income. The 5% withdrawal facility is therefore a valuable tax-planning feature.

Q May I take more than 5% from my with-profits bond?

A Some companies allow holders to withdraw more than 5% per year – 7.5% tends to be the maximum – but you should tread cautiously. By exceeding the 5% annual allowance, you may be exposing yourself to tax (see section on investment bonds). There is also a danger that such withdrawals will eat into the capital value of your investment. As a rule of thumb, withdrawals should not exceed the annual bonus credited to the bond.

Q What happens if I forget to make a 5% withdrawal in a year?

A No problem. You may carry it forward to the next year. So if you buy a bond for £10,000 and make no withdrawal until year four, you may withdraw £2,000 – £500 for each year the bond has been held.

Q So I can take 5% income from my with-profits investment bond without paying tax. What's the catch?

A There is no catch. But remember that with-profits bonds are not tax-free. Though there is no basic rate income tax or capital gains tax on the proceeds from a with-profits bond, annual withdrawals above the 5% per annum limit may attract a higher rate tax charge, and profits made on encashment may also result in a further tax charge. The tax treatment of with-profits bonds is no different from that for ALL investment bonds. See the section on investment bonds for a full explanation of the rules.

Q Do withdrawals from a with-profits bond affect an elderly person's entitlement to age allowance?

A No. Bond withdrawals up to the 5% limit are technically a return of an investor's capital. Since such withdrawals are not treated as income for tax purposes, they do not affect the right to age allowance for the elderly.

Q What happens if I die?

A With-profits investment bonds are non-qualifying life policies. Typically, life cover is nominal only, equivalent to 1% of the bond's value at the date of death. So when a policyholder dies, a sum equivalent to 101% of the bond's value is returned. A tax charge may be levied on any gains, but that will depend primarily upon a person's taxable income in the year of death.

Q With-profits investment bonds seem to be a good idea. How do I choose one?

A While charges – entry, annual and exit – and headline bonus rates should be looked at carefully, the past performance of an insurance company's with-profits fund should be analysed. This should provide an idea of the financial strength of the insurance company behind the bond. The best results are produced by large established companies that are financially strong. A recent survey by *Money Management* magazine identified NFU Mutual, Prudential, London Life and Scottish Widows as insurance companies that fit this double bill. Similarly, Standard & Poor's researcher Micropal identified Prudential, Scottish Widows, Scottish Equitable, CGU, Scottish Mutual, Clerical Medical, Scottish Provident, Friends Provident and Norwich Union. If you are unsure, speak to an independent financial adviser before choosing a specific bond.

Q How much will I have to invest?

A Insurance companies set their minimum investment levels, but £5,000 is a typical sum. Some companies will reduce their charges for bigger amounts – this means that more of your money is put to work immediately on your behalf.

Q May I make regular payments into my bond?

A No. Your investment is set up as a non-qualifying single-premium bond. If you wish to make regular payments into an investment scheme, consider products such as unit trusts and investment trusts. However, there is nothing to stop you taking out a series of with-profits investment bonds with the same or different insurance companies provided you meet the required minimum investment level.

Q What about possible windfalls?

A If your with-profits investment bond is managed by a mutual insurance company that is subsequently taken over or floated on the stock market, you may receive a windfall payment. But buying a with-profits investment bond in the hope of earning a windfall gain is not wise. You should buy only if it makes good investment sense.

Q How do I buy a bond?

A You may buy directly from the insurance company or through a sales representative of the organisation. But the best way is through an independent financial adviser. An IFA will not only be able to tell you whether a with-profits investment bond fits your long-term financial objectives, but will also recommend the best bond on offer.

Dos and Don'ts

- **DON'T** buy a with-profits investment bond simply because it offers the best headline bonus rate. More important factors, such as the insurance company's financial strength and its past performance record and charges, need to be considered. A timely and sober reminder of the importance of this is the recent sad demise of Equitable Life, now owned by Halifax.

- **DON'T** buy unless you are prepared to take an investment view of five years or more. If you withdraw your capital before five years, you are likely to be hit by the impact of initial charges and exit charges.

- **DON'T** forget the market value adjuster. While the word guarantee occurs frequently in the marketing literature of many with-profits bonds, don't forget that the insurance company has the right to reduce the value of your investment. It is a risk you must be aware of.

- **DON'T** forget the annual 5% withdrawal facility. It is a valuable tax-planning feature of a with-profits investment bond, especially for basic rate and higher rate taxpayers. But if you take advantage of this make sure the capital value of your investment is not eroded.

- **DO** remember that bond withdrawals up to the 5% annual limit do not affect an elderly person's right to age allowance.

- **DO** remember that returns from with-profits investment bonds are paid net of basic rate tax. Any further liability is deferred until the bond is encashed, or withdrawals are taken above the 5% allowance. Non-taxpayers may not reclaim tax and may well be advised to look for alternative investments.

- **DO** seek independent financial advice. With-profits investment bonds come in all shapes and sizes and some are no more than wolves dressed in sheep's clothing. A quality independent financial adviser should be able to sort out the good bonds from the bad.

Did you know?

- **DID** you know that various versions of a with-profits investment bond are available? There are conventional plans that invest wholly in the with-profits life fund of an insurance company, unitised plans that invest in an insurance company's unitised with-profits fund, and there are hybrid bonds that allow holders to invest in the with-profits fund plus a selection of other unit-linked funds.

- **DID** you know that an October 1998 survey of with-profits investment bonds by *Money Management* magazine revealed that on average, with-profits bonds were 55% invested in UK equities, 12% in overseas equities, 9% in property, 18% in fixed-interest securities and 5% in other assets? These figures confirm the broad spread of assets that with-profits investment bonds offer investors.

- **DID** you know that if a 49-year-old male had invested £10,000 in a with-profits investment bond in July 1998, he would have lost out had he encashed the investment a year later. *Money Management* magazine identified several bonds whose cash-in values after one year were less than £10,000 – Legal & General, Pearl, Scottish Mutual and Scottish Provident. These figures demonstrate conclusively that with-profits investment bonds should be viewed as long-term investments only. You should buy a bond only if you intend to hold it for at least five years.

So what now?

- **WITH**-profits investment bonds represent an ideal investment halfway house. They offer a taste of equity investment thrills without having to worry that your money is plunging in value in line with crashing stock markets. For investors who want more than what a conventional savings account has to offer, with-profits bonds are a logical choice.

Bonds

MANY investors start their savings life putting their hard-earned money in the local building society or bank. They then make the jump from deposits to equities, usually by taking out a tax-free Isa or a unit trust. However, for many people, this leap is one jump too far on the risk spectrum. One moment their capital is guaranteed. The next their financial fortune is dependent upon the ups and downs of the stock market.

For such people, the obvious halfway house is to consider a bond. Elsewhere in this book we have examined the virtues of several types of specialist bond – the with-profits bond, various National Savings bonds, guaranteed stock market bonds and building society bonds – but in this section we shall concentrate on the two big bond categories of the modern world. These are UK gilts and corporate bonds.

As we shall discuss, any balanced investment portfolio should include bonds.

Q Who issues bonds?

A Various organisations that want to borrow money. Government is a big issuer of bonds which are commonly referred to as gilt-edged securities or gilts. Big companies also raise finance by issuing bonds. These are often known as corporate bonds. Bonds are also issued by local authorities, overseas governments and overseas companies.

Q What is the deal?

A It's quite straightforward. In return for the loan of your money, the borrower (government, local authority or company) agrees to pay you a fixed rate of interest for a pre-determined period and to repay in full the money originally invested on a specified date. The fixed rate of interest is known as the 'coupon' while the date when you get your money back is called the 'maturity' or 'redemption' date. The attraction of this deal is that provided you hold the bonds to maturity, you know exactly what return you are going to get from your investment.

Q Is the return of capital a cast-iron guarantee?

A No, nor is the stream of regular income. Companies do go bust, both here and overseas, which can make bonds worthless. However, gilts offer a high degree of security because they are backed by the UK government while many UK company bonds are issued by some of the strongest companies in both the UK and in the world.

Q Do I have to hold a bond to maturity?

A Not at all. You can sell your bond before maturity as indeed you can buy a bond after it has been issued. Like equities, bonds are traded on the stock market. The price you pay – or obtain – for your bond will depend primarily on prevailing interest rates. As a general rule, when interest rates in the economy are rising, the price of bonds will fall because for the same amount of capital invested, you could get a better return elsewhere – hence people want out. In contrast, if interest rates are falling, the price of bonds will rise because bonds provide a better stream of income than you could get from alternative investments. By selling a bond before maturity, you could lose part of your original capital investment.

Q So I like the sound of government-backed UK gilts. Tell me more. How do I buy a gilt?

A There are essentially two ways to buy. You can buy newly issued stock from the Debt Management Office, part of the Bank of England. New stock is auctioned so you have to bid for it. There are no dealing charges on gilts bought in this way but you must bid for at least £1,000 of stock.

A better way is to buy stock which is already in issue and which is trading on the stock market. You can buy stock through a stockbroker or through the Bank of England brokerage service. The latter service makes sense for people who may only have small sums (in the region of £1,000) to invest. Commission rates charged by stockbrokers for UK gilt purchases or sales tend to be lower than for UK equities.

Q How long do I have to invest for?

A There is no set period. At any one point in time, there are gilts available with lifetimes of up to 20 years and more. Indeed, some stocks are called 'irredeemables', which means they have no redemption date so the only way you can cash in your investment is to sell them. Gilts are split into three distinct categories – shorts (five years or less to redemption); mediums (five to 15 years until redemption); and longs (more than 15 years to redemption). Again, you don't have to hold the gilts until maturity – you can sell them in the market through the Bank of England brokerage service or through a stockbroker.

Q What is the tax treatment?

A Income from gilts is normally paid gross which is convenient for non-taxpayers. However, income is taxable which means taxpayers have a tax bill to meet. Taxpayers can opt for income to be paid net of 20%. If they do this, lower rate or basic rate taxpayers have no further tax liability but higher rate taxpayers have extra to pay. Capital gains on gilts are tax-free. Also, there is no stamp duty payable on gilt purchases.

Q If I buy a UK gilt, my income is fixed until I redeem. What happens if returns are eroded by inflation?

A Tough. Your only option is to sell before the gilt matures. An alternative is to consider index-linked gilts where returns – both income and capital – are increased in line with inflation. These gilts can be bought and sold in the same way as for conventional UK gilts. As a result of the inflation protection that these gilts provide investors with, they tend to have lower coupons (fixed-interest rates) than those available on conventional gilts.

Q Can I buy gilts in a unit trust?

A Yes. Most leading investment houses such as JP Morgan Fleming and Schroder run gilt investment funds. By investing in such a unit trust you will be indirectly getting exposure to a broad portfolio of gilts. This has pluses and minuses. For a start, any income you receive will vary – you are not locking into a fixed income. Also, you will have to bear management charges – both initial and annual. However, you should benefit from the manager's investment expertise. Magazines such as *Money Management* list gilt unit trusts in the back of their magazine along with other investment funds.

Q What about bonds issued by companies?

A These are 'IOUs' issued by companies. Similar to a gilt, the company issuing a bond promises to pay a regular, fixed amount of interest known as the 'coupon'. This interest tends to be higher than for gilts, primarily because companies cannot offer the same level of security as the UK government, backers of gilts. The interest available from company bonds also varies between individual companies, reflecting the financial strength of the underlying countries. A company with solid financial backing will tend to pay a lower rate of interest than one deemed to be riskier.

Q Do prices for bonds fluctuate in the same manner as for gilts?

A Yes. Like gilts, bonds are traded on the stock market. And like gilts, their prices tend to fluctuate according to movements in interest rates. Rising interest rates usually result in falling corporate bond prices while falling interest rates cause corporate bond prices to rise.

Q Where do I stand from a tax point of view if I hold a corporate bond?

A Interest is paid net of 20% tax. This means basic rate taxpayers have no further tax to pay, higher rate taxpayers have extra to pay, while non-taxpayers can reclaim the tax. Capital gains are normally tax-free.

Q Can I buy corporate bonds as easily as I can buy gilts?

A No. Corporate bonds are usually traded in tranches of £100,000 which makes them off-limits for most private investors. Also, locking into just one corporate bond can be a risky business. You are putting a lot of investment eggs in just one basket.

Q So, if the purchase of individual corporate bonds is off limits to people like me, how can I get exposure to the income attractions of corporate bonds?

A Through a corporate bond unit trust. Most investment houses now operate corporate bond funds which invest in a broad spread of corporate bonds. Leading funds are offered by some of the country's top investment houses such as Fidelity, HSBC and M&G. You can make a one-off investment – typical minimum investment is £500 to £1,000 – or you can save on a regular basis from as little as £50.

Q Are there any drawbacks?

A Yes.

DRAWBACK 1: By buying into a corporate bond unit trust, you will not be locking into a fixed income. The income you receive will depend upon the bonds held by the fund manager.

DRAWBACK 2: You will have to pay management charges, comprising an initial charge and an annual management fee.

DRAWBACK 3: No two corporate bond funds are the same, which makes comparison difficult. Some funds pay above average income because they invest in riskier bonds – some based overseas. Others, which in terms of income look less appealing, are more conservatively managed – and more appropriate for many low-risk investors.

DRAWBACK 4: Funds apply different charging structures which can disguise potential risks. Some funds charge their annual management fees against the capital of the fund rather than the income generated. They do this in order to provide investors with the maximum possible income. However, many investors are unaware that the downside of such a charging structure is that their capital investment is being chipped away at.

Q And what about the pluses?

A There are a number.

PLUS POINT 1: Corporate bond unit trusts can be held inside a tax-free Isa. This means returns are tax-free. For many elderly people in search of income, this makes corporate bond Isas an attractive investment proposition. You can use your full Isa allowance

(£7,000) to invest in a corporate bond fund or you can use part of it.

PLUS POINT 2: Most corporate bond funds pay income at least half-yearly. Some will pay monthly or quarterly. This can make them an important part of an income portfolio.

PLUS POINT 3: You benefit from professional fund management. The manager of a corporate bond fund should be able to spot the good corporate bonds from the bad.

Q OK, I now know about gilts and corporate bonds. Are there other bonds I should be looking at?

A As explained at the start, there are several, some of which are explained in greater detail elsewhere in the book. To summarise:

BOND ONE: LOCAL AUTHORITY BONDS. A number of local authorities now issue local authority bonds. Investment is for a fixed term – usually between one and five years – with interest payments being fixed although some bonds can be bought and sold on the stock market. Interest is usually paid six-monthly and tends to be higher than for UK gilts because of the greater risks involved. Income is paid net of 20% tax which means basic rate taxpayers have no more tax to pay. Higher rate taxpayers have extra tax to pay while non-taxpayers can reclaim all of the tax. *Moneyfacts* (01603 476476) publishes monthly details on the local authority bonds available for investment.

BOND TWO: BANK AND BUILDING SOCIETY BONDS. A number of banks and building societies offer savings bonds which pay a rate of interest for a predetermined period, usually anywhere between six months and five years. Interest can be fixed during the bond's life. Alternatively, it may vary or go up in small increments – so-called escalator bonds. These bonds tend to pay lower rates of interest than other forms of bond because of the capital security offered by a bank or building society.

BOND THREE: GUARANTEED INCOME BONDS. These pay a fixed rate of interest over a predetermined period with income being paid on a monthly, quarterly or annual basis. These bonds are offered by insurance companies and at the end of the term an investor will receive their original investment back in full.

BOND FOUR: WITH-PROFITS BONDS. Again offered by insurance companies, these bonds build up annual bonuses by investing in a mix of financial assets such as equities, property and gilts. Investors can take an income from these bonds.

BOND FIVE: STOCK MARKET-LINKED BONDS. These bonds, offered by a number of insurance companies, pay an income during the course of their term. Then, provided the stock market index which the bond is linked to is higher on maturity than when the investment began, an investor will get all their original capital back. If the index has fallen, then you may lose part of your original capital.

BOND SIX: NATIONAL SAVINGS BONDS. National Savings offer a number of bonds including income bonds, capital bonds, fixed-rate savings bonds, pensioner and children's bonds.

BOND SEVEN: INVESTMENT BONDS. These are offered by insurance companies and provide investors with the opportunity to take tax-free income on a regular basis.

Dos and Don'ts

- DO keep an eye on the competitiveness of the income you get from any UK gilts you hold. Returns can be eaten away by inflation – unless you have bought an index-linked gilt.

- DO remember that like shares, there is a spread between the buying and selling prices for gilts. This means that buyers pay a little more than the quoted price while sellers obtain a little less. The spread tends not to be as wide as on UK equities.

- DO bear in mind that UK gilts can prove very useful financial tools for the elderly in search of income. For example, it is often possible to buy gilts which lock investors into an attractive interest rate in return for a small capital loss if they hold them until maturity.

- **DO** be careful when comparing the yields quoted by various corporate bond funds. Most investment houses quote running yields, which is an indication of the income that a fund is expected to pay. In contrast, the redemption yield is a measure of the expected annual return – including capital gains and losses – if all the fund's investments were held to maturity.

- **DON'T** attempt to trade in gilts unless you know exactly what you are doing. You can run up losses. If in any doubt, speak to an independent financial adviser or a stockbroker.

- **DON'T** get mesmerised by the coupon or interest rate available from a gilt. What is imperative is the so-called running yield on the investment – the investor's income return on their original investment. For example, if an investor pays £50 for £100 of nominal stock with a coupon of 3%, the running yield is 6%. In other words, the investor is generating an income equivalent to 6% on their original investment.

- **DO** your homework before investing in a corporate bond fund. Ask for a copy of the last unitholder's report and accounts so you can see what kinds of bonds the manager is investing in. Are there many overseas holdings or company names on the list that you have never heard before? Does the bond fund invest in other assets such as preference shares or the income shares of split capital investment trusts? Does the fund pay out income as regularly as you want it to do? How are charges levied against the fund? How has the fund performed against its peer group?

- **DO** be aware that if you invest in a corporate bond fund, your capital may be at risk. If capital security is paramount, you are better off looking at other investment opportunities.

Did you know?

- **DID** you know that you can get a form from your local post office telling you how to buy and sell UK gilts? You can then buy or sell via the post.

- **DID** you know that prospectuses for new issues of UK gilts are often printed in quality newspapers?

- **DID** you know that gilts with a maturity date will tell you so in their title? So Treasury 7% 2005 means that the government will pay £7 per £100 of nominal stock until 2005 when it will be redeemed. Some gilts will give two dates, for example, Treasury 7% 2006–2009. This means the government can choose a date between the beginning of 2006 and the end of 2009 when redemption will take place.

- **DID** you know that an investor can calculate the overall return he or she obtains from a UK gilt? This is called the yield to redemption and takes into account the income from the gilt plus any capital gain or loss if it is held until redemption. This figure is published daily in the price alongside the prices for individual gilts.

- **DID** you know that the Bank of England has published a guide to how gilts work and how to invest? It is called: 'Investing in gilts – the private investor's guide to British Government stock'. It is available from the Bank of England Registrars Department on 01452 398080.

- **DID** you know that the price of individual gilts is shown in quality newspapers on a daily basis?

- **DID** you know that no British Government stock has ever failed to pay interest or to repay capital?

- **DID** you know that gilts are all issued as units with a nominal or par value of £100?

- **DID** you know that each gilt has a coupon which is the amount of annual interest to be paid on £100 of stock? For example, a stock with a coupon of 7% pays £7 interest per annum for the duration of the loan.

- **DID** you know that interest from gilts is paid half-yearly on predetermined dates? You can buy a portfolio of gilts which, because of different interest payment dates, provide you with quarterly or a more regular source of income.

- **DID** you know that UK gilts go ex dividend before interest is due? If an investor sells when a UK gilt is declared ex dividend, he or she still receives the interest. If an investor sells before the gilt goes ex dividend, he or she will not receive the income – it will go to the buyer of the stock.

- **DID** you know that some banks and building societies will allow you to buy and sell UK gilts?

- **DID** you know that some UK corporate bond funds pay income on a monthly basis? They include Baillie Gifford Corporate Bond, CGU PPT Monthly Income Plus and Fidelity Moneybuilder Income. Funds which pay quarterly income include: Aberdeen Sterling Bond, Jupiter Corporate Bond and Standard Life Corporate Bond.

- **DID** you know that personal finance magazines such as *Money Management* list all corporate bond funds available together with how often income is paid and the fund's yield?

- **DID** you know that preference shares have the characteristics of both shares and bonds? Like shares, they usually have no redemption date. However, like bonds, interest payments are fixed. The interest payments of preference shareholders are paid by companies before those to ordinary shareholders by way of dividends – hence the title preference. Unlike corporate bonds, preference shares cannot be held inside a tax-free Isa. Further details on preference shares are given in the section on shares.

So what now?

- **NO** balanced investment portfolio should be without bonds – UK gilts or corporate bonds. Although not as secure as deposit accounts, these bonds do provide investors with the opportunity to earn attractive rates of interest – plus some capital growth in some instances – on their savings. However, as in most areas of personal finance, investors should tread carefully. Picking the most appropriate gilt or the best corporate bond can be a minefield. It is therefore probably best if you get professional independent financial advice.

Shares

SQUIRRELLING money away in the bank or building society makes great sense for all of us. Provided you pick the right account, you can earn a decent rate of interest while you have the comfort of a financial buffer which can be used to meet any unexpected financial emergency. And of course, your capital is not at risk.

However, putting money away in a savings account is not going to look after your long-term financial future. Unless you have your money in an account paying an attractive rate of interest, there is every chance that the value of your savings could fall in real returns because of the effects of inflation. In other words, the value of your accumulated deposit savings is worth less to you than to begin with.

For people interested in saving for the long term, they need to complement deposit savings with investments where the rewards – and risks – are potentially higher. One of these investments is shares.

Q What is a share?

A Shares are issued by companies to raise money. When you buy shares in a company, you become a part-owner and you share in its profits by means of dividend distributions. If it doesn't make profits, you don't get dividends. As an owner, you are also entitled to a share of the company's assets if it is wound up in the future. You are also invited to shareholders' meetings.

Q Are shares all of a similar type?

A No, but they fall into two broad churches. Church 1, the ordinary share, is the most popular. These are issued by more than 2,000 UK companies. Church 2 comprises overseas equities, which are ordinary shares issued by non-UK companies. Most people buy ordinary shares in UK companies simply because it is easier to do so and also because they are familiar with the businesses behind the shares.

Q How do I earn a return from holding shares?

A Returns come in two forms. First, as a shareholder, you will receive a dividend which is typically paid every six months. Companies are not obliged to pay dividends although most leading companies do so. Indeed, many companies make it their policy to grow their dividends on an annual basis. Secondly, you can also make capital gains. This is because shares are traded on the stock market and can both fall and rise in value. If you buy shares and then sell them in the future at a higher price, you have made a profit although this may result in a tax bill for capital gains.

Q Why do shares fall and rise in value?

A Many factors influence the price of individual shares. For a start, the stock market generally is influenced by big-picture factors such as the state of the economy, inflation and interest rates. If the economy is doing well, then usually the stock market will rise as people believe companies quoted on the stock market will deliver bigger profits and bigger dividends. Conversely, if the economy looks as if it is going to go into recession, maybe because of higher interest rates, then stock markets can fall.

World events can also impact on stock markets. Adverse events in the Far East and America, such as economic turmoil, can cause a crisis of confidence in the UK, leading to sharp stock market corrections.

The price of individual company shares is also influenced by more micro factors such as how the company is faring in the economy, how it is faring against competitors and its own prospects. If these look good, then more people will want to buy the company's shares than sell them, leading the share price to increase. Conversely, the more people want to sell a company's shares, the more the company's share price will fall.

Q Given shares fall, as well as rise, why take the risk when I can put my money in a building society and be assured that my capital is not at risk?

A It is proven that over the long term, shares outperform other forms of financial assets such as deposits and bonds. Barclays Capital, the investment banking division of Barclays Bank, analyses the performance of equities on an annual basis. In its 2000 study, it calculated that over the past 10 years, UK equities have enjoyed an annual real return – over and above inflation – of 10.7%. In contrast, gilts have enjoyed a comparable return of 8.3% while cash has delivered a real return of 4.5%.

Over the longer term, the case for equities is even more convincing. According to Barclays Capital, the annual return from UK equities over the past 50 years has averaged 8.1% compared to 1.1% for gilts and 1.3% for cash.

That is not to say that equities do not have their blips. In 1998, for example, gilts outperformed shares as an investment. But over the long term, shares can enhance your wealth.

Q OK. I'm convinced. How do I go about buying shares?

A There are four main ways to buy shares:

AVENUE 1: THROUGH A STOCKBROKER. If you want advice on what shares to buy, you can use a stockbroker. They will recommend shares that they feel meet your investment objectives. However, charges can be expensive and you will probably need at least £10,000 to start off with.

Advice tends to take two forms. There is the discretionary service where you grant full power to your stockbroker to buy and sell shares on your behalf. This is after you have laid down your investment requirements. Then there is the advisory service where the stockbroker will provide advice on specific stocks but the decision as to whether to buy and sell is left entirely to you.

The Association of Private Client Investment Managers and Stockbrokers (APCIMS) provides a directory of stockbrokers detailing the services they offer: 112 Middlesex Street, London E1 7HY (www.apcims.co.uk). This includes details of stockbrokers providing advisory and discretionary services.

AVENUE 2: THROUGH A BANK OR BUILDING SOCIETY. Your bank or building society will probably provide a share-dealing service although it is unlikely that you will be given investment advice. Some institutions will also limit the shares you can trade in – some restrict transactions to the top companies in the UK. Using your bank or building society makes sense for many people because they are dealing with an organisation they know and – hopefully – trust. The slight drawback is that charges may be higher than levied elsewhere.

AVENUE 3: THROUGH AN EXECUTION-ONLY STOCK-BROKER. Here, you are given no advice – simply the facility to buy and sell shares. Most of these services are run via the post or telephone and are usually inexpensive. Again, APCIMS provides a directory listing those brokers offering such services.

AVENUE 4: VIA THE INTERNET. This is becoming an increasingly popular way to buy and sell shares. Before trading, you will have to set up an account but once you have done this, costs can be extremely competitive. Leading players include: Barclays Stockbrokers (www.barclays-stockbrokers.co.uk), Charles Schwab (www.schwab-europe.com), DLJ Direct (www.DLJdirect.co.uk), E*Trade (www.etrade.co.uk), Halifax ShareXpress (www.sharexpress.co.uk), Hargreaves Lansdown (www.h-l.co.uk), Killik & Co (www.killik.co.uk), NatWest Stockbrokers (www.natweststockbrokers.co.uk), Stocktrade (www.stocktrade.co.uk) and the Share Centre (www.share.co.uk). Like Avenue 3, you will typically not get any advice if you buy shares on-line.

Share transactions tend to be conducted in two ways. The first is where you are given a real-time share price at which you can trade. You then have some 15 to 20 seconds to accept or reject the price. The second is where your order is delivered by e-mail. A human dealer then carries out the trade as they would if you were dealing by phone.

Q How much does it cost to buy and sell shares?

A Costs vary between brokers so it is imperative you shop around. Most levy commission rates which will reduce the more you have available to invest. For example, a deal of £15,000 may attract commission of 1.5% on the first £10,000 and then 0.5% on the next £5,000. Many brokers also stipulate a minimum commission payment which can deter small investors.

Commission is not the only cost. On purchases, not on sales, you must pay 0.5% stamp duty while there is also a spread between the prices at which you buy and sell shares. This can be 1.5% for shares in well-traded companies but much higher for smaller companies where shares are not often traded.

Other charges you may face include fees for running a nominee account (see below) and a £2 levy on trades above £10,000 (the so-called PTM levy applied to help fund the City's panel on takeovers and mergers). You may also be charged if you ask your stockbroker for reports and accounts of the companies you have bought shares in.

Q Will I get a share certificate when I purchase my shares?

A Probably not. Share certificates are becoming a relic of the past. Indeed, if you purchase shares through a stockbroker, there is every chance that you will do so through a nominee account where you will not receive share certificates.

Q What is a nominee account?

A It is a way of keeping life easier for both the stockbroker and you the customer. With a nominee account, you will typically receive an annual statement of all your transactions showing you the shares you have bought, any you have sold, and the current value of your holdings. You will also receive a consolidated tax certificate at the end of the year showing the dividends you have received and any tax credits.

Q What are the drawbacks?

A For a start, you don't own the shares directly – the broker does on your behalf. Some stockbrokers charge for offering the nominee service even though it may be the only service they offer. Also, any dividends you earn from your shareholdings will be automatically paid into the nominee account where they may earn low rates of interest. Some operators of nominee accounts also refuse to pass on shareholder perks and do not send out company accounts automatically. ProShare has a free fact sheet on nominee accounts which is available from: ProShare, Centurion House, 24 Monument Street, London EC3R 8AQ.

Q So that's it, nominee or share certificates?

A No. There is a third option called 'Crest'. Here you trade through Crest, the settlement system for UK shares. Your shares are held electronically but you have the same rights as if you held the shares directly. You can use this option by becoming a sponsored member of Crest. This is possible by paying a fee of around £10 to your stockbroker.

Q Once I have bought my shares, how can I monitor their progress?

A Most newspapers, including the tabloids, carry closing prices of major shares. Papers such as the *Financial Times* and the *Daily Telegraph* carry full listings. It is also possible to keep track of your shares by using the Internet. Good sites include: www.ft.com; www.carol.uk (company annual reports on line); www.esi.co.uk (electronic share information) and www.hemscott.com.

Q Where do I stand with regard to tax?

A Dividends count as income for tax purposes. They are paid after deduction of tax at 10%. Both starting rate and basic rate taxpayers have no further tax to pay. Non-taxpayers cannot reclaim the tax while higher rate taxpayers have a further tax to pay. In total, higher rate taxpayers pay tax on dividends of 32.5%. So, for example, if a higher rate taxpayer receives a dividend of £54, this equates to a gross dividend of £60, 10% (£6) having already been deducted. The further tax liability is £13.50 – in other words 22.5% of £60.

Capital gains on shares are taxable although you are able to use your annual capital gains tax allowance of £7,500 (tax year ended April 5, 2002) to offset any gains. See chapter 6: Getting to Grips with Tax.

Q Can I hold shares in an Isa?

A Yes and by doing so, you do not have to worry about tax. Currently, for the tax year ended April 5, 2002, you can invest the full annual allowance of £7,000 in shares. Alternatively, you can take out a mini-shares Isa where the maximum annual allowance is currently £3,000.

Q Can I buy foreign shares?

A Yes, some brokers specialise in this area. Again, APCIMS provides details of these companies. Leading players include Barclays Stockbrokers (www.barclays-stockbrokers.co.uk), Charles Schwab (www.schwab-europe.com) and Killik & Co. (www.killik.co.uk).

Q How does the payment system work for buying and selling shares?

A Since June 1995, five-day trading has been introduced. This means payment must take place five working days after shares are bought or sold. However, you are not obliged to use this system. You can use the slower 10-day settlement system although you may pay more in commission for using this. You might also get a poorer price for the shares you want to trade.

Dos and Don'ts

- **DO** your homework before buying any shares. Read the financial press to see if anything has been written about the company you are thinking of investing in. As well as the City pages of national newspapers, read through specialist magazines such as *Shares* and *Investors Chronicle*. Also, do your own homework – get hold of the last report and accounts and if it is a retail firm, go and visit one of its stores to see whether the business is thriving as you may have been led to believe.

  A number of websites can also help you do your homework on specific companies. They include: www.citywire.co.uk (offering news on director dealings for UK companies), www.sharepages.com (listing all announcements for companies trading on the London Stock Exchange) and www.hemscott.co.uk (basic information on publicly traded companies in the UK including historical financial results and analyst research).

- **DO** try to diversify your share holdings. If you purchase companies all in the same line of business, there is a risk that you could get caught out by a slump in that sector.

- **DO** concentrate, to begin with at least, on so-called blue-chip shares – shares of the country's leading companies. These will usually be companies with familiar names. Although the price of blue-chip shares can often fall out of proverbial bed, these types of shares are easy to buy and sell and information about them and their prospects are easy for the private investor to get hold of.

- **DON'T** buy individual shares unless you have done your homework and fully understand the risks involved. There is no point investing in shares unless you are prepared to lose what you have invested and you are prepared to make a long-term commitment.

- **DON'T** make individual shares your first port of equity call. It makes better sense, first of all, to buy a collective investment fund such as a unit trust or investment trust where your money is spread across a range of companies. Then, if you feel comfortable, move on to buying individual shares.

- **DON'T** hold shares obtained through a building society conversion – windfall shares – if you don't like taking risks with your money. If you didn't hold shares before the building society converted, you shouldn't be holding shares once the society has transformed itself to a plc. You are better off converting the shares into cash and putting the money in a good paying savings account.

- **DON'T** confuse stocks with shares. Stocks are fixed-interest securities such as gilts and bonds.

- **DON'T** forget that ordinary shares are not the only type of share available.

  PREFERENCE SHARES. These offer investors fixed dividend

payments so they can appeal to people requiring a regular income. The potential for capital return is minimal although these shares have 'preference' over ordinary shareholders if the company is wound up. Preference shareholders also have preference when it comes to income distribution from the company.

PARTICIPATING PREFERENCE SHARES. These offer investors fixed dividend payments plus the right to a limited share of profits.

CONVERTIBLES. Like preference shares, they pay a regular income. They also have a fixed redemption date at which time you have the right to convert to an ordinary share. This can prove attractive if the price is appealing on conversion.

WARRANTS. These confer the right, but not an obligation, on the holder to convert to a specific share at a predetermined price and date. Warrants are risky so tread carefully.

- **DON'T** dabble in penny shares unless you are prepared to lose your shirt. A number of investment newsletters promote the benefits of investing in penny shares on the basis that a small rise in the share value can lead to a massive percentage return for investors. However, for every penny share winner, there are 99 losers. Beware of false promises.

- **DON'T** be distracted by the nominal value of any shares you hold. If you receive 25p shares or 50p shares, it means nothing. What is far more important is the market value of the shares you hold.

Did you know?

- **DID** you know that for shares to be listed on the London Stock Exchange, they must fulfil certain conditions? The company whose shares are being listed must have a three-year track record as a company, they must make full disclosure of the company's financial affairs and they must offer at least 25% of the company's shares for public subscription.

- **DID** you know that companies which are unable to fulfil the conditions of joining the London Stock Exchange can join the Alternative Investment Market? This market, AIM, exists to help young companies raise finance through the sale of shares. Given companies offering shares through AIM usually have little track record, private investors should tread carefully. Steer clear, take professional investment advice, invest through a collective investment fund such as a unit trust or investment trust, thereby spreading risk, or use an enterprise investment trust (EIS) or venture capital trust (VCT). These two latter vehicles do offer private investors some tax breaks.

- **DID** you know that you can buy shares in new issues, companies which are coming to the market? Many of you will equate new issues with the privatisation issues of the 1980s. However, buying shares in a new issue in the expectation of immediate gains – and immediate profits – is a fool's game. Only buy a new issue if you genuinely think it is going to be a solid long-term investment. New issues are conducted in three main ways.

    There is an OFFER FOR SALE where you subscribe for shares at an agreed price. You then receive the shares you asked for, receive a reduced amount because of over-subscriptions for the shares on offer, or you receive none at all following a ballot as to who is going to get shares and who is not.

    Then there is the so-called TENDER where you apply for shares and nominate the price you are prepared to pay for the shares. If the price you are prepared to pay is above that agreed, you will receive a share allocation.

    Then there is a PLACING where shares are 'placed' with financial institutions, usually pension funds and insurance companies, who are willing to buy the shares. Placings discriminate against private investors because they are aimed at big City institutional investors.

- **DID** you know that sometimes companies will offer share-holders the right to buy more shares in the company? These share issues are called rights issues and are usually priced at a level below the prevailing share price so that investors take up the opportunity to buy more shares. So, for example, for every five shares you hold, you may be eligible to buy one more share. Whether you take up the rights issue is up to you – your decision will depend upon a number of factors such as whether you have sufficient funds available and whether you want to buy more shares.

- **DID** you know that some 12 million private investors now own shares directly?

- **DID** you know that most of us have exposure to the stock market even though we might not realise it? Most company pension schemes, endowment policies and personal pension plans are part invested in shares.

- **DID** you know that if you buy shares in some companies, you may be entitled to shareholder perks? These can take the form of discounts against holidays through to discounts against retail purchases. A number of guides are published on shareholder perks – foremost among them is that published by Hargreaves Lansdown (0117 980 9800).

- **DID** you know that all quoted shares in the UK are eligible to be held in a tax-free Isa? Also, you can hold shares traded on most foreign stock exchanges. An Isa cannot include shares traded on the Alternative Investment Market (AIM), Ofex or Tradepoint.

- **DID** you know that you can set up an investment club or share club, thereby making it fun to buy and sell shares? Investment clubs are one of the country's biggest growth areas. Set up by a group of friends or colleagues, you pool your cash so as to have greater buying power in the stock market. You also pool resources and share ideas. Typically, clubs meet once a month and each member pays a monthly contribution. These contributions are then pooled together and used to buy shares. Anyone over 18 can set up an investment club with membership ranging from 2 to 20. The best starting point is to call ProShare (020 7220 1730). This share ownership pressure group has mountains of information on how best to set up a club and the rules that should be laid down.

- **DID** you know that you can become a shareholder by joining your company's employee share scheme? Many leading companies now provide such schemes in order to maintain employee loyalty and to make employees feel a real part of the business. The most popular type of scheme is the Save As You Earn scheme. These schemes, which must be available to all employees, give staff the right, but not the obligation, to buy shares in the company they work for. Typically, you agree to buy the shares at an agreed price in the future and then invest a regular amount over a set period, ranging from between three and seven years. At the end of this period, you then have the option to buy the shares at the agreed price, or withdraw your savings plus interest.

  These schemes are usually great value because they give workers the opportunity to buy shares at a significant discount to their market value. If your employer offers such a scheme, it is well worth joining.

- **DID** you know that ordinary shareholders benefit from limited liability? This means that in the event of a company going into liquidation, ordinary shareholders do not have any liability for the company's debts. Their only risk is that the shares they own may be worthless.

So what now?

- **SHARES** should hold a place in any investment portfolio. However, don't jump in straight away. Try your luck to begin with by buying a unit trust, maybe one that tracks the performance of the UK stock market. If holding such a fund does not make you feel uncomfortable, then maybe move on to buying individual shares. But don't buy shares on a whim – do your homework, read the financial press and don't over-commit yourself to any one particular share.

  Information on shares abound. Two of the best organisations providing such information are the Association of Private Client Investment Managers and ProShare. There are no better starting places.

CHAPTER # 6
Getting to Grips with Tax

TAXPAYER

'Someone who works for the federal government, but doesn't have to take a civil service examination.'

Ronald Reagan

FEW of us are able – legitimately, that is – to escape the clutches of the taxman. We pay tax on a daily basis even though we don't realise it most of the time – every time, for example, that we pop into the local public house for half a bitter before going home; every time we fill the car with petrol and every time we dine out.

However, as this chapter will show, there are a number of ways you can reduce the tax you pay by prudent financial planning and by use of tax-friendly savings vehicles.

The chapter is divided into the following main headings:

1. INCOME TAX
2. SELF-ASSESSMENT
3. TAX ON SAVINGS
4. CAPITAL GAINS TAX
5. INHERITANCE TAX
6. TOP TAX SAVINGS TIPS

Income tax

Q Are we all liable to pay income tax?

A The answer, I am afraid to say, is yes although we all have personal allowances against which income can be offset. As a result of the existence of these allowances, many people do not have to pay income tax.

Income tax is levied on your earned income (income from work) and unearned income (income from investments) and is an annual tax. That is, the amount of income tax you have to pay varies from year to year depending upon changes announced in the Budget. The Budget, announced by the Chancellor of the Exchequer, is held in March and sets the income tax regime for the tax year starting April 6. Tax years run from April 6 to April 5 in the next year. So the tax year 2001–2002 relates to the tax year starting April 6, 2001 and ending April 5, 2002.

Q How do you calculate your liability to income tax?

A Your income tax liability in any tax year is determined by subtracting your personal allowances and any tax reliefs from your total income to arrive at a taxable income. Your taxable income is then divided into tax bands, each successive one of which has a larger tax rate.

INCOME comprises what you earn from your job or self-employment and what you receive from other sources such as investments. However, not all money – lottery winnings, for example – you receive is counted as income while income from savings may be tax-free, have already been taxed or received gross without any tax deducted.

RELIEFS are amounts you pay out and on which you get tax relief. They reduce your income before your tax bill is calculated. Pension contributions and donations to charity, for example, attract tax relief.

ALLOWANCES are amounts to which you are entitled because

of your personal circumstances. They reduce your income before your tax bill is calculated. Some allowances, such as age-related married couple's allowances, get a reduced rate of tax relief.

RATES OF TAX apply to your taxable income (income minus reliefs minus allowances). For the year ending April 5, 2002, they are as follows:

For taxable income between £0 and £1,880, 10% tax rate (STARTING RATE);

For taxable income between £1,881 and £29,400, 22% tax rate (BASIC RATE);

For taxable income over £29,400, 40% rate (HIGHER RATE).

Income

Q What counts as income for tax purposes?

A It is probably best to start by listing what money can be ignored.

Money that DOES NOT count as income includes:

1. Personal presents and small gifts (under £250).
2. Money gifted to you under a covenant.
3. Some maintenance payments.
4. Money you borrow.
5. Money you make selling something that has increased in value – this will fall into the capital gains tax net (see later in this chapter).
6. Large gifts of money and money you inherit.
7. Winnings from betting.
8. Lottery winnings.
9. Winnings from premium bonds.
10. Grants for education or certain home improvements.
11. Scholarships.
12. Court awards for compensation and damages.
13. Money from insurance claims.
14. Some social security benefits.
15. Up to £30,000 of redundancy pay.

16. Strike and unemployment pay from a trade union.
17. Some earnings from working abroad.
18. The first £4,250 of rent you get if you let a room in your home.
19. Income from National Savings certificates and Individual Savings Accounts.

Once you have ignored money that does not enter the income tax equation, you are then left with income that does count for tax purposes. The main sources of income that are subject to income tax include:

1. MONEY PAID TO YOU BY AN EMPLOYER. This will include not only your basic earnings but any payments with regard to overtime. Each year, you should receive a P60 from your employer. This will tell you how much income you have earned from employment and the tax you have paid at source through the Pay As You Earn (PAYE) system.

2. COMPANY PERKS. These typically include company cars and private medical insurance. Each year, your employer gives you a form P11D which details the taxable value of all your perks. You then pay tax on these perks.

3. FREELANCE EARNINGS. These may be earned in your spare time away from your main job. Such earnings will be taxable although you will be able to deduct expenses involved in carrying out the work, thereby reducing your liability to tax.

4. EARNINGS FROM SELF-EMPLOYMENT. Here you will be taxed on your taxable profits. Your liability to tax will be calculated on the basis of a tax return you are required to fill in.

5. PENSION INCOME. Income from a pension is subject to tax. This is irrespective of whether the pension is provided by the State (State Pension), an ex-employer (company pension) or

derived from a personal pension and paid in the form of an annuity. Either way, your pension is regarded as earned income.

6. RENT FROM LETTING PROPERTY. Income from letting property is liable to income tax although expenses incurred in letting the property can be deducted, thereby reducing your tax bill. As already mentioned, if you let a room in your house, you are able to receive rental income tax-free of up to £4,250 per year.

Q What rate of tax will I pay on income?

A It depends on your total income and also where the income comes from. The following checklist should help you:

1. EARNINGS FROM A JOB
   a. Tax already deducted? YES
   b. At what rate is tax deducted? STARTING/ BASIC/HIGHER
   c.   Further tax liability? NO
2. TAXABLE FRINGE BENEFITS (COMPANY CAR FOR EXAMPLE)
   a.   Tax already deducted? YES (from earnings)
   b.   At what rate is tax deducted? STARTING/ BASIC/HIGHER
   c.   Further tax liability? NO
3. PENSION FROM A FORMER EMPLOYER
   a.   Tax already deducted? YES
   b.   At what rate is tax deducted? STARTING/ BASIC/HIGHER
   c.   Further tax liability? NO
4. BANK/BUILDING SOCIETY INTEREST
   a.   Tax already deducted? YES (non-taxpayers can elect to receive gross interest)
   b.   At what rate is tax deducted? 20%

  c. Further tax liability? YES – HIGHER RATE TAXPAYERS ONLY

5. BRITISH GOVERNMENT STOCKS

  a. Tax already deducted? NO (can opt for interest taxed at 20%)

  b. At what rate is tax deducted? NONE (can opt for interest taxed at 20%)

  c. Further tax liability? YES (if tax paid already, higher rate taxpayers have further tax to pay)

6. INCOME FROM ANNUITY (NOT A PENSION ANNUITY)

  a. Tax already deducted? YES

  b. At what rate is tax deducted? BASIC

  c. Further tax liability? YES – HIGHER RATE TAXPAYERS ONLY

7. DIVIDENDS FROM SHARES

  a. Tax already deducted? YES (cannot be reclaimed by non-taxpayers)

  b. At what rate is tax deducted? 10%

  c. Further tax liability? YES – HIGHER RATE TAXPAYERS ONLY

8. INCOME FROM UNIT TRUSTS AND OPEN-ENDED INVESTMENT COMPANIES (OEICS)

  a. Tax already deducted? YES (cannot be reclaimed by non-taxpayers)

  b. At what rate is tax deducted? 10%

  c. Further tax liability? YES – HIGHER RATE TAXPAYERS ONLY

9. INCOME FROM AN EXECUTOR BEFORE A WILL IS SORTED OUT

  a. Tax already deducted? YES

  b. At what rate is tax deducted? BASIC RATE

  c. Further tax liability? YES – HIGHER RATE TAXPAYERS ONLY

10. INCOME FROM A TRUST

  a. Tax already deducted? YES

    b.   At what rate is tax deducted? Usually 34%

    c.   Further tax liability? YES – HIGHER RATE TAXPAYERS ONLY

11. INCOME FROM SELF-EMPLOYMENT
    a.   Tax already deducted? NO
    b.   At what rate is tax deducted? NONE
    c.   Further tax liability? YES

12. INCOME FROM A PARTNERSHIP
    a.   Tax already deducted? NO
    b.   At what rate is tax deducted? NONE
    c.   Further tax liability? YES

13. SOCIAL SECURITY BENEFITS
    a.   Tax already deducted? NO
    b.   At what rate is tax deducted? NONE
    c.   Further tax liability? YES

14. MAINTENANCE PAYMENTS
    a.   Tax already deducted? NO
    b.   At what rate is tax deducted? NONE
    c.   Further tax liability? NONE

15. RENT FROM PROPERTY?
    a.   Tax already deducted? NO
    b.   At what rate is tax deducted? NONE
    c.   Further tax liability? YES (tax-free income from rent a room up to £4,250)

Reliefs

Q What are tax reliefs?

A They are provided by the government to encourage you – not force you – to do certain things with your money – make your own pension provision for example or give money to charity. Encouragement is given by allowing you to deduct some or all of what you pay for these from your income before working out your income tax bill.

Q How do you get tax reliefs?

A You get tax relief in three main ways:

WAY ONE: You deduct the tax relief from the payment you make. So, for example, if you want to make a £100 payment to charity under the gift aid scheme and you are a basic rate taxpayer, you hand over £78.

WAY TWO: Through the PAYE system. So, for example, if you are making a £100 monthly contribution to your employer's pension scheme, and you are a higher rate taxpayer, you will only pay £60. The other £40 reduces your tax bill. The £100 deduction is made from your gross pay.

WAY THREE: Claiming it through your tax return.

Q What are the main tax reliefs available?

A Payments made into pension plans (employer or personal) and payments made to charities through covenants and gift aid. Tax relief is also available on investments into Enterprise Investment Schemes, interest on loans to pay inheritance tax and interest on business loans.

Allowances

Q So what income tax allowances are available?

A Every UK resident is given a personal allowance under which a certain amount of income each tax year is not subject to tax.
The main personal income tax allowances are as follows. The figures given all apply to the tax year ending April 5, 2002:

PERSONAL ALLOWANCE (basic) £4,535

For a husband and wife, each spouse is granted this allowance to offset against his or her income.

PERSONAL ALLOWANCES (age 65–74) £5,990

This is available to people aged 65 to 74. Whether you qualify for the full amount or a reduced amount depends on your total income – before tax income from all sources including pensions, part-time earnings and income from savings and investments minus any tax-allowable deductions such as payments you make to charity.

If your total income comes to more than £17,600, the allowance is reduced by £1 for every £2 of income over the £17,600 cap. Your allowance cannot be reduced beyond £4,535.

PERSONAL ALLOWANCES (age 75 and over) £6,260

This is available to those aged 75 and over. Again, the extra allowance is dependent upon your total income with the same allowance clawback rules applying as they do for the 65- to 74-year-olds.

MARRIED COUPLE'S ALLOWANCE (age 65 to 74) £5,365

This is available if either spouse is aged at least 65 on April 5, 2000 and is given at a rate of 10% of £5,365 (£536.50). The sum is used to reduce your final tax bill. It is always given to the husband and the amount of the allowance is calculated on the husband's total income. If the husband's income exceeds £17,600, his personal allowance is reduced first to account for excess income – in the same way as with the age allowances. When it has been pared back to the level of the basic personal allowance (£4,535), he may then start to lose the extra married couple's allowance. However, the married couple's allowance will not be reduced below the level of the basic married couple's allowance of £2,070.

Do note that one spouse has to be aged 65 before April 6, 2000 in order to receive married couple's allowance. Couples where either person does not reach the age of 65 on or after April 6, 2000 cannot claim married couple's allowance.

MARRIED COUPLE'S ALLOWANCE (age 75 and over) £5,435
This is available if either spouse is aged 75 or over and is given at a
rate of 10% of £5,435 (£543.50). The rules on restrictions are the
same as for the married couple's allowance – age 65 to 74.

Again, note that couples who did not reach age 65 on or after
April 6, 2000 cannot claim this allowance in the future.

How these rules work is best illustrated by way of example. In each
instance, let us assume that our case studies aged 65 or over all
reached the age of 65 prior to April 6, 2000, thereby making them
eligible for receipt of the married couple's allowance.

EXAMPLE 1: If a husband, Tim, aged 66, has a total income of
£18,000, he will receive the following allowances:
1. Personal Allowance of £5,790 (£5,990 minus £200).
   £5,990 represents the personal allowance for ages 65–74;
   £200 is the reduction for £400 of excess income over
   £17,600, the allowance being reduced at the rate of £1 for
   every £2 of income excess.
2. Married couple's age allowance of £5,365, leading to a tax
   bill reduction of £536.50 (10% of £5,365).

EXAMPLE 2: If a husband, Tom, aged 76, has a total income of
£25,000, he will receive the following allowances:
1. Personal Allowance of £4,535 (£6,260 minus £1,725)
   £6,260 represents the personal allowance for ages 75 and
   over; £1,725 is the reduction for £3,450 of excess income
   over £17,600 which reduces his personal allowance to the
   level of the basic personal allowance (£4,535). Remember,
   his personal allowance cannot fall below this level.
2. Married couple's age allowance of £3,460, leading to a tax
   deduction of £346. This is because Tom has £3,950 of
   excess income which must be used to reduce his married
   couple's allowance at the rate of £1 for every £2 of excess
   income. So his allowance is reduced from £5,435 by
   £1,975 to £3,460.

NOTE: If Tom's total income was in excess of £27,780, he would receive the basic personal allowance of £4,535 plus a married couple's age allowance of £2,070, leading to a tax deduction of £207 irrespective of the amount above £27,780. This is because the minimum married couple's allowance, set at £2,070, would kick in.

EXAMPLE 3: If Tom has the same income as before, £25,000, but is aged 61 and his wife Maureen is 67, Tom would still be eligible to receive the married couple's allowance because of Maureen's age.

Here Tom would receive the basic personal allowance of £4,535 by virtue of his age. His excess income over the income limit for age-related allowances is £7,400 (£25,000 minus £17,600). The married couple's allowance available would be the minimum of £2,070 leading to tax relief of £207.

Q Is it possible to maximise use of these allowances by transferring assets from one partner to another?

A Yes. It makes great sense, especially for those eligible to receive the higher age personal allowance and the married couple's allowance for the over 65s.

How a transfer of assets can keep personal allowances intact is best shown by way of example:

EXAMPLE: Let's assume that Terry, aged 67 and married to Tina, has total income of £21,000 of which £9,000 is from savings and investments. Tina, aged 65, on the other hand, has total income of £8,000.

The allowances that Terry and Tina would receive are as follows:

1. Terry would receive a personal allowance of £4,535 on account of the fact that his excess income above the income limit for age-related allowances is £3,400. This reduces his age-related allowance down from £5,990 to the basic level of £4,535.

2. Terry would receive a married couple's allowance of

£5,120, providing a tax deduction of £512. This is based on the fact that he has excess income of £490 after taking into account the £2,910 used to reduce his personal tax allowance down to the basic level. His married couple's allowance is therefore reduced (on the basis of a £1 allowance reduction for every £2 of excess income) from £5,365 by £245 to £5,120.

3.　Tina would receive a full age-related personal tax allowance of £5,990 on account of the fact that her total income is less than £17,600.

In total, Terry and Tina have lost allowances equivalent to £4,700.

However, Terry and Tina could keep their allowances intact by putting their savings and investments into joint names. By doing this, Terry receives £4,500 from these savings while Tina also receives £4,500. This means Terry now has a total income of £16,500 while Tina has £12,500.

Now, the allowances that Terry and Tina would receive are as follows:

1.　Terry would receive a full age-related personal allowance of £5,990 on account of the fact that his total income is less than the £17,600 limit for age-related allowances.
2.　Terry would also receive a married couple's allowance of £5,365, providing a tax deduction of £536.50. Again, given his total income is less than the £17,600 limit for age-related allowances, he is entitled to the full allowance.
3.　Tina would still receive a full age-related personal tax allowance of £5,990 on account of the fact that her income remains below £17,600.

Before Terry and Tina sorted out their savings, they had combined allowances of £15,645. After rearranging, their allowances total £17,345.

Q Are there any other allowances?

A There is the blind person's allowance. This is set at £1,450 for the tax year ending April 5, 2002. The allowance is payable if you are registered as blind with a local authority in England and Wales or unable to perform any work for which eyesight is essential in Scotland and Northern Ireland – where there is no register.

Fringe benefits

Q What are fringe benefits?

A They are perks provided by your employer in addition to your salary. Typical fringe benefits include employer's contributions to a pension scheme, a company car and an interest-free loan to cover the cost of a travel season ticket.

Q What is the tax situation regarding fringe benefits?

A Many fringe benefits are tax-free. Others are good value for employees because the taxable value put on them is less than it would cost you to pay for the benefit yourself.

Q So, what fringe benefits are tax-free?

A There is a whole host. They include:

1. Free or subsidised meals at work, provided they are available to all employees.
2. Changing room and shower facilities at work, provided they are available to all employees.
3. Luncheon vouchers up to a maximum of 15 pence a day.
4. Employer's contributions to a pension, life insurance or sick pay insurance policy.
5. Loans on preferential terms where the total loan

outstanding is not more than £5,000.

6. Routine medical check-ups or medical screening for you or your family.
7. Cost of medical treatment while working abroad.
8. Nurseries and play schemes run by your employer.
9. Living accommodation provided it is necessary for you to do your work or beneficial and customary for someone in your line of work.
10. Provision of car parking or bicycle-parking space at or near your work.
11. Cost of transport home if you are required to work late after public transport has closed down.
12. Entertainment for you or your family provided by someone other than your employer purely as a gesture of goodwill.
13. Annual parties provided by your employer for which the cost is no more than £75 a head per year to provide.
14. Sports facilities generally available to all staff and their families.
15. Relocation costs if you move house for your job, subject to a maximum of £8,000 per move.
16. Private use of a mobile provided by your employer.
17. Loan of a computer by your employer.

Q So what benefits are taxable?

A They break into four camps:

CAMP ONE: Assets transferred to you or payments made for you by your employer. Your employer may, for example, allow you to buy cheaply an item such as a television or furniture.

If you earn less than £8,500, the taxable value is the second-hand value of the payment in kind. Given this will be less than the cost of buying the good brand new, this can prove to your advantage.

If you earn £8,500 or more, the rules are stricter. Here you pay tax on the larger of the second-hand value or the cost to the employer of providing the asset.

If you are given a car or telephone or mobile phone, you are taxed on its second-hand value when you are given it, less anything you pay for it.

If you are given anything else that you have had the use of, the taxable value is the larger of the market value when given it or the market value of the asset when it was first loaned out less the total amount on which tax has already been charged. Any amount you pay is deducted from one of these sums to arrive at the taxable value.

If your employer pays any of your bills directly, such as your phone or credit card bill, you pay tax on the full amount paid.

CAMP TWO: Vouchers and credit cards. Here, you pay tax on the expense incurred by the person who provided them, less any amount that you have paid yourself.

CAMP THREE: Living accommodation. In some instances, living accommodation counts as a tax-free fringe benefit. Where it doesn't, the taxable value is based on the higher of the rateable value of the property or if the property is let, the rent paid for it. From the taxable value, you can deduct anything you pay for the accommodation.

CAMP FOUR: Mileage allowance. If you use your own car for work, most employers pay a mileage allowance. Any profit you make on the mileage allowance will be taxable. You can work out your profit in three different ways and you can choose which suits you best. The best starting point for this is Inland Revenue leaflet IR125: 'Using your car for work'.

Q What about company cars?

A Yes, they fall into a third category of fringe benefit: benefits which are tax-free if you earn at a rate of less than £8,500 and are not a director and which are taxable for everybody else. They include the following:

FRINGE BENEFIT 1: COMPANY CARS. The rules for taxing company cars are changing in April 2002.

The CURRENT system is as follows:

The baseline for a car's taxable value is 35% of its price. So a new car with a list price of £18,000 has a basic taxable value of £6,300. Any contribution you make towards the cost of the car is deducted from its price, up to a limit of £5,000.

The baseline tax then varies according to the number of business miles you drive in the car each tax year.

If you drive less than 2,500 miles, the tax charge is 35% of the price.

If you drive between 2,500 and 17,999 miles, the tax charge reduces to 25% of the price.

If you drive more than 18,000 miles, the tax charge is 15%.

If a car is more than four years old at the end of the tax year in question, you can deduct one-quarter of the taxable value you ended up with after any business mileage adjustment.

You are also taxed on free fuel you get although other running costs met by your employer, such as tax, servicing and insurance, are tax-free. Free car fuel is taxed according to a fixed scale of charges added to your taxable income – see appendix.

The FORTHCOMING system is as follows:

From April 6, 2002, the tax charge for a company car will be a percentage of the purchase price based on the car's carbon dioxide emissions. The charge will range from 15% to 35% (the most polluting) – see appendix.

Business mileage and age-related discounts will be abolished.

FRINGE BENEFIT 2: PRIVATE MEDICAL OR DENTAL INSURANCE. If your employer pays premiums for a private medical expenses policy or dental insurance for you, the amount is a taxable benefit. You pay tax on the cost to your employer, less any amount you pay for the benefit.

FRINGE BENEFIT 3: CHEAP OR FREE LOANS. If your employer provides a cheap or interest-free loan, you have to pay tax on the difference between the interest you pay and the interest worked out at an official rate – 6.25% for the tax year ending April 5, 2002. However, this rule is waived if the total loans you have outstanding are less than £5,000.

Tax liability

Q So I now know what constitutes taxable income and what reliefs and allowances are available. I am also aware of the tax situation regarding fringe benefits. How do I go about calculating what tax rate should apply to my income and how much tax on savings I should pay?

A This is best broken into three key stages. It is also best worked through by way of examples.

Stage 1: Calculation of your tax rate and tax bill before accounting for savings income and any adjustments for tax deductions

A. STEP ONE: Add up all your income that counts for tax purposes.
B. STEP TWO: Add up the taxable value of any fringe benefits.
C. STEP THREE: A + B = INCOME FOR TAX PURPOSES.
D. STEP FOUR: Add up your personal allowances and any other tax reliefs you can include in your tax-free band.
E. STEP FIVE: C – D = TAXABLE INCOME.
F. STEP SIX:
a. IF E is zero or a minus figure, you are a NON-TAXPAYER.
b. IF E is between £0 and £1,880, you are a LOWER RATE TAXPAYER.

c. IF E is more than £1,880 but less than £29,400, you are a BASIC RATE TAXPAYER.

d. IF E is more than £29,400, you are a HIGHER RATE TAXPAYER.

EXAMPLE 1: Bill, aged 33, has earnings of £25,000 in the tax year ended April 5, 2002. He has a company car with a taxable value of £6,000 and income from a cash Isa of £100. He has generated freelance earnings of £2,000. He also won £500 of premium bond prizes. He makes pension contributions of £1,250 per year.

A. STEP ONE: Add up all your income that counts for tax purposes.

Bill's income for tax purposes is £27,000 (earnings plus freelance earnings).

Income from the Isa can be ignored because it is tax-free. The premium bond prize can also be ignored because it is not deemed to be income.

B. STEP TWO: Add up the taxable value of any fringe benefits.

Bill's car has a taxable value of £6,000.

C. STEP THREE: A + B = INCOME FOR TAX PURPOSES.

Bill's income for tax purposes is £33,000.

D. STEP FOUR: Add up your personal allowances and any other tax reliefs you can include in your tax-free band.

Bill has a personal allowance of £4,535.

Bill has made pension contributions of £1,250.

E. STEP FIVE: C – D = TAXABLE INCOME.

Bill's taxable income is £27,215 (£33,000 minus £4,535 minus £1,250).

F. STEP SIX: IF E is more than £1,880 but less than £29,400, you are a BASIC RATE TAXPAYER.

Bill is a basic rate taxpayer.

On his taxable income up to £1,880, Bill will pay tax of £188 (10%).

On his taxable income of between £1,880 and £27,215 (£25,335), Bill will pay tax of £5,573.70 (22%).

Bill's tax bill before savings and any tax deductions is £5,761.70.

Key Stage 2: Calculation of your tax bill on savings

A. STEP ONE: Is your taxable income (STEP FIVE above) greater than £29,400 (the level at which higher rate tax kicks in)?
SCENARIO 1: If YES, your tax on savings is 40% of before tax savings (many savings have tax automatically deducted at 20% leaving higher rate taxpayers with a further 20% to pay).
SCENARIO 2: If NO, you add your income for tax purposes to your before-tax income from any savings.
a. If this figure is less than zero (in other words, your allowances exceed your total income), you do not pay tax on your savings.
b. If this figure is greater than zero but less than £29,400, then your tax bill on savings is 20%. Most savings vehicles automatically deduct at 20%, so no further tax payment is required.
c. If this figure is greater than £29,400, then part of your savings will be liable to 20% tax and part will be liable to 40% tax.

EXAMPLE 2: Let's take Bill again. As before, he is aged 33, has earnings of £25,000 in the tax year ended April 5, 2002. He has a company car with a taxable value of £6,000 and income from a cash Isa of £100. He has generated freelance earnings of £2,000. He also won £500 of premium bond prizes. He makes pension contributions equivalent to 5% of his salary (£1,250 a year). But this time, let's assume he has before-tax income from building society savings of £2,500.
STEP ONE: Bill's taxable income is £27,215: £33,000 of income for tax purposes (earnings plus freelance plus taxable value of car) minus £5,785 of a personal tax-free band (pension contributions plus personal allowance).
    Given it is below £29,400, Bill falls into Scenario 2.
SCENARIO 2: Bill has total income (taxable income plus pre-tax

savings income) of £29,715.

This means that £2,185 of Bill's pre-tax savings income (the amount of savings income that takes his income up to the upper band for basic rate tax of £29,400) will be subject to 20% tax (NOTE: not at 22%).

The balance of £315 (the amount of savings income that takes his income up above the threshold for higher rate tax of £29,400) will be subject to 40% tax.

Bill's total tax bill now comprises:

£1,880 of income taxed at 10%	£188
£25,335 of income taxed at 22%	£5,573.70
£2,185 of savings income taxed at 20%	£437
£315 of savings income taxed at 40%	£126
Bill's total tax bill is now	£6,324.70.

- **DO** note that Bill would already have paid tax on his £2,500 of savings at 20%. This sum (£500) would have been deducted at source. So he would only have to pay a further £63.

Key Stage 3: Calculation of tax deductions

Finally, you are able to reduce your tax bill by so-called tax deductions. The main tax deduction people can use to reduce their tax bill is the age-related married couple's allowance. Now only available to couples where at least one of the partners was 65 prior to April 6, 2000, the maximum deduction is £536.50 for those aged 65 to 74 and £543.50 for those aged 75 plus.

Dos and Don'ts

- **DO** remember that personal allowances reduce the amount of your income that will be liable for tax. In contrast, married couple's allowances reduce your final tax bill.

- **DO** check whether you are paying the right amount of tax. This is particularly important if you are employed and you do not receive an annual tax return to complete. You can do this by working out how much tax you think you should have paid (using key stages 1 to 3) and then marrying it up to the tax you have paid as an employee through PAYE and the tax you have paid on any savings.

If there is a major discrepancy, contact your tax office straight away. If you have been underpaying tax, you may face a penalty.

If you are overpaying, maybe because, for example, you have stopped receiving a company perk, the tax office will adjust your so-called tax code. Your tax code is used to calculate how much tax should be deducted from your pay by your employer and takes into account any tax allowances you are entitled to plus any extra income you may get from other sources which is untaxed as well as the taxable value of any company benefits.

- **DO** tell your tax office straight away if your work arrangements change in such a way that it will affect your tax bill. It will ensure any adjustments to your tax code are made straight away.

Did you know?

- **DID** you know that the married couple's allowance for the under 65s has been axed? This came into effect on April 6, 2000. The married couple's allowance is now only available to couples where at least one partner was aged 65 prior to April 6, 2000.

- **DID** you know that about six million people pay too much tax each year?

- **DID** you know that the government has now introduced tax credits? These work by giving you cash or tax reductions through the tax system. They include the Working Families Tax

Credit, the Disabled Persons Tax Credit and the Children's Tax Credit (introduced April 2001). Other tax credits are in the offing.

- **DID** you know that your employer must give you certain forms to help you in filling in any tax returns and to assist you in ensuring you are paying the right amount of tax? These include the P60 form (detailing your pay and tax paid during the tax year) and the P11D form (detailing any company benefits you have received during the tax year).

- **DID** you know that a 'pool car' is tax-free? To qualify, the car must not normally be kept overnight near your home, it must be used by more than one employee and any private use must be a consequence of business use.

- **DID** you know that a van provided by your employer for your private use is lightly taxed, compared to a company car? The basic taxable value of a van is only £500 and there is no tax charge for free fuel.

Self-assessment

THE self-assessment system for the collection of taxes was introduced in 1997. It puts the responsibility for declaring income and paying tax firmly and squarely on your shoulders. There are strict deadlines – set in Revenue stone – you must meet to send back your tax return and to pay any tax owing. Missing these deadlines can result in interest charges and fines so beware.

Q Does self-assessment affect everyone?

A No. If you are taxed via the PAYE (Pay As You Earn) system, there is a good chance that you will not have to fill in a self-assessment tax return. If you get income from other sources, where tax is taken at source, there is also a strong possibility that you will not have to get involved in self-assessment. Self-assessment primarily affects people who are higher rate taxpayers, self-employed, are a partner in a business, a company director or trustee or have complex tax affairs (for example, they receive additional income to that received under PAYE). People who receive income gross from savings which is taxable will also receive a tax form under self-assessment.

Q Does everyone get the same form under self-assessment?

A Everyone sent a tax form gets the basic eight-page return entitled 'Tax Return'. But there are supplementary pages (nine sets in total) that you may be required to fill in dependent upon your situation – if you are self-employed, for example, or in a business partnership. The Revenue should send you these but if they don't, request them as soon as you get your tax return so that you don't end up missing any deadlines. Supplementary pages can be ordered on 0845 9000 404 or by e-mail: saorderline.ir@gtnet.gov.uk. Alternatively, you can write to: PO Box 37, St Austell, PL 25 5YN.

Accompanying your tax return should be a tax return guide. This will explain how to complete your tax return.

Q When should I receive the tax form?

A In April every year. So the tax return for the tax year ending April 5, 2002 should be received during April 2002. The information you provide on this document will be used by you or by the taxman to work out your tax bill for the tax year ending April 5, 2002.

Q What happens if I don't send back my tax return?

A Don't even think about not returning it. If you get a self-assessment tax form, you must return it by January 31 at the latest together with a cheque for the tax due. So a tax return for the tax year ending April 5, 2002 should be returned no later than the end of January 2003. If you ignore the deadline, the Revenue starts to get heavy and will fine you for failing to meet the deadline. The Revenue also has the right to issue a determination – a best estimate of the tax you owe – which you are then obliged to pay.

Q Do I have to work out my tax bill as the term self-assessment implies?

A Not necessarily. If you get your tax return in by September 30 – four months early – the taxman will work it out for you. You will then have until January 31 to pay it. If you miss the September 30 deadline, you can still ask the Revenue to calculate your bill but there is no guarantee that you will receive your tax demand in time to meet the January 31 payment deadline. You could then end up paying interest on any unpaid tax.

Q What if I don't normally get a tax return but receive income which is not taxed at source?

A You must contact your tax office within six months of the tax year in which you received the money and inform them of the income received. So if you received the gross income in May 2001, you must tell the taxman by October 5, 2002.

Q What information will I need to work out my tax bill?

A You will need various forms that you should already have received such as a P60 (detailing income from your employment and the tax you have paid on it). If you have left employment, you will need a P45. Other essential forms are P11d or P9d which detail any benefits or expenses and P2 (your notice of tax coding). You will also need details of interest from any bank or building society savings accounts, dividends from shares, unit trusts or investment trusts and any other income you have received.

Q Once I have sent in my tax return, what happens?

A The Revenue will process your return . You will then receive a tax calculation form informing you of the total tax you owe for the tax year plus the payments, if any, you will have to make on account for the next tax year. You must challenge the tax calculation form if you don't agree with the figures or you simply don't understand it – write or phone your tax office for help.

Q What tax do I exactly have to pay by January 31?

A It depends. If you are employed, there is every likelihood that any extra tax due will be taken through the PAYE system – resulting in a monthly reduction in your take home pay.

For others, essentially the self-employed, the January 31 deadline requires you to pay in full the balance of any tax still owing from the previous tax year and make the first of two payments on account for the current tax year. The second instalment is payable by July 31.

This is best illustrated. For the tax year ending April 2002, you should receive a tax return in April 2002. The completion date will be the end of January 2003 or the end of September 2002 if you want the taxman to work out your bill. You will already have made an interim payment on account – in advance – for tax due in the year ending April 5, 2002 by January 31, 2002. This payment will be typically half the amount of tax you paid in the previous tax year – the year ended April 5, 2001.

You will then make the second interim payment on account – the other half – by the end of July 2002. The final payment for the tax year ending April 2002 will be made after you have completed your tax return – the deadline of course being January 2003.

In January 2003, you will also have to make a payment on account for tax due in the year ended April 5, 2003.

You will receive statements of account at the end of the calendar year and in the spring detailing how much you should pay by January 31 and July 31. These statements are estimates based on your previous tax bills and you can apply to have the payments reduced if your income has dropped. This is done by completing form SA303.

Q What happens if I don't pay on time?

A You will pay interest charges. On the other hand, any tax that you have overpaid will also earn interest, albeit at a lower level.

Q What happens if the taxman enquires into my return?

A Don't panic. Every year, a small selection of all returns are selected for enquiry. You will receive a written notice of an enquiry and may be asked to produce documents supporting your tax return. The enquiry will then be completed and you will be informed as to whether you owe any tax and if so be required to amend your self-assessment. If you are found to have been acting fraudulently or negligently, the Revenue has the right to issue a discovery assessment demanding that you pay the outstanding tax.

Tax enquiries cannot be conducted willy-nilly. A tax inspector can only enquire once into your tax return – he cannot come back a second time. Furthermore, there is a time limit on the issue of enquiries. If you have returned your tax return by January 31, the tax inspector has until the end of January the following year in which to launch an enquiry.

Dos and Don'ts

- **DO** inform the Revenue of any income you receive, especially if you don't normally receive a tax return. As already indicated, this must be declared within six months of the end of the tax year in which you received the income. Failure to do this can result in a hefty penalty plus interest charges. There are exceptions to this rule. For example, you don't have to notify your tax office of dividends received from shares if you are a basic rate taxpayer. This is because there is no further tax to pay. But you would have to if you were a higher rate taxpayer. This is because you have a further 32.5% to pay.

- **DO** keep all the documents you used to complete your tax return – dividend vouchers, bank statements – in a safe place. You may need to produce them if you are subject to a tax enquiry. Furthermore, failure to keep them may result in a penalty plus interest charges.

- **DO** keep a record of your working papers used to fill in your tax return – they will be needed if you are subject to a tax enquiry. In general terms, if you don't run your own business, you need to keep records for at least one year from the date you must file your tax return (January 31). However, if you are self-employed, you need to keep records for five years from the time you should have submitted your tax return (January 31).

- **DON'T** fail to check your statement of account detailing how much tax you will have to pay by January 31 and July 31. It may be possible to claim a reduction in payments although it is better to pay slightly more tax on account than too little. If you overpay, you will receive interest compensation but underpayments will result in interest charges.

- **DO** appeal against a fine for missing the deadline for filing tax returns if you have a genuine excuse. The Revenue does possess a sympathetic ear and will be flexible if you have been ill, suffered the loss of a close relative or had your tax records stolen or destroyed.

Did you know?

- **DID** you know that around one in 10 taxpayers fail to get to grips with self-assessment and end up paying a penalty for late delivery of their tax return?

- **DID** you know that a network of taxpayer enquiry centres now exists where taxpayers can talk to tax staff and sort out any queries?

- **DID** you know that the Revenue is encouraging people to send in their tax returns over the Internet and pay any tax due using a debit card? People who use this method will probably qualify for a small discount off their tax bill – the Revenue paid a £10 discount for people who filed their tax returns for the year ending April 5, 2000 in this way.

- **DID** you know that the Revenue provides a free software package to taxpayers to enable them to complete their tax returns? It is not suitable for everyone. Visit website www.inlandrevenue.gov.uk/sa.

- **DID** you know that the Inland Revenue grabs as much as £80 million from people who have either completed tax returns incorrectly or who have sent them in late?

- **DID** you know that employees who also receive additional taxable income from other sources can spread their future tax burden? Provided you complete your tax return by September 30, and the amount of tax due is less than £2,000, the Revenue will not ask you to pay tax on this extra income by the end of January 31 as is commonplace. Instead, it will be included in your PAYE code for the following tax year. You will therefore spread the payment of the tax over the entire tax year.

Tax on savings

THE choice of financial product available to the prudent saver is wider than ever before. There is something for everyone – deposit accounts for the risk averse through to shares for the adventurous. However, when choosing a savings vehicle, it is important that tax considerations are taken into account because different products attract different levels of tax. Indeed, some products escape the tax net altogether. By using such tax-free investments, you can protect a big chunk of your savings from the taxman.

The commentary below looks at savings and tax. Of course, the impact of tax on savings is also discussed in the individual chapters on savings later in the book.

Q Income from some investments is tax-free?

A Yes. Tax-free income from savings includes the following:

1. Interest on National Savings certificates and National Savings Children Bonus Bonds.
2. Interest and terminal bonuses on bank and building society Save-As-You-Earn schemes.
3. First £70 of interest each year from a National Savings Ordinary Account.
4. Income from a Personal Equity Plan.
5. Interest on a Tax Exempt Special Savings Account which is kept open for the full five years and where some of the interest is reinvested.
6. Income from an Individual Savings Account.
7. Dividends on ordinary shares in a venture capital trust.
8. Part of the income from an annuity – not a pension annuity.
9. Amount paid out by a regular premium life insurance policy such as an endowment provided it is no more than 5% per annum.

Q On savings and investments which are taxable, do I pay tax up front or do I wait until I get my tax return?
A Most investment income is now paid with tax deducted, which means that all bar higher rate taxpayers have no further tax to pay. This applies primarily to building society and bank accounts.

Q How much tax is deducted on my bank or building society account?

A It is deducted at 20%. There is no further tax to pay if you pay tax at the basic rate. If your income is insufficient to pay tax on or you pay tax on the rest of your income at 10%, you should be able to reclaim some or all of the tax which has been deducted.

EXAMPLE: Vivian has earnings of £4,500 in the tax year ending April 5, 2002. She also receives interest of £520 from her savings. Tax has been deducted at the rate of 20% but Vivian believes that she should be paying 10% on this money.

STEP ONE: Work out the amount of gross interest that Vivian received.

80% of X (gross interest) equals £520.

X equals £650 (£520 divided by 0.8).

In other words, Vivian has received gross interest of £650 on which she has paid tax of £130.

STEP TWO: Calculate tax rate which should apply.

Vivian has total income of £5,150 (£4,500 plus £650).

Vivian has a personal allowance of £4,535.

Vivian's taxable income is £615 (£5,150 minus £4,535).

Lower rate tax of 10% is due on the first £1,880 of taxable income.

Vivian should therefore have only paid £61.50 (10% tax on £615).

Vivian actually paid £130.

So Vivian is owed a tax rebate of £68.50 (£130 minus £61.50).

Q What if I am a higher rate taxpayer?

A You have a further tax charge. This will be paid either through PAYE or through the self-assessment tax system. How much additional tax you have to pay is best shown by way of example:

EXAMPLE: Carol has received £160 interest on her building society savings account for the tax year ending April 5, 2002. Tax has already been deducted at 20%.

STEP ONE: 20% of X equals £160.
STEP TWO: X (amount invested) equals £800.
STEP THREE: Total tax equals 40% of £800 equals £320.
STEP FOUR: Carol has already paid £160. Further tax charge is £160.

Q What is the tax situation regarding dividends from shares and authorised unit trusts?

A There is no further tax to pay if you are a lower or basic rate taxpayer. Tax, in the form of a tax credit, is already taken at a rate of 10%. However, if you are a taxpayer, there is a further tax charge, equivalent to 32.5%.

EXAMPLE: Mandy is a higher rate taxpayer and receives dividends from her shares of £1,600. What is her further liability to tax?

STEP ONE: Work out the grossed-up amount of Mandy's dividend.
Mandy received a net dividend of £1,600.
Net dividend is 90% of the gross dividend.
£1,600 equals 90% of X (gross dividend).
Gross dividend equals £1,778, tax credit is £178.
Total tax bill for Mandy is £578 (32.5% of £1,778).
Mandy has a tax credit of £178, so higher tax due is £400 (£578 minus £178).
Mandy is left with £1,200 (£1,600 minus £400).

Q Can I claim back the tax credit if I am a non-taxpayer?

A No. You are better off investing in Isas where the tax credit is reclaimed. This is the case until April 5, 2002.

Q You've dealt with building society accounts and shares. What about pensions?

A The government provides generous tax breaks to anyone saving through a pension. There is tax relief on contributions you make to a pension, any employer's contributions are not taxable as your income or as a fringe benefit, the fund your money goes into is tax-efficient and when it comes to taking benefits from your pension, you can take part of them tax-free. Further details are provided in the chapter on pensions.

Dos and Don'ts

- **DO** take advantage of the array of tax-free savings vehicles available.

- **DO** register for receipt of gross interest if you are a non-taxpayer. It's dead simple.

- **DON'T** pay tax on savings unless you truly have to. Use tax-free savings vehicles first.

Did you know?

- **DID** you know that you can claim back tax on savings by filling in form R40 from the Inland Revenue?

- **DID** you know that you can arrange to receive your savings without the payment of tax? This is possible by filling in form R85 available from banks, building societies and post offices as well as from tax offices. The Inland Revenue has published a useful booklet on tax and savings, IR110.

- **DID** you know that if you now buy gilts, either directly or via the National Savings Stock Register, interest is received gross. If you are a taxpayer, you will have to pay tax.

Capital gains tax

Q What is capital gains tax?

A It is a tax usually applied to assets you own which have increased in value and you then decide to sell them for a profit. The gain you make on the sale may be liable to capital gains tax. Capital gains tax is sometimes an issue for people who have held shares for a long time and who then decide to sell them. The tax also comes into play if you swap an asset for another or give an asset away. The key trigger for capital gains tax is if you 'dispose' of an asset.

Q How much is this tax?

A It can be a complicated tax to calculate but it is possible for you to be charged as much as 40% of any chargeable gain. However, don't panic. There are a number of factors which result in capital gains tax not being an issue for most people.

FACTOR 1: A number of assets are exempt from the capital gains tax net.

FACTOR 2: Everyone has an annual capital gains tax allowance which can be used to absorb most gains from asset sales.

FACTOR 3: The government allows you to use a combination of allowances and reliefs to reduce your liable gains to take into account the effects of inflation and how long you have held an asset.

FACTOR 4: Some transactions simply fall outside of the capital gains net.

Let's look at these factors in greater detail:

FACTOR 1: You don't have to worry about capital gains tax on any gains you make from the following assets:

Your home.

Private Cars.

Personal belongings (chattels) sold for less than £6,000.

A whole array of savings vehicles such as National Savings, Peps, Isas, Business Expansion Schemes, Enterprise Investment Schemes, shares in venture capital trusts, UK gilts.

There are a number of other exceptions but the key one for most people is your home.

FACTOR 2: The first slice of total chargeable gain in any tax year is free of capital gains tax. For the tax year ending April 5, 2002, this tax-free allowance is £7,500. You are not able to carry forward any unused part of this allowance to the next tax year. However, if you have made capital losses, you can offset these against any gains you have made. Furthermore, if in any tax year, your losses exceed your gains, you are able to carry over any net loss to reduce chargeable gains in later tax years.

EXAMPLE 1: Henry has made chargeable capital gains of £8,000 in the tax year beginning April 6, 2001. He has also made losses of £1,000. His net chargeable gain is £7,000, below the £7,500 threshold for capital gains tax. He escapes paying capital gains tax.

EXAMPLE 2: Tom has made chargeable capital gains of £9,000 in the tax year ending April 5, 2002. Given this exceeds his annual tax-free allowance of £7,500, he faces paying capital gains tax on £1,500. But if Tom in the previous tax year had incurred net capital losses of £3,000, he can use £1,500 of this amount to reduce his total chargeable gain for the tax year ending April 5, 2002 to £0. Tom still has £1,500 of unused losses to carry forward to the next tax year and beyond.

FACTOR 3: The capital gain or loss on an asset is not simply the change in value since you owned the asset. You are allowed to make adjustments to take into account the impact of inflation (indexation allowance) and how long you have held an asset for (taper relief).

The calculation, and it isn't simple, is best shown by way of example. Let's assume that Fred bought 6,000 shares at £1 a share in a small electrical company in March 1987. He then sold them for £29,000 in May 2001. Let's also assume, for simplicity's sake, that this is the only asset sale he has made for the tax year ending April 5, 2002 and he has no allowable losses from previous tax years.

STEP ONE: Establish the sale value of the shares.
Sale value is £29,000.

STEP TWO: Find out the amount Fred paid for the shares – special rules apply to assets owned before March 31, 1982 which will be discussed later.

Fred paid £6,000.

STEP THREE: Calculate the gross capital gain/loss (STEP ONE – STEP TWO).

Fred has a gross capital gain of £23,000 (£29,000 minus £6,000).

STEP FOUR: If Fred held the shares prior to April 5, 1998, he can reduce any gross capital gain by applying the indexation allowance to take into account the impact of inflation up to this date. Remember, the indexation allowance applies to assets owned between April 1, 1982 and March 31, 1998 – different rules apply to assets owned on or before March 31, 1998.

The indexation allowance factor for March 1987 is 0.616 (see appendix).

Fred's indexation allowance is therefore 0.616 x £6,000 = £3,696.

STEP FIVE: Find out Fred's chargeable gain.

Fred has a chargeable gain of £19,304. This is above the £7,500 capital gains tax allowance for the tax year ending April 5, 2002 so he will pay capital gains tax.

STEP SIX: Assess Fred's entitlement to taper relief. Taper relief reduces any chargeable gain based on how long an asset has been held after April 5, 1998. Fred has held his shares for three complete tax years. He also qualifies for one bonus year given he held the shares before March 17, 1998 and sold them after April 6, 1998. This means he is eligible for taper relief applying to assets held for four complete tax years. This is 10% (see appendix).

Fred's taper relief is 10% of the chargeable gain (£19,304). This works out at £1,930.40.

Fred's net tapered gain is therefore £17,373.60.

STEP SEVEN: Calculate Fred's liability to capital gains tax.

Fred has a capital gains tax allowance for the tax year ending April 5, 2002 of £7,500.

This means his capital gains liable for taxation are £9,873.60

(£17,373.60 minus £7,500).

STEP EIGHT: Calculate Fred's capital gains tax bill.

Fred's capital gains of £9,873.60 are added to his taxable income for the year (ending April 5, 2002) and taxed as if it was savings income.

So assuming Fred had taxable income of £9,000. The combined total would be £18,873.60 – within the upper limit for basic rate tax (up to £29,400). He would therefore pay capital gains tax of £1,974.72 (20% of £9,873.60).

However, if Fred had taxable income of £20,000, the combined total would be £29,873.60. This would result in a capital gains tax charge of £2,069.44 (£9,400 of gain taxed at 20% and £473.60 taxed at 40%).

It's all very complicated and you would be wise to obtain advice from a tax expert if you think you may have a large capital gains tax liability or you are thinking of selling an asset which you think will generate a capital gains tax liability.

FACTOR 4: Capital gains tax is not a factor when assets are passed on when someone dies (although inheritance tax may come into the equation), when gifts are made between spouses and gifts to charity.

Q Indexation allowance and taper relief are designed to reduce your capital gains tax liability. Are there any other ways to reduce this tax burden?

A There are some allowable expenses you can deduct in calculating the capital gain on an asset. They include acquisition costs, costs incurred in improving an asset and disposal costs. These can all reduce your capital gains tax bill as the following example shows.

EXAMPLE: Mhairi bought a second home in July 1987 for £60,000. When she bought the home, she incurred acquisition costs of £1,600 (a mix of legal fees, stamp duty and surveyors' fees). She then paid for improvements to the home, costing £5,500 in

September 1988. When she sold the house in May 2001 for £130,000, she incurred disposal costs of £2,300 (payments to estate agents and legal fees).

STEP ONE: Establish the sale value of Mhairi's second home.
    Sale value is £130,000.
STEP TWO: Find out the amount Mhairi paid for the second home.
    She paid £60,000.
STEP THREE: Calculate the gross capital gain/loss (STEP ONE – STEP TWO).
    Mhairi has a gross capital gain of £70,000 (£130,000 minus £60,000).
STEP FOUR: Total the allowable expenses.
    Mhairi has incurred allowable expenses of £9,400 (£1,600 plus £5,500 plus £2,300).
STEP FIVE: Calculate the net chargeable gain.
    Mhairi has a net chargeable gain of £60,600 (£70,000 minus £9,400).
STEP SIX: Calculate any indexation allowance.

Mhairi can claim indexation allowance to remove some of the capital gain. This only applies to costs incurred between April 1, 1982 and March 31, 1998.

    Indexation can be applied to the cost of the home (£60,000), acquisition costs (£1,600) and improvement costs (£5,500). It cannot be applied to the disposal costs because these were incurred in May 2001 – after the March 31, 1998 cut-off for indexation allowance.

    Mhairi's indexation allowance is as follows:
    £61,600 x 0.597 (indexation factor for July 1987).
    £5,500 x 0.5 (indexation factor for September 1988).
    The indexation allowance comes to £39,525.20 – see appendix for indexation factors.
STEP SEVEN: Reduce the net chargeable gain by the indexation allowance.
    Mhairi now has a net chargeable gain of £21,074.80 (£60,600

minus £39,525.20). This is above the £7,500 capital gains tax allowance for the tax year ending April 5, 2002 so she will have to pay capital gains tax – but considerably less than if the allowable expenses had not been taken into consideration.

STEP EIGHT: Assess Mhairi's entitlement to taper relief. Taper relief reduces any chargeable gain based on how long an asset has been held after April 5, 1998. Mhairi held her second home for three complete tax years. She also qualifies for one bonus year given she owned her home before March 17, 1998 and sold it after April 6, 1998. This means she is eligible for taper relief applying to assets held for four complete tax years. This is 10% – see appendix.

Mhairi's taper relief is 10% of the chargeable gain (£21,074.80). This works out at £2,107.48.

Mhairi's net tapered gain is therefore £18,967.32 (£21,074.80 minus £2,107.48).

STEP NINE: Calculate Mhairi's liability to capital gains tax.

Mhairi has a capital gains tax allowance for the tax year ending April 5, 2002 of £7,500.

This means her capital gains liable for taxation are £11,467.32 (£18,967.32 minus £7,500).

STEP TEN: Calculate Mhairi's capital gains tax bill.

Mhairi's capital gains of £11,467.32 are added to her taxable income for the year (ending April 5, 2002) and taxed as if it was savings income.

So assuming Mhairi has taxable income of £31,000, all the capital gain would be taxed at 40%. She would therefore pay tax of £4,587.

Q The indexation allowance applies to assets held between April 1, 1982 and March 31, 1998. What about assets held before this date?

A If you owned an asset on or before March 31, 1982, only the gain since that date is liable to capital gains tax. Any gain made before April 1, 1982 is tax-free. The initial value for capital gains tax purposes is usually assumed to be the market value on March 31, 1982. Expenses incurred on or before that date cannot be deducted for capital gains tax purposes.

However, it is possible that use of the March 31, 1982 value will artificially inflate your gain or loss. For example, you may have bought an asset prior to March 31, 1982 which then fell in value up to March 31, 1982 but then rose in value. By using the March 31, 1982 market value, you will be increasing your liability to capital gains tax.

As a result of this, the Revenue allows you to work out two figures for gains or losses incurred on assets held prior to April 1, 1982 – (1) the chargeable gain using the market value on March 31, 1982 but ignoring any costs incurred on or before that date; and (2) the actual gain using the original cost you paid for it and allowing for allowable expenses incurred on or before March 31, 1982.

If both (1) and (2) produce a gain, the smaller gain is used to calculate your capital gains tax bill.

If both (1) and (2) produce a loss, the smaller loss is allowable.

If (1) and (2) produce a gain and a loss or vice versa, the disposal is assumed to produce no gain or loss.

This calculation is called the 'kink' test.

EXAMPLE: Jane bought a second house in June 1978 for £15,200. She spent £1,000 on improvements a year later in June 1979. The home's value on March 31, 1982 was £13,000. She eventually sold the home for £110,000 in May 2001.

Under (1), the chargeable gain is £97,000 (£110,000 minus £13,000).

Under (2), the chargeable gain is £93,800 (£110,000 minus £15,200 minus £1,000).

Given (2) produces the smaller capital gain, this will be used to calculate Jane's capital gains tax bill.

Jane's capital gains tax is then calculated as follows:
STEP ONE: Calculate any indexation allowance.

Jane can claim indexation allowance to remove some of the capital gain. Indexation can be applied to the cost of the home (£15,200) and the improvement costs of £1,000. It is assumed to apply from March 31, 1982.

Jane's indexation allowance is as follows:

£16,200 x 1.047 (indexation factor for March 1982).

The indexation allowance comes to £16,961.40 – see appendix for indexation factors.

STEP TWO: Reduce the chargeable gain by the indexation allowance.

Jane now has a net chargeable gain of £76,838.60 (£93,800 minus £16,961.40). This is above the £7,500 capital gains tax allowance for the tax year ending April 5, 2002 so she will have to pay capital gains tax.

STEP THREE: Assess Jane's entitlement to taper relief. Taper relief reduces any chargeable gain based on how long an asset has been held after April 5, 1998. Jane held her home for three complete tax years. She also qualifies for one bonus year given she owned her home before March 17, 1998 and sold it after April 6, 1998. This means she is eligible for taper relief applying to assets held for four complete tax years. This is 10% – see appendix.

Jane's taper relief is 10% of the chargeable gain (£76,838.60). This works out at £7,683.86.

Jane's net tapered gain is therefore £69,154.74 (£76,838.60 minus £7,683.86).

STEP FOUR: Calculate Jane's liability to capital gains tax.

Jane has a capital gains tax allowance for the tax year ending April 5, 2002 of £7,500.

This means her capital gains liable for taxation are £61,654.74 (£69,154.74 minus £7,500).

STEP FIVE: Calculate Jane's capital gains tax bill.

Jane's capital gains of £61,654.74 are added to her taxable income for the year (ending April 5, 2002) and taxed as if it was savings income.

So assuming Jane has taxable income of £40,000, all the capital gain would be taxed at 40%. She would therefore pay tax of £24,661.90.

Q So for assets held on or before March 31, 1982, I have to apply the so-called kink test?

A No, in a fit of kindness, the Revenue does allow you to make a so-called 'rebasing election'. This means all assets owned on or before March 31, 1982 will be based on their market value at March 31, 1982. Once you have made such an election, there is no turning back. If Jane above had made this election, her final capital gains tax bill would have worked out as follows:

Jane's rebased chargeable gain is £97,000 (£110,000, the sale price, minus £13,000 – the market value at March 31, 1982). The improvement costs are ignored because they were incurred before March 31, 1982.

Jane's capital gains tax is then calculated as follows:

STEP ONE: Calculate any indexation allowance.

Jane can claim indexation allowance to remove some of the capital gain. Indexation can be applied to the market value of the home (£13,000) on March 31, 1982.

Jane's indexation allowance is as follows:

£13,000 x 1.047 (indexation factor for March 1982).

The indexation allowance comes to £13,611 – see appendix for indexation factors.

STEP TWO: Reduce the chargeable gain by the indexation allowance.

Jane now has a net chargeable gain of £83,389 (£97,000 minus £13,611). This is above the £7,500 capital gains tax allowance for the tax year ending April 5, 2002 so she will have to pay capital gains tax.

STEP THREE: Assess Jane's entitlement to taper relief. Taper relief reduces any chargeable gain based on how long an asset has been held after April 5, 1998. Jane held her home for three complete tax years. She also qualifies for one bonus year given she owned her home before March 17, 1998 and sold it after April 6, 1998. This means she is eligible for taper relief applying to assets held for three complete tax years. This is 10% (see appendix).

Jane's taper relief is 10% of the chargeable gain (£83,389). This works out at £98,338.90.

Jane's net tapered gain is therefore £75,050.10 (£83,389 minus £8,338.90).

STEP FOUR: Calculate Jane's liability to capital gains tax.

Jane has a capital gains tax allowance for the tax year ending April 5, 2002 of £7,500.

This means her capital gains liable for taxation are £67,550.10 (£75,050.10 minus £7,500).

STEP FIVE: Calculate Jane's capital gains tax bill.

Jane's capital gains of £67,550.10 are added to her taxable income for the year (ending April 5, 2002) and taxed as if it was savings income.

So assuming Jane has taxable income of £40,000, all the capital gain would be taxed at 40%. She would therefore pay tax of £27,020.04.

In this instance, Jane's rebasing election would actually have worked against her because she would have ended up paying more capital gains tax than she would have done if she had decided to apply the 'kink' test. This drills home the point that in assessing your liability to capital gains tax, it is best to obtain professional taxation advice.

Q What happens if I sell shares or holdings in unit trusts, for example, which I bought in batches over a period of time? How do I go about calculating my capital gains tax liability?

A Like anything to do with capital gains tax, it's not easy. The Revenue matches sales with purchases in the following order:

FIRST: Shares/units acquired on the same day.

SECOND: Shares acquired at any time in the next 30 days. This has been introduced to stop the practice of so-called 'bed and breakfasting' where shares were sold towards the end of the tax year to soak up any unused tax-free capital gains tax allowance and then bought back early in the new tax year.

THIRD: Shares acquired before the day of sale and after April 5, 1998 with the most recent purchases counting first.

FOURTH: Shares acquired between April 6, 1982 and April 5, 1998. Shares bought during this period qualify for indexation allowance and taper relief. Shares bought during this period are treated as one asset when working out gains or losses (see example). FIFTH: Shares purchased between April 6, 1965 and April 5, 1982. As with other assets, shares bought during this period can have gains based on their market value on March 31, 1982 or their cost at the time of purchase.

SIXTH: Shares acquired on or before April 5, 1965. These are deemed to be the last shares to be sold with the last to be bought prior to April 5, 1965 being assumed the first to be offloaded. You can elect for these shares to have gains based on their market value on March 31, 1982. This will invariably make sense because it will bump up your initial cost for capital gains tax purposes, thereby reducing your capital gains liability.

EXAMPLE 1: Millicent bought 3,000 shares in Boing Plc in May 1984 at a cost of £3,000. In May 1986, she bought another 2,000 shares in the same company at a cost of £12,000. She sold 1,500 shares in May 2001 for £150,000.

STEP ONE: Given all of Millicent's shares were bought between April 6, 1982 and April 5, 1998, it is necessary to treat all her shares as a single asset.

STEP TWO: Calculate the average cost.

Millicent paid £15,000 for 5,000 shares. The average cost per share is £3.

STEP THREE: Calculate the average indexation allowance.

Indexation factor for Millicent's 3,000 shares bought for £3,000 in May 1984 is 0.828.

The indexation allowance is therefore £2,484 (£3,000 x 0.828).

Indexation factor for Millicent's 2,000 shares bought for £12,000 in May 1986 is 0.662.

The indexation allowance is therefore £7,944 (£12,000 x 0.662).

Millicent's total indexation allowance on her 5,000 shares is £10,428 (£2,484 + £7,944).

Average indexation allowance for each of Millicent's 5,000 shares is £2.09 (£10,428 divided by 5,000).

STEP FOUR: Calculate Millicent's capital gains tax bill on the sale of 1,500 shares.

Initial cost of Millicent's 1,500 shares is £4,500 (1,500 x £3).

Indexation allowance is £3,135 (1,500 x £2.09).

Millicent's gross capital gain is £145,500 (£150,000 minus £4,500).

Millicent's net chargeable gain after indexation is £142,365 (£145,500 minus £3,135).

Millicent is also entitled to taper relief. Taper relief reduces any chargeable gain based on how long an asset has been held after April 5, 1998. She has held her shares for three complete tax years. She also qualifies for one bonus year given she owned her shares before March 17, 1998 and sold them after April 6, 1998. This means she is eligible for taper relief applying to assets held for four complete tax years. This is 10% (see appendix).

Millicent's taper relief is 10% of the chargeable gain (£142,365). This works out at £14,236.50.

Millicent's tapered gain is therefore £128,128.50 (£142,365 minus £14,236.50).

Millicent has a capital gains tax allowance for the tax year ending April 5, 2002 of £7,500.

This means her capital gains liable for taxation are £120,628.50 (£128,128.50 minus £7,500).

Millicent's capital gains of £120,628.50 are added to her taxable income for the year (ending April 5, 2002) and taxed as if it was savings income.

So assuming Millicent has taxable income of £100,000, all the capital gain would be taxed at 40%. She would therefore pay tax of £48,251.40.

EXAMPLE 2: Millicent bought 3,000 shares in Boing Plc in May 1979 at a cost of £3,000. In May 1986, she bought another 2,000 shares in the same company at a cost of £12,000. She sold 2,500 shares in May 2001 for £50,000. Let's assume that the market value of Millicent's 3,000 shares bought in May 1979 was £6,000 on March 31, 1982 and that she has made a rebasing election.

STEP ONE: Millicent first has to match disposals with acquisitions.

2,000 shares for disposal can be matched with shares bought in May 1986 (that is, acquired between April 6, 1982 and April 5, 1998).

500 shares for disposal can be matched with 500 of the 3,000 shares bought in May 1979 (that is, acquired between April 6, 1965 and April 5, 1982).

STEP TWO: Calculation of gain on 2,000 shares bought in May 1986.

Indexation factor for May 1986 is 0.662.

Indexation allowance is £7,944 (£12,000 x 0.662).

STEP THREE: Calculation of gain on 500 shares bought in May 1979.

Market value of 3,000 shares on March 31, 1982 is £6,000.

Market value per share is £2.

Market value of 500 shares is therefore £1,000.

Indexation factor for March 1982 is 1.047 (see appendix).

Indexation allowance is £1,047 (£1,000 x 1.047).

STEP FOUR: Calculate Millicent's capital gains tax bill on the sale of 2,500 shares.

Initial cost of Millicent's 2,500 shares is £13,000 (£12,000 + £1,000).

Indexation allowance is £8,991 (£1,047 + £7,944).

Millicent's gross capital gain is £137,000 (£150,000 minus £13,000).

Millicent's net chargeable gain after indexation is £128,009 (£137,000 minus £8,991).

Millicent is also entitled to taper relief. Taper relief reduces any chargeable gain based on how long an asset has been held after April 5, 1998. She has held her shares for three complete tax years. She also qualifies for one bonus year given she owned her shares before March 17, 1998 and sold them after April 6, 1998. This means she is eligible for taper relief applying to assets held for four complete tax years. This is 10% (see appendix).

Millicent's taper relief is 10% of the chargeable gain (£128,009). This works out at £12,800.90.

Millicent's tapered gain is therefore £115,208.10 (£128,009

minus £12,800.90).

Millicent has a capital gains tax allowance for the tax year ending April 5, 2002 of £7,500.

This means her capital gains liable for taxation are £107,708.10 (£115,208.10 minus £7,500).

Millicent's capital gains of £107,708.10 are added to her taxable income for the year (ending April 5, 2002) and taxed as if it was savings income.

So assuming Millicent has taxable income of £100,000, all the capital gain would be taxed at 40%. She would therefore pay tax of £43,083.24.

Q What is the capital gains tax position regarding share rights issues?

A The extra shares are allocated to the shares they belong to. For example, if you bought 50 shares in Xtreme Plc in May 1984 and the same number in July 1998, the rights issue is split between the shares acquired after April 5, 1998 (July 1998) and those acquired between April 6, 1982 and April 5, 1998 (May 1984). Taper relief on the new shares is calculated from the time the shares they relate to were acquired.

Q What is the position regarding personal possessions and capital gains tax?

A As already mentioned in FACTOR 1, personal possessions which are sold for less than £6,000 escape the capital gains tax net. Personal possessions are often referred to as chattels and typically include furniture, paintings and silverware. They do not include assets with a life less than 50 years such as television and cars.

Q What happens if a chattel or personal possession is sold for more than £6,000?

A The taxable gain is restricted to 5/3 of the surplus over £6,000.

EXAMPLE: Vivian bought a painting for £2,500 and sold it for £8,000.

The sale price is above £6,000, so the sale is not tax-free.

The capital gain on the sale of the chattel is £5,500.

However, for capital gains tax purposes, the gain cannot be more than 5/3 of the surplus over £6,000.

In Vivian's case, the surplus is £2,000 and the gain liable to capital gains tax is £3,333.33.

Q What happens if a chattel is sold at a loss?

A You can claim a loss for capital gains tax purposes but the loss is calculated as if you achieved £6,000 from the sale of the possession.

EXAMPLE: Vivian bought a painting for £11,000 and then was forced to sell it at a rock-bottom price of £4,000.

The capital loss on the sale of the chattel is £7,000.

However, for capital gains tax purposes, the sale price is assumed to be £6,000.

Vivian's capital loss for capital gains tax purposes is therefore £5,000.

Dos and Don'ts

- **DO** ensure you don't hand over more in capital gains tax than you should do. Ensure you claim all your allowable expenses, indexation allowance and taper relief. Use your annual capital gains tax allowance and don't forget about losses which you can offset against gains.

- **DO** remember that husbands and wives each have an annual capital gains tax allowance. Use them both.

- **DO** keep full records of assets you acquire which may fall into the capital gains tax net. This includes receipts for allowable expenses.

- **DO** remember that if a married couple dispose of assets to each other, this is ignored for the purposes of capital gains tax.

- **DO** get taxation help if you are worried about capital gains on the proceeds from a monthly savings scheme set up with a unit trust or investment trust company. The calculation of gains can prove a minefield although the Revenue does allow a simplified method of calculation to be used in some circumstances.

- **DO** be aware that when insurance companies and building societies convert to a plc, the proceeds from these conversions may result in a potential capital gains tax liability. The converting mutual society should inform you of the taxation implications of any windfall (cash or shares) you receive.

- **DO** get hold of the various Inland Revenue leaflets on capital gains tax. They are useful and are available from your local tax office.

- **DON'T** panic if you own shares in a company which is then taken over. This has no impact on capital gains tax although if as a result of the takeover you receive part cash, this will count as a disposal for capital gains tax purposes.

Did you know?

- **DID** you know that if you gift an asset to a charity, it will fall outside the capital gains tax net? As a result, if you are thinking of gifting an asset which is showing a loss, it might make more sense to sell the asset and then give the proceeds to the charity.

  EXAMPLE: Joan wants to gift a second property she owns to a charity for the homeless. The house is run down and as a result, she stands to lose £20,000 if it is sold. Joan also owns shares with chargeable gains of £25,000. If she gifts the home, the transaction falls outside of the capital gains tax regime. She would then still be liable for the gains on the shares when she came to sell them. An alternative strategy would be to sell the home, thereby creating an allowable loss for capital gains tax purposes. This loss could then be used to offset gains from selling the shares, thereby minimising her overall liability to capital gains tax. The money she obtained from the sale of the home could then be gifted directly to the charity.

- **DID** you know that any capital gains tax for the tax year ending April 5, 2002 has to be paid by the end of January 2003?

- **DID** you know that husbands and wives are treated as two separate individuals for tax purposes? This means they have separate tax-free allowances and each is responsible for paying their own capital gains tax bills. If assets are held jointly by a married couple, capital gains are split on a 50:50 basis. The only exception to this rule is where a married couple have already informed their tax office that they want to hold assets on an unequal basis. In this instance, capital gains are divided according to the agreed asset split.

- **DID** you know that where assets are held in trust, the rate of capital gains tax paid by trustees is 34%? Trusts are entitled to a capital gains tax allowance which for most is half the amount available for individuals. So, for the tax year ending April 5, 2002, the first £3,600 of net chargeable gains are free of tax for a trust. There are exceptions to this rule.

- **DID** you know that taper relief is also available on the disposal of business assets?

- **DID** you know that capital gains tax can be payable when shares acquired through an employee share scheme are sold? Taper relief is available on such sales although it is possible to escape capital gains tax altogether by instead transferring such shares into a tax-free Isa. Inland Revenue help sheet IR287 ('Employee share schemes and capital gains tax') provides full details.

- **DID** you know that if you pay for new shares through cash instalments, indexation allowance and taper relief on the full purchase price runs from the date when the shares were acquired ONLY if all the instalments are paid within a year. The exception is shares bought in a privatised company where payments were made in instalments. Here, indexation and taper relief runs from the date you acquired the shares.

- **DID** you know that you can defer paying capital gains tax bills by investing in the ordinary shares of unquoted companies and some companies listed on the Alternative Investment Market? Making investments in Enterprise Investment Schemes and Venture Capital Trusts also enables you to do this.

Inheritance tax

Q What is inheritance tax?

A It is primarily a tax on what you leave when you die.

Q How is it applied?

A It is charged at a hefty rate of 40% of the value of your estate over £242,000 (on deaths in the tax year ending April 5, 2002). Your estate encompasses your home, possessions, investments and any payments paid out by life insurance policies (unless they are written under trust). Debts such as outstanding mortages and funeral expenses are deducted from the total to find the value of your estate.

Q Are there any exemptions?

A Yes, there are a number. The main ones are: anything you leave to your husband or wife; anything left to a UK charity; and anything left to certain national institutions such as the National

Trust, National Gallery and British Museum (also to their Scottish, Welsh and Nothern Ireland counterparts). These bequests and legacies are deducted from the value of your estate before the tax bill for inheritance tax is calculated.

Q Are there any sums that need to be added to the estate before inheritance tax is calculated?

A Yes, if you made any gifts to people in the seven years before your death which are not exempt, these must be added to the value of your estate. These gifts are commonly referred to as 'potentially exempt transfers' (PETs). If inheritance tax is payable on a gift made before your death, it must be paid by the person you made the gift to. They may in turn be able to reduce the amount payable in tax by claiming tapering relief. This is available on gifts where the time between the gift being made and death was more than three years. Between three and four years, 80% of inheritance tax is payable; between four and five, 60% is payable; between 5 and 6, 40% is payable and between 6 and 7, 20% is payable. One further point: the proceeds of any life insurance policies not written in trust must be included in any inheritance tax calculation.

EXAMPLE 1: Sandra died in July 2001 leaving an estate worth £330,000. In June 1996, she made a taxable gift of £18,000 to grandchild Matthew. In August 1998, she made another taxable gift to grandchild Mark of £256,000.

Sandra's first gift of £12,000 (£18,000 minus the £3,000 gift allowance for both tax years 1995/6 and 1996/7 as per page 297) to Matthew is below the £242,000 threshold for inheritance tax when she died in July 2001. There is no tax to pay.

Sandra's second gift (minus a further £6,000 of gift allowances) to Mark took her taxable gifts to £262,000. This is above the £242,000 threshold. Inheritance tax is payable.

The tax payable is 40% of £20,000 (£262,000 minus £242,000) which comes to £8,000. Mark must pay this tax. Given he has had the gift for less than three years, there is no tapering relief and so he must pay the full £8,000.

The amount of Sandra's estate liable for inheritance tax is £350,000 (£330,000 + £12,000 + £250,000 minus £242,000).

Inheritance tax payable is £140,000 (40% of £350,000). Matthew's share is £0, Mark's share is £8,000 while the balance of £132,000 must be paid out of Sandra's estate.

EXAMPLE 2: Here the situation is the same as in EXAMPLE 1 but this time Mark received his taxable gift in August 1996.

In this instance, Mark is able to claim tapering relief on account of the fact that the time between the gift being made and Sandra's death was more than four years. The percentage of inheritance tax payable is thus 60%.

Mark must therefore pay £4,800 (60 per cent of £8,000)

Inheritance tax payable is £140,000 (40% of £350,000). Matthew's share is £0, Mark's share is £8,000 (tapered down to £4,800) while the balance of £132,000 must be paid out of Sandra's estate.

EXAMPLE 3: Here the situation is the same as in EXAMPLE 1 but this time in June 1996, she made a taxable gift of £256,000 to grandchild Matthew. In August 1998, she made another taxable gift to grandchild Mark of £18,000.

Sandra's first gift of £250,000 (net of annual gift allowances as per page 297) to Matthew is above the £242,000 threshold for inheritance tax when she died in July 2001. Inheritance tax is payable on the gift.

The tax payable is 40% of £8,000 (£250,000 − £242,000) which comes to £3,200.

Matthew has had the gift for more than five years so he is eligible for tapering relief.

Matthew must only pay 40% of the inheritance tax payable (£3,200) which comes to £1,280.

Sandra's second gift to Mark (again, net of £6,000 of allowances) took her taxable gifts to £262,000. His gift was made above the £242,000 threshold. Inheritance tax is again payable.

The tax payable is 40% of £12,000 which comes to £4,800.

Mark must pay this tax. Given he has had the gift for less than three years, there is no tapering relief and so he must pay the full £4,800.

The amount of Sandra's estate liable for inheritance tax is £350,000 (£330,000 + £250,000 + £12,000 minus £242,000).

Inheritance tax payable is £140,000 (40% of £350,000).

Matthew's share is £3,200 (tapered down to £1,280), Mark's share is £4,800 and the balance of £132,000 must be paid out of Sandra's estate.

Q Fine, I now know how inheritance tax is levied. Is it simply a case of waiting for the grim reaper and letting the taxman have his slice?

A Not at all. There are a number of steps you can take to ensure you reduce your estate's liability to inheritance tax.

STEP ONE: MAKE A WILL. By making a will, it forces you to think about what you own and how you want your estate to be disposed of after you die.

STEP TWO: MAKE GIFTS. By making gifts during your lifetime, you can minimise the inheritance tax payable on your estate upon your death.

Gifts fall into two camps:

TAX-FREE GIFTS. These are immediately exempt from the inheritance tax net. They include:

1. Small gifts worth up to £250 to any number of people in any tax year. An individual gift cannot exceed £250.
2. Gifts made out of your normal income. These gifts must come out of your normal after-tax income and not be made from your capital. After paying for the gift, you must have enough income left to maintain your normal standard of living.
3. Gifts made on marriage. Parents are allowed to give £5,000 to their children when they get married – each parent being allowed to make a separate gift. Grandparents are also allowed to give £2,500 each while any other relative or friend can give £1,000. The gift must be made before the

wedding day.

4. Gifts for the maintenance of your family including, for example, to children under 18 or still in further education.

5. Gifts to UK charities, recognised political parties and certain national institutions (as already mentioned).

6. Gifts between husband and wife.

7. Gifts of up to £3,000 in total to anyone. If you don't use all of the £3,000 exemption in one tax year, you are able to carry forward the unused part to the next tax year only. But the current tax year's exemption must be used first.

POTENTIALLY EXEMPT TRANSFERS. If you make gifts other than those available under the various tax-free headings, they fall out of the inheritance tax reckoning if you live for more than seven years after making them. If you die before seven years, they are taken into consideration when computing the inheritance tax bill on your estate. However, as we have already shown, tax is only payable on gifts if they exceed the nil-rate band of £242,000 and then tapering relief is available. Tax on such gifts is paid by the recipient of the gift (See EXAMPLES 1 to 3 previously).

STEP THREE: CONSIDER TAKING OUT AN INSURANCE POLICY. It is possible to take out insurance in order to provide the means to pay a future inheritance tax bill. The idea is that the policy is written in trust, thereby ensuring the proceeds fall outside your estate when you die. The proceeds instead go directly to the beneficiary of the trust. If you pay the policy premiums out of your normal expenditure out of income, they can be treated as tax-free lifetime gifts.

STEP FOUR: CONSIDER OWNING YOUR HOME ON A 'TENANTS IN COMMON BASIS'. Most couples own their home on a joint tenancy basis which means a spouse's half of the property is automatically passed on to the other when they die. This transfer is free of inheritance tax but it means the surviving spouse's estate is enlarged, making it more likely to be subject to inheritance tax in the future.

An alternative is to hold the home on a 'tenants in common' basis. Here, each partner owns a discrete 50% share of the property which they can pass on as they wish on death. Typically, a spouse will bequeath half of their half-share in the property to the children. By doing this, the surviving spouse's estate is reduced by the value of the property bequeathed while leaving the widow or widower to live in the home for the rest of their life.

Although ownership of a home on a tenants in common basis can make good sense for inheritance tax purposes, it should not be entered into lightly. Take professional advice.

STEP FIVE: USE TRUSTS. It is possible to use trusts in order to escape or minimise inheritance tax. The idea is that assets are put into trust for the benefit of children or grandchildren, thereby reducing your assets liable for inheritance tax. Again, the use of trusts should only be considered after taking expert advice.

Dos and Don'ts

- **DO** make a will. If you die without making a will, your estate will be divided up according to pre-defined rules. The rules as they apply to England and Wales are as follows:

  IF YOU ARE MARRIED WITH CHILDREN. If your estate is worth more than £125,000, your spouse gets all the personal effects, the first £125,000 and a 'life interest' (income but not the capital) in half the rest. The children, assuming they survive to age 18, get the balance in equal shares and the remainder of your estate when your spouse dies. If your children died before you, their children step into their shoes.

  If your estate is worth less than £125,000, everything goes to your spouse.

  IF YOU ARE MARRIED WITHOUT CHILDREN. Your spouse gets the personal belongings, the first £200,000 and half the balance. The rest goes to relatives in a pecking order which starts with your parents, moves on to your brothers and sisters (if your parents are dead), moves on to your nieces or nephews (if your brothers and sisters are dead) and so on. If your parents are dead and you have no brothers and sisters, your spouse receives everything.

IF YOU ARE SINGLE. Here the estate goes to your children. If you have no children, your estate goes to your parents. If they are dead, it goes to your brothers and sisters. If they are dead, it goes to their children. If you have no brothers or sisters, it goes to your grandparents. If they are dead, it goes to your uncles and aunts or their children or children's children. If you have no living relatives within these definitions, your estate goes to the Crown.

IF YOU ARE LIVING WITH SOMEONE. Here your partner has no rights under the laws of intestacy. However, under the Inheritance Act, your partner has similar rights to spouses as long as they lived with you as common law man or wife for at least two years prior to death.

In Scotland, the intestacy laws are as follows:

If you are married, your surviving spouse is entitled to the first £130,000 worth of the family home and the first £22,000 of the home's fixtures and fittings. If you have no children, the spouse is also entitled to the first £58,000 of assets (such as shares and savings accounts). If you have children, the spouse is restricted to the first £35,000 of assets. These are commonly referred to as 'prior rights'.

Irrespective of whether you leave a will in Scotland, spouses and children are entitled to so-called 'legal' rights. This means that if you have no children, your spouse is entitled to half of your movable estate (everything except land and buildings). If you have a spouse and children, your spouse's legal rights are one-third of the movable estate and your children's are also a third – shared between them. If you have children but no spouse, your children are entitled to half the movable estate.

Children and spouses have the option to exercise this legal right. If they don't, then the estate is divided in accordance with the terms of the will.

If you are single without children, the estate passes to your brothers and sisters, or their children; if none, to parents or grandparents – and down the family line until some relative is found. If there is no one, the estate passes to the Crown.

Q If an estate is liable for inheritance tax, when must the tax be paid?

A It is due six months after the end of the month in which the death occurred. Interest is charged if this deadline is missed.

Dos and Don'ts

- **DO** remember that if you make a will, you will have to appoint executors. These people, usually relatives, will deal with your estate and ensure your wishes are carried out properly. Executors can be beneficiaries of a will. You can also appoint a professional executor such as a solicitor with their fees paid for out of your estate.

- **DO** ensure your will is signed by yourself and witnessed by two people who will not be beneficiaries, nor their spouses.

- **DO** ensure your will is stored safely and that your executors are aware of where it is, together with any documents needed to aid the carrying out of the will.

- **DO** ensure that your will states that it revokes all others.

- **DO** take advantage of the various tax-free gifts you can make – provided you don't leave yourself financially embarrassed.

- **DON'T** get too uptight about inheritance tax. Provided you plan properly, it is possible to escape the inheritance tax net. Indeed, only one in 45 estates fall into the inheritance tax net.

- **DON'T** give away money simply to avoid inheritance tax at any cost. There is little point leaving yourself in financial straits as a result of gifting away as much of your estate as possible.

- **DON'T** delay making larger gifts if you have the financial resource to do so. The earlier you make them, the greater the chance you will have of ensuring the gift is exempt from inheritance tax. Remember, such larger gifts escape inheritance tax if you survive seven years after making the gift.

Did you know?

- **DID** you know that at least half the adults in the UK have yet to make a will? This means they run the risk of dying 'intestate'. If you die intestate, your estate is divided up according to the rules of intestacy as opposed to your wishes. This could impact adversely on the inheritance tax bill your estate may end picking up.

- **DID** you know that there are various ways to make a will? You can go to a specialist agency (some of which are run by the larger charities) or even do it yourself by obtaining a will-writing kit. However, for most people it still makes sense to use a solicitor, especially if your affairs may be somewhat complex.

- **DID** you know that in England and Wales, but not in Scotland, a will is automatically invalidated if you remarry or marry?

- **DID** you know that you can make alterations to a will by adding a so-called 'codicil' – a supplement? Like your original will, this must be witnessed. If the changes you make are extensive, it makes more sense to make a new will altogether.

- **DID** you know that it is possible for a deed of variation to be executed up to two years after your death? This deed will alter the distribution of assets laid down in your will. It has to be signed by all beneficiaries who will lose out from the variation being implemented and is generally used to avoid or reduce inheritance tax.

- **DID** you know that you can't give something away and then keep rights over it? So, for example, you can't give your home to your children on the condition that you can go on living in it until your death. This is deemed to be a 'gift with reservation' and would be recognised for inheritance tax purposes. In other words, its value would be added to your estate when you died.

Top tax savings tips

IT'S not difficult to save tax. Here is a list of top tips, many of which are based on the previous five sections. Even if you only act on a handful of those listed, you will be well on the way to improving your personal finance affairs:

- **TIP ONE:** Keep proper tax records, including your working papers and relevant documents such as savings certificates. Remember, you can be fined by the taxman for not keeping proper records.

- **TIP TWO:** Don't be late sending in your tax return. You risk a fine for being late.

- **TIP THREE:** Don't forget that you can send in your tax return over the Internet, thereby getting £10 knocked off your bill.

- **TIP FOUR:** Don't be frightened to check any documents that the taxman sends you such as a notice of coding or a tax calculation. Remember, taxmen do make mistakes.

- **TIP FIVE:** Don't sit on your hands if you think you are being asked to pay too much tax on account. Ask to pay less.

- **TIP SIX:** If you're feeling charitable, be tax-efficient. Consider payroll gifting or Gift Aid.

- **TIP SEVEN:** If you are married, ensure your finances are organised so that investment income is paid to the partner who pays less tax.

- **TIP EIGHT:** Keep good records of your business miles so you can substantiate your claims.

- **TIP NINE:** Do remember that from April 2002 the tax you pay on your company car will depend on its carbon dioxide emissions.

- **TIP TEN:** The government provides lots of tax incentives for you to contribute to a pension. Take advantage.

- **TIP ELEVEN:** If you are a non-taxpayer, do ensure you receive interest from your savings free of tax.

- **TIP TWELVE:** If you are a taxpayer, do take advantage of the various tax-free savings schemes available such as Isas.

- **TIP THIRTEEN:** If you let out a room, do remember that you can take £4,250 of gross rent a year tax-free.

- **TIP FOURTEEN:** Do try to use your annual capital gains tax allowances.

- **TIP FIFTEEN:** If you own valuables such as antiques, keep careful records of what they cost you to buy and maintain. Such expenses may help reduce any capital gains tax bill payable when you come to sell them.

- **TIP SIXTEEN:** Make a will.

- **TIP SEVENTEEN:** Don't forget that you can make a nunber of gifts which will reduce any future liability to inheritance tax.

So what now?

- **TAX** is an intimidating subject. This chapter has only scratched at the surface of an area of personal finance which is too complex by far. As mentioned throughout the chapter, the Revenue has produced a breathtaking number of leaflets on you and tax, covering all areas of personal finance. It would pay you to invest in those booklets which cover the taxation areas you are most interested in. Get down to your local tax office as soon as possible or visit the Revenue's useful website: www.inlandrevenue.gov.uk.

CHAPTER **7**

Pensions

RETIREMENT

'The ugliest word in the language.'

Ernest Hemingway

SAVING for retirement may not seem appealing in your twenties and thirties when maybe you are starting a family and buying your first home, but it can be one of the best financial moves you will ever make. Today, it is a sad fact of life that too many people retire to a life of near poverty relying upon an inadequate state pension and little else besides. In a nutshell, they have failed to take good financial care of themselves.

However, your retirement should not – and does not have to – be a time of financial hardship. By squirrelling away small sums of money while you are working, you can ensure that your retirement years are money-worry free, and you can do all those things you never had a chance to do during your working life – such as going on that world cruise or visiting long-lost relatives on the other side of the globe.

The best way to save for retirement is through a pension set up by your employer or one which you have taken out off your own back – a stakeholder or personal pension for example. This is because the government provides generous tax breaks to those people who save through these investment vehicles. It does this primarily because it does not want people to be a burden on the state in retirement.

Unfortunately, the pensions market is extremely complicated, offering a range of schemes dependent upon whether you are employed or self-employed. Stakeholder pensions were thrown into the pensions melting pot in April 2001, making the market even more confusing.

As a result, while buying a pension makes great sense, you should not leap into the first plan that hits your personal radar screen. You should only make pension provision after careful consideration and preferably after obtaining pensions advice from an independent financial adviser.

This chapter is divided into three key parts – state pensions, company pensions, personal pensions and stakeholder pensions.

State pensions

Q I'm OK – I've worked all my life and paid my National Insurance contributions on the nail. Surely, the state will provide me with a pension which will allow me to enjoy financial security during my retirement?

A Unfortunately, the answer is no. The basic state pension is currently just £72.50 a week (year to April 5, 2002) or £3,770 a year. For a married couple, the basic pension is £115.90 a week (year to April 5, 2002) or £6,026.80 a year. These payments are insufficient on their own to ensure you are financially secure in retirement – a fact recognised by the government, which has now introduced a so-called minimum income guarantee.

Furthermore, not everybody is eligible for a full state pension so don't think you have an automatic right to a state pension. Only those who have paid enough National Insurance contributions during their working life will qualify. To receive the full basic pension, you will have to pay National Insurance contributions for at least 90% of the tax years in your so-called 'working life'. If you pay contributions for less than a quarter of your working life, then there is a strong possibility that you will get no basic state pension whatsoever.

Q What is meant by my working life?

A It is the tax years from the time you reach 16 through to the complete tax year before you reach state pension age. Men are deemed to have a working life of 49 years while a woman's working life may range from 44 to 49 years. This is because men are eligible to receive a state pension when they reach the age of 65. Women are currently eligible at age 60 although this is being raised to 65. This will mean that any woman born after March 5, 1955 will not receive a state pension until age 65.

Q Is there any way I can ensure a maximum basic state pension when I retire?

A The key is to ensure you pay National Insurance contributions – and for all 52 weeks of the tax year. For the employed, this means paying class 1 National Insurance contributions which should be deducted automatically from your pay by your employer. For the self-employed, this means paying class 2 contributions.

Q Are the rules for state pensions the same for women and men?

A No. For men, their eligibility to a basic state pension depends primarily on the number of years they have paid National Insurance contributions. For women, the rules are more complicated.

> GROUP 1: Women who have worked all or most of their working life and paid class 1 contributions should get a full basic state pension in their own right at age 60.

> GROUP 2: Women who have only worked for part of their adult life will either receive a reduced pension based on their own contribution record which they can claim at age 60. Alternatively, they can receive a pension based on their husband's contribution record although they cannot claim this until their husband reaches the age of 65.

GROUP 3: Married women who have never worked are also entitled to a pension based on their husband's contribution record. However, to receive this, the husband must have reached the age of 65, retired and be in receipt of a basic state pension. The woman must be aged 60. If she is aged less than 60, her husband may be able to claim a pensions supplement if she does not work or her earnings are minimal. If she is 60 but her husband has yet to reach state retirement age, she must wait until her husband reaches age 65 before she can receive a share of the married couple's pension.

Q What happens if I'm unemployed? Am I losing out on future state pension entitlement?

A In some circumstances, you will be credited with National Insurance contributions which will go towards working out your state pension – even though you haven't paid them as a result of not working. People who fall into this category include the following:

GROUP 1: Those who are claiming certain state benefits such as Jobseeker's Allowance, maternity allowance or incapacity benefit.

GROUP 2: Men within five years of state pension age (65) and unemployed.

GROUP 3: Those who spent their 16th, 17th and 18th birthdays at school and who were born after April 5, 1957.

GROUP 4: Those who took part in an approved training course and who were born after April 5, 1957.

As far as non-working mothers are concerned, they qualify for something called Home Responsibilities Protection which reduces the number of National Insurance contribution years they require to obtain a given level of state pension. People who stay at home to look after a sick or elderly relative may also be eligible for HRP.

Q Is it possible to make up for years in which National Insurance contributions were not paid, thereby ensuring a bigger state pension at retirement?

A Yes, backdating is possible through the payment of class 3 National Insurance contributions. However, you can only go back a maximum six years. Before making these voluntary contributions, it is best to obtain a forecast of your likely state pension. This can be done by completing form BR19 available from your local Benefits Agency and sending it to the Retirement Pension Forecast and Advice Service. By doing this, you will get a clear idea of whether backdated contributions are worthwhile.

Q What happens to my state pension if I die before reaching state retirement age?

A It depends whether you leave behind a widow or widower. A widow may be entitled to a combination of a tax-free widow's payment, a widow's mother's allowance (if caring for children) and a widow's pension (payable to those aged 45 and over who are not looking after children). However, these payments will depend to a large extent upon your National Insurance contribution record before your death. Widowers receive no form of widower's pension although this is due to change in April 2001 when both widows and widowers will be eligible to receive a combination of a bereavement payment, a widowed parent's allowance and a bereavement allowance.

Q What happens to my pension if I die after retiring?

A If your widow/widower gets less than the full-rate basic state pension, they can claim a combined pension using your contribution record. But they can only claim up to an amount equivalent to the maximum single person's basic state pension – £72.50 per week (year to April 5, 2002).

Q What happens if I have to retire early through ill health or simply because I want to? Can I take my state pension early?

A The simple answer is no. You can't take your pension until state retirement age. If you decide to retire voluntarily, you should consider continuing to pay National Insurance Contributions (class 3) so as to ensure you receive the maximum state pension possible. If you retired early because of ill health, you may be able to obtain other state benefits such as incapacity benefit or income support to tide you through until you receive your state pension.

Q So the state gives us a pretty raw pensions deal?

A If truth be told, the answer is yes. However, the basic state pension is not the only pension that you are eligible to receive from the government. Some people may be entitled to a state graduated pension if they worked between the years 1961 and 1975. But many more people are entitled to a second state pension – the State Earnings Related Scheme.

Q Who is eligible to receive Serps?

A Serps started in 1978 and anyone who is employed should be building up a Serps pension provided they are earning more than the so-called 'lower earnings limit' – currently set at £76 a week (year to April 5, 2002). As its name implies, Serps pensions are linked to your earnings – in very basic terms, the more you earn, the more entitlement you are building up to a Serps pension.

However, not everyone who is employed will be in Serps. Many people are 'contracted out' of Serps. This means that instead of a Serps pension, they are building up an equivalent pension in an employer's pension scheme (a contracted-out employer's pension scheme) or a personal pension.

If you are in a contracted-out employer's pension scheme, you are automatically contracted out of Serps by your employer. People who have contracted out of Serps and taken out a personal pension

– also referred to as a rebate only or appropriate personal pension – will have done so voluntarily. However, contracting out does not make sense for many people and it can pay to contract back in.

Q What about the self-employed?

A No. They are not entitled to a Serps pension.

Q Can I work out my entitlement to a Serps pension?

A Not unless you are a rocket scientist. You are better off completing form BR19 – already referred to – and returning it to the Retirement Pension Forecast and Advice Service. It will provide you with an estimate of the Serps entitlement that you have already built up together with a projection of the entitlement that you may have by retirement.

Q How is a Serps pension paid?

A Along with your basic state pension. Payments are also increased each year in line with inflation.

Q Serps seems very messy and complicated. Are there moves to revamp it?

A Yes. The government has said it intends to replace Serps with a state second pension. This new scheme, scheduled for introduction in 2002, is designed to give better pensions to people on low earnings. This new scheme will not impact adversely on anyone's existing entitlement to a Serps pension.

Q OK, so how do I get my state pension, be it a basic pension or a combination of a basic pension, Serps and a graduated pension?

A You should be contacted by the Department of Social Security prior to reaching retirement age. You will be asked to complete a claim form (BR1). If this form doesn't reach you four months before retirement, contact the DSS – the last thing you want is for your pension to be delayed. After completing form BR1, the DSS should contact you and tell you how much state pension you will be getting. When it comes to receiving your pension, you can choose to have your pension paid directly into a bank or building society account. Alternatively, you can ask for a pension book which will entitle you to obtain your pension from your local post office.

Q So in a nutshell, are you telling me that I shouldn't rely upon the state pension to see me through retirement?

A Exactly. Although governments of all political persuasions have said that the basic state pension is here to stay, its value is being chipped away at all the time. In the recent past the link with increases in national earnings has been broken, eroding the purchasing power of the state pension. Also, a woman's right to obtain a pension at age 60 is slowly but surely being withdrawn. There is nothing to stop future governments making other changes which devalue the value of the state pension.

If you want to ensure a financially healthy retirement, you have no choice but to go it alone and save through a private pension scheme.

Dos and Don'ts

- **DO** obtain details of the progression of your state pension by completing form BR19 available from your local Benefits Agency. It will cost you nothing, other than time, to complete and by taking action on the back of the information returned, you might provide yourself with a better pension in retirement.

- **DO** check whether you are paying class 1 reduced rate National Insurance contributions – paid primarily by married women. If you fall into this category, you must be aware that your contributions are not going towards the building of a basic pension for yourself. Instead, you will have to rely upon your husband's contribution record for a pension. For some women, it will pay them to switch to full-rate class 1 National Insurance contributions. Only go down this route if you have spoken first to the Contributions Agency, part of the Department of Social Security. The CA is usually located in the same building as your local Benefits Agency.

- **DO** be aware of the fact that the state retirement age for women is to rise to age 65. The change will be phased in over 10 years, beginning in 2010. Women born before April 6, 1950 will not be affected by the change.

- **DO** be aware of the fact that married women and widows who do not qualify for a basic state pension in their own right may be entitled to a basic pension on their husband's contribution record – at about 60% of the level to which he is entitled.

- **DO** be aware of the fact that your state pension is taxable although for most people tax will not be an issue because they will be below the income tax threshold.

- **DO** check out where you stand with regard to your state pension if you decide to work abroad. It is possible, for example, for social security contributions made in another country to go towards your UK state pension. The DSS overseas branch should be able to help.

Did you know?

- **DID** you know that the full basic state pension was equivalent to 22% of average earnings in 1975? Today, it represents only 17% of average earnings and this is expected to fall to just 7% by the year 2030. Don't rely upon it to see you through retirement.

- **DID** you know that the basic state pension is increased each April in line with inflation, not average earnings?

- **DID** you know that it is possible for a married couple to qualify both for a full state pension based on their own National Insurance contribution record? So instead of receiving a married couple's pension of £6,026.80 (for year to April 5, 2002) per year, they will receive £7,540 – twice the single person's pension of £3,770.

- **DID** you know that a married woman is now entitled to have her part of the joint pension (£43.40) offset against her own personal allowance? This can prove tax-efficient.

- **DID** you know that state pensioners qualify for an extra pension of 25p a week when they reach the age of 80? Indeed, at age 80, if you do not qualify for a state basic pension or you receive a small one, you may be entitled to an 'over 80s pension'. This pension is not based on your past National Insurance contributions. In the tax year 2001–2002, this pension is set at £43.65 for a single person and £72.55 for a married couple.

- **DID** you know that you can defer taking your state pension for a maximum five years? For a man, this means you can defer until age 70, for a woman until age 65. If you defer, your eventual pension will be increased by 7.5% for each year of delay. So the maximum uplift you will get is 37.5%. People sometimes defer their pension because they are still working at age 65 and do not want to pay tax on their state pension. However, by deferring, you could lose out if, for example, you were to die shortly after taking your delayed pension. You should not go down this route without reading Benefits Agency leaflet NI92 – 'Giving up your right to retirement pension to earn extra'.

- **DID** you know that from 2010 the amount earned by deferring your state pension will be increased from 7.5% to 10%? The five-year limit on deferral will also be scrapped.

- **DID** you know that the government has introduced a minimum income guarantee which ensures that single pensioners and pensioner couples receive at least £92.15 and £140.55 a week respectively? This guarantee, however, is means-tested and is dependent upon any savings you may have.

So what now?

- **YOUR** local Benefits Agency should have a raft of useful leaflets on state pensions. They include:

  CA01 – National Insurance contributions (NICs) for employees
  CA02 – NICs for self-employed people with small earnings
  CA03 – NICs for self-employed people (class 2 and 4)
  CA07 – Unpaid and late-paid contributions
  CA08 – NIC (voluntary contributions)
  CA09 – National Insurance for widows
  CA12 – Training for further employment and your NI record
  CA13 – NIC for married women
  GL14 – Widowed?
  NI92 – Giving up your right to retirement pension to earn extra
  NI196 – Social Security benefit rates
  NP45 – A guide to widows' benefits
  RM1 – Retirement
  RM2 – Approaching retirement
  RM3 – Retired?
  NP46 – A guide to retirement pension
  PM2 – You and state pensions

  If your local Benefits Agency does not have some of these, contact the DSS Pension Information Line on 0845 7313233 (website: www.dss.gov.uk).
  For anyone about to take their state pension or who wants to find out the progress of their state pension, these leaflets are required reading.

Company pensions

Q OK, the state gives me a poor pensions deal. How can I ensure a decent pension when I retire?

A If you work for a company, there is a fair chance that it will run a pension scheme. If you are eligible to join it, and you should be, do so because it will prove one of the best ways to supplement the pensions deal you will get from the state upon retirement. The pension scheme will be run independently of your employer's company. It will be set up under trust and run by trustees, appointed from the company's management and from scheme members. It is the job of the trustees to manage the fund and to ensure that benefit promises are maintained.

Q Why should I join?

A The government makes available attractive tax incentives in order to encourage employees to join their company pension schemes. You would be foolish to jettison them.

FIRST: Income tax relief is given on personal contributions into company pension schemes at your highest tax rate. So for a basic rate taxpayer, a £100 contribution only costs £78. For higher rate taxpayers, the deal is even better. A £100 contribution costs only £60. These contributions will be taken from your gross pay.

SECOND: The pension fund is exempt from capital gains tax and some of the income generated also builds up tax-free, providing excellent growth prospects for your money.

THIRD: When you come to retire and take your pension benefits, a proportion of them can be taken in the shape of a tax-free lump sum.

The other attraction of company pension schemes is that the employer may enhance your pension, either by making additional payments on your behalf or by meeting the costs of running the pension scheme. You will not be taxed on any payments made by your employer on your behalf into the pension scheme. Indeed, some companies provide 'non-contributory' pension schemes where you do not have to pay anything towards your pension.

Also, most company pension schemes offer additional benefits other than the provision of a pension. If you die or become ill before retirement, the scheme may pay benefits to you (if you are still alive) or your surviving spouse or dependants. These may include a widow's/widower's pension if you die, a lump-sum payment if you die or a pension if you have to retire early because of ill health.

Q How can I join my company's pension scheme?

A You will be invited to join, normally when you first start with the company. Sometimes, you may have to serve a probationary period before being eligible to join. Ask at your job interview or as soon as you join the company. Once you have joined, you should receive a scheme booklet detailing how the scheme works and the benefits payable. It will also include important information on when you can take your pension as well as additional benefits such as death in service and widow's/widower's pension entitlements. Read the booklet and then put it away in a safe place.

You do not have to join the company pension scheme but you should think twice before turning your nose up at it. Indeed, the government is looking at whether employees should be compelled to join their company's pension scheme.

Q What happens if my employer does not run a company pension scheme?

A You will have to make your own pension arrangements, probably through a personal pension. However, as a result of new stakeholder pension rules introduced by the government, most businesses, both small and big, are being forced to give workers the option to save through a pension.

From October 2001, any employer with five or more employees will have to offer workers access to a cost-friendly stakeholder pension if it does not already provide an occupational or group personal pension scheme to which it contributes a sum equivalent to 3% of workers' earnings. Also, if there is a waiting period in excess of a year before employees are allowed to join their company pension scheme, a stakeholder pension must be offered.

The only companies which will be exempt from stakeholder are those employing less than five workers and those where all employees earn less than the National Insurance lower earnings limit (currently £76 a week).

Under stakeholder, employees will be able to make contributions from as little as £20 (both for regular and one-off payments). Workers will also be able to start and stop contributions into their scheme whenever they want, without penalty. They will also be able to transfer stakeholder plans to another provider if performance does not come up to scratch. Management charges on stakeholder will be capped at 1% per annum.

Contributions made by workers under stakeholder will be paid net of basic rate tax relief. So a basic rate taxpaying worker who wants to invest £100 a month in a stakeholder pension need only contribute £78 because of the 22% tax relief. A higher tax rate worker must reclaim the extra 18% tax relief through their self-assessment tax return.

The amount workers contribute to a stakeholder pension will be dependent upon age and earnings. The under 35s, for example, will be able to contribute 17.5% of earnings while those aged 61 and over will be able to contribute 40%. These contribution rules are the same as those governing personal pensions – see later on in the chapter.

Finally, benefits from a stakeholder pension can be taken between the ages of 50 and 75. As with personal pensions, 25% of the fund can be taken as tax-free cash while the balance must be used to buy an annuity.

Full details on stakeholder pensions will be provided later on in the chapter.

Q If my company offers an occupational pension scheme, how much do I need to put into it?

A The company will stipulate the percentage of your earnings that will go into the company pension scheme. The typical amount is 5% which is taken from your gross salary. However, the maximum permitted is 15% of your earnings. This is exclusive of any payments that your employer may make into your pension on your behalf. As explained later, you can make top-up payments through so-called Additional Voluntary Contributions or Free Standing Additional Voluntary Contributions.

Q Is there a limit on the amount of pension I can obtain from a company pension scheme?

A Yes.The Inland Revenue puts a limit on the benefits payable primarily because of the generous tax breaks on offer. The exact limits depend upon when you joined the company pension and when the scheme was set up. But in most cases the maximum pension payable is equivalent to two-thirds of your so-called 'final salary'. The limit on the tax-free lump sum payable will be typically 1.5 times your final salary.

Your pension and tax-free lump sum may, however, be restricted by a so-called pensions earnings cap. This is currently set at £95,400 (tax year ended April 5, 2002). This means that the maximum pension, two-thirds of final salary, is £63,600 while the maximum tax-free lump sum allowed is £143,100. However, this cap is only applied to members of schemes set up after March 13, 1989 and to new employees joining pension schemes from June 1, 1989. Your scheme details should explain the rules pertaining to you.

The definition of so-called final salary varies but will usually be based on your highest earnings in any one year out of the last five years before retirement or the highest yearly average of your earnings during a three-year period ending any time within the last 10 years before retirement.

These maximum pension limits are generous given that normally the maximum pension and tax-free lump sum build up over 40 years. Pension typically builds up at a rate of one-sixtieth of final salary for each year you're with the employer. The tax-free lump sum builds up at a rate of three-eightieths for every year served.

Your pension scheme booklet should outline the maximum pension and tax-free lump sum payable.

Q When will I receive my company pension?

A Your employer will have a normal retirement age at which time it will start paying your pension. This will usually be age 65 – for both men and women – although some schemes have a normal retirement age of 60. You cannot take a pension from your company unless you no longer work for them although this rule may change in the future. If you take early retirement, you may be able to obtain a pension earlier than the scheme's designated normal retirement age but it will be lower to reflect the fact that you have had less service and you are accessing your pension earlier than scheduled. Many pension schemes apply what is called an early retirement factor to reflect the fact that you are taking your pension early and can be high as 4% per year – 4% for each year not worked until retirement.

Q Are all company pension schemes the same?

A No. Company pension schemes tend to fall into two camps – final salary and money purchase schemes.

FINAL SALARY: The most common is the final salary or the defined benefit or salary related scheme. Here, your pension is calculated as a proportion of your final salary and is dependent upon the number of years you have worked for the company and been a member of the pension scheme and the fraction of final pay on which the scheme is based – known as the 'accrual rate'. Typically, final salary schemes are based on one-sixtieth. So, if you have worked for 20 years, you will receive a pension equivalent to a third (20/60th) of your final salary, irrespective of how much you have paid into the pension scheme.

The advantage of this type of company pension scheme is that there are certainties – you know that if you work so many years, you will be entitled to a certain level of pension. In other words, they are a low-risk way of you saving for retirement. You will obtain the promised pension irrespective of how well or badly your pension contributions have been invested. It is the employer that bears all the investment risk because it is committed to paying in whatever it takes to ensure that pension promises are kept.

MONEY PURCHASE: In contrast, with a money purchase pension scheme, your contributions – and those made by your employer on your behalf – will be invested in a pool of assets and it is the growth in the value of these assets which will determine the amount of pension you receive at retirement.

Although easier to understand, money purchase schemes are less predictable than final salary schemes. This makes pension planning more difficult. Your pension will depend directly upon the performance of the pension fund. If it performs well, you should be rewarded with a good pension. If it doesn't, then you will suffer financially at retirement.

Another unpredictable factor is when your pension is turned into a pension income. At retirement, your pension fund will be used to purchase an annuity – a lifetime pension income. Annuity rates can vary greatly from year to year which means you could retire in a year when annuity rates are poor, resulting in a lower lifetime income than if you had retired when annuity rates were higher.

Company pension schemes are increasingly being set up on a money purchase basis because they shift any investment risk onto the shoulders of the pension members. With a money purchase scheme, an employer knows the cost of contributions that must be made on employers' behalf.

Q Are there any other types of company pension arrangement?

A Yes.

TYPE 1: A relatively new version of the company pension is the GROUP PERSONAL PENSION. This is a money purchase type arrangement where the pension you ultimately receive will depend upon the retirement pot you have managed to accumulate and the annuity rates on offer when you decide to hang your boots up. A group personal pension plan is similar to a personal pension (see later) in that you have an individual plan. The only difference is that your employer will have chosen the plan's provider on your behalf – and that of all the other workers. You will, however, be able to choose the underlying fund into which your contributions are invested. So, for example, you could opt for a managed fund while a co-worker could have their contributions invested in a fund with exposure to UK equities.

Group personal pensions tend to have lower charges than individual personal pensions. The contributions you can make are determined by the limits governing personal pensions which means 17.5% of earnings for the under 35s rising to 40% for those aged 61 and over.

Most group personal pensions have been set up by employers because they are far cheaper than conventional money purchase schemes or final salary schemes. Indeed, most employers do not currently support employees' contributions with top-up payments. However, stakeholder is changing all that. If an employer with more than five workers does not make contributions on employees' behalf equivalent to 3% of their pay, they must provide a stakeholder alternative.

TYPE 2: For senior exectives and directors of businesses, EXECUTIVE PENSION plans are an option. The rules governing contribution limits and benefit levels under executive pensions are far more flexible than under other pension arrangements. They are particularly advantageous to employees, for example, who have worked for a long time but maybe were unable to make pension contributions in the early days as a result of establishing the business. Contributions can be made based on the employee's length of service. Also, contributions are allowable as a business expense and can be offset against corporation tax in the case of companies or income tax for partnerships and sole proprietors.

As under other company schemes, the maximum pension allowed under an executive scheme is two-thirds of final salary and part of the pension can be taken as tax-free cash.

TYPE 3: SMALL SELF-ADMINISTERED SCHEMES are attractive to directors who want to use their pension fund to invest in their business. Typically, the pension fund's assets are used to buy the company's office premises. The business then rents the property from the pension fund. A SSAS can also be invested in shares, investment funds and cash.

Such schemes usually have a maximum of 12 members. All members must be trustees and they are collectively responsible for running the scheme. There must also be an independent trustee – a so-called pensioner trustee.

TYPE 4: For some highly paid employees, employers are prepared to set up so-called FUNDED UNAPPROVED RETIREMENT BENEFIT schemes. These are appropriate for employees who earn in excess of the pension earnings cap (£95,400 for the tax year ending April 5, 2002). Here the employer pays contributions relating to the unpensioned tier of earnings into a fund which is written in trust for the employee. There is no formal limit on either the contributions or the amount of pension that can be provided. The fund can be used to buy an annuity or it can be taken as a tax-free lump sum. This is because Furbs are funded from net income.

Types 2 through to 4 are all pension arrangements designed for high earners and company directors. They should only be entered into after speaking to a good independent financial adviser.

Q You say that most companies ask you to pay a percentage of your gross salary, usually 5%, into the company pension scheme. Is there any way you can save more in order to generate a bigger pension?

A Yes. Some final salary schemes allow you to buy extra years of pension entitlement – the pensions administrator will be able to tell you if this is possible. But for most employees the best option to top up their pension is to make what are called Additional Voluntary Contributions which in effect build you an additional pension fund. These contributions can be made in two ways – through an in-house AVC run by your employer or through a so-called free-standing AVC operated by an insurance company or investment house.

If you take out an AVC or FSAVC, you get the same tax benefits on your contributions as you do when paying into an occupational pension scheme – namely tax relief at your highest marginal rate of tax. But you cannot use an AVC or FSAVC to generate tax-free cash when you come to retire. Your contributions go purely towards building your pension. The only exception to this rule are members of AVC schemes contributing before April 1987 – their AVC contributions can be used to provide tax-free cash.

One point you need to be aware of is that if you take out an AVC or FSAVC, you cannot access them until age 50 at the earliest. It may make better sense instead to put any excess savings into a tax-free Isa where you can access your money when you want to.

Q How much can I put into AVCs or FSAVCs?

A The Inland Revenue allows you to put up to 15% of your salary in a combination of an occupational pension scheme and AVCs. So if you are currently paying 5% of your salary into a company pension scheme, you can top up using AVCs to the tune of a further 10%. If you are on a salary of £20,000, this would mean that you could make AVCs of £2,000.

One point often overlooked is that the 15% limit is based on your gross remuneration – which includes any bonuses you may earn and any fringe benefits – and not your basic salary. This can result in a greater scope to make AVC contributions than you first thought.

So, for example, if you earn basic pay of £20,000, bonuses of £7,500 and fringe benefits taxable at £2,500, your gross remuneration would be £30,000. This would mean a total entitlement to pension contributions of £4,500 – 15% of £30,000. If your contribution into the company pension scheme is based on 4% of your basic payment, this would mean that you have scope to make AVCs of £3,700 – £4,500 less the £800 of contributions going into the main pension fund.

Most people will have plenty of scope to make AVCs but if you are in doubt, ask your pension scheme administrator who will be able to tell you where you stand exactly. You may be limited if you have already built up a sizeable fund which means you are up against maximum approvable pension benefits. You can also not make payments into an AVC in respect of earnings over the pensions earning cap of £95,400 (tax year ending April 5, 2002) unless you joined your pension scheme before June 1989 and the scheme was up and running before March 14, 1989.

Payments into FSAVCs and AVCs can be made on a regular savings basis or by investing a lump sum – subject to minimum premium levels.

Q What is best, an AVC or a FSAVC?

A Both AVCs and FSAVCs have their pluses and minuses.

1. CHARGES: Charges on AVCs tend to be lower. This is because employers sometimes subsidise the costs or negotiate lower costs on your behalf.
2. PERSONAL CHOICE: It is the trustees of your company pension scheme who decide which firm operates the in-house AVC scheme – you have no choice in the matter. With a FSAVC, it is you who chooses to manage the scheme. It could

be an investment house you have a high regard for or your favourite insurance company.

3. INVESTMENT CHOICE: FSAVCs tend to offer greater investment choice. Most in-house AVC schemes are conservatively managed. Your money is usually invested in one of the following: deposit accounts, with profits schemes or a managed fund investing in a broad range of assets including property, shares and bonds. FSAVCs provide greater choice, enabling you to invest in riskier investments such as funds investing in North American companies, smaller companies and European markets.

4. PORTABILITY: If you save through an in-house AVC, it remains linked to your company pension scheme. So if you change jobs, you cannot continue to pay into the AVC. Instead, you will have to start a new AVC scheme with your new employer. With a FSAVC, the fund builds up separately from your company pension scheme. So if you move employers, you can continue paying into the scheme.

5. CONFIDENTALITY: With a FSAVC, you are in control and your employer need not know that you have such an investment. This is not the case with an AVC. In other words, an FSAVC is personal to you.

6. TAX: With an AVC, a higher rate taxpayer receives instant tax relief on their contribution. This is because it is paid through their payroll. FSAVC contributions are paid net of basic rate tax relief at source. Any higher rate relief has to be claimed through the self-assessment tax system.

If an adviser – a company representative or an independent financial adviser – tries to sell you a FSAVC, they must explain why it is a better choice than the company pension AVC. In most cases it will not be. If they persist, ask them to produce written recommendations as to why they suggest it.

Q How do I receive a pension from an AVC or FSAVC?

A Nearly all AVC arrangements are money purchase based. So your contributions are invested and when it comes to accessing your fund, it is converted into pension scheme via the purchase of a pension annuity. Obviously, the bigger the fund, the better the annuity that can be bought. However, all annuities are dependent upon prevailing interest rates. So beware of buying an annuity at an inappropriate time.

Q What happens to my company pension if I change jobs?

A If you have belonged to the pension scheme for less than two years, you have the right to a refund of your contributions less 20% tax. However, many companies will allow you instead to preserve your pension with the company or use the value of the accumulated pension – the transfer value – to buy into a new scheme.

FINAL SALARY: If you have contributed to your company pension for more than two years, then you are entitled to what is called a preserved pension. This will be based on the number of years that you were a member of the pension scheme, the normal accrual rate applied by your scheme (for example, one-sixtieth or one-eightieth) and your final salary at the time of leaving the scheme.

At one time, this preserved pension would have been frozen and resultingly eroded in value by inflation. But now, preserved pensions built up from January 1, 1985 must be increased each year in line with inflation up to a maximum of 5% – some schemes are more generous. These increases must be applied until you retire and take your pension.

MONEY PURCHASE: Again, if you have belonged to your pension scheme for at least two years, you are entitled to a preserved pension. The pension fund you leave will simply remain invested and hopefully grow in value. There will be no new contributions paid into the pension on your behalf by your ex-employer but be mindful that your pension will still attract charges.

Q Instead of preserving my pension when I move employers, can I move my pension?

A Yes, you have the right to have your pension rights converted into a 'transfer value' (a lump sum) and invested in another pension scheme such as a new employer's pension scheme, a personal pension or a so-called Section 32 contract. However, it may be the case that your new employer refuses to accept your pension transfer value so you must check beforehand.

There are also special rules relating to the transfer of so-called 'contracted-out' benefits – the pension benefits which your ex-employer may have built up on your behalf to replace Serps. so-called contracted-out pension schemes promise to provide members with benefits at least equal to those which would be payable if they remained in Serps. Your ex-employer should tell you where you stand on these accumulated benefits.

Q What is a Section 32 contract?

A In very simple terms, they are a special type of personal pension designed to accept transfer values from employers' pension schemes. They are offered by most leading pension providers.

Q So does transferring a pension make sense?

A Deciding whether to transfer a pension is a difficult task and most people should take independent financial advice. But anyone transferring should bear the following in mind:

POINTER 1: If your ex-employer's scheme is a final salary scheme, the transfer value may not take into account discretionary benefits – benefits which the scheme may give you but is not obliged to do so such as discretionary increases to your pension once you retire.

POINTER 2: Before transferring between employer pension schemes, you need to weigh up the benefits you will lose in your old scheme against the benefits you can buy in the new scheme.

There is little point transferring if the benefits available in the new scheme are less attractive.

POINTER 3: If you transfer into a new employer's final salary scheme, you will normally purchase added years in exchange for your transfer value. This will mean you will get a bigger pension when you retire. If you are transferring benefits from one final salary scheme to another, your transfer value will normally buy less years than the number of years you had in your former employer's pension scheme. This is because each year in the new pension scheme is expected to provide you with a higher pension based on your salary at retirement – as opposed to your final salary when you left your former employer's scheme.

POINTER 4: If you transfer from a final salary scheme to a money purchase scheme or a personal pension scheme, remember that you will be giving up a guaranteed pension in exchange for a pension dependent upon the vagaries of investment markets.

POINTER 5: If you transfer from a final salary scheme to a Section 32 buy-out contract, you can arrange for the plan to provide you with minimum guarantees. However, this will mean your transfer value being invested in low-risk investments which could result in a lower pension at retirement than if the money had been invested in a personal pension with a broader investment risk.

POINTER 6: Do remember that if you transfer your pension scheme to a Section 32 buy-out or a personal pension, you will have to bear the plan's running costs. Some personal pension plans have high running costs so beware.

As a general rule, you will usually be better off leaving your pension where it is. If you are advised to transfer your existing pension to a personal pension or a Section 32 buy-out, it may be worth obtaining a second opinion. Only transfer if you are convinced personally that it is the right move for you. Again, get any recommendation to transfer in writing.

Q Can I opt out of a company pension scheme and instead save through a personal pension?

A The answer is yes although you would be mad to do so. You would be losing out on a whole raft of benefits that a personal pension is not going to provide you with – life insurance for example. If an adviser recommends that you should opt out of a company pension scheme in favour of a personal pension, ask them to put their reasons why in writing.

Q What if I have a complaint with my company scheme?

A First, you should contact your pensions administrator at work who will provide details of the formal complaints procedure which is a requirement under pensions law. If your problem is not resolved after going down this route, you should then contact the Pensions Advisory Service (OPAS). It will mediate between you and the pension scheme and it may refer you to the Pensions Ombudsman. OPAS can be contacted on: 020 7233 8080 while the Pensions Ombudsman can be contacted on 020 7834 9144.

This route is also the complaints channel to go down if you have a problem with your AVC. If you have a problem with your FSAVC, you should contact the adviser who sold you the plan or contact the product provider.

Dos and Don'ts

- **DO** think twice before deciding not to join your employer's pension scheme. If you don't join your company pension scheme, you are effectively taking a pay cut. As well as not benefiting from your employer's pension contributions, you are missing out on other important benefits contained within your pension.

- **DO** ask questions before joining a company pension scheme.

  QUESTION 1: Is it final salary or money purchase? If it is final salary, how is my pension calculated, will it be increased post retirement to take account of inflation and what happens if I wish to retire early or late or am enforced to retire early as a result of ill health? If it is money purchase, where exactly will my money be invested and who are the external investment managers?

QUESTION 2: Is it contracted out of Serps?

QUESTION 3: What percentage of my salary will be used to fund pension contributions? And what level of contributions will be made on my behalf by my employer?

QUESTION 4: What happens to my pension if I die before, or in, retirement?

QUESTION 5: What happens to my pension contributions if I am laid off work without pay or am forced to go on short-time working?

- **DO** remember that when you move jobs and decide to leave your accumulated pension where it is, your pension will not simply provide you with a future pension when you retire. It should still provide you with a menagerie of other benefits such as a pension if you are forced to retire early because of ill health and a pension for your spouse or other dependants if you die. If you have a preserved pension, you should familiarise yourself with the full range of benefits available under the scheme. Also, keep in touch with the pension administrators, informing them of any changes of address.

- **DO** obtain professional advice if you are thinking of transferring the benefits from an existing company pension scheme. This is particularly important if you are thinking of transferring benefits from a final salary pension scheme because of the attractive benefits that you could be giving up.

  Advice on transfers can be obtained either from a company representative – typically working for an insurance company – or an independent financial adviser. Firms of independent financial advisers can only give advice on transfers if they have someone on the staff who has gained extra qualifications in this specialist area. You can check whether this is the case by contacting regulator the Financial Services Authority on 0845 606 1234. An adviser recommending a transfer to a personal pension or a Section 32 buy-out contract must provide you with a written detailed analysis explaining his recommendation. This must include an explanation of the pluses and minuses associated with both leaving your benefits where they are and of transferring them. This analysis must show you the rate at which your investments need to grow to match the benefits you are giving up by transferring.

- **DO** be aware of the fact that if you contribute to a FSAVC, you will have to certify that you are not contributing to another FSAVC scheme – you can only contribute to one FSAVC at a time. This is if your gross contributions are below £2,400. If your contributions are above this figure, the provider of the FSAVC must check that you are not overfunding your pension by contacting your company pension scheme. This is known as the 'headroom' check. If you are over-funding your pension, surplus funds will be returned subject to a tax charge of 33% (for basic rate taxpayers) 47.9% (higher rate taxpayers).

- **DO** remember that you can change the provider of your FSAVC if you do not think the performance is up to scratch. In moving your pensions pot from one provider to another, do bear in mind that you will probably have to pay more set-up charges.

- **DO** keep details of any previous pensions you have had with companies you have worked with in the past. However small the pension payable from these schemes may be, remember that it is your money and it will be money you are grateful for in retirement. If you have lost track of any company pensions, contact the Pensions Schemes Registry which will help you trace them. It can be contacted at: PO Box 1NN, Newcastle upon Tyne, Tyne and Wear NE99 1NN (0191 225 6316). Website: www.opra.co.uk.

- **DON'T** transfer benefits from a public sector pension scheme – benefits built up by local and central government workers such as the police, nurses and teachers. The only exception to this rule is if you wish to transfer from one public sector pension scheme to another. Here there is often a special arrangement called a 'transfer' club which protects your pension rights when transferring.

- **DON'T** automatically take tax-free cash from your pension at your retirement. It may be better to take all the pension fund in the form of pension income. Remember, the more tax-free cash you take, the less pension income you will have.

- **DON'T** go and take out your own pension plan if your employer says you cannot join the company pension scheme straight away. It is better to wait and join the company scheme as soon as you can.

Did you know?

- **DID** you know that about 10.7 million people are now members of company pension schemes?

- **DID** you know that many company pension schemes now automatically enter new employees into the company pension scheme?

- **DID** you know that most company pension schemes offer a range of benefits that extend beyond a pension at retirement. Additional benefits can include:

  1. A reduced pension if you choose to retire early.
  2. A pension if you have to retire early as a result of ill health.
  3. A pension for your widow/widower if you die before retirement.
  4. A pension for your widow/widower if you die after retirement.

5. A pension for other dependants, such as an unmarried partner, if you die.
6. A lump sum paid to your dependants if you die before retirement.
7. Increases to pensions once they start to be paid.

- **DID** you know that your employer is obliged to furnish you with certain pensions information if you are eligible to join the pension scheme? This includes:

> 1. EXPLANATORY BOOKLET: This will give you basic key information about the pension scheme including the type of scheme (final salary or money purchase) and the benefits payable on retirement, early retirement or death. This booklet should be received when you first join the company or shortly afterwards.
> 2. ANNUAL BENEFITS STATEMENT: This will indicate how your individual pension is progressing and is required by law for members of money purchase schemes. It will help you assess whether your retirement plans are on schedule or if you need to make additional pensions provision.
> 3. TRUSTEES' REPORT AND SCHEME ACCOUNTS: This will show you how the company pension scheme is performing overall taking into account investment growth, contributions received and pensions paid. Although many pension schemes send out a summary report as a matter of course, you do have the right under law to request the full trustees' report and scheme accounts.
> 4. OPTIONS ON LEAVING THE COMPANY PENSION SCHEME: This should spell out your available pension options – keep the pension preserved or transfer it – and provide you with a transfer value. This information has to be made available to you by law.
> 5. SCHEME CHANGES: This will spell out major scheme changes – such as a change of investment managers, a

move from final salary to money purchase – and again is required by law.

If you have any queries over your pension, you should speak to your personnel department in the first instance. You may then want to speak to the pensions administrator or the trustees of the scheme.

- **DID** you know that the Occupational Pensions Regulatory Authority (Opra) is the regulator responsible for ensuring that occupational pension schemes operate within the law? Opra can be contacted on: 01273 627600 (website: http://www.opra.co.uk).

- **DID** you know that any employer who runs an occupational pension scheme must by law offer an in-house AVC scheme? Details of the AVC should be included in your pension scheme booklet.

- **DID** you know that recent rule changes now allow you to take benefits from an AVC between the ages of 50 and 75 and independently from when you take benefits from the main company pension scheme?

- **DID** you know that some company pension schemes are a combination of money purchase and final salary? So-called hybrid schemes will ensure you receive the better of the final salary scheme or the money purchase scheme – whichever pays the better pension at the time of your retirement. Other schemes provide new employees with the option of joining a money purchase scheme to begin with and then the option to join a final salary scheme at a later stage.

- **DID** you know that there are government proposals in train which will enable you to obtain an annual pension forecast? This will detail the pension you have built up from all sources, including the state, company pensions and personal pensions. It will also provide you with details of the kind of pension you are likely to receive if you retire at the state retirement age.

- **DID** you know that rules now exist to ensure both parties to a divorce get a fair pensions deal? Until recently, pensions were invariably overlooked when couples divorced. This often resulted in many women facing an impoverished life in retirement as their former spouses walked off with all the pension assets.

  Thankfully, the rules have been toughened up. Now, part of a pension can be 'earmarked' for the benefit of a former spouse. This means that when the pension scheme member retires, a share of the retirement benefits becomes payable directly to the former partner.

  More recently, pensions splitting has been introduced. Rather than having to wait until their former spouse retires in order to obtain control of their pension, pension assets are split at divorce. This means that each spouse then has a pension of their own.

So what next?

- **JOINING** a company pension scheme is one of the best personal finance moves that you can make towards a rewarding retirement. If you get the chance to join a scheme, do so – don't turn it down.

  Also, don't be put off by the barrage of jargon surrounding such schemes – such as money purchase, final salary, accrual rates and transfers. Hopefully, by breaking through some of this jargon, this section will ensure you go down the company pension route with more confidence than you would have done previously.

  If you need more information on company pensions, the Financial Services Regulator has produced a number of excellent booklets on different aspects. They include:

  FSA guide to pensions

FSA guide to the risks of pension transfers
FSA guide to boosting your occupational pension

These can be ordered by ringing 0845 606 1234.

The Department of Social Security has also published a number of useful pensions fact sheets including:

PM1: 'Don't leave your pension to chance' (a general guide to pensions)
PM3: 'You and occupational pensions'

These can be ordered on 0845 731 32 33.

Stakeholder pensions and personal pensions

Q OK, I'm one of the unlucky ones. I don't have access to a company pension scheme. What can I do other than rely upon the ever diminishing state pension?

A STEP ONE: First of all, you should look at STAKEHOLDER PENSIONS. These were introduced in April 2001 by the government and are designed to get more people to save for retirement.

If you are an employee, your employer must in most cases offer a stakeholder scheme by October 2001 – see the section on company pensions.

The rules on stakeholder are relatively straightforward. Such schemes are offered on a money purchase basis and operated primarily by some of the country's leading insurance companies. At retirement, the fund you have built up will currently be used to buy an annuity. You will also be allowed to take up to 25% of the pot as tax-free cash.

You are allowed to contribute at least £3,600 a year

automatically into a stakeholder pension. But unlike with personal pensions and company pensions, these contributions do not have to come out of earned income. This means, for example, that non-working partners and the unemployed will be able to pay into stakeholder pensions. Furthermore, there is no minimum age limit, which means parents will be able to pay money into a stakeholder plan for a child.

Contributions above £3,600 can be made under stakeholder but only if you fall within the contribution limits for personal pensions (see later). These start at 17.5% of earnings up to age 35 rising to 40% for ages 61 and over. These contributions will also be allowed to continue for up to five years after earnings have ceased.

Contributions are paid by everyone net of basic rate relief. This means that a £100 gross contribution costs a basic rate taxpayer £78. Higher rate taxpayers reclaim their extra tax relief through their self-assessment tax returns.

Stakeholder pensions provide buyers with a number of assurances. First, they must be cost-friendly. Only one charge can be levied, capped at 1% per annum. The minimum contribution level must be £20 or lower and you can contribute whenever you want to. There is no compulsion, for example, to save on a regular monthly basis even though it may be prudent to do so.

The choice of fund type under stakeholder will be similar to that available under personal pensions (see later) although probably not as wide given the 1% cap on the annual management charge.

STEP TWO: Look at PERSONAL PENSIONS. Personal pensions were launched in 1988 as part of a government initiative to extend individual pension choice. They replaced self-employed retirement annuities – so-called Section 226 retirement annuities – and are aimed at the employed who do not have access to a company pension and the self-employed who have to make their own pension provision.

Q How do personal pensions work?

A Personal pensions do not provide a pension linked to salary like many company pension schemes. Instead, they work on a 'money purchase' or 'defined contribution basis', which means that your contributions are invested to build up a fund which at retirement can be used to purchase a pension annuity – a lifetime income. The pension income you eventually derive from your personal pension will depend upon a number of factors including: the amount of contributions you have made, the charges the pension provider has deducted from your plan, the performance of your plan, the pension fund size at retirement, and annuity rates at the time you convert your fund into a regular guaranteed income stream.

Q Are there attractive tax breaks for people prepared to save for retirement through a personal pension – in the same way as there are for people saving through company pensions?

A Yes. Contributions qualify for tax relief at your highest marginal rate of tax, the pension fund grows virtually free of tax and when you come to retire, you can take up to 25% of your final retirement fund as tax-free cash. The balance must be used to purchase an annuity. This annuity must be purchased between the ages of 50 and 75. Annuity income is taxed as earned income.

Q How much can I contribute to a personal pension?

A The amount you can contribute depends upon how old you are. The older you are, the higher the percentage of so-called 'net relevant earnings' you can contribute to a personal pension. For the self-employed, net relevant earnings are loosely defined as annual earnings. For the employed, they are again generally defined as gross earnings.

The maximum annual contributions to a personal pension, given as a percentage of net relevant earnings, are as follows. Up to age 35: 17.5%; 36–45: 20%; 46–50: 25%; 51–55: 30%; 56–60: 35%; 61–74: 40%.

Q Can employers contribute to a personal pension?

A Yes, although any contributions made must be made within the maximum annual contribution limits.

Q Is there a cap on the amount of money you can put into a personal pension?

A Yes. High earners are restricted by the so-called 'earnings cap'. For the tax year ended April 5, 2002, this is set at £95,400. So, if you are aged 33 and have net relevant earnings of £100,000, the maximum you can put into your personal pension is £16,695 – 17.5% of £95,400.

Q What if I am still contributing to an old style personal pension – a Section 226 policy. Am I governed by the same maximum contribution limits?

A No. The percentage of net relevant earnings you can put into an old-style personal pension is lower at all ages. Up to age 50, the percentage is 17.5%. For those aged between 51 and 55 the percentage is 20% while for those aged between 56 and 60 and 61 and 74, the percentages are 22.5% and 27.5% respectively.

However, there are plus points. There is no earnings cap, which means high earners can make bigger contributions into these plans. Also, it is possible to obtain more than 25% of your final retirement fund in the form of tax-free cash.

Q Company pensions offer a range of additional benefits such as life insurance. Are these available under a personal pension?

A You can buy life insurance under your personal pension wrapper but you have to pay for it. It is possible to use up to 5% of the annual contribution limit to pay for life assurance. This can prove cost-effective because you get tax relief on the premiums you pay. However, some term rates offered by pension providers can be expensive, which offsets the tax benefits.

You can also purchase so-called 'waiver of premium insurance', which will ensure your pension contributions are paid if you suffer from a serious illness. If you are no longer able to work, contributions will be paid until your retirement age.

Q Do I have to make personal pension contributions through one plan?

A No, you can contribute to as many plans as you wish. However, setting up a series of plans may not be cost-effective because you may end up paying a series of set-up charges which you would avoid with just the one plan.

Q Given the introduction of stakeholder pensions, why should I bother with a personal pension?

A Good question. Personal pensions sold since April 1999 have had to be stakeholder-friendly and the regulators have insisted that these plans must allow policyholders to switch to a stakeholder scheme without being materially disadvantaged.

As a general rule, if you have been contributing to a personal pension for a while, it makes sense to seek independent financial advice as to whether you should continue with the policy or divert new premiums into a stakeholder pension.

Q If I want to buy a personal pension, where do I go?

A A good question. Providers of personal pensions proliferate. Although the main providers remain insurance companies – for example, Standard Life, Friends Provident – other companies have entered the arena. They include retailers (Marks & Spencer), banks (Abbey National) and investment houses (Edinburgh Fund Managers). Although it is now possible to buy many of these plans on an execution-only basis, it is probably best in the first instance to seek the professional help of an independent financial adviser. They should be able to seek out a plan which fits best with your financial objectives.

Q What kinds of personal pension plan are available?

A You need to make two key decisions.

DECISION 1: Do I contribute on an irregular or regular basis? If you do not think you can make a regular contribution to a personal pension plan – maybe because your income fluctuates markedly from month to month – then you are better off with a SINGLE PREMIUM plan or a RECURRING SINGLE PREMIUM plan where you make one-off payments or a series of one-off payments. Alternatively, if you prefer to squirrel away a little every month, then a REGULAR PREMIUM plan suits best. Minimum contributions for regular premiums plans (typically £50) are far lower than for single premium plans (typically £500). The downside is that regular premium plans seem to attract more pension charges.

DECISION 2: Where should my money be invested? Yet again, choice abounds. Plans tend to fall into the following categories:

1. UNIT-LINKED: These plans are sold by insurance companies. Here you buy units in a fund and their value then rises or falls according to the performance of the underlying assets. Funds range from deposit funds (low-risk) through to UK equity funds and more esoteric, high-risk funds such as emerging market funds. All insurance companies tend to offer broadly 'managed' funds – a jack of all investment trades – which usually invest in a range of the other funds. These 'managed' funds tend to be the first port of call for most pension investors because of their broad investment remit.

2. UNIT TRUSTS: These pension plans are offered by unit trust companies such as Invesco Perpetual. They work in much the same way as unit-linked plans in that your pension contributions buy units in a fund, these units then fluctuate in price according to the value of the underlying assets held within the fund. Fund choice is wide, ranging from cash through to fixed-interest and equities, both overseas and UK.

3. INVESTMENT TRUSTS: These plans are provided by

investment trust companies. Leading players include: Alliance, Edinburgh Fund Managers, Fleming and Foreign & Colonial. Pension contributions are invested in a fund whose shares are quoted on the stock market. Fund choice is again wide.

4. WITH-PROFITS: These used to be the main choice for people putting money into a personal pension. Offered by insurance companies, contributions are invested in a with-profits fund which in turn is invested in a broad spread of financial assets – from property through to gilts and equities. Your pension plan then increases in value every year through the addition of bonuses (annual or reversionary bonuses) to the sum assured (the minimum guaranteed payout at retirement). Upon retirement, the plan also benefits from a terminal or final bonus which is added to the final retirement pot. Although with-profits personal pensions do provide investors with a level of assurance, they are not transparent. It is impossible to see how your pension plan is progressing other than when you receive your annual bonus statement. With unit-linked plans it is possible to follow the unit price of your pension by looking in the financial pages of national newspapers on a daily basis. It is also difficult for people to work out how much their retirement pot is going to be, especially where insurance companies put great emphasis on terminal bonus payouts.

Just to confuse matters further, a new type of with-profits pension has emerged in the shape of the UNITISED WITH-PROFITS PLAN. Here there is no sum assured as with a conventional with-profits policy. Either the unit price of your plan increases as bonuses are declared. Or you receive bonuses in the form of extra units. As with a conventional plan, a final bonus is received upon retirement. Most insurance companies have now gone down this with-profits route including CGU, Friends Provident, Legal & General, Scottish Mutual and Standard Life.

5. GUARANTEED EQUITY FUNDS: These relative new-comers to the personal pensions world provide investors with funds which protect their contributions in the event of stock

market falls. In return for this, investors do not enjoy all the gains if stock markets race ahead. A number of companies including Scottish Mutual have successfully moved into this territory. They appeal to investors who are cautious about how their money is invested.

6. LIFESTYLE FUNDS: These match the type of fund your pension money is invested in to your age and time from retirement. In broad terms, your money is invested initially in equities and then as you get closer to retirement, your money is moved across into funds with greater exposure to bonds, gilts and cash. These funds can prove useful, ensuring that your final pensions pot is not ravaged by a sudden stock market fall.

7. SELF-INVESTED PERSONAL PENSIONS: These provide you with far greater investment scope than with a traditional personal pension. Here your pension plan is administered by a life office but the choice of investments is left to you or a stockbroker or investment specialist. By using a so-called SIPP, you do not restrict yourself to the pension funds offered by one company – you have free rein to include individual shares, unit trusts and investment trusts in your pension portfolio. You can even buy commercial property within a SIPP.

Q What about personal pension charges?

A They vary considerably but as a general rule, charges for monthly premium plans are higher than for single premium plans. With a monthly premium plan, you will suffer an up-front sales charge on premiums, often reduced contributions in the early years to pay for the adviser's commission, an annual management charge applied to the pension fund value and also a policy fee. This latter charge is often a fixed fee applied monthly which discriminates against people who make smaller pension contributions. On single premium plans, charges tend to be far simpler: an up-front sales charge and an annual management fee.

The one good bit of news is that charges for personal pensions have fallen sharply in recent years. With the advent of stakeholder pensions, pension companies have had no choice but to bring personal pension charges more closely in line with those for stakeholder.

Q Right. I've bought my personal pension. What happens if it isn't performing up to scratch?

A You have a number of options.

OPTION 1: You can transfer your fund to another one offered by the pensions company and then make contributions into the new fund.

OPTION 2: You can keep your money where it is but make contributions into another fund offered by the same pensions provider.

OPTION 3: You can cease contributions and start another pension plan with another provider.

OPTION 4: You can transfer your plan to another provider.

If you pursue any of these options, do check to see that you are not being stung with charges. Transfer penalties, when you transfer from one provider to another, can be heavy and make a significant indentation on your pensions pot. If in doubt, seek independent financial advice.

Q I've survived until retirement. How do I transform my pension pot into a lifetime income?

A There are several steps you must take to ensure you obtain an appropriate pension.

STEP ONE: First of all, you need to obtain details of the pension pot available at retirement. This will be sent by your pensions provider. It should explain the tax-free cash you are eligible to take and the annuity options available to you. Don't act on this straight away – it will pay you to stand back and consider all your options. The illustrations given by your insurance company are often inappropriate to your individual financial circumstances. They also usually represent poor value for money.

STEP TWO: You need to consider first of all whether you need tax-free cash or whether you are prepared to use the whole of your pension pot to convert to a lifetime income. Most people take the maximum tax-free cash possible, not just to go out and spend but to invest in other assets. The choice is yours. If in doubt, speak to a professional independent financial adviser.

STEP THREE: After deciding about tax-free cash, you need to go about getting the best annuity deal. This is absolutely critical for a number of reasons. For a start, once you have bought an annuity, you cannot exchange it – you are lumped with it for life. Secondly, there is a massive gap between the best and worst pension annuity deals available. Lock into a rum deal and it will affect your financial affairs for the rest of your life.

As ever with pensions, there are numerous options available to those wanting to turn their pension fund into pension income:

OPTION 1: BUY A CONVENTIONAL ANNUITY FROM YOUR PENSION PROVIDER. This will be the deal offered by your pension fund manager in its illustration. The deal will provide you with a guaranteed lifetime income. However, there are bells and whistles which you need to be aware of.

For a start, most quotations and illustrations are based on a SINGLE LIFE basis, woefully inappropriate for most people who are married. A single life pension annuity dies with the annuitant. In contrast, a JOINT LIFE pension annuity pays a full or reduced pension to your spouse if you die. Single life quotes are given because the rates look better than if illustrations for a joint life pension annuity were shown.

You should also be aware that you can buy GUARANTEES with your pension. Usually five years and sometimes as long as 10 years, these ensure that if you die soon after taking out your annuity, payments continue until the end of the guarantee period.

Also, most annuities pay a level rate of income. However, you can buy ESCALATING annuities which increase by either a fixed rate per annum or by the rate of inflation. However, the cost of such an option can be prohibitive leading to a very poor starting pension annuity.

Your pension provider should be able to provide you with these options. However, it is unlikely that your pension provider, however wonderfully it has looked after your money, will provide you with the best annuity deal. It pays you to shop around.

OPTION 2: SHOP AROUND. Everyone has the right to shop around at retirement for the most appropriate, and best value for money, pension annuity. It is called using the 'open market option'. Even if your pension provider hits you with penalties for taking your fund elsewhere, it will invariably pay you to shop around.

A number of companies have emerged to specialise in this area. They include: ANNUITY BUREAU (020 7902 2300) and ANNUITY DIRECT (020 7684 5000).

These companies will not only hunt down the companies with the best annuity deals but will also ensure you are aware of other important annuity ingredients such as guarantees, inflation protection and widow's protection.

OPTION 3: GO UNCONVENTIONAL. It is now possible to purchase an investment-linked annuity. Here your fund is invested in a with-profits or unit-linked fund. The annuity you then derive is dependent upon the performance of the investment fund.

A. WITH-PROFITS ANNUITY: Here you select the level of your first year's income by choosing an 'anticipated bonus rate' which must be within the provider's current range. The higher ABR you choose, the higher your initial income will be. Then, each year, the with-profits provider will declare the bonus level it has achieved in the preceding year. If this is less than your chosen ABR, your income will fall for the next 12 months. Conversely, if it is higher, your income will rise.

Some with-profits annuities now offer minimum income guarantees.

Obviously, the great attraction of with-profits annuities is that you are not locking into a level income but giving yourself the opportunity to see your income rise. But there are risks, primarily to see your income fall.

A number of companies now offer with-profits pension annuities. They include: CGU Life, Legal & General (0845 765 4465), Liverpool Victoria, Norwich Union (0845 773 8393), Prudential (0845 712 5270), Scottish Mutual, Scottish Widows (0131 655 6000) and Standard Life (0131 225 2552).

You should not buy a with-profits pensions annuity without seeking professional independent financial advice. The Annuity Bureau (020 7902 2300) provides advice in this area as should any decent independent financial adviser.

B. UNIT-LINKED ANNUITIES: Here, in very broad terms, your annuity is comprised of units in a chosen investment fund. The annuity payments you then receive depend upon the investment performance of the underlying units. As with with-profits annuities, you can choose the starting income you want by selecting an 'anticipated growth rate'. The higher the AGR you select, the higher the income you obtain from the beginning. But the quid pro quo is that if the AGR is not met by the underlying investment fund, your income will then start to fall.

Some companies take unit-linked annuities a step further by offering SELF-INVESTED UNIT-LINKED ANNUITIES. Here, rather than invest in one pension fund, you have the freedom to invest in a wider range of investments including shares, unit trusts and investment trusts.

No one should go down the unit-linked pension annuity route without first speaking to an independent financial adviser. However, in general terms, unit-linked annuities are most appropriate for younger people who (a) can afford to have their annuity linked to the fortune of financial assets (b) would otherwise be penalised for purchasing a conventional pension annuity because of their age.

OPTION 4: PHASED RETIREMENT AND INCOME DRAWDOWN. These are both ways of controlling the income you obtain from your pension fund while leaving the fund fully invested.

A. PHASED RETIREMENT: Here, your pension plan is divided into a series of mini-policies – often referred to as segments or clusters. Each year, you use some of these segments to obtain a mix of tax-free cash and a pension annuity. Meanwhile, the rest of the pension pot remains invested. The idea is that the older you get, the annuities you will be able to purchase – all other things being equal – will be higher. Furthermore, the balance of the pension fund you have invested in will benefit from solid investment performance.

There are a number of important additional points. ONE: Do bear in mind that with such a scheme, you cannot take your tax-free cash upfront. You release it over a period of time. TWO: Such an arrangement offers full tax-free cash to your beneficiaries on death, avoiding inheritance tax. This is a big plus point compared to a conventional annuity where the annuity dies with you or your spouse. THREE: Your entire fund has to be converted to pension annuities by the time you have reached age 75. FOUR: These plans are risky and so professional advice should be sought. Your pension fund can suffer from poor performance, especially if stock markets go belly up. Also, there is no guarantee that annuity rates are going to move in your favour as you get older.

B. INCOME DRAWDOWN OR PENSION INCOME

WITHDRAWAL: Here you can take your tax-free cash up front. You then draw an income from your pension fund which remains invested. The amount of income you can take must be within minimum and maximum levels laid down by the Inland Revenue. At age 75, you must use the remaining fund to purchase a conventional pension annuity.

Like phased retirement, income drawdown has drawbacks and plus points.

PLUS POINT 1: Your fund remains invested, thereby hopefully benefiting from continued investment growth.
PLUS POINT 2: The death benefits are attractive. A spouse, for example, can continue to draw an income from the plan, use the fund to buy an annuity or take the fund as cash less a 35% tax charge.
DRAWBACK 1: The income you take may erode the value of the pension fund, leaving you with a much reduced pension pot when you come to convert it into an annuity.
DRAWBACK 2: Charges can be high. Charges equivalent to between 3% and 6% of your original pension pot can be taken initially. Furthermore, your pension pot may then suffer an annual management charge of anything between 1% and 2%.

Annuity Bureau, an annuity specialist, says that the ideal person for an income drawdown scheme is a young retiree aged under 68 years who has a substantial pension fund, is not averse to risk and has other retirement income. In contrast, someone unsuitable for such a scheme would be a conservative investor aged 70 plus.

Annuity Bureau's sister company, the Income Drawdown Advisory Service (020 7401 2040), specialises in this area.

Dos and Don'ts

- **DO** consider a stakeholder pension before you buy a personal pension. Stakeholder plans are cost-friendly and are designed for you, not for the benefit of the provider. In short, stakeholder pensions have:
  - a single annual management charge of 1%;
  - no other charges such as policy fees or bid-offer spreads;
  - a minimum savings requirement of no more than £20;
  - the right for 100% of your contributions to be invested from the word go;
  - the facility for you to stop and start your savings without penalty;
  - the facility to increase or decrease your savings at any time without penalty;
  - the facilty to allow you to transfer your plan to another provider without penalty.

- **DO** check the small print of any old-style personal pension you hold. Some of these policies provide a very poor deal if you die before retirement. With a personal pension, the value of your accumulated fund goes back to your estate. But with some old-style plans, only contributions plus interest are returned. Such a poor financial deal has caused much financial heartbreak in the past – ensure you don't fall victim. Some pension providers will rewrite your plan so that the fund value will be paid out in the event of your early death. It can also pay to transfer the plan to a personal pension where the fund value is automatically paid out in the event of early death. However, don't do this without first taking professional independent financial advice.

- **DO** ensure any old-style personal pension you hold is written under trust. If it is not, you could be leaving dependants with furture inheritance tax problems.

- **DO** use an independent financial adviser to help you with personal pensions. There is no doubting the fact that personal pensions are complex and swathed in complex rules – a good independent financial adviser, and not all are good, should be able to find you a plan which meets with your needs.

- **DO** your homework before buying a personal pension, even if you ask an independent financial adviser to help you. Check out the past performance numbers to see whether they stack up against competing plans. If they don't, ask why the adviser is recommending such a plan. Equally, check out the company's charges to see if they are competitive. *Money Management*, a personal finance magazine, produces a comprehensive survey every year – published in its October edition – analysing the personal pension good guys and bad guys. Get a copy of it.

- **DO** ensure the personal pension plan you buy is as flexible as possible. A good personal pension plan should allow you to stop and restart contributions without penalty as well as allow you to increase or decrease payments according to changing financial circumstances. A good plan should also allow you to transfer your pension to another provider without penalty.

- **DO** ask your employer to contribute to a personal pension if he does not provide a company pension scheme. Remember, if you don't ask, you don't get.

- **DO** ensure your personal pension is invested in the right assets. There is no point starting a personal pension in your 20s and having the money invested in a fixed-interest fund. It is far better to have your money invested initially in equities so that you can benefit from the long-term returns they can generate. Then as you get closer to retirement, you can shift your pensions portfolio into less risky financial assets such as with-profits, fixed-interest and cash.

- **DO** remember that a good pension fund manager will not necessarily provide you with a good annuity. Shop around by using your open market option.

- **DO** remember that the tax-free cash from a personal pension is yours to enjoy. You are under no obligation to reinvest it – and many financial advisers will push you to do so, not necessarily just for your benefit. If you want to spend it on a holiday or on clearing your mortgage, do so.

- **DO** check to see whether your pension provider applies penalties if you decide to buy an annuity from another company. This can make moving your money elsewhere not as attractive as it might first appear.

- **DO** remember that income from a pension annuity is taxable as earned income but is not subject to National Insurance. Income is taxed at your highest rate of tax.

- **DO** check to see whether your pension provider offered you a guaranteed annuity rate when you took out your pension. These can be very attractive. Indeed, a number of insurers, primarily Equitable Life, have found the guarantees so onerous that they have tried to wriggle out of them. A guaranteed annuity pays a guaranteed annuity rate, irrespective of prevailing interest rates. Recently, such guarantees have ensured superior annuities for holders of such policies.

- **DON'T** buy a personal pension if your employer offers a company pension scheme. It is seldom the case that you are better off doing your own thing – company pension schemes offer a range of extras which a personal pension simply cannot offer you – such as employer contributions, death and disability cover and dependants' pensions.

- **DON'T** top up an existing pensions policy without first finding out the charges you will incur. Some pension providers still levy a whole raft of new charges on premium increases, thereby giving you bad value for money. A better option is to direct any premium increase into a new stakeholder pension. In some instances, it may also make sense to stop paying into a personal pension – making the policy paid-up – and putting further contributions into a new stakeholder plan.

- **DON'T** forget about pension plans you have set up in the past and maybe have stopped contributing to. Many of these plans were bad value for money because of heavy charges. It may make sense in some instances to transfer these policies to new friendlier pension plans. You should only do this after speaking to a good independent financial adviser.

- **DON'T** just assume that a personal pension is for the self-employed or for workers whose employers do not provide a company pension scheme. Personal pensions can be appropriate for certain other categories of people including:

CATEGORY ONE: Those people who are unable to join their company pension scheme straight away either because they are too young or because they are contract workers. In these circumstances, it can pay to make personal pension contributions until you are allowed to join the company pension scheme.

CATEGORY TWO: Those people who have additional freelance earnings on top of a salary from their main employment. Personal pension contributions can be made against these additional earnings.

CATEGORY THREE: Those people who belong to an occupational scheme which only provides death and dependants' benefits. Here, because no pension is being offered, it is possible to make personal pension contributions.

- **DON'T** get mixed up with a Self-Invested Personal Pension unless you have least £10,000 to invest. Setting-up charges can be steep.

- **DON'T** confuse pension annuities with purchased life annuities. Pension annuities are compulsory purchase annuities – you have no choice but to turn your pension fund into a lifetime income before age 75. In contrast, a purchased life annuity is a voluntary arrangement whereby you invest a lump sum and in return you obtain an income. Part of the income paid out is regarded as a return of capital and is tax-free. Tax is deducted from the interest element only.

- **DON'T** dismiss conventional pension annuities lightly. Some of the newer devices designed to get an income from your pension pot incorporate a high level of risk – something you may not wish to take on board. If you cannot afford to take financial risks in retirement, or simply want financial certainty in your retirement, a conventional pension annuity is for you.

- **DON'T** buy an income drawdown scheme which is invested in with-profits. The mathematics just do not stack up. In order for your income not to take great chunks out of your pension fund, you need your fund to be invested in equities.

- **DON'T** sit on your hands if you think you have been missold a personal pension in the past as a result of being asked to transfer out of or opt out of a company pension scheme. Contact the Financial Services Authority's helpline on 0845 606 1234.

Did you know?

- **DID** you know that stakeholder pensions are being offered by affinity groups and trade unions?

- **DID** you know that the government hopes to attract more than five million people into pensions as a result of charge-friendly, consumer-friendly stakeholder pensions?

- **DID** you know that people with no earnings, such as non-working parents, can take out a stakeholder pension?

- **DID** you know that stakeholder pensions can be set up for children?

- **DID** you know that when you buy a pension, you will get a document called a key features document? This spells out the charges contained within the plan and the impact of charges on future returns assuming annual investment growth of 7%. By comparing documents issued by different pension providers, it is possible to get an idea of which companies offer best value for money – although no idea can be gauged as to which company is going to invest your pension the best.

- **DID** you know that personal pensions can be used to accept transfers from a preserved company pension scheme or another personal pension plan? Transfers rarely make good financial sense, especially when transferring from a company scheme to a personal one so tread very carefully.

- **DID** you know that you can use a personal pension to fund a mortgage? The idea is that when you come to retirement, you pay off the interest-only mortgage with the tax-free cash from the pension. In the meantime, you pay interest payments on the mortgage. At retirement, while the tax-free cash is used to pay off the mortgage, the pension annuity provides you with a lifetime income. Pension mortgages are inflexible vehicles and should in most instances be avoided. A pension should be used to fund your retirement, not as a means to fund the purchase of a home.

- **DID** you know that it is still possible to carry back pension contributions into previous tax years to soak up unused tax relief? If you want to do this, speak to a good independent financial adviser.

- **DID** you know that many pension plans still levy unfriendly charges such as policy fees, capital units (units which attract excessive charges), and reduced allocation? These pensions may have been taken out a long time ago. It will pay you to check out whether these plans are worth holding on to or maybe transferring to another provider. It will also pay you to see whether it is worth making the policy paid-up and diverting future payments into a new cost-friendly plan such as a stakeholder plan.

- **DID** you know that it is possible to contribute to both a Section

226 retirement annuity contract (an old-style personal pension) and a personal pension?

- **DID** you know that in the October 2000 survey of personal pensions conducted by *Money Management* magazine the following companies were mentioned for solid performing with-profits pensions established by way of a regular premium? They were: Axa Sun Life, Co-operative Insurance and Liverpool Victoria. For single premium plans, the following companies received *Money Management*'s seal of approval. They were: Axa Sun Life, NFU Mutual, Scottish Amicable, Standard Life and Wesleyan Assurance.

- **DID** you know that you can now buy personal pensions where you can have access to the investment skills of some of the country's leading fund managers? These pension funds offer unit-linked funds managed by external fund managers. So, for example, Skandia Life, one of the leading players in this market, offers managed pension funds managed by a host of top fund managers including Fidelity, Henderson, Mercury, Newton and Perpetual. A number of companies have joined Skandia in offering such external fund links including Professional Life, Scottish Amicable and Scottish Equitable. Charges for these types of plan can be more expensive than for conventional unit-linked funds but the idea is that these extra charges will be more than made up for with superior investment performance. Also, with such an umbrella personal pension plan, you have far greater flexibility when it comes to transferring your plan. You can simply transfer your money, or contributions, to another manager offered under the personal pension umbrella.

- **DID** you know that you can choose to have income from a pension annuity paid monthly, quarterly or annually? It is up to you.

- **DID** you know that a number of companies offer IMPAIRED LIFE pension annuities? These pay enhanced annuity rates if you have a medical condition that is likely to shorten your life expectancy. Companies that specialise in this area include: Axa Sun Life (0117 989 9000); Scottish Widows (0131 655 6000); Britannic Retirement Solutions (0845 300 3321); GE Life (0800 169 1111) and Pension Annuity Friendly Society (020 7680 8960).

- **DID** you know that a number of companies offer SMOKERS annuities? Like impaired annuities, they pay higher annuity rates on the basis that the annuitant has a shortened life expectancy. Companies that offer enhanced annuity rates for smokers include: Britannic Retirement Solutions (0845 300 3321) and GE Life (0800 169 1111).

- **DID** you know that most pension annuities are paid monthly in advance? That means that the first payment of income will be on the same date as the annuity is effected. Some annuities, however, are paid in arrears which means people have to wait one month before receiving their first payment.

- **DID** you know that some pension annuities are offered on a 'with proportion' basis. This means that if an annuitant dies and has an annuity paid in arrears, a payment will be made in proportion to the time elapsed between the last payment and the date of death.

- **DID** you know that standard pension annuities are extremely safe? There is not one instance in the UK where a standard pension annuity has defaulted in payment.

- **DID** you know that the income you obtain from your annuity will depend upon a number of factors, some of which are sadly out of your control? Generally speaking, the younger you are, the poorer annuity deal you will get. This is because you are expected to live longer than someone taking out an annuity 15 years your senior. Women get offered poorer annuity deals than men of the same age because women live longer than men. Also, the economic environment plays a big part in the annuity deal you get. In general terms, low interest rates mean poor annuity rates while higher interest rates mean better annuity deals on the table.

So what now?

- **LIKE** it or like it not, funding your own pension for retirement is now a necessity, not a luxury. The government has done its bit by introducing cost-friendly stakeholder pensions which have had the effect of reducing charges on personal pensions.

  It's now up to you.

CHAPTER **8**

The Golden
Nuggets

BUDGET

'A mathematical confirmation of
your worst suspicions.'

A. A. Latimer

SINCE *Financial Mail on Sunday* was born in early 1994, there is no
doubt that the personal finance sector has undergone a quiet
revolution and transformed itself into one of the country's most
competitive marketplaces.

Gone are the days when you had to queue up for a mortgage
and be grateful that you were granted an interview. And gone are the
days when you had no choice but to go to a bank for a bank account
and a building society for a deposit account and be content with the
deal offered.

Today, instead, competition is rife. The previous barriers which
existed, which meant insurance had to be sold by insurers and
mortgages by building societies, have long been blown away. And
with their removal, new players have come storming into the arena
intent on putting the interests of customers first. The consumer is
suddenly king.

So we now have companies, traditionally renowned for selling
insurance, moving into new territories such as banking and

mortgages. Equally, we have companies firmly established on Britain's high streets entering personal finance territory. This new wave of competition, which shows no sign of abating, is simply great news for consumers.

In the following chapter, we will show you 60 different ways in which you can improve your financial lot. Many of these 'golden personal finance nuggets' stem from the increased competition which now exists in the personal finance arena. Some of these tips have already been pointed out in previous chapters on specific subjects such as mortgages and insurance. Some have not because they fall outside the mainstream areas of personal finance advice. All have appeared as key personal finance advice in the pages of *Financial Mail on Sunday* over the past seven years.

Even if you only decide to act on one or a number of the 'golden personal finance nuggets' provided below, you will be better off financially for doing so.

Golden nugget 1: get the best from your savings

FOR far too long, too many savers have been receiving a poor savings deal from their bank or building society, in many instances earning less than 1% gross interest from their deposit savings. Thankfully, by shopping around, savers can now enjoy higher interest rates.

New entrants into the savings market, such as insurance companies, supermarkets and companies more renowned for their aircraft and music, have put the focus back on the saver through the offering of attractive savings rates. These new players include Virgin, Standard Life and Prudential's Egg.

Moving your hard-earned savings to a financial player which puts your interests before their profits is hassle free, involves no risk whatsoever and will furnish you with a long-term improvement in your savings income.

And if you feel guilty that in moving, you are being disloyal to the bank or building society you have been with for a near lifetime, think again. Remember, it is your loyalty that the financial institution has played upon in order to give you such a rotten long-term savings deal in the past. You owe them nothing.

Did you know? – Fact 1

- **DID** you know that most financial sections of national newspapers now include best-buy savings tables? These tables enable you to ascertain which companies are offering the best deals as well as gauge what kind of deal you are currently getting from the savings institution looking after your money. *Moneyfacts*, a monthly publication, includes comprehensive details on savings rates available from most savings institutions. Further details from: Moneyfacts Publications, Moneyfacts House, 66-70 Thorpe Road, Norwich NR1 1BJ (01603 476 476).

Golden nugget 2: don't pay tax on your savings if you don't have to

IF you are a non-taxpayer, ensure that you are not paying tax on interest from any building society or bank deposits.

Interest from building society or bank deposit savings is automatically paid net of 20% tax. But non-taxpayers do not have to suffer the tax in the first place. All they need to do in order to qualify for tax to be paid gross is to complete a form R85 available from their bank or building society or failing that from their local tax office.

Tax is a big enough burden for all of us without paying it unnecessarily.

Did you know? – Fact 2

- **DID** you know that basic rate taxpayers do not have to pay any more tax on interest from their savings? On the other hand, higher rate taxpayers have to cough up an additional 20%.

Golden nugget 3: keep a date with Tessa

WHILE April 6,1999 heralded the new dawn of the tax-free Isa, it certainly did not herald the final curtain call for Peps and Tessas, the vehicles which Isas replaced. You ignore your Peps and Tessas at your peril.

While Pep investors can improve their lot by transferring plans to benefit from improved performance – see GOLDEN NUGGET TEN – Tessa savers should keep doing what they have always been doing and that is squirrelling their money away in this deposit-based tax-free savings pot.

Anyone who took out a Tessa prior to April 6, 1999 can invest a maximum of £9,000 over the course of the next five years. This money will build up tax-free. So, if you've got a Tessa, use it.

Furthermore, anyone who took out a follow-on Tessa prior to April 6,1999 can invest the difference between the £9,000 maximum cap and the capital they transferred initially into the plan. So if, for example, they transferred £6,000, they can invest a further £3,000 over the course of the next five years.

In continuing to build up your Tessa tax-free pot, you will be protecting more of your savings from the scourge of the taxman. Furthermore, once your plan matures, you will have the ability to transfer the capital – in effect the contributions you have made over the five-year period – into a cash Isa, thereby maintaining the tax-free status of your savings. Alternatively, you can simply enjoy the fruits of your savings.

Did you know? – Fact 3

- DID you know that any contributions you make towards a Tessa will have no bearing whatsoever on your ability to contribute to an Isa? As a result, provided your household budget can stand the strain, you can contribute to both an Isa and a Tessa at the same time.

Golden nugget 4: discover whether you are paying over the odds for life assurance

MOST of us, especially if we are married and have children, will have bought life assurance in order to provide financial protection in the event of death. But few of us will have checked to see whether the premiums we are paying for cover today remain competitive.

If you bought term assurance, the best-value life cover around and the most straightforward, in the 1980s or early 1990s, there is a good chance that you are now paying over the odds for cover. Term assurance premiums have come tumbling down over the past few years as a result of increased competition and reduced concerns over the impact of illnesses such as AIDS on claims.

As a result, by cancelling cover with your existing insurer in favour of term assurance with an insurer with keener premiums, you can save yourself a lot of money. Critically, you can shave pounds off your monthly premium costs without reducing the level of life cover you and your family have. One word of warning, keep your existing cover going until your new policy is in force.

Did you know? – Fact 4

- **DID** you know that some companies now monitor term assurance rates on a regular basis and can provide you with quotes on the telephone, thereby enabling you straight away to see whether you can benefit from a better deal? Leading player in this field is Term Direct (020 7684 8000). The Association of British Insurers has also produced a number of useful leaflets on life assurance. Further details from: ABI, 51 Gresham Street, London EC2V 7HQ.

Golden nugget 5: home in on best-value cover

MANY homebuyers purchase home insurance when they arrange a mortgage with a lender. Indeed, it is often a condition of a lender granting a loan that home insurance is also bought through them at the same time. Unfortunately, what these same homebuyers fail to realise is that the only reason why their mortgage deal looks so attractive is because they are paying over the odds for their home insurance. They then perpetuate this financial folly by clinging on to this expensive home insurance year in and year out.

If you fit this description or you simply accept the premium hike that your home insurer informs you of on an annual basis without batting an eyelid, it is time for financial action. By shopping around for better value insurance when your policy comes up for annual renewal, you can literally shave hundreds of pounds off your annual home insurance costs.

You can get an independent financial adviser to do the shopping around for you. They will scour the market on your behalf in search of the best home insurance deal for you. They should also ensure the new cover you obtain is not cheaper simply because it is full of exclusions and mighty excesses.

Alternatively, you can approach a selection of insurance companies which sell direct to the public. By buying direct, you can save yourself money because the insurance company is not having to pay a middleman such as a bank or building society for arranging the sale. But in buying direct, take your time and don't be frightened to ring several direct insurers for quotes.

The key is not to accept home insurance renewal notices as done-deals. Shop around and tell your insurer you are doing so. If nothing else, you are sending out a strong signal to your insurer that it cannot take your business for granted.

Did you know? – Fact 5

- **DID** you know that some bank and building societies will charge you a fixed fee if you move your home insurance elsewhere? Alas, do not despair. Did you also know that many insurers will pay this moving fee on your behalf if you take out its home insurance? Typically, this charge is in the region of £25.

Golden nugget 6: prepare for the unthinkable

ALTHOUGH we all think we are invincible, statistics tell us a different tale. According to Department of Social Security figures, you are 16 times more likely to be unable to work for more than six months as a result of illness than you are to die before the age of 65.

Unfortunately, too few of us have financial protection in place to cope with the financial problems that long-term illness can bring. While employers can come to the rescue, the state will only do so as a last resort. As for the self-employed, without an employer behind them, they can be particularly vulnerable to the consequences of long-term illness, especially if they are a one-man band.

An array of insurance is now available to soften the financial blow of long-term illness. There is permanent health insurance which aims to replace your income while you are off work; critical illness cover which pays out a lump sum on the diagnosis of certain serious illnesses; and for homeowners there is mortgage payment protection which will meet your mortgage payments in the event of long-term illness.

Although such insurance is unglamorous and should only be bought through an independent financial adviser who can ensure you end up with cover which dovetails with your existing insurance, it does give you vital peace of mind. Don't ignore it.

Did you know? – Fact 6

- **DID** you know that many famous people have survived major illnesses only to come back fitter than ever? Singer and film star

Olivia Newton-John and Wendy Richards of *EastEnders* and *Are You Being Served?* fame have both survived cancer while politician Michael Heseltine and film star and singer Adam Faith have both survived heart attacks.

Golden nugget 7: cut your mortgage costs

IF you have a mortgage where you pay the lender's standard variable interest rate, there is a good chance that you could reduce your monthly mortgage outgoings considerably by changing lenders and taking advantage of a cheaper loan.

As a result of the fierce competitiveness of the mortgage market, lenders are literally falling over each other to get your business. It is a mortgage buyer's market, hence some of the fantastic remortgage deals around.

Remortgaging is not without its pitfalls, nor its associated costs, but a good mortgage broker should be able to assess quite quickly whether remortgaging will pay for you. Furthermore, if it is for you, they should then be able to navigate you through the remortgage waters.

In short, if you are paying a lender's variable rate mortgage, you would be a fool not to explore the remortgage option. You have little to lose and potentially you could save yourself a lot of money.

Did you know? – Fact 7

- **DID** you know that a number of independent mortgage brokers specialise in remortgaging? Two of the country's leading brokers are Bath-based London & Country Mortgages and London-based Savills Private Finance.

Golden nugget 8: think modern mortgages

IF you are thinking about taking out a new mortgage, consider one of the new-style flexible mortgages.

A number of new entrants have come into the mortgage market in recent years with loans designed to cope with the modern working world. Unlike traditional mortgages, these new-style loans enable you to make early repayments of capital without penalty. Furthermore, interest is calculated on a daily basis which means your interest payments come down immediately in response to reductions in your outstanding loan.

With traditional standard variable rate mortgages set up on a capital repayment basis, your outstanding loan is only reduced once a year even though your monthly repayments are in theory part capital repayment and part interest charges. As a result, you in effect pay interest on money you no longer owe. It is a scandal – plain and simple.

Most flexible loans also allow you to suspend mortgage payments for a while and overpay if your household budget can cope with it. Some provide you with a cheque book so that you can draw funds against the mortgage account.

A number of companies have made flexible mortgages their speciality including Direct Line, Legal & General, Prudential's Egg, Royal Bank of Scotland, Standard Life, Virgin and Woolwich. Although such loans are not for everyone, they can save you masses of interest charges in the long run.

Did you know? – Fact 8

- **DID** you know that industry experts believe Britain's homeowners pay £350 million per year in excess interest charges as a result of having standard variable rate mortgages where interest is calculated on an annual rather than a daily basis? A good independent mortgage broker, including Savills Private Finance and London & Country Mortgages, will be able to tell you whether you are paying over the odds for your mortgage and advise you on the appropriateness of a more flexible loan.

Golden nugget 9: avoid redemption penalties like the plague

WHILE special mortgage deals are available in abundance, don't be overwhelmed by attractive headline rates – because they usually hide a snake-pit full of biting early redemption penalties.

Many lenders have made it their goal to appear in the best-buy mortgage tables in national newspapers. A best-buy appearance usually guarantees them massive new business. But such offers do not come without a cost to new borrowers.

In order to make up for the attractive up-front interest rate, these lenders usually ply their loans with onerous early redemption penalties which means you cannot escape the loan in the early years without having to pay a big penalty. There is also no guarantee that the interest rate will be competitive once the special deal expires.

As a rule of thumb, any loan which carries redemption penalties beyond the term of the special deal should be kicked into touch. So if you are offered a three-year fixed-rate mortgage with early redemption penalties in the first five years, look elsewhere.

As a matter of course, you should fully understand the size and length of early redemption penalties before you accept any mortgage offer. If in doubt, get the lender or a good mortgage broker to spell them out in pence and pound notes so that you know exactly where you stand.

Did you know? – Fact 9

- **DID** you know that early redemption penalties can be expressed in a multitude of ways? Most lenders express them in terms of monthly interest charges. So a mortgage with a 90-day redemption penalty means you will have to pay the equivalent of three months' interest to get out of the loan early. But others use more complex calculations involving interest rate differentials and the amount of time left until the special mortgage deal – the fixed-rate period, for example – expires.

Golden nugget 10: don't forget your Pep

FROM April 6, 1999, it has not been possible to put any more money into a tax-free Personal Equity Plan. If you have wanted to continue saving on a tax-free basis, then new-style Individual Savings Accounts have been your answer.

Yet it is imperative that you do not leave your Peps to wallow, especially if they form an important component of your investment portfolio. Although Peps remain tax-free, this tax freedom provides no protection against poor investment management. And unfortunately too many people currently hold their money in poorly performing Peps. Alas, there is a solution.

Although you can no longer contribute to a Pep, you do have the right to transfer a Pep to a new manager in order to benefit, hopefully, from improved investment performance. Transfers are easy to arrange although there are a couple of pitfalls awaiting the uninitiated.

First, transfer charges have to be taken into consideration – you can get clobbered by both exit charges levied by your old Pep manager and by entry charges demanded by your new manager. Also, you have to transfer an entire year's plan at a time – you can't transfer part of a plan accumulated in a particular tax year and leave the rest where it is.

Pep transfers are your escape route from poor investment performance. Use it – don't settle for second best.

Did you know? – Fact 10

- **DID** you know that the tax treatment of your Pep is identical to that for new-fangled Isas? That means there is no capital gains tax to pay on any investment growth while income continues to roll up tax-free.

Golden nugget 11: don't rush into an Isa head-first

ALTHOUGH Isas are the new tax-free savings kids on the block, there is no reason why you should rush out and buy the first offering you set your eyes on. Indeed, holding back should be a positive advantage. By delaying your Isa purchase until more Isa plans become available, you should then be able to pick the best from the whole bunch rather than the best from a half-formed bunch.

Furthermore, unlike Peps and Tessas, the Isa rules are somewhat complicated, which is another good reason for holding fire. By choosing a particular Isa route, you could inadvertently preclude yourself from some investment options.

The rules are as follows. You can invest £7,000 in an Isa. A maximum of £3,000 can be cash and a maximum of £1,000 can be invested in insurance. The balance – £3,000 – or indeed the entire £7,000 can be invested in equities such as shares, unit trusts and investment trusts.

Fine so far. You then essentially have two choices. You can opt to have your Isa pot managed by just one company who will put your money where you want it – a so-called maxi Isa.

Alternatively, you can elect to have the three separate Isa elements – cash, insurance and equities – managed by different companies. This is the so-called mini Isa approach. But remember, if you choose this latter route, you can only invest a maximum of £3,000 in equity-related products as opposed to £7,000 under a maxi Isa. This may not appeal to many investors who have grown up on the back of Peps and the returns they have enjoyed from such equity-based plans.

In a nutshell, hang fire on Isas until you really know how and where you want your money invested. Already, many people have taken out mini cash Isas, failing to realise that in doing so they have restricted their ability to get equity exposure. Don't join this crowd unless you are sure you really want to.

Did you know? – Fact 11

- **DID** you know that Isas are available in all kinds of places – from banks, building societies through to supermarkets? Furthermore, anyone over the age of 18 (16 for cash Isas) and ordinarily resident in the UK for tax purposes can take out an Isa. All leading national newspapers carry extensive editorial within their personal finance pages on Isas – it is essential reading for anyone looking to buy an Isa.

Golden nugget 12: think trusts

IF you are thinking of buying equities for the long term, you really should consider the merits of unit trusts and investment trusts run by some of the country's leading investment groups.

Both unit trusts and investment trusts are collective investments, which means the managers pool investors' money and use it to invest in a broad span of company shares. So when you invest in a unit trust or investment trust, you are obtaining exposure to a wide spread of companies, thereby diluting your investment risk. These companies may be big blue-chip concerns or international giants. Alternatively, they may be little-known smaller companies.

Whatever the underlying investment, the hope is that your holding will increase in value over time, thereby increasing your own personal wealth.

Both the unit trust and investment trust industries have a proud record of delivering solid returns for investors without charging the purchaser the earth. And apart from the occasional hiccup, both industries are relatively scandal free. Critically, they represent a sounder investment option than putting your faith in the fortunes of one or a narrow range of shares.

And one last thought – trusts can be held inside a tax-free Isa.

Did you know? – Fact 12

- **DID** you know that both the Association of Unit Trusts and Investment Funds and the Association of Investment Trusts publish useful guides to the virtues of both unit trusts and investment trusts? Further details from: The Unit Trust Information Service, 65 Kingsway, London WC2B 6TD; AITC, Durrant House, 8–13 Chiswell Street, London EClY 4YY. Furthermore, a number of leading monthly personal finance magazines publish performance tables which will enable you to keep a tab on the performance of your trust – unit trust or investment trust. They include *Money Management*, *Bloomberg Money* and *What Investment?*

Golden nugget 13: think regular

DON'T think that just because you haven't got £1,000 to put into an investment you will be unable to get a slice of the investment action. Far from it. One of the best ways to buy a unit trust or investment trust is through a regular savings scheme.

Most trust managers now offer regular savings schemes as a matter of course, enabling you to save from £50 per month. Indeed, some companies will allow you to save even less. Money is taken from your bank account every month, either by standing order or direct debit, and steadily over time, almost without feeling it, you will build a sizeable investment fund.

Although there is little to choose between unit trusts and investment trusts, savings schemes run by most investment trust companies tend to offer best value for money, primarily because the costs are so cheap. Indeed, some investment trusts will charge you no more than stamp duty on your monthly purchase of shares.

There can be few better financial deals doing the rounds.

And one final point. Remember that if you save through a unit trust or investment trust within the tax-free wrapper of an Isa, any gains will be tax-free.

Did you know? – Fact 13

- **DID** you know that both the Association of Unit Trusts and Investment Funds and the Association of Investment Trusts publish booklets on the benefits of regular saving through unit trusts and investment trusts? Further details from: The Unit Trust Information Service, 65 Kingsway, London WC2B, 6TD; AITC, Durrant House, 8–13 Chiswell Street, London EC1Y 4YY. Past performance numbers on regular saving into unit trusts and investment trusts are not readily published although magazines such as *Money Management* do publish surveys on an irregular basis.

Golden nugget 14: be a general, not for a day but for the long term

BUYING a unit trust or investment trust can be a daunting exercise, what with the breadth of choice available. Do you invest in an overseas trust, an exciting emerging markets trust, a smaller companies trust or a UK equity income fund?

One of the unsung heroes of the investment trust sector is the generalist trust or world fund. These trusts, most of which have been around since the late 1800s, make their living by investing in all the major stock markets of the world as well as in a selection of the up-and-coming markets. As a result, they seldom let investors down, nor do they shout from the top of the performance tables or scream with anguish from the bottom of the tables.

By investing conservatively across the world, generalist investment trusts make a perfect investment vehicle for first-time investors. They also act as the perfect core to an investment portfolio.

Also in their favour is the fact that many of the generalist trusts are of considerable size – some £1 billion – which is a big comfort factor for investors.

Despite their unsexy name, a generalist trust should be the first equity port of call for most investors. Big generalist trusts include Foreign & Colonial, Alliance, Monks, Second Alliance and Scottish Investment Trust.

And of course, such trusts can be bought through cost-effective regular savings schemes as well as form the investment component of a tax-free Isa.

Did you know? – Fact 14

- **DID** you know that the country's oldest investment trust, Foreign & Colonial, is a generalist? Formed back in 1868, Foreign & Colonial investment trust now has assets under management in excess of £2 billion and invests worldwide. The Association of Investment Trust Companies has published an informative guide to 'generalist' trusts. Write to: AITC, Durrant House, 8–13 Chiswell Street, London EC1Y 4YY. The past performance of generalist investment trusts can be scrutinised by looking at the performance tables in leading personal finance magazines such as *Money Management* and *Bloomberg Money*.

Golden nugget 15: don't be mesmerised by investment charges

FIERCE competition within the unit trust world has resulted in some companies reducing their charges in recent years in order to encourage new investors on board. A number of companies have cut their initial charges back to zero, meaning that all of your money is invested from day one rather than the customary 94.5%.

Yet, while such price competition is great news, do not be led into believing that low charges automatically equate with superior investment returns because they do not. In choosing a unit trust as a home for your long-term savings, other considerations are far more important – such as the fund's ability to meet your investment needs, its past investment record and more importantly its future prospects.

Paying little or nothing for a unit trust can make financial sense. But it will count for nothing if your investment then subsequently fails to perform. Some of the country's best and most successful investment houses levy an initial charge and an annual management charge because they use the fees to invest in some of the country's top investment managers. Leading investment groups such as Jupiter and Invesco Perpetual have adopted this approach to very good effect.

Provided you do a little homework, or speak to an independent financial adviser well versed in the unit trust world, you shouldn't be offput paying a 5.5% initial charge for buying a decent unit trust with a strong track record.

Did you know? – Fact 15

- **DID** you know that the Association of Unit Trusts and Investment Funds has published a booklet providing key details for all unit trust groups including charges? Copies are available from: The Unit Trust Information Service, 65 Kingsway, London WC2B 6TD.

Golden nugget 16: don't panic when stock markets go haywire

WHILE investing in equities makes great long-term sense, do not assume that everything will go smoothly because it won't. Investing in equities is a little like a roller-coaster ride with sudden dips to catch the unexpected and take the breath away.

The key is to hold on through the dips. Don't pile out at the bottom because you will only lose money. If you can cling on, your share or trust fortunes should come good again. Remember, a share loss is only a loss once you have crystallised it – in other words, once you have actually sold your investment. While you continue to hold it, your losses are paper losses only.

Equally as important, if you save via a unit trust, investment trust or Isa savings scheme, keep the plans going through thick and thin. When stock markets dip in fortunes, regular savings schemes come into their own because they buy more units or shares for you. This approach will stand you in good stead in the long term.

Did you know? – Fact 16

- **DID** you know that research by leading investment group Fidelity proved that it pays to be a patient long-term investor rather than one who responds to market falls by getting out of the market, only to return when fortunes have turned for the better?

Golden nugget 17: don't be sucked into hot investment themes

ALTHOUGH unit trusts and investment trusts are great long-term investment vehicles, they can be subject to aggressive marketing – usually at a time when it is least attractive for you to pile your money in.

As a result, tread very carefully. Don't be enticed by compelling past performance numbers quoted in alluring financial adverts, especially when they relate to trusts with restricted investment objectives such as emerging market funds, technology funds or single country funds. Such trusts have a habit of falling in price far quicker than they rise in value. Unfortunately, the adverts don't tell you that fact in the same bold print as they shout about past performance achievements.

If past performance figures look almost too good to be true, they usually signal one overwhelming fact – that such numbers are unsustainable and that the investment bubble is about to burst.

If you do fancy exposure to such volatile trusts with exotic-sounding names, then commit no more than a fraction of your new savings budget to them. And invest through a regular savings scheme, thereby ensuring you do not end up investing all your hard-earned money just prior to a stiff market correction. Don't invest any more than you can afford to lose.

Did you know? – Fact 17

- **DID** you know that most investors who put money into Far Eastern investment funds five years ago are still standing on heavy losses? At the time, few investors doubted the sustainability of the Far Eastern economic miracle, egged on in no small way by advertisers anxious to sell their investment funds. Today, most investors won't touch the area with a proverbial bargepole.

Golden nugget 18: don't let the tax tail wag the investment dog

WHILE 'tax-free' is an appealing sales label, don't buy an investment or savings product simply on the basis of a tax-free wrapper because you could end up sorely disappointed.

There is little point, for example, in a non-taxpayer taking out a cash Isa if they can get a better interest rate elsewhere. They could be better off in a high-paying deposit account held outside an Isa with interest being paid gross.

Similarly, there is little point taking out a friendly society tax-free savings bond if the charges absorb all the tax-free benefits – as many plans have indeed done in the past. And tax-free National Savings savings certificates are not worth holding unless the interest rates on offer are competitive. As for venture capital trusts and enterprise investment schemes, they should only be approached with a tax adviser in tow.

Tax freedom on savings is a big benefit; especially for taxpayers, if it goes hand in hand with good investment returns. But it counts for nothing if it acts as a smokescreen for a rank bad financial product.

Did you know? – Fact 18

- **DID** you know that you can invest tax-free £10,000 in both the current issues of National Savings index-linked and fixed-interest certificates? Furthermore, you can squirrel away £25 per month or £270 per year into a friendly society 10-year-tax exempt plan. But as already advised, don't do so unless you are sure that you are getting a good deal.

Golden nugget 19: don't mix insurance and investments

IT is a fact of personal finance life that products which combine life assurance with an element of investment usually represent bad value for money. Products which fit into this category include friendly society tax-free investment plans, whole-of-life policies and endowments.

When insurance companies combine life assurance with investments, it is usually an excuse for them to swamp policies with excessive charges. As a purchaser, at worst you end up with expensive life assurance. At best, you end up with an expensive investment. In other words, you fall between two stools – those belonging to insurance and investment.

There is a school of personal finance thought that says that you should never mix savings and insurance within the same financial plan. If you want life cover, opt for straightforward term assurance. If you want an investment, select from an Isa, unit or investment trust. It is a view worth abiding with.

Did you know? – Fact 19

- **DID** you know that an ideal way for a family to obtain life cover is through the purchase of a family income benefit policy? These cheap and cheerful term assurance policies will provide an income until a predetermined date in the future in the event of your death before the policy term expires. Such policies, available from leading insurance companies, can be written on a joint basis, which means income payments are made if you or your partner dies. They can also be written to coincide with the expected period of dependency of the youngest child in the family. They are great value for money.

Golden nugget 20: don't jettison endowments without thinking first

ALTHOUGH many endowment policies have performed adequately well it is a fact that many have failed to live up to the expectations hyped up by commission-hungry insurance salesmen in the late 1970s and 1980s.

If you have a poorly performing endowment, or you can no longer afford the monthly premiums or you want to invest the premiums elsewhere, don't immediately surrender the policy back to the insurance company without first taking a deep breath of air.

A number of companies, so-called second-hand endowment specialists, will now buy the policy off you and provide you with a better payout than that available through surrendering.

Although these companies will not accept all endowments, it is an option worth exploring. After regulatory pressures most insurance companies now point out the second-hand policy route to policyholders prior to meeting their request to surrender their plans.

Remember, no surrender until you have discovered whether you can get a better deal by selling your policy on.

Did you know? – Fact 20

- **DID** you know that research by the regulators has shown that some 25% of endowment policyholders are likely to surrender their policy within two years? Unless you are sure that you will stick the 25-year term, avoid endowments like the plague.

Golden nugget 21: remember the children

WHILE saving for your own financial future has to be one of your paramount financial objectives, don't forget to put a little aside for your children. By saving for kids as soon as they are born, you can give your money every chance of growing into a worthwhile savings pot.

Savings vehicles for children abound, including children's savings accounts (complete with kiddies' gifts) and children's friendly society 10-year tax-free investment plans. But better investments are unit trusts and National Savings children's bonus bonds.

You can buy a unit trust for a child simply by buying units in your name but then adding the child's initials to indicate who owns the units. This is known as a designated account. When the child is old enough – usually 18 – they can then claim the units by filling in a simple stock transfer form. Given the unit trust should remain invested for a long time, the opportunity for solid investment growth is high.

National Savings children's bonus bonds are a more conservative investment. They can be bought for anyone under the age of 16 and offer a guaranteed rate of interest for five years. Interest is automatically reinvested in the bond each year to increase its capital value. At the end of five years, you are then sent details of the guaranteed interest rate for the next five years. The bonds automatically mature on the holder's 21st birthday and all proceeds are tax-free.

With bonds costing £25, they represent a great little investment. Stakeholder pensions can also be taken out for children as can cash-based Isas (for those aged 16 and over).

Did you know? – Fact 21

- **DID** you know that if a parent gives their child money to invest, the parent is liable to tax on all the interest if it is more than £100 in any one tax year? But interest on National Savings children's bonus bonds is exempt from this rule.

Golden nugget 22: if you like a flutter, go premium

AS an alternative to the National Lottery draw, you should consider premium bonds. Although the big prizes are not as alluring as the National Lottery – a mere £1 million top prize every month – you do have the assurance that you can get your stake back whenever you want to as well as have the chance every month to win one of more than 500,000 prizes ranging from £50 to £100,000. And if you are lucky enough to win, the winnings are tax-free, which means they do not have to be declared on your tax form.

If you like a gamble and have £100 available to invest, premium bonds could just be right up your street.

Did you know? – Fact 22

- **DID** you know that you can hold a maximum of £20,000 in National Savings' premium bonds? For wealthier people who can afford to purchase a large chunk of bonds, they make good sense because the probability of them winning a tax-free prize is enhanced.

Golden nugget 23: contribute to a company pension scheme

IF you work for a company which runs an occupational pension scheme, don't delay in joining it – it's simply the best pensions deal around and the best way of you preparing financially for retirement.

In joining your company pension scheme, not only will you benefit from tax relief on contributions you make into the scheme but most employers worth their salt will boost the payments you make into the scheme with contributions made on your behalf. Look at this employer contribution as a form of extra pay.

If you aren't a member, ask your personnel department why not. Some schemes exclude part-time workers although this is now the exception rather than the norm. Others will not accept you as a scheme member until you have served an initial probationary period at the company.

The quicker you join your employer's company pension scheme, the longer time your pension pot has in order to provide you with a half-decent pension on retirement.

If your employer does not offer a company pension scheme, or if you are self-employed, then you should make your own pension provision by taking out a personal pension. Anyone under the age of 35 can put up to 17.5% of annual earnings into a personal pension, rising to 40% at ages 61 to 74. And contributions qualify for tax relief at your highest rate of tax.

Did you know? – Fact 23

- **DID** you know that you are not restricted to the personal contributions you make into your company's pension scheme? The current rules allow you to increase your payments, subject to an overall ceiling equivalent to 15% of your salary, by making so-called additional voluntary contributions. By doing this, you will be boosting your prospects of a financially healthy retirement.

Golden nugget 24: you're never too young to start a pension

THE longer you delay putting money into a pension, the worse off you will be when you reach retirement age – it's an undisputed fact.

For example, a man paying £100 a month into a personal pension at age 20, with contributions increasing 5% per year, could build a retirement fund worth £635,000 by the time he is aged 60 assuming annual investment growth of 9%. This, in turn, would generate an annual pension upon retirement worth £40,300, increasing by 5% per annum.

But a man delaying until age 30 before making identical

pension contributions would only generate a retirement fund of £242,000. This would buy him a lifetime annual income of £15,400 – less than half that secured by the man starting at age 20.

For women, pensions delay represents an even bigger problem because the pension income they can secure from a retirement fund is less than that for a man – primarily because women live longer than men.

The pensions message is simple – get saving now.

Did you know? – Fact 24

- **DID** you know that the pensions rules positively encourage you to save more as you get older? Although you are limited to squirrelling away 17.5% of your earnings below the age of 35, this percentage increases to 25% at age 46 and 30% at age 51.

Golden nugget 25: shop around at retirement

ALTHOUGH funding a pension adequately is vital to a financially secure retirement, equally important is ensuring you maximise the pension income from your pension pot when you retire.

Anyone who has a personal pension – old-style or new-style – or is a member of a money purchase pension scheme has to purchase a pension annuity with their pension fund. This will provide them with a guaranteed lifetime income.

But not everyone knows that in purchasing this annuity, they have the right to refuse to buy the annuity offered by their pension fund manager and instead go elsewhere in search of better value.

Exercising the open-market option, as this pension annuity shopping around is referred to, makes great financial sense. It is a fact that the best pension fund managers do not necessarily offer the best annuity deals.

And by shopping around, you can not only secure a higher annuity rate but usually a more appropriate annuity deal – one, for example, that acknowledges that you have a partner who does not want to be left in the financial lurch if you die in retirement taking your annuity with you.

Exercise your rights and shop around for the best annuity deal in town.

Did you know? – Fact 25

- **DID** you know that a number of companies now exist purely to ensure you end up with an appropriate annuity deal? Leading annuity specialists include the London-based triumvirate, Annuity Solutions, Annuity Direct and The Annuity Bureau.

Golden nugget 26: pay less for your plastic

OVER the past five years, the credit card industry in this country has undergone a dramatic transformation. Previously dominated by the mighty clearing banks who believed they could charge customers what they pleased, the credit card market is now as competitive as it has ever been with new customer-focused entrants flooding in almost daily. Hard luck banks, good news for credit card holders.

If you have a credit card issued by one of the major banks, and you use it to borrow, there is a good chance that you can shave your interest bills sharply by transferring your balance to a new provider – one of the new American banks, for example.

In transferring, not only will many of the new card issuers offer you lower long-term interest rates but they will also apply a special discounted interest rate to the card balance you transfer across. As a result, you win two times over.

Transferring a credit card balance to a new card issuer is a painless exercise for everyone bar the company losing your business. And don't worry if by transferring you lose out on membership of a card loyalty scheme – just think of the interest payments you will be saving.

Did you know? – Fact 26

- **DID** you know that the Credit Card Research Group has a mountain of information available on credit cards? Contact the CCRG at: 2 Ridgmount Street, London WC1E 7AA (020 7436 9937). For details of up-to-date credit card interest rates, contact Moneyfacts Publications at: Moneyfacts House, 68–70 Thorpe Road, Norwich NR1 1BJ (01603 476 476).

Golden nugget 27: ask questions

IF you are uncomfortable with any detail of a financial product you are about to buy – be it a mortgage, investment or insurance-based plan – hang fire.

Do not proceed until you have got satisfactory answers to the concerns you have. And if not forthcoming, you are better off looking elsewhere.

Confusing terms and conditions usually provide a good indication that a product is not what it purports to be.

Did you know? – Fact 27

- **DID** you know that if you buy a product which you subsequently believe was not appropriate for your circumstances or the company or salesman concerned failed to alert you to certain drawbacks you have the right to complain? The complaints procedures in the UK personal finance marketplace are now more formalised than ever before. If you have a complaint, put it down in writing and send it to the adviser or company which sold you the product. It is then duty bound to investigate your complaint and to tell you where you can go – an Ombudsman Bureau for example – if you want your complaint investigated independently.

Golden nugget 28: forget the all-singing alarm clocks and all-dancing leather wallets

IF you are offered a free gift for purchasing a financial product, don't be taken in. The free offering, be it a leather wallet, an alarm clock or a calculator, is usually a smokescreen for a rank bad investment.

Such gifts are usually offered in mailings issued by friendly societies and some insurance companies. The best place for such mailings is the dustbin.

Remember, your financial future is worth more than a new alarm clock. And remember, while the gift may be promoted as 'free', you will end up paying for it – either in high charges or mediocre investment returns.

Did you know? – Fact 28

- **DID** you know that no half-decent financial services company has to 'bribe' investors to buy their products with free gifts? If a financial product is good enough, it should stand up on its own two legs – plain and simple.

Golden nugget 29: if in doubt, speak to a professional

WHILE it is becoming increasingly easy to buy financial products directly – over the telephone, via the post or via the Internet – there is no substitute at the end of the day for professional independent financial advice, especially in complex areas such as pensions.

A good independent financial adviser – and please note not all advisers are good – will sit down with you and discuss your financial objectives before recommending a particular investment and financial protection strategy. This strategy will be based on the best of the products available from across the entire marketplace.

Furthermore, once the adviser has put a financial battle plan in place, they will keep an eye on your finances on a regular basis to ensure they dovetail with your changing lifestyle and employment prospects.

Independent financial advice is simply the best type of financial advice available. If you don't know one, speak to relatives or friends and ask them whether they have used an independent financial adviser in the past. Word-of-mouth recommendation is the best way to find an adviser.

Did you know? – Fact 29

- **DID** you know that not all advisers are independent? Many so-called advisers are insurance salesmen or tied agents, which means they can only sell the products of one company, even if better products exist elsewhere. Before obtaining financial advice, find out the status of the person you are dealing with.

Golden nugget 30: buy travel insurance annually

IF you travel abroad more than once a year, especially outside Europe, you can make substantial savings by buying an annual worldwide travel policy rather than taking out insurance every time you book a holiday.

Annual policies are available on both an individual or family basis and will cover you for any trips you make during the year. Most insurers will charge you extra if you want the policy to cover winter sports or motoring abroad, although some will reduce premiums if you do not require cover for personal baggage – for example, where this is already covered by household contents insurance.

In choosing an annual travel policy, don't go for the one with the cheapest premium. Check that the cover offered is adequate – no two plans are the same – and that you are happy with the excesses which the insurer will apply if you make a claim.

Although no two annual travel policies are the same, most policies will cover you against medical and air ambulance costs, personal accident and personal liability, legal expenses and hospital costs. They also cover you against holiday cancellation, holiday curtailment, loss of passport and travel delay.

Did you know? – Fact 30:

- **DID** you know that annual travel policies are now available from most high street banks and building societies? However, it is probably best – and cheaper – to buy via a direct insurer over the telephone.

Golden nugget 31: make a will

IF you want to ensure your wealth is passed on to people that matter most to you, it is vital that you make a will. If you die without leaving a will, you will be deemed to have died 'intestate', which means your wealth will be divided up between the surviving members of your family according to preset rules. If you do not have any family, your wealth will go straight to the 'crown' (the government). Furthermore, the rules of intestacy are cast in stone and do not recognise unmarried partners, friends or charities.

Making a will is not difficult or expensive. Although will-writing services now proliferate, you are best getting a local solicitor to draw up a will. It should not cost you more than £150.

Did you know? – Fact 31:

- **DID** you know that 70% of the population do not have a will? In other words, seven out of 10 people will have no say over how their wealth is distributed when they die.

Golden nugget 32: choose your cash machine carefully

ALTHOUGH cash machines now proliferate, to be found as readily at your local petrol station as at the local supermarket, don't think that such wider choice comes without a cost. Some banks now levy charges on customers who use other banks' cash machines to obtain cash. Charges are usually levied where a cash machine is to be found in a shop, pub or bookmaker.

Before using your cash card, check out which cash machines you can use without incurring charges. Most banks now have agreements with competitors which mean customers of both can use each other's cash machine networks without being charged. Your bank should be able to provide you with such information straight away.

Did you know? Fact 32

- **DID** you know that most banks and building societies are members of independent cash machine network Link, which means customers have access to more than 250,000 cash machines?

Golden nugget 33: give to charity tax-efficiently

WHILE it may be convenient to get rid of your loose change by popping it in a charity box, a far better way to give to charity is through making a donation at work. Many companies now offer workers payroll giving schemes which allow them to make charitable donations on a regular, hassle-free basis. Once the arrangement is set up, there is no further paperwork to worry about and you will not miss the money.

More importantly, payroll giving is tax-efficient. Payments are taken from your gross pay, which means they cost you less than the charity is benefiting. A higher rate taxpayer, for example, will only pay £6 for a £10 donation. Furthermore, the government is currently boosting payroll donation by a further 10%, which means a £10 donation is worth £11 in the hands of the charity.

Did you know? Fact 33

- **DID** you know that 400,000 people make regular donations to charities through payroll giving? If you are one of them, good on you. If you are not, join your company's scheme now. If your company does not operate a scheme, urge them to do so.

Golden nugget 34: take the pain out of charity giving by opening a CAF acount

IF you want to make hassle-free donations to charity and have total control and flexibility over where your payments are going, open an account with the Charities Aid Foundation. You make payments into your account, maybe from a bank account, on a regular basis (it is up to you), and CAF then recovers any tax on your behalf and credits it to your account (22% if you are a basic rate taxpayer, 40% if you are a higher rate taxpayer). You then use the cheque book provided to make donations to any charities you desire. CAF makes a deduction equivalent to 5% of contributions to cover expenses.

Did you know? – Fact 34

- **DID** you know that you can also use your CAF account to pay annual membership fees to charitable bodies such as the National Trust or the Royal Society for the Protection of Birds? Further details on 01732 520 055.

Golden nugget 35: offload any unwanted shares to Sharegift

IT is now possible to gift small parcels of shares you no longer need, or which are uneconomic to sell, through a scheme called Sharegift. The scheme will sell the shares and then give the proceeds to charity. You get full income tax relief on the gifting of the shares and you will have no liability to capital gains tax on any accumulated gains.

Did you know?– Fact 35

- **DID** you know that further details on Sharegift can be obtained by ringing 020 7337 0501?

Golden nugget 36: get your pet insured

INSURING a cat or dog can leave change from a fiver every month but scandalously only 15% of domestic cats and dogs are currently insured. If you are a pet owner sitting in the 85% camp, make it your priority to purchase insurance. It won't break the bank and it will take the pain out of any unforeseen vet bills in the future.

Did you know?– Fact 36

- **DID** you know that treating a dog's broken leg can cost anything between £400 and £1,000? With pet insurance, most of this cost, bar a small excess, would be met by the insurer.

Golden nugget 37: protect your no-claims discount on your car insurance

LOSING your no-claims bonus on your car insurance can cost you dearly in terms of higher motor premiums when you come to renew your policy. But you can protect your no-claims bonus by the purchase of no-claims protection cover. Typically, this will add an additional 15% to your motor premiums. But without it, the making of a claim will cost you two years' discount, worth up to 25% of the premium. Most insurance companies will offer you such cover but you may have to demonstrate four years of no claims before being eligible to purchase it.

Did you know? – Fact 37

- **DID** you know that up to 80% of those motorists eligible now take out no-claims bonus protection? If you qualify for it, buy it.

Golden nugget 38: keep on track with an index-tracking investment fund

UNIT trusts, Open-Ended Investment Companies and investment trusts are a great way to obtain exposure to the stock market. Unfortunately, it is a fact that many of these funds are run by managers who fail to outperform the stock market indices they set out to beat. In light of this woeful underperformance, it is no surprise that index-tracking investment funds have come to the fore. In a nutshell, index-tracking funds are designed to track the performance of a chosen market such as the FTSE 100 or the FTSE All-Share. Indeed, there are some funds that track other markets such as those in Europe or Japan.

Index-tracking funds are popular because they take some degree of risk out of the investment equation. If the stock market goes up, then an index fund tracking that market will go up by the same amount – plain and simple. That is not necessarily the case with a fund run by a manager – a so-called active fund – which might actually go down in value because of the manager's particular choice of shares. Also many active fund managers are dogged by inconsistency – they outperform for a year and then underperform for the following year. In contrast, an index-tracking fund will deliver you what the stock market does – nothing more, nothing less.

An index-tracking fund makes a great bolthole for an investment portfolio. You can then build around it by purchasing actively managed funds run by some of the country's investment stars – there a number of them around. Also the costs of buying an index-tracking fund are usually much cheaper than equivalent costs for buying an actively managed fund. Many index-tracking companies levy no or minimal initial costs while annual management charges are usually no more than 1% – especially when it comes to tracking funds which move in line with UK stock markets.

Did you know?– Fact 38

- **DID** you know that you can buy index-tracking funds in several areas of personal finance? You can purchase index-tracking unit trusts, investment trusts and Open-Ended Investment Companies. You can also use an index-tracking fund as part of your annual tax-free Isa allowance. You can also buy index-tracking insurance funds and personal pension funds. Index-tracking funds are run by many investment houses including many familiar household names. Players include: Abbey National, Alliance & Leicester, Bank of Scotland, Barclays, CGU, Deutsche, Direct Line, Fidelity, Friends Provident, Gartmore, Guardian, Halifax, HSBC, Legal & General, M&G, NatWest, Norwich Union, NPI, Royal & SunAlliance, Scottish Amicable, Scottish Equitable, Scottish Mutual, Scottish Widows, Sovereign, St James Place, Tesco, Virgin and Woolwich.

Golden nugget 39: bat cleverly with your private medical insurance

IT is a fact of life that private medical insurance is expensive. It is also a fact of life that premiums can be cut if customers are prepared to scale back on the amount of cover provided by their insurance.

BARGAIN NUMBER 1: Cut-price policies can now be bought which only cover a set number of conditons and surgical procedures – those where National Health Service waiting lists are longest. By restricting cover, the insurer is able to keep down premiums.

BARGAIN NUMBER 2: Other policies give customers the option of using the NHS (if the waiting time, for example, is acceptable) or going private. If they opt for NHS treatment, they receive a cash payment. Again, by limiting the amount of private cover on offer, the insurer is able to reduce premiums.

BARGAIN NUMBER 3: A number of insurers now allow customers to pay a large sum – upwards of £1,000 – towards their private medical treatment. Insurance then covers any sum above this amount.

Did you know? – Fact 39

- **DID** you know that inflation has driven private medical insurance premiums through the roof in recent years? Inflation has caused premiums to rise by between 7% and 10% per annum over the past few years.

Golden nugget 40: don't rule out pay as you go for medical treatment

YOU don't have to buy private medical insurance in order to enjoy private treatment. A number of hospital groups now allow you to pay as you go – in effect obtain treatment on demand. If you are diagnosed in need of treatment or an operation, the hospital will quote you a fixed price. This will cover the cost of surgery, payments for doctors and anaesthetists, and the cost of recuperation in a hospital bed. You can pay via savings or via loan agreements offered by the hospital. If you require a loan, you will probably be asked for a deposit of at least 10%.

Did you know? – Fact 40

- **DID** you know that most of the leading hospital groups now provide so-called pay-as-you-go schemes? Bupa (0845 600 8822), Nuffield Hospitals (0800 688 699) and BMI Healthcare (020 7419 6000) are all leading providers. An alternative approach is to go via an intermediary such as GoPrivate (0870 241 2728), an offshoot of Exeter Friendly Society. It will shop around the hospitals in order to get you the best price for the treatment you require.

Golden nugget 41: a holiday does not necessarily have to cost you an arm and a leg

A DREAM holiday does not have to make a big dent in your savings or deplete your bank account. There are now available a number of holiday options which allow you to travel for next to nothing:

TIP ONE: HOME-SWAP. Here, you agree to swap homes with another family from overseas for a fixed period. The swap is made through a house-swapping agency, which charges you a registration fee for joining the club. By home-swapping, you will not have to pay any accommodation bills although you will have to pay for the cost of travel. You can also be assured that someone is looking after your property while you are on holiday. Leading home swapping agencies include HomeLinkInternational (01344 842 642) website www.homelink.org and Intervac International Home Exchange (01225 892 208), website www.intervac.com.

TIP TWO: HOME-SIT. Here, you agree to be a home-sitter for a fixed period. You are in effect a caretaker for one or two weeks, agreeing to follow to the letter the homeowner's instructions. You may also be asked to do light domestic duties such as take phone messages, water plants and look after pets. Unlike home-swap, your travel costs will be met and you should also receive a small allowance to cover the costs of your home-sitting stay.

Given the heavy responsibilities placed upon home-sitters, you cannot easily become a home-sitter. Good home-sitting firms require excellent references and will only take on their books people aged 40 and over. Some will allow sitters to be accompanied by spouses or partners although no allowances will be paid to the extra person. Homesitters is the UK's biggest home-sitting agency. Further details on 01296 630 730 or website www.homesitters.co.uk.

TIP THREE: GO TO WORK ON HOLIDAY. Once aimed just at young people, working holidays are now available in abundance, covering everything from looking after a herd of pedigree sheep in the Alps for a few hours each day through to working on organic farms. They are really only suitable for single people. What costs are covered will vary so check out beforehand. Books such as *Summer Jobs Abroad* and *International Voluntary Work* are a mine of useful information and updated every year. Both books are published by Vacation Work and available at leading bookshops.

TIP FOUR: CONSERVE THE ENVIRONMENT. The British Trust for Conservation Volunteers offers people the opportunity to help conserve the environment by taking part in projects in the UK or overseas. People can enjoy activities such as clearing woods, drystone walling and foothpath repair. Although you will have to pay to go on such a conservation break and pay your own travel costs, the costs are minimal. The British Trust for Conservation Volunteers can be contacted on 01491 839 766 or via website: www.btcv.org.

Did you know? – Fact 41

- **DID** you know that agencies that arrange home-swaps can offer properties as far afield as the Caribbean and Australia? Home-swaps can allow you to see the world without breaking the bank.

Golden nugget 42: draw up a cohabitation agreement if you are not married and living with a partner

THERE are many myths surrounding the rights of partners who have lived together for a long time in a relationship. One such myth is that if a woman lives with a man for at least seven years, they are a common-law wife and as a result have the same rights as a married woman. Unfortunately this is not the case, which can cause big financial problems when couples split up. Indeed, the only guaranteed right an unmarried partner has is maintenance payments if there are children in the relationship.

One sound way for unmarried couples to protect themselves from financial hiccups if their relationship goes awry is to draw up a cohabitation agreement. By arranging such an agreement, a couple lay down in the form of a contract how their assets will be divided in the case of a relationship breakdown. Although not a binding agreement in law, the existence of a cohabitation agreement should prevent matters from going to court.

Each partner should have their own lawyer draw up their side of the agreement. The agreement should include the disclosure of all financial assets and debts, and a course of action in the event of unforeseen events such as the birth of children, getting married, disability, death or the end of the relationship.

Cohabitation agreements should cost no more than £1,000 and maybe as little as £200.

Did you know? – Fact 42

- **DID** you know that people living together are nine times more likely to break up than married couples?

Golden nugget 43: get your credit rating checked out

YOU now have the right to obtain details of your so-called credit worthiness – use it. This should especially be the case for people who have been turned down for credit – for example, a credit card or a personal loan – in the recent past and are baffled why. Both Equifax and Experian, the country's two leading credit reference agencies, will supply copies of your credit files on request for a small fee. These credit files form the basis for decisions taken by companies to lend money to you.

If your file contains incorrect information, you can apply to have the details amended. The most common problem arises when people share an address with a poor creditor and as a result get an impaired credit scoring. By asking for a notice of dissociation, your credit file will be separated immediately from that of the poor creditor.

Did you know? – Fact 43

- **DID** you know that it only costs a few pounds to obtain a copy of your credit file? Further details can be obtained from: Equifax Consumer Advice Department, PO Box 3001, Glasgow G81 2DT (08700 100 583) or Experian Consumer Help Service, PO Box 8000, Nottingham NG1 5GX (0115 976 8747).

Golden nugget 44: don't forget insurance when you're moving home

MOVING home can be a daunting enough experience without having to worry about whether your top-of-the-market dining table is going to be scratched in transit. However, you can now buy cheap but effective removals insurance which will cover the cost of any breakages or damage caused as a result of employing a removals firm to move your possessions. Although household insurance policies do sometimes provide cover for losses incurred during a house move, cover can be patchy and exclusions rife so a stand-alone policy often makes better sense.

Did you know? – Fact 44

- **DID** you know that the leading providers of removals insurance are the British Association of Removers (020 8861 3331) and 1st Quote (020 8590 8412).

Golden nugget 45: invest your child benefit on your child's behalf

ALTHOUGH many parents rely upon child benefit to boost their household income, others see it as a welcome monthly financial perk. For those in the latter category, it makes great sense to invest the benefit on behalf of their children, thereby providing them with a welcome present when they reach 18 and go out on their own into the real world.

Child benefit is currently £15 per week for a first child and £10 a week for younger siblings. These are sums which if invested early enough could provide sizeable lump sums in the future. Ideal homes for child benefit money are savings schemes linked to unit trusts and investment trusts. Other sensible homes include children's savings accounts, National Savings' children bonus bonds and tax-free friendly society accounts.

Did you know? – Fact 45

- **DID** you know that *Moneyfacts* provides details of all children's savings accounts including current interest rates? Further details on 01603 476 476. The Association of Investment Trust Companies also provides a useful fact sheet on children and savings (0800 085 8520).

Golden nugget 46: don't squander a windfall

THERE is no doubt that building societies and insurance companies will continue to demutualise. This will result in windfalls for qualifying members. If you are fortunate enough to receive a windfall, don't go out and spend it straight away. Think about using all or some of it in other ways – such as paying off a chunk of your mortgage, using it to carry out a home improvement, paying off credit card debt, using it to fund a pension or to invest for the future in an investment fund such as a unit trust or investment trust.

Did you know? – Fact 46

- **DID** you know that some windfalls from insurance company demutualisations have exceeded £100,000?

Golden nugget 47: don't forget the car import option

IT can now pay many people to buy a car from overseas rather than through a car dealership. Prices on the continent can be as much as 60% cheaper. Over the past year, a number of websites have sprung up in order to make the importation of a car as easy as possible with companies such as Virgin and Direct Line getting involved. Sites vary in how far they will help you. Some will point you in the direction of a continental dealer and then it is up to you to haggle over the price and arrange collection. Others will offer the full service, delivering your car. Websites involved in this area include: www.autobytel.co.uk; www.autohit.com; www.autolocate.co.uk; www.broadspeed.com; www.carbusters.com;www.carimporting. co.uk; www.jamjar.com; www.oneswoop.com; www.virgincars. com.

One note of caution. While buying an imported car can save you pounds, do tread carefully. Do ensure you are saving yourself money while keeping an eye out for hidden extras such as road tax, delivery costs, registration and administration fees.

Did you know? – Fact 47

- **DID** you know that the web can also help you cut the cost of your petrol? Website www.petrolbusters.com allows you to type in your postcode and establish where in your area you can get the cheapest petrol.

Golden nugget 48: loyalty can pay

SOME building societies have tried to counter the threat of carpetbaggers and their target of juicy windfalls by coming up with their own reward schemes for loyal customers. These can take the shape of annual loyalty bonuses, one-off bonuses, discounts off mortgage rates or enhanced savings rates. No one should choose a building society purely because they offer such a scheme. Shopping around in search of best-value products is a better financial strategy. However, for people who like the convenience and mutual structure of a building society, these loyalty schemes can be the icing on the cake.

Did you know? – Fact 48

- **DID** you know that Britannia, Coventry, Skipton and West Bromwich building societies all pay bonuses to long-term members? Britannia, for example, pays an annual bonus dependent upon the size of a borrower's mortgage or balance in an investment account. In contrast, Coventry reduces standard variable mortgage rates for loyal borrowers while paying loyal savers enhanced interest rates.

Golden nugget 49: claim your rightful windfall

IT is estimated that billions of pounds are lying unclaimed in the coffers of banks, building societies and insurance companies – and some of it could belong to you. This money may take the form of unclaimed building society windfall shares, forgotten bank and building society accounts, unclaimed National Savings certificates, premium bond prizes or unclaimed insurance policy payouts. Unclaimed financial assets usually result from people moving home and failing to tell a company they have done so.

Experts state that 12% of unclaimed asset searches they conduct on behalf of clients result in a payout. So if you think you may have forgotten financial treasures, it could pay you to take action – you have little to lose. Contact the company direct.

Did you know? – Fact 49

- **DID** you know that a number of companies now exist purely to track down unclaimed assets on behalf of clients? They include: Asset Search (0161 839 4664); Trust Research Services (01732 741 411) and Unclaimed Assets Register (0870 241 1713; website: www.uar.co.uk).

  If you are tracking down a dormant bank account, banks have a standard form to help people. This is available through local branches or through the British Bankers' Association (Pinners Hall, 105–108 Old Broad Street, London EC2N 1EX; website: www.bankfacts.org.uk).

  For details on building societies (those, for example, that have merged or been taken over), contact the Building Societies Association on 0207 437 0655 or visit website: www.bsa.org.uk. Unclaimed building society conversion windfalls remain at former building societies Abbey National, Alliance & Leicester, Birmingham Midshires, Halifax, Northern Rock and Woolwich.

  For unclaimed equity investments, individual company

shares can be traced through the company's share register. The main registrars used by stock market-listed companies are Lloyds TSB Registrars (01903 502 541); Computershare Services (0870 702 0000); and IRG (020 8650 4866). If the company has merged or dissolved, you may be able to trace it through Companies House in Cardiff.

Misplaced unit trusts can be traced through the Association of Unit Trusts and Investment Funds (020 7831 0898) while unclaimed investment trust shares can be tracked down through the Association of Investment Trust Companies (0800 085 8520).

With regard to National Savings, contact the savings organisation on website: www.nationalsavings.co.uk.

Golden nugget 50: surf the web for travel insurance

WHILE travel insurance cover offered by your travel agent is often shockingly expensive, you don't have to accept it. Annual travel insurance bought separately is – nine times out of ten – a far better deal as explained in Golden Nugget thirty. However, you can go one step further and cut insurance costs further – by surfing the Net. Website travel insurance is often best value for money although holidaymakers should not just chase the cheapest deal available. Ensure the cover offered is adequate. Policies can be purchased to dovetail with your specific holiday arrangements or on an annual basis.

Website travel insurance providers fall into three camps – the first comprises traditional insurers such as Royal & SunAlliance, Woolwich and Preferential; the second is composed of the Internet arms of tele-insurance companies such as Direct Line and Columbus Direct; and the third comprises intermediaries whose websites carry a selection of policies from numerous insurers.

In searching these travel insurance sites out, you have little to lose – and a lot of money to save.

Did you know? – Fact 50

- **DID** you know that there are more than a dozen websites providing travel insurance quotes? They include: Bishopsgate (www.bishopsgate.co.uk); CGU Direct (www.cgu-direct.co.uk); Columbus (www.columbusdirect.co.uk); Direct Line (www.directline.co.uk); Eagle Star (www.eaglestar. co.uk); Preferential (www.preferential.co.uk); RapidInsure (www.rapidinsure.co.uk); Rough Guide (www.roughguide. co.uk); Royal & SunAlliance (www.royalsunalliance.co.uk); Trailfinders (www.trailfinders.co.uk); Screentrade (www. screentrade.co.uk). For backpackers, cover can be arranged through Sta Travel (www.sta-travel.com) and Endsleigh (www.endsleigh.co.uk).

Golden nugget 51: don't just rely upon E111

MANY people travel in Europe relying upon form E111 to get them out of trouble if they fall ill or have an accident. However, such a tactic is a highly dangerous one.

In theory, an E111 form entitles travellers to free medical treatment. However, not all European countries have signed up to the reciprocal arrangement between European health services which allows for free treatment. France and Germany, for example, have a good track record in accepting these forms while Spain doesn't. Furthermore an E111 form does not cover you for extra travel and accommodation expenses or repatriation costs. Nor does it cover you for additional hotel and travel expenses if you are forced to return home because of illness or death of a friend, relative or business partner.

Anyone travelling abroad should take out travel insurance as well as complete form E111. Form E111 is available from your local post office.

Did you know? – Fact 51

- **DID** you know that some travel insurers will waive any medical excess under their policies if you have also completed an E111 form?

Golden nugget 52: if you're elderly, don't let your travel insurer take advantage of you

MANY insurance companies discriminate against the elderly when it comes to travel insurance. Some companies simply refuse to insure the over 65s while others increase premiums substantially – sometimes doubling premiums.

However, such discrimination is not universal. Some companies, and not necessarily the obvious ones, go out of their way to court the elderly traveller. They are worth tracking down. They include the Retirement Insurance Advisory Service, Direct Line and Nationwide building society. Age Concern and Saga also target the elderly but their premiums, especially for the over 75s, can be expensive so be careful.

Did you know? – Fact 52

- **DID** you know that you can cut your travel insurance bill by asking for specific cover to be excluded from your travel insurance? For example, you may not want cover for lost baggage because your household insurance already provides such cover.

Golden nugget 53: treat store cards with great care

STORE cards can seem a tempting way to make purchases, especially when the store assistant tempts you with a discount if you sign up for the in-house credit card. However, tread carefully because if you use the card to borrow, you can be stung for sky-high interest rates. Store cards are one of the most expensive ways to borrow on plastic with interest rates being impervious to downward movements in base rates within the wider economy.

Did you know? – Fact 53

- **DID** you know that you can transfer debt built up on a store credit card to a cheaper credit card? Many credit card companies apply special low rates to balances transferred from other cards although these rates only tend to last for a set period – typically six months. If you are determined to keep your store card, and you use it to borrow, then consider arranging for the minimum balance to be paid by direct debit. Some store cards – not all – reduce interest rates for cardholders who agree to this arrangement. Details on store cards can be obtained from *Moneyfacts* on 01603 476 476.

Golden nugget 54: don't forget the endowment policy loan route

BORROWING money against an endowment policy can be a useful way to raise money. Most endowment providers will now offer loans against their own policies but there are hurdles to overcome. For a start, the policy must be 'assigned' to the policy loan provider as security against the loan taken out. Given many endowment policyholders have their plans assigned to a mortgage lender, taking out a loan is not an option available to them. Also, loans are not available on all types of endowment policy. With-profits policies are OK but unit-linked plans are not. Loans available on endowment policies can have attractive interest rates but it is imperative you check them out before diving in.

Did you know? – Fact 54

- **DID** you know that some financial institutions such as Newcastle building society and Scottish Widows bank will offer loans against other providers' policies?

Golden nugget 55: did you buy term assurance through an insurance salesman? If yes, read on

SHOPPING around for cheaper term assurance can save you pounds – as explained in Golden Nugget four. However, don't expect any help from your insurance salesman. If you bought term assurance through an insurance salesman in the past, there is every likelihood that you could now get cheaper cover. You are not being told about this because it is not in the financial interests of the insurance salesman to do so. Act now.

Did you know? – Fact 55

- **DID** you know that by shopping around for cheaper term assurance, you could cut your monthly premiums by up to 30%?

Golden nugget 56: remember share exchange

MANY people hold a hotch-potch of shares acquired as a result of building society conversions. However, many of these people would be better off swapping their shares for a holding in a collective investment such as a unit trust or investment trust. Most trust companies now offer 'share exchange' schemes enabling people to swap their holding in one company for a holding in a trust with exposure to the fortunes of many companies.

Share exchange schemes are not offered for free. You will typically pay a sales charge per holding offloaded plus a purchase charge including stamp duty of 0.5%. Most investment companies will also insist on a minimum size deal which can be as high as £1,000. But they are a solid way of diversifying your investment portfolio.

Did you know? – Fact 56

- **DID** you know that the share exchange scheme run by Alliance, a Dundee-based investment trust company, enables you to exchange holdings in individual shares into trusts run by other managers as well as its own funds? Share exchange can also be used as a way to invest in a tax-free Isa. Both the Association of Investment Trust Companies (0800 085 8520) and the Association of Unit Trusts and Investment Funds (020 7831 0898) have details on investment companies offering share exchange schemes.

Golden nugget 57: cut your fuel bills by conserving energy

WHILE changing gas or electricity supplier can cut your energy bills, most people often overlook more basic ways of reducing outgoings. Simply by taking a number of energy-saving steps, you can make significant inroads into expensive bills. There is no need to adopt a spartan lifestyle. Energy-savings tips include: turning off the television fully, cutting down on the time you tumble-dry clothes, taking a shower rather than a bath, turning down the central heating by a small amount, using long-life, low-energy light bulbs or investing in better insulation, a central heating boiler or thermostats.

Did you know? – Fact 57

- **DID** you know that grants are available for people who take energy conservation steps – such as putting in insulation? These government grants, available under the Home Energy Efficiency Scheme (0800 952 0600), are open to people claiming certain benefits in England. In Scotland, grants are available under Warm Deal (0800 072 0150), run by non-profit organisation Eaga. Eastern Energy produces a useful leaflet on energy efficiency (0845 762 6513).

Golden nugget 58: don't forget the insurer's helpline

PICKING a plumber at random from the telephone directory in the event of a household emergency can end up a costly move. However, homeowners should first of all check to see whether their household insurance offers a domestic helpline service. These helplines can usually put policyholders in touch with contractors who have been vetted for fairness and honesty. They can also impart good advice at a time when reason can go out of the window.

Did you know? – Fact 58

- **DID** you know that Domestic & General, a leading insurer of domestic appliances, has launched a website-based service which puts people in touch with quality repairers for electrical appliances, including PCs and gas central heating boilers? The site, called flyingtoolbox.com, rates contractors according to feedback from customers who have already used them.

Golden nugget 59: understand what cooling-off means

INVESTMENT companies are obliged to give investors a short breathing space when they place their money in a fund, enabling them to pull out if they decide to put their money elsewhere or simply not go ahead with the deal. However, such a breathing space is not necessarily cost-free. Investment houses currently employ two systems.

Under so-called deferred entry, or 'cooling off', investors' money is placed in a special deposit account. If they then decide not to go ahead with the deal, they have the right to get their money back in full. This right varies in length between 7 and 14 days.

Under the second system, a 14-day cancellation period, investors' cash is invested immediately. If an investor then does not want to proceed with the deal, they can get their money back with no initial charges taken. However, if the fund's price has fallen during the time the money has been invested, an investor will not get back the value of their initial investment. In contrast, if the market has risen and an investor still wants to get out, they will simply receive back the value of their initial investment.

Did you know? – Fact 59

- **DID** you know that if you buy an investment fund on an execution-only basis – that is, without advice – you are not entitled to any breathing space? However, some groups offer it as a matter of course – check this fact out before you invest.

Golden nugget 60: think isas and the Internet

MOST investment houses are now linked to the Internet providing you with details about the products they offer. Some companies also allow you to buy your Isas on-line. Two of the most innovative companies in this area have been Fidelity and Egg (Prudential's Internet arm) who now allow you to construct Isas based around the best Isas available in the marketplace. You don't have to restrict yourself to one company's unit trusts as is the practice if you buy an Isa direct from a provider.

Did you know? – Fact 60.

Further details on these so-called fund supermarkets are available from www.egg.com and www.fundsnetwork.co.uk

So what now?

ONE final golden nugget but probably the most important one. Whatever you may wish to purchase in the personal finance world, be it an investment fund or a pension, don't be bullied into buying an inappropriate one. Remember, it's your hard earned money and you owe it yourself to have it looked after it properly. If you have any doubts about the intended home for your money, take a deep breath and go elsewhere. Caveat emptor.

CHAPTER **9**

Completing the Personal Finance Jigsaw

COIN

'Something that's useful for getting the wrong number in a telephone box.'

Jack Cruise

PERSONAL finance is a daunting subject area and to do proper justice to it, a book along the lines of the massive tome *War and Peace* would be required. Indeed, nearly every week there is a new development within the personal finance world – a result of provider innovation, regulatory demand or government interference.

In the previous chapter, we identified 60 top ideas for improving your personal wealth or ensuring you don't tread on a personal finance mine. In this chapter, we identify 20 areas of personal finance which you may never have stumbled across before but which may interest you. These topics range from unusual insurances through to new investment opportunities.

Jigsaw piece 1: spread betting

A number of companies now allow you to bet on the future movement of individual shares or stock market indices as well as the outcome of specific sporting events. Essentially, betting on a share's movement, so-called spread betting, is no different from buying the share and holding it. But there is no tax liability. Instead, duty on bets is paid in advance by the spread betting company.

Unlike fixed-odds betting that relies on a specified outcome, say the chances of a particular horse winning the Grand National, with spread betting you might predict the number of horses that will finish a race. So a spread betting bookmaker might give a price of between 13 and 15 horses to cross the line for £10 a horse. A punter predicting that fewer than 13 horses will finish will bet low or 'sell' at 13. This means that if eight horses cross the line, the difference between that result and the sell price of 13 is five. That will be multiplied by pounds per point (£10), giving a win of £50. But if 18 horses cross the line, the gambler loses £50 – £10 for each additional horse over 13.

The more you are right with spread betting the more money you win. But the opposite also applies – the more you are wrong the more you lose. You can, however, curtail any losses by asking the spread betting company to apply a guaranteed stop – a level of losses you are not prepared to exceed. In doing this, you will curtail your gains on the upside.

Spread betting is not for investment beginners, nor for people with faint hearts. Unless you are prepared to spend a lot of time analysing particular shares or stock markets, you should give it a wide berth.

FURTHER DETAILS: There are five main spread betting firms. They are: City Index (020 7861 5000); Financial Spreads (08000 969 620); IG Index (020 7896 0011); Index Direct (0800 358 5599); Sporting Index (08000 969 607).

Jigsaw piece 2: base-rate tracker mortgages

BASE-rate tracking mortgages have been launched by lenders to counteract the criticism levelled at them by borrowers with standard variable rate mortgages – namely that when interest rates fall, lenders will fail to respond with a corresponding mortgage rate reduction. With a base-rate tracking mortgage, the mortgage rate is tied to the Bank of England base-rate. If base rate moves up or down, so does the interest rate on the mortgage by the same amount. So a 0.5% reduction in base rate results in a 0.5% cut in the lender's mortgage rate.

While base-rate mortgages ensure the benefit of interest rate reductions in the wider economy are passed on to borrowers, they are not without their flaws. Critically, they do not protect borrowers against rising interest rates – as do fixed-rate mortgages and to a degree capped-rate mortgages.

FURTHER DETAILS: Most mainstream lenders now offer base-rate tracking home loans. A good independent mortgage adviser should be able to point out the best deals.

Jigsaw piece 3: buy-to-let mortgages

A NUMBER of lenders now offer buy-to-let mortgages to people who want to invest in flats and houses in order to generate additional income. With such mortgages, you put down a sizeable deposit, usually 25% to 50% of a property's value, and borrow the rest. The idea then is to let out the property so that the income generated covers the mortgage interest plus other expenses. What is left after tax is profit.

In going down the buy-to-let route, do be cautious. In calculating your likely returns, allow for the costs of maintenance, managing the property and insurance. And factor into the sums that your property is likely to be empty for at least one month in every 12.

Also, don't underestimate the time involved in being a landlord.

Managing a property involves spending plenty of time finding and vetting tenants, dealing with repairs and keeping an eye on the place. You can alternatively turn to a managing agent to do the managing for you but you will have to hand over between 10% and 15% of the rental income.

FURTHER DETAILS: The Association of Residential Letting has produced a useful booklet on buy to let. Copies are available by ringing 01923 896 555.

Jigsaw piece 4: equity release

FOR many elderly people, maximising their income in retirement is a priority. One way of achieving this goal is by releasing equity from your home in order to generate a regular income or a lump-sum payment.

Home income plans, as they are generically referred to, are suitable for the over 60s. Schemes come in all shapes and sizes but tend to fall into two camps. There are cash schemes, which allow you to retain ownership of your home while using part of the property's value to generate a lump-sum payment. Although interest is charged on the loan that you take out, these charges are not taken until the house is sold or on death. There are also reversion schemes, which involve selling all or part of your home in return for an income or lump sum. As with cash schemes, you can remain in your home.

Equity release schemes are attractive but they should not be entered into lightly. You should speak to a solicitor before agreeing to sign up for such a deal. You should also speak to dependants because at the end of the day, it is they who will effectively bear the cost of any equity you decide to release from your home.

FURTHER DETAILS: The country's leading specialist in equity release is Hinton & Wild (0800 32 88 432).

Jigsaw piece 5: football affinity products

THE recent surge in football interest has resulted in a number of football clubs looking for new opportunities to make money from their fan base. One of the 'opportunities' they have stumbled upon is the football club savings account and the football club credit card. Both financial products work in similar fashion. When you open an account or are accepted for a card, the club receives a payment from the company operating the product. It also receives a payment related to the amount you then spend on your credit card or tuck away in the savings account.

As far as fans are concerned, football-related financial products do have some benefits. Some football clubs offer holders of such products discounts on club merchandise or season tickets. But if you are looking for a best credit card deal or an attractive savings rate, they are not for you. Most football credit cards are expensive while the rates available from football savings accounts are at best meagre and uncompetitive. If truth be told, better products lie elsewhere.

FURTHER DETAILS: Your football club will gladly inform you of any branded financial products it markets. But do remember: just because your club is top of the league does not mean that the savings or credit card deal it is going to give you is top drawer.

Jigsaw piece 6: ethical investments

A NUMBER of financial companies now allow you to invest with a conscience by offering so-called ethical funds. Although ethical funds come in all shapes and sizes, they all tend to adopt one of two approaches to investment. They either exclude investing in companies which fall foul of certain predetermined ethical criteria – a company, for example, selling armaments or involved in alcohol or tobacco production. Or they invest in companies which meet certain ethical criteria such as helping improve the environment, reduce waste or conserve energy.

Ethical unit trusts, investment trusts, pensions and insurance funds are now all available from some of the country's leading investment houses. Although the past performance record of such funds is somewhat chequered, there is no proven evidence to suggest that an ethical investor has to sacrifice investment returns in order to invest with a conscience.

In opting for a specific ethical investment product, do check that the fund is run according to your wishes. Some ethical funds are more ethical than others – the company's product literature should spell out the rules that the ethical fund observes.

FURTHER DETAILS: A number of independent financial advisers now specialise in ethical investment. The leading player is Bristol based Holden Meehan (0117 925 2874). Companies which offer ethical investments include: Allchurches, Clerical Medical (part of Halifax), Credit Suisse, Friends Provident, Jupiter, NPI and Scottish Equitable.

Jigsaw piece 7: pet insurance

THERE is no National Health Service available for pets. And a visit to the vet does not come cheap, which makes it worthwhile considering pet insurance.

As well as covering the cost of unexpected vet's bills (not those for vaccinations, spaying, neutering or nailclipping), pet insurance also provides a range of other useful cover – cover for legal fees if your dog upsets the postman, the cost of advertising if you happen to lose your pet and kennel fees if you have to go into hospital and there is no one available to look after your pet.

A number of companies now offer pet insurance including many household names such as Churchill, Direct Line, Nationwide and Woolwich. Although dogs and cats form the bulk of pets insured, some insurance companies will cover any pet – from rabbits to snakes.

Although premiums are not expensive, it will pay you to shop around. Policies do differ markedly. Ensure before you sign on the dotted line that you are happy with the excess you will have to pay if you make a claim. Also check out the maximum amount it will pay for vet's fees – some insurers cap individual claims or set a limit on the amount that can be claimed per year. Finally, check through the policy details so that you know what is and what is not covered by your policy.

FURTHER DETAILS: Companies which offer pet insurance include: AIMS (0800 834 866); B Portwood (0191 477 2231); Churchill (0121 224 6747); DBI Insurance (0845 073 3999); Direct Line (0845 246 8705); Healthy Pets (01730 301 420); Hill House Hammond Pet Care Plus (0845 300 1422); Nationwide building society (0845 603 9189); Paws (0121 626 7891/7892); Pedigree Chum Healthcare (0870 243 0090); Pethealth Insurance (0800 9520050); Pethealthcare (0800 300 885); Petplan (0800 072 7000); Petshield (0800 072 1006); Pet Protect (0800 650 056); Sainsbury's (0800 056 5758); Woolwich (0870 606 1034); Equine & Livestock Insurance (0870 742 3800) specialises in insurance for horses and ponies while Cliverton (01263 860 388) and Exotic Direct (01444 482 946) both insure exotic pets. Golden Valley (01981 240 536) specialises in cover for birds.

Jigsaw piece 8: charity giving

PUTTING coins into a collecting box is a traditional way of supporting charities. But there are other ways of making charitable donations, some of which can provide you with generous tax breaks.

GOOD GIVING TIP 1: GIVE THROUGH YOUR PAYROLL. Almost 400,000 people give more than £30 million a year to charities via payroll deductions. Payments are made from your gross – rather then taxed – pay. This means that a basic rate taxpayer who gives £10 a month to charity only pays £7.80 net of tax while a top rate taxpayer pays £6 net of tax. As an additional boost, the government has also agreed to provide a 10% bonus to all payroll donations. This means a pre-tax £10 donation boosts a charity's coffers to the tune of £11.

GOOD GIVING TIP 2: CONSIDER TAKING OUT AN AFFINITY CREDIT CARD. There are more than 1,200 affinity credit cards on the market linked to high-profile charities such as the RSPCA, Marie Curie Cancer Care, Great Ormond Street Hospital for Sick Children, Guide Dogs for the Blind and the Third World charity Action Aid.

The credit cards all work in the same way. For every £100 you spend on your card, your chosen charity receives a sum in the order of £0.25. It also receives a small payment when you first take out the card (anything between £2.50 and £5) as well as an annual payment (between £1 and £2). Of course, if you clear your credit card balance on a monthly basis, your charitable giving ends up costing you nothing.

GOOD GIVING TIP 3: CONTEMPLATE GIFT AID. Through gift aid, the taxman will give a charity the basic rate of income tax that donors have paid on their one-off contribution. So if a basic rate taxpayer makes a donation through gift aid, a charity can claim a further amount equivalent to tax at 22%. So a £100 donation becomes £128.21 in the hands of the charity. For higher rate taxpayers, they can reclaim for themselves the difference between basic and higher rate tax – 18%. So, for a donation of £100, the charity receives £128.21 while the higher rate taxpayer reclaims some £23. There are no limits – minimum or maximum – on the amount donated through gift aid. The Inland Revenue produces a useful leaflet on gift aid (IR113).

GOOD GIVING TIP 4: MAKE A GIFT IN YOUR WILL. Although we are happy to donate to charity during our lifetime, few of us are prepared to give to good causes in our wills. Only one in three people who make wills leave charitable legacies. However, leaving a legacy is tax-efficient. All legacies are free of inheritance tax – in other words, they are taken off the total estate before the tax is calculated. So, for example, an estate valued at £300,000 would attract tax at 40% on the amount above the inheritance tax threshold of £242,000. But the surplus above £242,000 could be bequeathed to a charity, thereby excluding the estate from any inheritance tax.

GOOD GIVING TIP 5: CHARITABLE TRUSTS. For people with a sizeable sum that they wish to donate to charity, the setting up of a charitable trust can make good sense. These trusts benefit from full breaks on income tax and capital gains tax and the donor has control over how the assets are distributed. You will need at least £40,000 to put into a trust. This is because setting-up costs are not cheap – anything between £1,000 and £2,000 – and there will also be running costs as independent trustees control the trust's purse strings.

To qualify for a charitable trust, you must get permission from the Charity Commission. It will need to be convinced that the trust's money will ultimately be used to fight poverty, go towards education or religion, or be of benefit to the community. The trust must then be given approval from the Inland Revenue.

As with gift aid, every £100 donated by a basic rate taxpayer allows the trust to reclaim £28.21 from the taxman. A higher rate taxpayer can reclaim a further £23.08. All growth within the trust is free of capital gains tax with the trust's assets being allowed to be invested in standard investments such as stocks and shares.

Setting up a trust is a decision that should not be taken lightly. This is because once you have set up a trust, you cannot get at the money to use for your own purposes.

GOOD GIVING TIP 6: GIFTS OF SHARES. You can gift shares you own to a charity. The full market value of the shares is treated as the value for tax purposes and you can recover 22% income tax relief while higher rate taxpayers can recover an extra 18%. You will not be liable for tax on any accumulated capital gains.

FURTHER DETAILS: The Charities Aid Foundation has a useful website at: www.givingtoday.org. Its give as you earn guide is available by contacting 01732 520 019. If you want to check if a charity in England or Wales is registered, visit the site: www.charity-commission.gov.uk. To check Scottish charities, call 0131 226 2626. The major suppliers of affinity credit cards are MBNA, Bank of Scotland and American-owned HFC Bank. The Charity Commission can be contacted on 0870 333 0123 or website www.charity-commission.gov.uk.

Jigsaw piece 9: holiday money

YOU cannot go on an overseas holiday without buying the local currency. By following a few basic steps, you can ensure that you get a fair currency deal and have few money troubles on your holidays.

STEP 1: Before getting to your holiday destination, find out what forms of payment are most widely accepted and also the availability of cash machines. This information should be readily available from your holiday company or bank – and it will dictate your holiday money strategy. There is no point, for example, relying upon plastic if you intend to spend your holiday at a resort where cash machines have yet to make an appearance and credit card purchases are the exception rather than the norm.

STEP 2: Take some foreign currency with you. Although buying foreign currency in the UK tends to be more expensive than buying it abroad, you should take some with you. There is nothing worse than arriving at a foreign airport without a bean to pay for a taxi from the airport or in order to get a much needed drink. Foreign currency can be bought from banks, banking societies, bureaux de change and major travel agents. You can pay by cash, cheque, debit card or credit card. Charges vary but you will probably end up paying commission (anything between 1% and 3%) with a minimum charge of anything from £1.

STEP 3: Spread your currency net by taking with you various payment/cash withdrawal options. Once abroad, you will probably be able to use several payment/cash withdrawal options including credit card, debit card, travellers' cheques and eurocheques. Credit cards and debit cards are usually the cheapest holiday payment forms:

Credit cards: If you have one, take it on holiday – you will be able to use it to pay for purchases as well as get cash from cash machines that display your card's logo, very useful in an emergency. On cash withdrawals, you will typically pay a 1.5% cash handling charge. You may also pay interest charges – some credit card companies charge you interest from the day that you make the withdrawal. There may also be a loading charge applied, which means the exchange rate used to convert your purchase back into sterling will be stacked against you. Your credit card company should tell you the loading charges it applies, if you ask them. If you have a number of cards, it will pay you to take that card where loading charges are least onerous.

Debit cards: Again, a debit card is a useful holiday tool, enabling you to obtain cash from foreign cash machines as well as pay for purchases. As with credit cards, there will be a loading charge applied to the cost of transactions when converted into sterling. For cash withdrawals, a cash handling charge will also be levied.

Travellers' cheques: These are particularly useful in places where plastic payment is not yet the norm. Although you might incur a charge both when you buy them and use them, they are secure, enabling you to get a quick refund and replacement if they are lost or stolen. Available from banks, building societies and bureaux de change, travellers' cheques can be bought in fixed denominations of sterling, dollars, euros and other foreign currency. The provider should tell you which currency is best for you in light of your holiday destination.

Eurocheques: These enable you to write out cheques in the local currency and are backed by a eurocheque card which acts as a guarantee. You should ask your bank whether it issues such cheques but they are not a cheap currency option – you will pay an annual fee for the card, a handling charge each time you write out a cheque as well as foreign exchange commission and a loading charge.

STEP FOUR: Before going on holiday, make a note detailing all your credit cards, debit cards and travellers' cheques. This could prove invaluable if you lose any of them on your holidays. Also, ensure you make a note of all the emergency telephone numbers for your various bits of plastic – again invaluable if you lose them. Also, ensure you have enough money in your current account or spending power left on your credit card so that you will have no problems obtaining cash while you are away.

Jigsaw piece 10: zero dividend preference shares

ZERO dividend preference shares are a relatively new development in the personal finance world. A product of the investment trust industry, they enable investors to lock into an attractive annual return over a set period of time. Although returns are not guaranteed, zeros often offer more competitive returns than other low-risk investments such as gilts and corporate bonds although they are non-income producing.

Zeros are offered as part of split capital investment trusts alongside other classes of share such as capital shares and income shares. As their name implies, an investor receives no dividends on their holdings. Instead, they receive first call on the trust's assets when it is wound up at a set time in the future. The return earned is classed as capital growth so there is no income tax to be paid. Capital gains tax may be payable although everyone has an annual capital gains tax allowance of £7,500, which should mean returns are enjoyed tax-free.

The beauty of zeros is that when someone buys them, they can find out the expected annual return they will enjoy if they hold them until the trust's life comes to an end. This is because every zero has a redemption price (the predetermined price per share a zero shareholder is expected to obtain at the trust's wind-up) and a wind-up date (the date at which the trust will be wound up and assets distributed to shareholders). By relating the price you bought your zero at to the redemption price and the wind-up date, you can calculate the so-called gross redemption yield – the annual return, before tax, that you are likely to enjoy from your zero.

This is best illustrated. If a zero has a current share price of £2.39, a redemption price of £3.25 and a wind-up date three years and eight months into the future, the gross redemption yield will be 9.8%. This is because for your outlay of £2.39, you will enjoy a return of £0.86 over the next 3.67 years, a sum equivalent to £0.23 per year. On an investment of £2.39, this is equivalent to a return of 9.8%.

It must be stressed that returns from zeros are not guaranteed. If the underlying investment trust does not deliver sound enough performance, it might not generate enough assets at wind-up to pay zero shareholders in full. But a person buying zeros can get a good idea of how likely it is for their investment to be paid out in full by obtaining details of the so-called hurdle rate. This figure indicates how the trust's assets must perform between the date of purchasing the zero and the trust's wind-up in order to meet the target price of the zero.

A negative hurdle rate is good – it means the trust's asset price can fall and the zero's predetermined price will still be paid out. A positive hurdle rate means the trust's assets must increase before the official wind-up date for the zero's maturity price to be met. Usually, zeros with higher than average gross redemption yields have positive hurdle rates – in other words, they carry more risk.

Before buying a zero, it is essential you find out details of the current gross redemption yield and the hurdle rate. You should then compare these against other zeros.

Zeros are offered by most of the country's top investment trust houses including Aberdeen, Fleming, Gartmore, Henderson, Jupiter and Schroder. They can be bought through a stockbroker and once you have bought them, you can monitor their price through the stock market pages of the financial press.

Zeros are ideal to meet expected bills in the future such as school fees. One final point – you don't have to hold a zero until the so-called maturity date. You can sell them through a stockbroker at any time.

FURTHER DETAILS: The Association of Investment Trust Companies provides useful details on zero dividend preference shares including those companies that issue them. Call 0800 707 707 or visit website www.itsonline.co.uk.

Exeter Fund Managers also runs a unit trust which invests in a range of zeros. It is called the Exeter Zero Preference Unit Trust.

Jigsaw piece 11: self-build

BUILDING your own home may seem no more than a pipe dream but some 25,000 people a year embark upon such a task. Although most of these people do not physically build their own dream home – they get labourers to put their dreams into fruition – they do have to find suitable land, get planning permission for development and obtain finance to complete the building.

Many banks and building societies now offer self-build mortgages for people who want to build their own homes. They include all the big names such as Halifax, Nationwide and Bradford & Bingley. Typically, they will lend between 25% and 80% of the value of land and between 65% and 95% of the cost of building the home. The money is usually paid in tranches as certain key work is completed.

FURTHER DETAILS: Self-build should not be taken lightly and should not be embarked upon without seeking professional advice from a raft of professionals including surveyors, architects and planning consultants. For good solid information on building your own home, the best starting point is Buildstore on 01506 417 130. For key details on self-build mortgage providers, consult *Moneyfacts* magazine (01603 476 476).

Jigsaw piece 12: cycle insurance

GOVERNMENT ministers may continually encourage us to get on our bike, and new cycle routes are being built every year to make a cyclist's life a happier one, but you shouldn't hit the pedals without adequate cycle insurance. Unbeknown to most, cyclists have the same responsibilities as motorists, which means they can be held liable if they cause accidents or damage to other vehicles. The key difference is that cycle insurance is not compulsory.

Most household insurance policies do provide limited cover for the cyclist – for example, third-party cover for accidents that are their fault and the theft of a bike from a home or garden. But if your bike is stolen away from home, there is a good chance that your home insurer will not pay up unless they are specified under the personal all-risks section. Also, most home insurance policies have a maximum limit on the value of bike insured.

Cycle insurance is the answer, especially for people with high-value bikes or who cycle off-road or take part in races or time trials.

A good starting point is the Cyclists' Touring Club, which caters mainly for leisure cyclists. By becoming a member, you automatically obtain third-party cover in the UK. It also sells cycle insurance policies under the Cyclecover brand, which can be extended to cover racing. Discounts are available if more than one bike is owned at the same address.

By joining the British Cycling Federation, you will also receive automatic third-party cover. You can also obtain theft and accidental damage insurance. Other insurers are the Environmental Transport Association and Sportscover Direct.

FURTHER DETAILS: British Cycling Federation (0161 230 2301); Cyclists' Touring Club (01483 417 217); Environmental Transport Association (01932 828 882); Sportscover Direct (0117 922 6222).

Jigsaw piece 13: divorce

EACH year, more than 150,000 couples split up, often resulting in financial chaos and huge costs as a result of having to employ expensive lawyers and financial advisers. Although the hiring of a lawyer is essential, divorcing couples can keep a lid on costs by adopting the following five-part plan:

PART ONE: Before visiting a solicitor, try to sit down and agree how to split assets – it will save you huge solicitors' bills in the long run.

PART TWO: Sort out how you are going to deal with your children. Who are they going to live with and what amount will be paid in terms of maintenance? The Child Support Agency (website www.dss.gov.uk/csa) will suggest a sum if agreement cannot be reached.

PART THREE: Sort out what is going to happen to the marital home. Should it be sold or should it form part of the divorce settlement?

PART FOUR: Be prepared to disclose all your assets – and debts – at the time of separation. This should include all assets – pensions included – and debts held in single or joint names. New rules govern pensions that ensure a fair deal for both sides.

PART FIVE: Work out a financial budget detailing how much you will need to live on after the split.

Jigsaw piece 14: prize insurance

OFFERING a big prize at a village fête or a golf day normally ensures a healthy turnout. And if you are organising such an event, you don't have to pay through the roof in order to offer such a juicy reward – instead you can take out an insurance policy which will pay out in the event of the prize being won. All you have to do as organiser is pay for the insurance cover, which will be inexpensive provided the odds of contestants winning are long.

A typical event where insurance is bought is a golf day where the achieving of a hole-in-one at a specified par three hole will result in the winning of a big cash prize or car. However, insurance companies specialising in this area will also cover competitions such as roll-the-dice (where you need the dice to all turn up sixes) and crack-the-safe (guessing the figures on a combination lock).

FURTHER DETAILS: The following companies specialise in the provision of insurance against the winning of big prizes: Hamilton & Wellard Underwriting Agency (0500 053 982); National Hole-in-One Association (0800 833 863); Worldwide Hole'n One (01727 843 686).

Jigsaw piece 15: credit unions

CREDIT unions are becoming a popular way for people to save and borrow, especially in areas where banks have removed their branch networks. Members of a credit union are united by a common bond, such as their occupation or where they live. The aim of a credit union is to encourage people to save on a regular basis. After saving for a regular period of time, usually 13 weeks, members are allowed to borrow. Loan rates cannot be more than 1% a month which works out at 12.68% a year and loans must be repaid over a maximum period of two years. Savers receive dividends, the amount dependent upon the strength of the credit union. Children can save with credit unions but they cannot borrow.

So-called regeneration trusts are also emerging. Their role is primarily to provide business lending to individuals and small businesses.

FURTHER DETAILS: The Association of British Credit Unions Ltd is the best starting point for anyone interested in joining a credit union. Contact ABCUL on 0161 832 3694 or visit website www.abcul.org. Details on regeneration trusts can be obtained by contacting Karl Dyson, University of Salford, The Crescent, Salford M5 4WT.

Jigsaw piece 16: orphan assets

A number of insurance companies have established substantial reserves over the past years. These reserves, which have built up within their with-profits life funds, are now being distributed to policyholders by some insurance companies. This is because they are deemed to be orphan assets and are not needed to meet the reasonable expectations of existing policyholders. The Treasury has recommended that orphan assets are distributed 90% to policyholders and 10% to shareholders although distribution schemes so far devised by insurance companies have not worked to this ratio. These assets may be distributed in the form of cash or extra policy bonuses, or a mix of the two. Orphan assets are a windfall.

FURTHER DETAILS: Most of the big insurance companies have substantial orphan assets including Prudential and CGNU. Chartwell Investment Management has published a guide on orphan assets. Copies are available from 9 Kingsmead Square, Bath BA1 2AB (01225 321 700).

Jigsaw piece 17: financing the cost of a car

THERE are a number of schemes now available which enable you to fund the purchase of a car. There are five broad schemes:

SCHEME 1: HIRE PURCHASE. This is the traditional way of financing a new car. You put down a deposit – typically a minimum of 10% – and then you pay off the balance in fixed monthly instalments which include interest charges. Hire purchase agreements can run from 12 to 48 months. At the end of the agreement, you can keep the car by paying a small fee – typically £25. Hire purchase agreements are typically offered by the car dealership from whom you decide to purchase the car.

SCHEME 2: PERSONAL CONTRACT PURCHASE. This is a variation on hire purchase but here the monthly payments are lower. This is because payments are worked out on the difference between the cost of the car (minus any deposit you put down) and a so-called 'minimum guaranteed future value' – MGFV. This latter sum is the minimum amount a dealership thinks the car will be worth at the end of the personal contract purchase agreement.

At the end of the agreement, you then have a choice: you can pay the MGFV and become the owner of the car. Alternatively, you can give the car back and walk away or trade the car in, using any extra equity in the car to offset against another deposit.

Although personal contract purchase can lead to lower monthly payments, there are drawbacks. At the end of the agreement, you can be left with a car which is worth far less than the MGFV because of plunging second-hand values. This means you have no alternative but to hand back the keys. Also, companies that offer these schemes will often insist on drivers agreeing to certain conditions such as a maximum mileage per year. Exceeding this limit can lead to a fine.

SCHEME 3: CAR PURCHASE PLAN. This is a variation on the personal contract purchase idea. Here, you take out a loan – no deposit is required – but defer the payment of a final lump sum until the end of the deal. This sum is based on the car's expected future value at that time. At the end of the deal, you can sell the car to clear the deferred amount or continue to make payments until the loan is cleared. Alliance & Leicester is the leading player in this market.

SCHEME 4: PERSONAL LOANS. These unsecured loans are provided by most banks and building societies and can offer attractive interest rates. The maximum loan offered is usually £25,000.

SCHEME 5: PERSONAL CONTRACT HIRE. Here, you lease the car so you never own the vehicle. At the end of the agreement, you simply give the car back. Although monthly repayments include the cost of servicing and maintenance, the fact that you never own the car means repayments are competitive against other forms of leasing. PriceWaterhouse Coopers is a leading player in this market (www.lease123.com).

FURTHER DETAILS: For details of best personal loans, contact *Moneyfacts* (01603 476 476). Individual car dealerships will have details of finance agreements available on their range of cars.

Jigsaw piece 18: sending money abroad

SENDING money abroad to a loved one as a result of a crisis happens to us all at some stage in our lives. Typically, a son or a daughter has had their wallet or purse stolen, leaving them overseas without two pennies – or two pesetas – to rub together. Thankfully, a number of companies enable you to get money out quickly.

Leading player is Western Union which has some 90,000 agents in some 200 countries. You simply visit one of its branches, fill out a form stating to whom and where the money is to go and pay by cash or credit card. The recipient will be asked for identification although if this has also been stolen, Western Union will arrange for a four-word ID question to be transmitted thereby ensuring the money does not end up in the wrong hands. An example would be: 'father's job: taxi driver'.

Western Union also allows people to make money tranmission orders over the telephone (0800 833 833). Although the service is not cheap, it can prove a financial lifeline.

FURTHER DETAILS: Apart from Western Union, other companies which offer money transmission services include: the Post Office, Thomas Cook, American Express (members only), and most leading banks including Alliance & Leicester, Bank of Scotland, Barclays, Co-op, HSBC, NatWest and Lloyds TSB.

Jigsaw piece 19: basic banking

MOST of the major high street banks have, until recently, shunned people with poor credit histories. However, as a result of government pressure, a number of the big banks are now offering basic banking facilities – no-frills current accounts – to people who want to jump on the banking ladder. Although these accounts differ between providers, they tend to offer limited or no overdraft facilities, thereby making it difficult for people to go into the red. Customers are usually given a cash machine card and are allowed to set up direct debits or standing orders.

FURTHER DETAILS: Details of these basic bank accounts are available direct from high street banks. Leading players include NatWest (Step account) and Royal Bank of Scotland (Key account).

Jigsaw piece 20: boat insurance

THERE is no legal requirement for boat owners to have insurance although it is compulsory on some waterways and key marinas. However, it makes sense to have cover because if you hit another boat or injure someone without insurance, you could have to pay out a small fortune in damages.

A typical boat insurance policy will include third-party liability insurance, which will pay for accidents or injuries caused to other people or property. It will also include accidental damage to a boat, theft, fire, lightning and flood. Cover can also embrace salvage cover in case a boat breaks down and has to be rescued or towed.

FURTHER DETAILS: Boat insurance can be bought through most insurance brokers. However, a number of insurance companies, including GJW Direct, CGU and Navigators & General, now sell direct to the public.

CHAPTER # 10
Life Cycle

ACTUARY

'Someone who cannot stand the excitement of chartered accountancy.'

Glan Thomas

DURING our lives, our financial aspirations and needs change. In our late teens and early 20s, for example, it's all about trying to control debts resulting from going to college. At the other end of the spectrum, in our 60s, it's all about ensuring we have enough income to live on.

In this chapter, we look at the key financial decisions – 50 steps – which we need to take at key stages of our life. The information presented is meant to be no more than a checklist – no two individuals' financial circumstances are alike.

If the information presented does no more than jolt you into taking action – maybe starting a pension, for example – the purpose of the chapter will have been fulfilled.

Age 0 to 18 (no responsibilities)

STEP 1: If you are an adult with children, ensure you save on your children's behalf. Take advantage of tax-friendly children's savings schemes offered by National Savings and friendly societies. Also, don't forget new stakeholder pensions which can be taken out on behalf of children as well as cash-based Isas for the over 16s. Open children's savings accounts and encourage your young ones to save. Get them into good financial habits at an early stage.

STEP 2: If you want to save for your children's further education, start saving as early as possible. Take independent financial advice because there is a vast array of plans available to meet this goal – from endowments through to bonds designed to meet further educational costs. Financial arrangements may be available via the school you have targeted for your children.

STEP 3: Remember, Isas can now be taken out by 16-year-olds. Take advantage. Also adults can take out stakeholder pensions on their children's behalf. The earlier you start squirrelling away money, the greater the chance you give it of growing.

In your late teens and early 20s (footloose and fancy free)

STEP 4: Forget about saving in your late teens and early 20s. For most people, the key financial decision they must take at this age is financing their way through college or university. Although the government still typically pays about three-quarters of the cost of tuition fees, a quarter has to be met by you. How much precisely will depend on your family's income – the more they earn, the bigger the proportion of tuition fees will have to be met by yourself. By applying to your local educational authority, you will find out how much help you are going to get.

STEP 5: Then there are living costs. For most people, funding these costs will only be possible by applying for a student loan through your local education authority. These loans are available to cover your living costs while you are studying with the interest charged pegged to the rate of inflation. How much loan you qualify for will depend on where you are studying (living away and studying in London will make you eligible for a larger loan), your income and the income of your parents. The loan will have to start to be repaid after you have finished college and once you start earning more than £10,000 a year.

STEP 6: Some students, such as the disabled and those with dependants, may be able to apply for other grants. They should contact their local education authority.

It is also possible to obtain finance by getting a company to finance you through university. Sponsorship and incentives are also available to those who are interested in joining the army, becoming medics or teachers.

STEP 7: If you have chosen to work rather than seek further education, enjoy yourself. Financial planning should be as basic as it comes. Don't think investments or insurance beyond saving for your next fun holiday. Just don't spend more than you earn.

In your 20s (still footloose and fancy free)

STEP 8: Pay off debts from your student days. You don't want them hanging around your neck – and you can't run away from them.

STEP 9: Try to budget. Money is often tight in your 20s, so it will pay to keep control of your money.

STEP 10: Ensure you have a bank account which you feel comfortable with, which has low charges and maybe pays you interest on funds you have in it.

STEP 11: Try to build an emergency savings fund in a savings account. It will come in handy if you need cash in a hurry – maybe to meet an unexpected bill.

STEP 12: Open up a regular savings account. It will help when you come to putting down a deposit on a first home. Usually, the bigger the deposit you can put down on a home, the better the mortgage deal you will get.

STEP 13: Think about pensions. Although retirement may seem a long way away, it is never too early to start a pension. If your employer has a scheme, join it. If not, take one out yourself. A stakeholder pension may make great sense.

STEP 14: Don't buy life insurance unless you have dependants. However, consider critical illness cover and/or income replacement if you have financial commitments.

STEP 15: Don't buy any savings- and insurance-linked savings plans. Again, you are throwing good money down the proverbial financial drain.

STEP 16: Enjoy yourself. You only live once!

In your 30s (married with family and new-found responsibilities)

STEP 17: Ensure you have adequate life insurance. It's a must for those with children. You don't want your family suffering financially if you are unfortunate to pass away early.

STEP 18: Think about other forms of protection insurance such as critical illness, income replacement and mortgage payment protection. Although expensive, protection insurance can provide a lifeline if you suffer from serious illness and you are unable to work for a long time, putting your family under serious financial stress.

STEP 19: Think about private medical insurance. Although something of a luxury, it is cheaper when you are younger. If your company offers cover through a group scheme, take it for you and your family.

STEP 20: Ensure you have the right mortgage. Don't pay over the odds for a mortgage. If necessary, shop around and remortgage. It's painless and can save you a small fortune.

STEP 21: Take out a will. If you have a family, this is imperative. It's easy to do and not expensive. Use a solicitor. It might cost more than using a will-writing service but it's something you need to get right.

STEP 22: Ensure your pension is progressing nicely. If you are in a company pension scheme, consider topping up via an Additional Voluntary Contribution Scheme or a free-standing AVC.

STEP 23: Consider a tax-free Isa and other investments such as unit trusts and investment trusts. These are all long-term investments and should perform better over the long term than deposit savings.

STEP 24: If you are borrowing via a credit card, ensure you are doing so as cheaply as possible. Shop around for a better credit card deal – credit card transfers are easy to arrange.

In your 40s (establishing yourself for the rest of your financial life)

STEP 25: Ensure you are maximising your pension contributions, either by making additional contributions (if a member of a company pension scheme) or ensuring your personal contributions are increasing every year. Remember, with personal pension contributions, the percentage of your earnings that can be squirrelled away inside a pension increases with age. If in doubt, speak to an independent financial adviser who should be able to tell you whether your pensions planning is on track.

STEP 26: Ensure you still have adequate life insurance. It may also pay you to rebroke your term assurance to another insurance company, thereby reducing premiums and extending cover.

STEP 27: If you haven't bought protection insurance, think about buying it now – long-term illness can strike you in your 40s so don't be complacent.

STEP 28: Ensure your will is up to date. You have the right to change it.

STEP 29: Ensure your mortgage is on track – especially if it is interest only. Get a financial expert to check whether all is progressing well or whether you need to take corrective action. You don't want a mortgage hanging around your neck at retirement.

STEP 30: Pay off part of your mortgage if you can. Reducing your debt makes sense – at any stage of life.

STEP 31: Keep on investing. Although retirement is a way away, saving via a tax-free Isa and unit trusts and investment trusts makes great sense.

In your 50s (setting yourself up for retirement)

STEP 32: Get an idea of the state pension you will be entitled to by completing form BR19. It doesn't cost you anything to get hold of this forecast.

STEP 33: Review your pension arrangements, including pensions built up under previous employers. If necessary, step up your contributions now to ensure you are storing up an adequate pension in retirement. Remember, in your 50s, you can put more into a pension than you could in your earlier years – the government is far more generous.

STEP 34: Review your investments. If they are all of a risky nature, consider transferring some of them into less risky assets such as bonds, gilts and with-profits, thereby spreading your risk. However, don't stop investing in equities or collective investments such as unit trusts or investment trusts. You still have a long time until you retire – hopefully.

STEP 35: If you can, clear your mortgage. You don't want a mortgage hanging around your neck at retirement.

STEP 36: Ensure you are not paying unnecessary tax on your savings and investments. Consider transferring assets to the spouse who is paying less or no tax. Also ensure you are utilising your tax-free investment allowances such as Isas.

STEP 37: Think about inheritance tax. Now might be a good time to think about gifting assets to relatives, thereby ensuring you are protecting yourself and your family from inheritance tax.

STEP 38: Start thinking about long-term-care insurance. The earlier you start a plan, the cheaper it will be.

Your 60s and beyond (time to enjoy the fruits of your hard labour)

STEP 39: Ensure you get the maximum income from your pension at retirement. If you have a personal pension, ensure you purchase the best-value pension annuity by shopping around.

STEP 40: Claim your state pension – it's yours.

STEP 41: Claim any benefits you are entitled to – don't be ashamed of doing this. It is your right.

STEP 42: Ensure your savings are arranged in such a way that you are not paying unnecessary tax.

STEP 43: Think income. Consider changing the way your assets are invested so that they are geared more towards generating income. Corporate bonds, gilts and with-profits should all be considered.

STEP 44: Be wary of investing in shares. You don't need sleepless nights worrying how your investment portfolio is performing.

STEP 45: If you are eligible to receive gross interest from your savings, ensure you receive it by filling in the necessary forms.

STEP 46: Keep thinking tax-free when it comes to savings and investments. Isas can still play an important part in your retirement strategy, providing you with income.

STEP 47: If you are equity rich, cash poor, consider a home income plan.

STEP 48: Check your will so that everything is to your liking. Make any changes that are necessary.

STEP 49: Think about taking out a pre-payment funeral plan. Yes, it sounds ghoulish but by taking out such a plan now, it means your funeral arrangements will all be sorted out when your final day comes, thereby relieving some of the stress for your loved ones.

STEP 50: Most of all, enjoy yourself in retirement. Take those holidays you have been dreaming about for years. Join the local bridge club, local golf club. Live for today, not tomorrow.

CHAPTER **11**
Top Providers

STOCKBROKER

'A man who can take a bankroll and
run it into a shoestring.'

Alexander Woollcott

THE one criticism you cannot level at the financial services industry
is the amount of choice on offer. The industry is literally brimming
over with suppliers eager to sell their wares – from insurance
companies and building societies through to retail giants such as
Tesco and Marks & Spencer.

Although no one company holds sway over the personal
finance world, there are companies which seem to do certain things
better than others, be it managing unit trusts or investment trusts, or
offering standard variable rate mortgages.

The following chapter looks at those companies which excel in
their particular fields. The choices are part judgemental, part based
on former experience and part based on speaking to a phalanx of
top professional financial advisers. Indeed, details of top
independent financial advisers are also provided.

In some areas it is impossible to identify top players, essentially
because the markets are so fragmented.

If your particular product choice is not included, don't despair
at all. Ask 10 top advisers for their opinion and they will come up
with 10 different answers. It's what makes the personal finance
world such a fascinating one.

Unit trusts/open-ended investment companies

THE unit trust world is a crowded one consisting of more than 180 different investment houses and nearly 2,000 individual funds. This makes choice a difficult exercise.

As a general rule, insurance companies and banks make poor investment houses. The best unit trust providers tend to be those which specialise purely in investment management.

Over the past 10 years, there is no doubt that an elite division of unit trust companies has evolved. Its members include:

ABERDEEN UNIT TRUST MANAGERS
ADDRESS: One Bow Churchyard
London EC4M 9HH
TELEPHONE: 020 7463 6000
WEBSITE: www.aberdeen-asset.com
PLUS FACTORS: Particularly liked for its bond and technology expertise. Offers a full range of funds which can be bought on a regular savings basis or through a tax-free Isa.

FIDELITY INVESTMENT SERVICES
ADDRESS: 25 Lovat Lane
London EC3R 8LL
TELEPHONE: 020 7283 9911
WEBSITE: www.fidelity.co.uk
PLUS FACTORS: An excellent all-rounder with a full range of funds encompassing index-tracking funds and some of the country's most consistent performers. A number of its Moneybuilder funds have no initial charges. Funds can be bought through a savings scheme or held within a tax-free Isa.

GARTMORE FUND MANAGERS
ADDRESS: 8 Fenchurch Place
London EC3M 4PH

TELEPHONE: 020 7782 2000
WEBSITE: www.gartmore.com
PLUS FACTORS: An investment house offering a full range of funds including index-tracking funds and noted for its strong investment performance in Europe. Funds can be bought on a regular basis or held inside a tax-free Isa.

INVESCO FUND MANAGERS
ADDRESS: 11 Devonshire Square
London EC2M 4YR
TELEPHONE: 020 7626 3434
WEBSITE: www.invesco.co.uk
PLUS FACTORS: Now owned by Amvescap, this company has literally reinvented itself – from being a company with brilliant marketing but lousy investment performance to an investment house focused on obtaining top-drawer returns for investors. Excellent record in Europe, albeit dented in the past year, and offers one of the few unit trusts, Rupert Children's Fund, exclusively available to children. Funds can be bought through a savings scheme or held inside a tax-free Isa. It has now acquired Perpetual.

JUPITER UNIT TRUST MANAGERS
ADDRESS: 4 Grosvenor Place
London SW1X 7TJ
TELEPHONE: 020 7412 0703
WEBSITE: www.jupiterifa.co.uk
PLUS FACTORS: An investment house which has emerged almost out of the blue in recent years. Renowned for its excellent team of fund managers leading to the outstanding long-term performance of such funds as Jupiter Income. Recently, the company has lost its way as a result of putting marketing interests at the top of its pile – in other words, putting the acquisition of new business before the interests of existing investors. It has also lost a number of key fund managers. Offers a regular savings scheme and Isas.

NEWTON FUND MANAGERS
ADDRESS: 71 Queen Victoria Street
London EC4V 4DR
TELEPHONE: 020 7332 9000
WEBSITE: www.newton.co.uk
PLUS FACTORS: Owned by the Mellon Bank Corporation, this company goes about its business quietly, delivering consistently good returns for investors. Renowned for its management of income funds. Offers both regular savings facilities and tax-free Isa wrap-arounds.

INVESCO PERPETUAL UNIT TRUST MANAGEMENT
ADDRESS: Perpetual Park
Perpetual Park Drive
Henley-on-Thames
Oxfordshire RG9 1HH
TELEPHONE: 01491 417 000
WEBSITE: www.invescoperpetual.co.uk
PLUS FACTORS: One of the few investment houses to have thrived by operating out of London. Has an outstanding investment team although it did go off the boil during 1999. Offers a user-friendly savings facility (with an extremely low minimum monthly savings requirement of £20) and an Isa scheme. Now part of the Invesco group.

SCHRODER UNIT TRUSTS LTD
ADDRESS: 33 Gutter Lane
London EC2V 8AS
TELEPHONE: 020 7658 6000
WEBSITE: www.schroders.com/uk/retail funds
PLUS FACTORS: A group with a full range of investment funds. Offers both regular savings facilities and tax-free Isas.

There is also a band of emerging unit trust companies with some good performance numbers behind them. They include:

ABN AMRO FUND MANAGERS LTD
TELEPHONE: 020 7678 4521
(great UK record and possesses two of the best fund managers in the country)

ARTEMIS UNIT TRUST MANAGERS
(0845 458 4595)
(good UK investment team which learnt its trade at Ivory & Sime)

BWD RENSBURG UNIT TRUST MANAGERS
TELEPHONE: 0113 245 4488
(UK specialist with a strong record in income investment)

INVESTEC FUND MANAGERS
TELEPHONE: 020 7597 1800
(a good record in the management of bond funds)

LEGGMASON INVESTORS
TELEPHONE: 020 7070 7500
(strong record in the UK and in the management of utility stocks)

LIONTRUST INVESTMENT FUNDS LTD
TELEPHONE: 020 7412 1700
(UK fund management specialist)

SOCIETE GENERALE UNIT TRUSTS LTD
TELEPHONE: 020 7815 8600
(new to unit trusts but with some outstanding managers who have done it all before such as Nicola Horlick and technology expert Alan Torry)

VIRGIN DIRECT UNIT TRUST MANAGERS
TELEPHONE: 08456 101 030
(for investors who like their investments plain and simple – an excellent provider of index-tracking funds)

Investment trusts

ALTHOUGH there are nowhere near as many investment trusts as there are unit trusts, there is no doubt that some investment trust houses are better than others. Not just better because of superior investment performance but because they seem determined to court the private investor through cost-effective savings plans and charge-friendly Isas.

An elite division of investment trust companies would include the following:

ALLIANCE TRUST
ADDRESS: Meadow House
64 Reform Street
Dundee DD1 1TJ
TELEPHONE: 01382 201 700
PLUS FACTORS: A company which offers two investment trusts perfect for private investors – Alliance and Second Alliance. These trusts are invested worldwide and are supported by an imaginative savings scheme (enabling investors to invest in other shares and trusts) and a similarly flexible Isa.

BAILLIE GIFFORD
ADDRESS: 1 Rutland Court
Edinburgh EH3 8EY
TELEPHONE: 0500 418 008
PLUS FACTORS: A Scottish-based investment house which goes about its business without the marketing hype of many of its rivals. The group offers a broad selection of investment trusts including long-established trusts such as Monks and Scottish Mortgage which, believe it not, are invested across the world's major stock markets. Offers both a savings scheme and an Isa. A group renowned for conservative investment management which should find appeal with many investors.

EDINBURGH FUND MANAGERS
ADDRESS: Donaldson House
97 Haymarket Terrace
Edinburgh EH12 5HD
TELEPHONE: 0131 313 1000
WEBSITE: www.edfd.com
PLUS FACTORS: An investment house renowned for its collection of specialist investment trusts investing in the Far East and South America. Offers a cost-effective regular savings scheme with the minimum monthly contribution set at £30 and an Isa where the minimum monthly payment is £50. Also offers a share exchange plan and accommodates parents who want to save for children.

GARTMORE INVESTMENT
ADDRESS: 8 Fenchurch Place
London EC3M 4PH
TELEPHONE: 0800 289 336
WEBSITE: www.gartmore.co.uk
PLUS FACTORS: A company with a broad range of trusts and something of a specialist in the management of split capital investment trusts. Good track record in Europe through Gartmore European and one of the only groups to offer a retail investment trust investing in Ireland (Gartmore Irish Growth). Offers both Isas and a savings scheme.

FLEMING ASSET MANAGEMENT
ADDRESS: 10 Aldermanbury
London EC2V 7RF
TELEPHONE: 0800 403 030
WEBSITE: www.chasefleming.com
PLUS FACTORS: An investment trust house which offers something for everyone – from UK invested funds (Fleming Claverhouse) through to the unusual (Fleming Chinese and Fleming Indian). A very private investor-focused house which offers both Isas and a

regular savings plan. Also encourages investors to attend share-holder meetings. Now part of JP Morgan Fleming Asset Management.

FOREIGN & COLONIAL MANAGEMENT
ADDRESS: Exchange House
Primrose Street
London EC2A 2NY
TELEPHONE: 0845 600 3030
WEBSITE: www.fandc.co.uk
PLUS FACTORS: An investment trust house which has been at the forefront of making trusts accessible to the private investor. The trust stable is built around the formidable Foreign & Colonial Investment Trust – a perfect first-time investment – although there are other trusts on offer, specialising in geographic areas (for example, Eurotrust) and specific sectors (Special Utilities). Offers both an Isa and a regular savings scheme.

HENDERSON INVESTORS
ADDRESS: 3 Finsbury Avenue
London EC2M 2PA
TELEPHONE: 0800 106 106
WEBSITE: www.henderson.com
PLUS FACTORS: Offers a broad range of trusts including well-respected Bankers' (internationally invested) and Witan (again internationally invested). Provides both Isa and regular savings options.

INVESCO ASSET MANAGEMENT
ADDRESS: 11 Devonshire Square
London EC2M 4YR
TELEPHONE: 020 7626 3434
WEBSITE: www.invesco.co.uk/investmenttrusts
PLUS FACTORS: An investment trust group with much improved investment performance. Has a strong investment emphasis on Asia with trusts such as Invesco Asia, Invesco Japan Discovery,

Invesco Tokyo and GT Japan. Offers both a savings plan and an Isa facility.

MARTIN CURRIE INVESTMENT MANAGEMENT
ADDRESS: Saltire Court
20 Castle Terrace
Edinburgh EH1 2ES
TELEPHONE: 0808 100 2125
WEBSITE: www.martincurrie.com
PLUS FACTORS: An investment group with a low profile but some half-decent investment trusts. Offers a flexible savings plan with a low monthly savings requirement of £30.

SCOTTISH INVESTMENT TRUST
ADDRESS: 6 Albyn Place
Edinburgh EH2 4NL
TELEPHONE: 0131 225 7781
WEBSITE: www.sit.co.uk
PLUS FACTORS: This is a one-trust stable based around the long-standing Scottish Investment Trust, a worldwide invested fund. The savings scheme is both inexpensive and private investor-friendly with a minimum monthly savings requirement of only £25. There is also an Isa plan based around the conservatively invested trust.

Personal pensions

THE personal pensions market has undergone a dramatic transformation in recent years in response to regulatory pressure for greater charges disclosure and the advent of stakeholder pensions. As a result, many companies have had no choice but to give customers a better deal – those who haven't managed to do so have been driven out of business.

In identifying top personal pension providers, there is only one personal finance bible to which you should refer. It is *Money*

Management magazine which has made it its role in life to give consumers full information on the acceptability of individual personal pension plans. On a regular yearly basis, *Money Management* scrutinises those personal pension plans available on a number of points – past performance and the impact of charges on plans taken out now, both in the early years and at retirement. By doing this, it arrives at a list of 'five star' companies – companies which it believes offer customers best personal pensions value for money.

In its 2000 survey, *Money Management* classified five star personal pension providers as follows: 'Companies must have 50% or more of their 5 and 10 year unit linked results above average, which must include above-average performance for the principal managed fund over 5 years, plus below-average charges for open market options [the fund available at retirement upon which the purchase of an annuity is based] and transfer values.'

The companies awarded five stars were as follows:

Monthly premiums

ABBEY NATIONAL LIFE
ADDRESS: 287–301 St Vincent Street
Glasgow G2 5NB
TELEPHONE: 0141 275 8000

EAGLE STAR DIRECT
ADDRESS: Montpellier Drive
Cheltenham GL53 7LQ
TELEPHONE: 01242 221 311

EDINBURGH FUND MANAGERS
ADDRESS: 97 Haymarket Terrace
Edinburgh EH12 5HD
TELEPHONE: 0800 028 6789

FRIENDS PROVIDENT
ADDRESS: Castle Street
Salisbury, Wilts SP1 3SH
TELEPHONE: 0870 608 3678

MARKS & SPENCER
ADDRESS: King's Meadow
Chester Business Park
Chester CH99 9LS
TELEPHONE: 0800 363 420

NFU MUTUAL
ADDRESS: Tiddington Road
Stratford-upon-Avon CV37 7BJ
TELEPHONE: 0800 622 323

PORTFOLIO FUND MANAGEMENT
ADDRESS: 64 London Wall
London EC2M 5TP
TELEPHONE: 020 7638 0808

SKANDIA PROFESSIONAL
ADDRESS: PO BOX 37
Skandia House
Portland Terrace
Southampton SO14 7AY
TELEPHONE: 0800 181 396

Single premiums

ABBEY NATIONAL LIFE
ADDRESS: 287–301 St Vincent Street
Glasgow G2 5NB
TELEPHONE: 0141 275 8000

EAGLE STAR DIRECT
ADDRESS: Montpellier Drive
Cheltenham GL53 7LQ
TELEPHONE: 01242 221 311

FRIENDS PROVIDENT
ADDRESS: Castle Street
Salisbury, Wilts
TELEPHONE: 0870 608 3678

MARKS & SPENCER
ADDRESS: King's Meadow
Chester Business Park
Chester CH99 9LS
TELEPHONE: 0800 363 420

NFU MUTUAL
ADDRESS: Tiddington Road
Stratford-upon-Avon
TELEPHONE: 0800 622 323

Money Management stresses that its five star list is based on a series of assumptions which if altered could lead to other companies being awarded five stars. But its analysis of personal pension value for money is simply the most comprehensive conducted.

Independent financial advisers

INDEPENDENT financial advisers are much criticised but a good adviser is worth his or her weight in gold. Over the past 14 years, I have had personal dealings with hundreds of advisers. These are the crème de la crème.

FIONA PRICE & PARTNERS
ADDRESS: 29 Ely Place
London EC1N 6TD
TELEPHONE: 020 7611 4700
(specialists in dealing with advice for women)

HOLDEN MEEHAN
ADDRESS: 283–287 High Holborn
London WC1V 7HP
TELEPHONE: 020 7692 1700
(all-round advisers but with specialism in ethical investments)

AIS PENSIONS
ADDRESS: Imperial House
41 Gap Road
London SW19 8JE
TELEPHONE: 020 8543 6698
(pensions specialists)

BESTINVEST
ADDRESS: 20 Mason's Yard
London SW1Y 6BU
TELEPHONE: 020 7321 0100
(investment experts)

ALAN STEEL ASSET MANAGEMENT
ADDRESS: Nobel House
Linlithgow EH49 7HU
TELEPHONE: 01506 842 365
(all-round specialists)

CLANCY'S FINANCIAL & BUSINESS ADVISERS
ADDRESS: Station House
Wylam
Northumberland NE41 8HR
TELEPHONE: 01661 853 838

NORWEST CONSULTANTS
ADDRESS: 7–9 Stanmore Hill
Stanmore
Middlesex HA7 3DP
TELEPHONE: 020 8954 5474

PREETY TECHNICAL
ADDRESS: 1 Seething Lane
London EC3N 4NH
TELEPHONE: 020 7734 9899

DENNEHY WELLER & CO.
ADDRESS: 75 High Street
Chislehurst
Kent BR7 5AG
TELEPHONE: 020 8467 1666

LOWLAND
ADDRESS: 1 Green Street
Galashiels TD1 3AE
TELEPHONE: 01896 751 007

PLAN INVEST
ADDRESS: Plan Invest House
9 King Edward Street
Macclesfield
Cheshire SK10 1AQ
TELEPHONE: 01625 429 217
(strong in the area of investment)

DIANE SAUNDERS FINANCIAL ADVISERS
ADDRESS: 351 Harrogate Road
Leeds LS17 6PZ
TELEPHONE: 0113 266 9595
(strong in the area of protection insurance)

UNITAS
ADDRESS: 9 Henderson Avenue
Scunthorpe
North Lincolnshire DN15 7RH
TELEPHONE: 01724 849 481
(specialists in unit trusts)

HIGHCLERE FINANCIAL SERVICES
ADDRESS: 42 London Road
Apsley
Hemel Hempstead, Herts HP3 9SB
TELEPHONE: 01442 234 800
(specialist in protection insurance)

Mortgage advisers

GOOD mortgage advisers are few and far between. However, a select band stand apart from the madding crowd. These advisers will shop around for a mortgage most appropriate to your circumstances – and don't be deterred by where they are based. They will conduct business over the telephone.

LONDON & COUNTRY MORTGAGES
ADDRESS: Beazer House
Lower Bristol Road
Bath BA2 3BA
TELEPHONE: 01225 408 000

BRADFORD & BINGLEY
ADDRESS: PO Box 88
Croft Road
Crossflatts
Bingley
West Yorkshire BD16 2UA
TELEPHONE: 01274 555 555

(provides independent financial advice on mortgages throughout its branch network, under the Marketplace label)

SAVILLS PRIVATE FINANCE
ADDRESS: 25 Finsbury Circus
London EC2M 7EE
TELEPHONE: 0870 900 7762

Savings accounts

The deposit savings market is fragmented, making choice of best provider a nigh impossible task. Although an organisation may, for example, offer good savings rates on particular products, it may then spoil this by paying measly rates on other accounts.

Irrespective of which savings account you take out, it is imperative that you check that it remains competitive. All too often, new savings accounts are offered which pay solid rates of interest, only for these rates to become uncompetitive over time and to be superseded by better deals, either from competing organisations or from the same institution.

Bank accounts

FEW bank accounts have offered customers a fair deal in recent years. Charges have been excessive while interest paid on credit balances has been at best paltry.

The best bank accounts are now offered by new players in the current account market. Some of these players are Internet-based, which means they are not appropriate for many people who prefer to do their banking on a face-to-face basis.

Internet players include cahoot (www.cahoot.com) and smile (www.smile.co.uk).

Mortgages

LIKE savings accounts, it is impossible to compile a top mortgage providers' list. Most mortgage providers offer a vast range of products, some of which can provide value for money while others may be expensive. Some products may look inexpensive but then contain a nasty array of redemption penalties.

Building societies

BUILDING societies may be a dwindling breed but many of those which cling onto their mutual status provide customers with an array of good value for money products. If you have a local building society, you would be well to use its services. However, a number of building societies do stand out from the madding crowd:

NATIONWIDE BUILDING SOCIETY
ADDRESS: Nationwide House
Pipers Way
Swindon SN38 1NW
NUMBER OF BRANCHES: 681
TELEPHONE: 01793 513 513
WEBSITE: www.nationwide.co.uk
PLUS FACTORS: It is the biggest and also the best building society around. It has established beyond doubt that a well-run building society can deliver to members in terms of competitively priced products. Whatever Nationwide does, it seems to put members (customers) first. You can't go far wrong with this organisation, whether it is e-banking you want to get into or just a traditional branch-based account.

YORKSHIRE BUILDING SOCIETY
ADDRESS: Yorkshire House
Yorkshire Drive

Bradford
West Yorkshire BD5 8LJ
NUMBER OF BRANCHES: 132
TELEPHONE: 01274 740 740
WEBSITE: www.ybs.co.uk
PLUS FACTORS: Another building society in the Nationwide mould. It is true to its mutual status and puts customers first.

COVENTRY BUILDING SOCIETY
ADDRESS: Economic House
PO Box 9
High Street
Coventry CV1 5QN
NUMBER OF BRANCHES: 50
TELEPHONE: 0845 766 5522
WEBSITE: www.coventrybuildingsociety.co.uk
PLUS FACTORS: Concentrates on offering good value for money savings accounts and mortgages. Also rewards loyal customers with mortgage discounts or enhanced savings rates.

ECOLOGY BUILDING SOCIETY
ADDRESS: 18 Station Road
Cross Hills
Keighley
West Yorkshire BD20 7EH
NUMBER OF BRANCHES: 1
TELEPHONE: 01535 635 933
WEBSITE: www.ecology.co.uk
PLUS FACTORS: Very big into offering self-build mortgages for those borrowers building eco-friendly homes. It is the only building society of its kind and has carved out a niche for itself.

MARKET HARBOROUGH BUILDING SOCIETY
ADDRESS: Welland House
The Square
Market Harborough

Leicestershire LE16 7PD
NUMBER OF BRANCHES: 9
TELEPHONE: 01858 463 244
WEBSITE: www.mhbs.co.uk
PLUS FACTORS: An innovative building society which uses the Internet to distribute its products.

NORWICH & PETERBOROUGH BUILDING SOCIETY
ADDRESS: Peterborough Business Park
Lynch Wood
Peterborough
Cambridgeshire PE2 6WZ
NUMBER OF BRANCHES: 63
TELEPHONE: 01733 372372
WEBSITE: www.npbs.co.uk
PLUS FACTORS: Good regional building society with a strong presence in the self-build market.

STAFFORDSHIRE BUILDING SOCIETY
ADDRESS: PO Box 66
84 Salop Street
Wolverhampton WV3 0SA
NUMBER OF BRANCHES: 49
TELEPHONE: 01902 317 317
WEBSITE: www.staffordshirebuildingsociety.co.uk
PLUS FACTORS: Solid regional building society.

Credit cards

UNTIL recently, the credit card market remained in the hands of the big banks. However, spurred on from overseas, competition has blossomed resulting in customers being able to get a fairer credit card deal. Although most credit card companies are now constantly launching new cards or new card transfer deals in an attempt to attract new business, a number of card companies have emerged as giving customers a better deal. They include:

CAPITAL ONE

EGG (www.egg.com)

GOLDFISH CARD

NATIONWIDE

RBS ADVANTA

SMILE (www.smile.co.uk)

Protection insurance

IDENTIFYING best-value protection insurance is as difficult as it comes. The number of factors that need to go into the melting pot – such as age, medical history, sex, smoker or non-smoker – means that there is no top list of overall providers. While some companies may offer best value insurance to non-smoking women in their 30s, others may offer best terms to smokers.

Alan Lakey of Highclere Financial Services in Apsley, Hertsfordshire, has identified some of the best providers. But, as he stresses, any buyer of protection insurance should not blindly take out one of these plans. Their own individual circumstances need to be taken into account before arriving at best-value-for-money insurance.

1. CRITICAL ILLNESS (plans paying out a lump sum on diagnosis of a critical illness)

Best plans are from:

Skandia Life

Scottish Provident

Pegasus

Swiss Life

Cheaper plans which merit attention include those from:

Permanent Insurance

Zurich Life
Bupa
Legal & General

For smokers who have to pay more for cover, worthwhile plans are available from:
Swiss Life
Bupa
Zurich Life
Scottish Equitable

2. PERMANENT HEALTH INSURANCE (plans paying an income in the event of illness)

Again, the best-value-for-money insurance depends upon many factors including occupation. What is imperative is that a plan is purchased where cover pays out as soon as you are unable to carry out your own occupation – as opposed to any occupation.

Highclere Financial Services says the best plans are available from:
Swiss Life
Permanent Insurance
Zurich Life
Royal & SunAlliance

3. MORTGAGE PROTECTION INSURANCE (covers your mortgage in the event of long-term illness)

Best-value plans are available from:
Legal & General
Norwich Union
Swiss Life
Scottish Provident
Friends Provident

Annuity advisers

THE ANNUITY BUREAU
ADDRESS: Enterprise House
The Tower
11 York Road
London SE1 7NX
TELEPHONE: 020 7902 2300
WEBSITE: www.annuity-bureau.co.uk

ANNUITY DIRECT
ADDRESS: 32 Scrutton Street
London EC2A 4RQ
TELEPHONE: 020 7684 5000
WEBSITE: www.annuitydirect.co.uk

Home income plans

SAFE HOME INCOME PLANS (SHIP)
ADDRESS: 1st Floor
Parker Court
Knapp Lane
Cheltenham
GL50 3QJ
TELEPHONE: 01242 1539494
WEBSITE: www.ship-ltd.co.uk

CHAPTER

12

How to Buy

WEALTH

> 'Any income that's at least $100 more a year than the income of one's wife's sister's husband.'

> *H. L. Mencken*

BUYING financial products is now as easy as spending money you do not have. Take mortgages, for example. Thirty years ago, it was not unusual for people to queue for hours outside their local building society in the hope of obtaining a mortgage. But now mortgage providers, be they banks, insurance companies or building societies, are literally falling over each other to sell you a mortgage. The same goes for many other key financial products such as credit cards, personal loans and savings plans.

However, the buying of financial products is no longer a problem. It is the purchase of appropriate products that is the key issue – many people end up with a hotch-potch of insurance and savings plans primarily because they adopt a piecemeal approach to their finances. They buy products, many on impulse, without prioritising and without contemplating their whole financial picture. And often, it is only after squirrelling away sums of money in a plan for a while that they realise the product they have bought is not going to meet their key financial needs or even worse they can no longer afford the premiums.

In getting to grips with the different ways in which financial products can be bought, it is essential you find the route that you feel most comfortable with. But don't end up buying financial products simply for the sake of buying them – ask yourself the question: is this product appropriate for my burning financial needs?

Straight from the supplier:

Many people prefer to take their own financial decisions and make their own financial choices. That usually means buying directly from a financial services provider.

Fine – most financial services companies have no problem selling direct to you and often prefer to deal with you in this way because they have no agent or intermediary to pay. In other words, they can keep more profit for themselves.

A number of companies, 'direct' providers, now specialise in selling only direct to the consumer, and pass on some of their cost savings to customers by way of low charges. For the purchaser who knows what they want, these direct providers can provide value for money.

There are many ways in which you can buy financial products directly:

Via an advert

Many companies advertise their financial wares in national newspapers or specialist personal finance magazines. Few ask you for money there and then. Most instead invite you to send off for further details, either by completing a coupon or ringing a freephone.

Buying on the back of adverts is OK but don't be hoodwinked into purchasing something you don't really want or might not be the best around. Adverts always paint the rosiest picture possible about a product – and don't inform you about similar products available which could provide you with better value for money. It will pay you to shop around.

Many financial services adverts also go on about how investors have enjoyed strong returns in the recent past. However, past investment success is not always a sign of great investment times ahead. Indeed, back in early 1987, unit trust companies had a field day advertising funds with impressive performance records. Unfortunately, these returns were made on the back of a stock market bubble which burst in October 1987, leaving many investors pulled into funds by persuasive adverts with their fingers seriously burnt.

Via a mailshot

MANY companies generate a lot of their business by conducting mailshots – either by post or by inserting mailings inside newspapers. Credit card companies, friendly societies and insurance companies selling a mix of insurance and savings are past masters at the mailshot – again, like adverts in newspapers, tread carefully.

Many mailshots, especially those issued by insurance companies, offer potential customers the opportunity to obtain a free gift if they take out the product offered – an alarm clock or a gift voucher are often promised. Don't let these offerings entice you or cloud your judgement – the financial product has to be suitable, plain and simple.

Buying financial products by mailshot may not be a recipe for disaster but it is certainly a recipe for obtaining poor value for money. Mailshots are best put in the bin.

Via the Internet

MANY financial services companies now allow you to buy their products over the Internet – everything from mortgages to unit trusts. Buying over the Internet can prove cheaper than other purchase options but the price for this cheapness is the lack of advice available. If you know what you want, the Net can prove cost-effective. If you are unsure, then you are better off going to an expert.

The other big worry with the Internet is the security of buying on-line. In the majority of cases, buying on-line is as safe as houses but you do need to be careful.

Follow these 10 tips and you will not go far wrong:

TIP ONE: On the page that asks for your details, look for a locked padlock at the bottom of your browser to ensure you are on a secure server.

TIP TWO: Check the url or web address to see that you are on a secure server. It should read https:// and not http://. https:// is the definitive sign of a safe page.

TIP THREE: Always pay with plastic. That way, you can get a refund if it all goes wrong.

TIP FOUR: Never send your credit card details via e-mail.

TIP FIVE: Consider obtaining a separate credit card with a low-spending limit for on-line purchases. This is a good way to both protect yourself and not be too tempted to overstep your budget.

TIP SIX: Look out for 'safe shopping' endorsements from consumer watchdogs such as the *Which?* web trader seal.

TIP SEVEN: Always check your credit card statements to be sure that there are no unauthorised transactions.

TIP EIGHT: Do business with companies you know. Many high street names, for example, have websites. If you don't know the company, give it a ring to ensure that the company's details are correct and that it is indeed a legitimate business.

TIP NINE: Shop at websites based in the UK. Many overseas-based websites will charge you excessive shipping fees for any products you buy on the web.

TIP TEN: Keep a record of all communications you receive during the course of your on-line transactions.

Via a salesman

MANY banks and insurance companies run direct sales forces whose role in life is to sell you their products. Go into a Barclays branch, for example, and there is a probability that a salesman will attempt to sell you the company's range of savings or insurance products.

These salesmen, often referred to as tied agents or appointed representatives, are now required to pass certain exams before they can be unleashed on the general public. And many do a good job, making people aware of the benefits of undersold insurance products such as critical illness and permanent health insurance.

However, in buying from an insurance salesman, do be aware that you will only be recommended the products of the company he works for. That is irrespective of whether they offer value for money or that other companies' products provide better value for money.

In nearly every instance, it will pay you to compare the advice and products offered by an insurance salesman with that provided by other companies. Shopping around will invariably pay, even though it may be time-consuming.

Via an independent financial adviser

THE best way to purchase financial products, especially protection and savings products, is through an independent financial adviser. The role of an independent financial adviser is to scour the entire marketplace and recommend the most suitable products offered by the country's army of insurance companies and investment houses – taking into account your financial circumstances and your financial needs. To put this into context, this contrasts with the role of a tied agent of a bank or insurance company who can only recommend the products of the company he works for.

In searching for an appropriate independent financial adviser, do the following:

TIP ONE: SPEAK TO FRIENDS. Word-of-mouth recommendation from a friend is often the best way to find an independent financial adviser. If your friend has had a good level of service from an adviser you can bet your bottom dollar that you will receive a similar quality service.

TIP TWO: GET THEM TO PROVE WHETHER THEY'RE ANY GOOD. When contacting an adviser for the first time, ask them whether they are prepared to put you in contact with existing clients satisfied with the firm's services. Also, ask them whether they specialise in the area of advice you are interested in. There is no point in you going to an adviser specialising in pensions if it is insurance that you are after.

TIP THREE: GET THEM TO SHOW THEIR PROFESSIONAL CREDENTIALS. Once you meet the adviser who may be looking after your financial affairs, don't be frightened to ask them to prove their professional worth. All independent financial advisers now have to pass certain examinations designed to show that they know the personal finance world inside out. But some are less qualified than others even though they may have a string of letters after their name.

Independent financial advisers with basic qualifications in financial advice will possess one of the following – and have the letters after their name to prove it:

FPC: Financial Planning Certificate

CeFA:Certificate for Financial Advisers

IAC: Investment Advice Certificate

CIP: Certificate in Investment Planning

MLIA (Dip): Member of the Life Insurance Association.

Advisers who have gone on to pass more demanding exams will possess any of the following:

AFPC: Advanced Financial Planning Certificate

MSFA: Member of the Society of Financial Advisers

ASFA: Associate of the Society of Financial Advisers

ACII: Associate of the Chartered Insurance Institute

PIC: Professional Investment Certificate

AIFP: Associate of the Institute of Financial Planning

MSI (Dip): Member of the Securities Institute and Diploma

ALIA (Dip): Associate of the Life Assurance Association

FLIA (Dip): Fellow of the Life Insurance Association.

A small band of advisers will have passed so-called 'elite' exams. They will have the following letters after their names:

FSFA: Fellow of the Society of Financial Advisers

FIFP: Fellow of the Institute of Financial Planning

FCII: Fellow of the Chartered Insurance Institute

FIA/FFA: Fellow of the Institute or Faculty of Actuaries.

The Society of Financial Advisers runs the 'Find an Adviser Service', which puts the public in contact with an adviser who has taken higher qualifications (020 7417 4419).

TIP FOUR: ASK HOW THEY ARE REMUNERATED. Advisers can be paid by way of commission from the companies whose products they recommend. Alternatively, they will charge you a fee levied on an agreed hourly rate. Both payment methods have their pros and cons and only you can decide what is best for you. Fees do tend to be more expensive although fee-charging advisers have no vested interest in recommending specific products to you. Some advisers, and I stress some, not all, who take commission can be prone to make product recommendations on the back of the size of commission offered by the provider – so beware.

Via a direct broker

MANY advisers now allow you to buy specific products directly from them without having to take advice. In conducting business this way, on an execution-only basis, the adviser is able to keep costs down and this will often result in lower charges for the customer. This is happening increasingly with sales of tax-free Isas. Many advisers allow people to purchase Isas on a non-advice basis. The cost of buying an Isa this way is often cheaper than buying it directly from the provider.

For people who know what they want, the use of a direct broker can make financial sense. But remember, you have to be sure of what you are buying and you have no fall-back if the investment subsequently performs like a dog.

CHAPTER # 13

Useful
Addresses

INCOME

'What you can't live without – or
within.'

Vern McLellan

A NUMBER of organisations now exist which provide useful information and advice on personal finance issues. These bodies, be they trade associations representing the interests of a particular area of personal finance or charities, can help you enormously in getting to grips with personal finance. They can also give out invaluable advice, often for free.

The following organisations all provide an important function in the personal finance marketplace.

AGE CONCERN
ADDRESS: Age Concern Information Line
Linhay House
Ashburton
Devon TQ13 7UP
TELEPHONE: 0800 009 966 (7 a.m.–7 p.m.)
SERVICE: Provides advice to elderly people on a whole range of issues, from pensions, state benefits, home income plans through to

inheritance planning. Publishes a whole range of useful leaflets and bookets on personal finance issues surrounding the elderly.

AGE CONCERN SCOTLAND
ADDRESS: 113 Rose Street
Edinburgh EH2 3DT
TELEPHONE: 0131 220 3345 (Monday–Friday, 9 a.m.–5 p.m.)
FAX: 0131 220 2779
E-MAIL: ucs@ccis.org.uk
SERVICE: Provides advice to elderly people on a whole range of issues, from pensions, state benefits, home income plans through to inheritance planning. Publishes a whole range of useful leaflets and bookets on personal finance issues surrounding the elderly.

ASSOCIATION OF BRITISH INSURERS
ADDRESS: Consumer Information Department
51 Gresham Street
London EC2V 7HQ
TELEPHONE: 020 7600 3333
FAX: 020 7696 8999
E-MAIL: info@abi.org.uk
WEBSITE: http://www.abi.org.uk
SERVICE: Provides useful fact sheets and booklets on a whole range of insurance matters – from mortgage payment protection, life insurance through to medical insurance.

ASSOCIATION OF INVESTMENT TRUST COMPANIES
ADDRESS: Durrant House
8–13 Chiswell Street
London EC1Y 4YY
TELEPHONE: 0800 085 8520
FAX: 020 7282 5556
E-MAIL: info@aitc.co.uk
WEBSITE: http://www.aitc.co.uk
SERVICE: Provides information on all things investment trusts, including a range of fact sheets and booklets, covering details of

investment trust companies and aspects of investment trusts – regular savings schemes, using trusts to save for children and using an investment trust to repay a mortgage.

ASSOCIATION OF SOLICITOR INVESTMENT
ADDRESS: Chiddingstone Causeway
Tonbridge
Kent TN11 8JX
TELEPHONE: 01892 870 065
DETAILS: Details of solicitors who provide independent financial advice.

ASSOCIATION FOR PAYMENT CLEARING SERVICES (APACS)
ADDRESS: Mercury House
Triton Court
14 Finsbury Square
London EC2A 1LQ
TELEPHONE: 020 7711 6234
FAX: 020 7711 6276
E-MAIL: publicaffairs@apacs.org.uk
WEBSITE: http://www.apacs.org.uk
SERVICE: Provides general information on the cheque clearing system and direct debits.

ASSOCIATION OF CHARTERED CERTIFIED ACCOUNTANTS
ADDRESS: 29 Lincoln's Inn Fields
London WC2A 3EE
TELEPHONE: 020 7242 6855
WEBSITE ADDRESS: http://www.acca.org.uk

ASSOCIATION OF POLICY MARKET MAKERS
ADDRESS: Holywell Centre
1 Phipp Stret
London EC2A 4PS
TELEPHONE: 020 7739 3949

FAX: 020 7613 2990
E-MAIL: apmm@dircon.co.uk
WEBSITE: http://www.apmm.co.uk
SERVICE: Provides information on the sale and purchase of endowment policies.

ASSOCIATION OF PRIVATE CLIENT INVESTMENT MANAGERS AND STOCKBROKERS
ADDRESS: 112 Middlesex Street
London E1 7HY
TELEPHONE: 020 7247 7080
FAX: 020 7377 0939
E-MAIL: info@apcims.co.uk
WEBSITE: http:/www.apcims.co.uk
SERVICE: Provides information on how to find a stockbroker or investment manager.

ASSOCIATION OF RESIDENTIAL LETTING AGENTS
ADDRESS: Maple House
53–55 Woodside Road
Amersham, Bucks HP6 6AA
TELEPHONE: 01923 896 555
WEBSITE: http://www.arla.co.uk
SERVICES: Trade body representing interests of letting agents.

ASSOCIATION OF UNIT TRUSTS AND INVESTMENT FUNDS
ADDRESS: 65 Kingsway
London WC2B 6TD
TELEPHONE: 020 8207 1361
E-MAIL: autif@investmentfunds.org.uk
WEBSITE: http://www.investmentfunds.org.uk
SERVICE: Provides useful fact sheets and booklets on all things unit trusts and open-ended investment companies.

BANK OF ENGLAND

A. GILTS
1. ADDRESS: UK Debt Management Office
Cheapside House
138 Cheapside, London EC2V 6BB
TELEPHONE: 020 7862 6501
SERVICE: General enquiries about gilts.

2. ADDRESS: Bank of England Registrar's Department
Southgate House
Southgate Street
Gloucester GL1 1UW
TELEPHONE: 01452 398 080
SERVICE: Help with holdings of specific gilts. Also provides details
of new gilt issues.

3. ADDRESS: Bank of England Registrar's Department
Southgate House
Southgate Street
Gloucester GL1 IUW
TELEPHONE: 01452 398 333
SERVICE: Information on buying and selling of gilts.

4. ADDRESS: Bank of England Gilt-Edged and Money Markets
Division
Threadneedle Street
London EC2R 8AH
SERVICE: Enquiries about index-linked gilts.

B. OTHER
5. TELEPHONE: 0113 244 1711
SERVICE: Mutilated banknote request forms.

6. TELEPHONE: 020 7601 4012/4878
SERVICE: Publications and general enquiries.

BRITISH BANKERS' ASSOCIATION
ADDRESS: Pinners Hall
105–108 Old Broad Street
London EC2N 1EX
TELEPHONE: 020 7216 8801
WEBSITE: http://www.bankfacts.org.uk
SERVICE: Provides a series of fact sheets on key banking issues, everything from applying for credit through to understanding personal bank loans.

BUILDING SOCIETIES ASSOCIATION
ADDRESS: 3 Savile Row
London W1X 1AF
TELEPHONE: 020 7437 0655
WEBSITE: http://www.bsa.org.uk
SERVICE: Provides fact sheets on all things building societies.

CHARTERED INSTITUTE OF TAXATION AND ASSOCI-
ATION OF TAX TECHNICIANS
ADDRESS: 12 Upper Belgrave Street
London SW1X 8BB
TELEPHONE: 020 7235 9381
WEBSITE ADDRESS: http://tax.org.uk
SERVICES: Details of tax advisers.

CHILD SUPPORT AGENCY
TELEPHONE: 08457 133 133
WEBSITE: http://www.dss.gov.uk/csa
ADDRESS:
1. EASTERN: Belfast CSAC
Great Northern Tower
17–21 Great Victoria Street
Belfast BT2 7AD
(0845 713 3133)
2. SOUTH-EAST: Hastings CSAC
Ashdown House

Sedlescombe Road North
St Leonards on Sea
East Sussex TN37 7NL
(0845 713 4000)
3. MIDLANDS: Dudley CSAC
2 Weston Road
Crewe CW98 1BD
(0845 713 1000)
4. SOUTH-WEST: Plymouth CSAC
Clearbrook House
Towerfield Drive
Bickleigh Down Business Park
Plymouth PL6 7TN
(0845 713 7000)
5. SCOTLAND: Falkirk CSAC
Parklands
Callendar Business Park
Callendar Road
Falkirk FK1 1XT
(0845 713 6000)
6. WALES AND NORTH WEST: Birkenhead CSAC
2 Weston Road
Crewe CW98 1BD
(0845 713 8000)
SERVICE: Fact sheets and specific advice on anything to do with the
assessment, collection and enforcement of maintenance payments.

CITIZENS ADVICE BUREAUX – ENGLAND, WALES AND
NORTHERN IRELAND
WEBSITE: http://www.nacab.org.uk
SERVICE: Help and guidance on personal finance matters,
including money problems and right to state pensions. Advice is
given from more than 700 nationwide bureaux and 1,100 other
outlets.

CITIZENS ADVICE BUREAUX – SCOTLAND
TELEPHONE: 0131 667 0156
WEBSITE: http://www.cas.org.uk, http://www.nacab.org.uk, http://www.adviceguide.org.uk
SERVICE: Help and guidance on personal finance matters, including money problems and right to state pensions. Advice is given from more than 50 bureaux.

CONSUMER CREDIT COUNSELLING SERVICE
TELEPHONE: 0800 138 1111
E-MAIL: info@ccs.co.uk
SERVICE: Advice for people with debt problems.

CONSUMERS' ASSOCIATION
TELEPHONE: 0845 301 0010
WEBSITE: http://www.which.net
SERVICE: Provider of personal finance advice and research. Publisher of *Which?* magazine and numerous personal finance books.

COUNCIL OF MORTGAGE LENDERS
ADDRESS: 3 Savile Row
TELEPHONE: 020 7437 0075
London W1S 3PB
E-MAIL: info@cml.org.uk
WEBSITE: http://www.cml.org.uk
SERVICE: Fact sheets and leaflets pertaining to the mortgage market.

CREDIT ACTION
ADDRESS: Credit Action
6 Regent Terrace
Cambridge CB2 1AA
TELEPHONE: 0800 591 084 (National Debt Helpline); 01223 324 034 (office)
E-MAIL: credit.action@dial.pipex.com
WEBSITE: http://www.creditaction.com

SERVICE: Information and guidance for people with debt problems.

DISABILITY ALLIANCE
ADDRESS: 88–94 Wentworth Street
London E1 7SA
TELEPHONE: 020 7247 8776
FAX: 020 7247 8765
SERVICE: Information on welfare benefits available to disabled people and their carers.

DISABILITY WALES
ADDRESS: Wernddu Court
Caerffili Business Park
Van Road
Caerffili CF83 3ED
TELEPHONE: 0800 731 6282
FAX: 029 2088 8702
E-MAIL: info@dwac.demon.co.uk
SERVICE: Fact sheets and leaflets available to disabled people, their families, personal assistants and carers.

EQUIFAX EUROPE
ADDRESS: Dept 1E
PO Box 3001
Glasgow G81 2DT
TELEPHONE: 08705 783783
SERVICES: Copy of enquirer's own credit record for £2 statutory fee.

ETHICAL INVESTMENT RESEARCH SERVICE
ADDRESS: 80–84 Bondway
London SW8 1SF
TELEPHONE: 0845 606 0324
WEBSITE: http://www.eiris.u-net.com

SERVICE: Details on advisers who offer advice on ethical investments. Also, publisher of *Money and Ethics*, a guide to choosing an ethical fund.

EXPERIAN
ADDRESS: PO Box 8000
Nottingham NG1 5GX
TELEPHONE: 0115 941 0888
SERVICES: Copy of enquirer's own credit record for £2 statutory fee.

FEDERATION OF INFORMATION AND ADVICE CENTRES
ADDRESS: 4 Deans Court
St Paul's Churchyard
London EC4V 5AA
TELEPHONE: 020 7489 1800
FAX: 020 7489 1804
E-MAIL: national@fiac.org.uk/london@fiac.org.uk
WEBSITE: http://www.fiac.org.uk
SERVICE: Fact sheets and booklets, primarily relating to debt problems.

FINANCIAL SERVICES AUTHORITY
ADDRESS: 25 The North Colonnade
London E14 5HS
TELEPHONE: 0845 606 1234
FAX: 020 7676 1099
E-MAIL: enquiries@fsa.gov.uk
WEBSITE: http://www.fsa.gov.uk
SERVICE: Fact sheets and booklets concerning personal finance and regulation of financial services companies.

HELP THE AGED (WELFARE ADVICE)
ADDRESS: 207–21 Pentonville Road
London N1 9UZ
TELEPHONE: 0808 800 6565

SERVICE: Advice on state benefits, pensions, funding of residential care and grants.

HELP THE AGED (PAID-FOR ADVICE)
ADDRESS: 207–21 Pentonville Road
London N1 9UZ
TELEPHONE: 020 7278 1114
FAX: 020 7278 1116
WEBSITE: http://www.helptheaged.org.uk
SERVICE: Details on insurance, retirement property, tax and care fees.

IFA PROMOTION
ADDRESS: 113–117 Farringdon Road
London EC1R 3BX
TELEPHONE: 020 7833 3131 (find an IFA consumer hotline – 0800 085 3250)
WEBSITE: http://www.ifap.org.uk (www.unbiased.co.uk)
SERVICE: Details on independent financial advisers.

INLAND REVENUE
WEBSITE: http://www.inlandrevenue.gov.uk
SERVICES: Fact sheets and booklets pertaining to personal finance and tax.

INSTITUTE OF CHARTERED ACCOUNTANTS (ENGLAND & WALES)
ADDRESS: Moorgate Place
London EC2P 2BJ
TELEPHONE: 020 7920 8100
WEBSITE: http://www.icaew.co.uk
SERVICES: Details on chartered accountants.

INSTITUTE OF CHARTERED ACCOUNTANTS (SCOTLAND)
ADDRESS: 21 Haymarket Yards
Edinburgh EH12 5BH

TELEPHONE: 0131 347 0100
SERVICES: Details on chartered accountants.

INSTITUTE OF FINANCIAL PLANNING
ADDRESS: Whitefriars Centre
Lewins Mead
Bristol BS1 2NT
TELEPHONE: 0117 945 2470
SERVICE: Details on independent financial advisers.

INSURANCE OMBUDSMAN BUREAU
ADDRESS: South Quay Plaza
183 Marsh Wall
London E14 9SR
TELEPHONE: 0845 600 6666
FAX: 020 7964 1001
E-MAIL: complaint@theiob.org.uk; advice@theiob.org.uk
WEBSITE: http://www.theiob.org.uk
SERVICES: Adjudication of complaints between consumers and insurance companies. Will form part of the Financial Ombudsman Service.

INVESTMENT OMBUDSMAN
ADDRESS: South Quay Plaza
183 Marsh Wall
London E14 9SR
TELEPHONE: 020 7796 3065
FAX: 020 7964 1001
SERVICE: Adjudication of complaints between consumers and firms managing investments. Will form part of the Financial Ombudsman Service.

LOCAL LAW CENTRES
ADDRESS: Law Centres Federation
Duchess House
18–19 Warren Street
London W1P 5DB

TELEPHONE: 020 7387 8570 (will provide list of local law centres)
E-MAIL: lcf-london@dial.pipex.com
WEBSITE: http://www.lawcentres.org.uk
SERVICE: State benefits but in relation to obtaining legal rights.

LONDON INTERNATIONAL FINANCIAL FUTURES AND
TRADED OPTIONS EXCHANGE
ADDRESS: Cannon Bridge
London EC4R 3XX
TELEPHONE: 020 7623 0444
FAX: 020 7588 3624
E-MAIL: enquiries@liffe.com
WEBSITE: http://www.liffe.com
SERVICES: Booklets and fact sheets on traded options and financial
futures.

LONDON STOCK EXCHANGE
ADDRESS: Old Broad Street
London EC2N 1HP
TELEPHONE: 020 7797 1000
WEBSITE: http://www.londonstockexchange.com
SERVICES: Information on shares and other stock market
investments.

MONEY MANAGEMENT COUNCIL
ADDRESS: PO Box 77
Hertford
Herts SG14 2HW
TELEPHONE: 01992 503 448
WEBSITE: http://www.moneyeducation.co.uk
SERVICES: Fact sheets on money matters.

MORTGAGE CODE ARBITRATION SCHEME
ADDRESS: 12 Bloomsbury Square
London WC1A 2LP
TELEPHONE: 020 7421 7444

FAX: 020 7404 4023
E-MAIL: info@arbitrators.org
WEBSITE: http://www.arbitrators.org
SERVICES: Dealing with mortgage complaints concerning mortgage intermediaries.

MORTGAGE CODE COMPLIANCE BOARD
ADDRESS: University Court
Stafford
Staffordshire ST18 0GN
TELEPHONE: 01785 218200
FAX: 01785 218249
SERVICES: Details of which lenders or intermediaries are registered under the Mortgage Code.

NATIONAL ASSOCIATION OF BANK/INSURANCE CUSTOMERS
ADDRESS: PO Box 15
Caldicot
Newport NP26 5YD
TELEPHONE: 01291 430 009
FAX: 07070 712 322
E-MAIL: bank.help@virgin.net; insurance.help@virgin.net
WEBSITE: http://freespace.virgin.net/bank.help
SERVICES: Fact sheets and booklets and organisers of seminars on banking and insurance.

NATIONAL ASSOCIATION OF ESTATE AGENTS
ADDRESS: Arbon House
21 Jury Street
Warwick CV34 4EH
TELEPHONE: 01926 496800
WEBSITE: www.naea.co.uk
SERVICES: Trade body representing interests of estate agents.

NATIONAL COUNCIL FOR ONE PARENT FAMILIES
ADDRESS: 255 Kentish Town Road, London NW5 2LX
TELEPHONE: 0800 018 5026/020 7428 5428
SERVICES: Advice and support for lone parents encompassing employment, housing, finance, legal and welfare issues.

NATIONAL DEBTLINE
TELEPHONE: 0808 808 4000
SERVICES: Specialist advice on dealing with debt problems.

NATIONAL DIRECTORY OF FEE-BASED ADVISERS
ADDRESS: Matrix Data Services
Freepost
Gossard House
7–8 Savile Row
London W1X 1AF
TELEPHONE: 0870 013 1925
SERVICES: Details of fee-based advisers – rather than commission-based advisers.

OCCUPATIONAL PENSIONS REGULATORY AUTHORITY
ADDRESS: Invicta House
Trafalgar Place
Brighton BN1 4DW
TELEPHONE: 01273 627 600
FAX: 01273 627 688
E-MAIL: helpdesk@opra.gov.uk
WEBSITE: http://www.opra.gov.uk
SERVICES: Fact sheets and booklets relating to operation of company pension schemes.

OCCUPATIONAL PENSIONS ADVISORY SERVICE
ADDRESS: 11 Belgrave Road
London SW1V 1RB
TELEPHONE: 020 7233 8080
WEBSITE: http://www.opas.org.uk

SERVICES: Deals with complaints against company pension schemes.

OPRA PENSION SCHEMES REGISTRY
ADDRESS: PO Box 1NN
Newcastle-upon-Tyne NE99 1NN
TELEPHONE: 0191 225 6316
WEBSITE: http://www.opra.gov.uk/psr.shtml
SERVICES: Tracing of pension schemes for members of the public.

OFFICE FOR THE SUPERVISION OF SOLICITORS
ADDRESS: Victoria Court
8 Dormer Place
Leamington Spa
Warks CV32 5AE
TELEPHONE: 01926 822 007
SERVICES: Deals with complaints against solicitors.

OFFICE OF THE BANKING OMBUDSMAN
ADDRESS: PO BOX 4
South Quay Plaza
183 Marsh Wall
London E14 9SR
TELEPHONE: 0845 766 0902
FAX: 020 7405 5052
E-MAIL: banking.ombudsman@financial-ombudsman.org.uk
WEBSITE: http://www.obo.org.uk
SERVICES: Deals with complaints against banks by customers. Will form part of the Financial Ombudsman Service.

OFFICE OF THE BUILDING SOCIETIES OMBUDSMAN
ADDRESS: South Quay Plaza
183 Marsh Wall
London E14 9SR
TELEPHONE: 020 7931 0044
FAX: 020 7931 8485

E-MAIL: bldgsocombudsman@easynet.co.uk
SERVICES: Deals with complaints against building societies by customers. Will form part of the Financial Ombudsman Service.

OFFICE OF FAIR TRADING
ADDRESS: Fleetbank House
2–6 Salisbury Square
London EC4Y 8JX
TELEPHONE: 0845 722 4499
FAX: 020 7211 8800
E-MAIL: enquiries@oft.gov.uk
WEBSITE: http://www.oft.gov.uk
SERVICES: Provision of general information through fact sheets and leaflets.

OFFICE OF PENSIONS ADVISORY SERVICE
ADDRESS: 11 Belgrave Road
London SW1V 1RB
TELEPHONE: 020 7233 8080
FAX: 020 7233 8016
E-MAIL: opas@iclwebkit.co.uk
WEBSITE: http://www.opas.org.uk
SERVICES: Deals with general queries and problems relating to pension schemes.

OMBUDSMAN FOR ESTATE AGENTS
ADDRESS: Beckett House
4 Bridge Street
Salisbury
Wilts SP1 2LX
TELEPHONE: 01722 333 306
SERVICES: Deals with complaints against estate agents.

PENSIONS COMPENSATION BOARD
ADDRESS: 11 Belgrave Road
London SW1V 1RB

TELEPHONE: 020 7828 9794

SERVICES: Compensation scheme covering occupational pension schemes.

PENSIONS OMBUDSMAN

ADDRESS: 11 Belgrave Road

London SW1V 1RB

TELEPHONE: 020 7834 9144

FAX: 020 7821 0065

SERVICES: Resolves disputes between pension schemes and their members.

PERSONAL INSURANCE ARBITRATION SERVICE

ADDRESS: 12 Bloomsbury Square

London WC1A 2LP

TELEPHONE: 020 7421 7444

FAX: 020 7404 4023

E-MAIL: info@arbitrators.org

WEBSITE: http://www.arbitrators.org

SERVICES: Deals with complaints against non-investment type of insurance. Will form part of the Financial Ombudsman Service.

PERSONAL INVESTMENT AUTHORITY OMBUDSMAN BUREAU

ADDRESS: South Quay Plaza

183 Marsh Wall

London E14 9SR

TELEPHONE: 020 7712 8700

FAX: 020 7216 0016

E-MAIL: postsort@piacmb.demon.co.uk

SERVICES: Deals with complaints against firms authorised by the Personal Investment Authority – primarily firms selling personal pensions, life insurance, unit trusts and investment trusts. Will form part of the Financial Ombudsman Service.

PRE-RETIREMENT ASSOCIATION
ADDRESS: 9 Chesham Road
Guildford
Surrey GU1 3LS
TELEPHONE: 01483 301170
WEBSITE: http://www.pra.uk.com
DETAILS: Help in preparing for retirement including the running of courses.

PROSHARE
ADDRESS: Library Chambers
13 & 14 Basinghall Street
London EC2V 5HU
TELEPHONE: 020 7394 5200
FAX: 020 7600 0947
E-MAIL: info@proshare.org.uk
WEBSITE: http://www.proshare.org.uk
SERVICES: Fact sheets pertaining to stock market investments.

RETIREMENT PENSION FORECAST AND ADVICE SERVICE
ADDRESS: Pensions and Overseas Benefits Directorate
Tyneview Park
Whitley Road
Newcastle-upon-Tyne NE98 1YX
TELEPHONE: 0191 218 7585
E-MAIL: baadmin@baadmin.demon.co.uk
WEBSITE: http://www.dss.gov.uk
SERVICES: Printed forecast of state pension in today's money. Also advice on how to boost state basic pension. Completion of form BR19 is necessary, available from local Benefits agency.

SAFE HOME INCOME PLANS (SHIP)
ADDRESS: 1st Floor
Parker Court
Knapp Lane
Cheltenham

GL50 3QJ
TELEPHONE: 01242 539494
FAX: 01242 539494
WEBSITE: http://www.ship-ltd.co.uk
SERVICES: Details on home income plans for the elderly.

SECURITIES AND FUTURES AUTHORITY COMPLAINTS BUREAU
ADDRESS: 25 The North Colonnade
Canary Wharf
London E14 5HS
TELEPHONE: 020 7676 1000
FAX: 020 7676 9712
WEBSITE: http://www.sfa.org.uk
SERVICES: Handling of complaints between member firms and consumers. Will form part of the Financial Ombudsman Service.

SHELTER NATIONAL CAMPAIGN FOR HOMELESS PEOPLE
ADDRESS: 88 Old Street
London EC1V 9HU
TELEPHONE: 0808 800 4444
E-MAIL: info@shelter.org.uk
WEBSITE: http://www.shelter.org.uk
SERVICES: Advice relating to housing-related benefits and debt problems.

SOCIETY OF FINANCIAL ADVISERS
ADDRESS: 20 Aldermanbury
London EC2V 7HY
TELEPHONE: 020 7417 4419
WEBSITE: http://www.sofa.org
SERVICES: Offers details on how to find a financial adviser.

SOLICITORS FOR INDEPENDENT FINANCIAL ADVICE
TELEPHONE: 01372 721172
WEBSITE: http://www.solicitor-ifa.co.uk

SERVICES: Details of solicitors who provide independent financial advice.

TAXAID
ADDRESS: Linburn House
342 Kilburn High Road
London NW6 2QJ
TELEPHONE: 020 7624 3768/020 7624 5216
WEBSITE: http://www.taxaid.org.uk
SERVICES: Personal taxation advice.

TRADING STANDARDS OFFICES
ADDRESS: (via local council)
SERVICES: Details on local provision of credit, borrowing and debt, mortgages and general insurance.

WAR PENSIONERS' WELFARE SERVICE
ADDRESS: Norcross
Blackpool
FY5 3WP
TELEPHONE: 0800 169 2277
E-MAIL: warpensions@gtnet.gov.uk
WEBSITE: http://www.dss.gov.uk/wpa
SERVICES: Details relating to war disablement pensions, war widow's pensions and related benefits.

YOUTH ACCESS
ADDRESS: Youth Access
2 Taylors Yard
67 Alderbrook Road
London SW12 8AD
TELEPHONE: 020 8772 9900
FAX: 020 8772 9746
SERVICES: Advice on money matters for young people.

CHAPTER # 14

Useful Personal Finance Reading

INCOME TAX

'The hardest thing in the world to understand.'

Albert Einstein

ALTHOUGH this book should arm you with sufficient information to tackle the personal finance market with comfort, it will not provide you with all the answers. Nor, by its very nature, can it keep you abreast of all the latest products available in the marketplace or the latest personal finance developments – for example, the most up-to-date performance numbers for unit trusts or building society conversions.

To fill this hole, you need to refer to regular personal finance publications which can be a mine of information. You can also obtain the latest up-to-date personal finance news by using the web.

The following books, magazines, newspapers and websites are some of the best available in personal finance.

Books

WHICH? (numerous guides including: *THE WHICH? GUIDE TO MONEY; THE WHICH? GUIDE TO PENSIONS; THE*

WHICH? GUIDE TO INSURANCE; THE WHICH? GUIDE TO SHARES; THE WHICH? WAY TO SAVE TAX; THE WHICH? WAY TO SAVE AND INVEST)

ADDRESS: *Which?*

Dept TAZM

Castlemead

Gascoyne Way

Hertford X, SG14 1YB

INFORMATION: *Which?* books are easy to read and as informative as you are going to find.

GOOD NON-RETIREMENT GUIDE – Rosemary Brown

(Kogan Page)

INFORMATION: A fact-packed book for those people approaching retirement or who have already retired. Covers everything from pensions to investments and tax as well as reviews leisure activities. Updated every year.

THE MONEYZONE

(*Financial Times* Prentice Hall)

INFORMATION: A must buy for anyone who wants to gets to grips with the perplexities of money from an early age. Written in plain English, which cannot be said of many personal finance books.

TAX GUIDE

(Profile Books)

INFORMATION: The bible when it comes to anything on tax. Not a particularly easy book to navigate but the information is all there. Uses some good case studies in order to explain how different taxes bite.

Magazines

MONEYFACTS

ADDRESS: Moneyfacts House

66–70 Thorpe Road

Norwich NR1 1BJ
TELEPHONE: 01603 476 100
PUBLICATION: Monthly
AVAILABILITY: By subscription
INFORMATION: A personal finance bible, providing up-to-date details on everything to do with savings, mortgages, credit cards and loans.

MONEY MANAGEMENT
ADDRESS: Maple House
149 Tottenham Court Road
London W1P 9LL
TELEPHONE: 01444 445 520
PUBLICATION: Monthly
AVAILABILITY: Leading newsagents and by subscription
INFORMATION: Conducts the most comprehensive surveys on personal finance products – on everything from personal pensions to Isas – thereby enabling people to make better financial decisions. Also includes past performance tables incorporating unit trusts, investment trusts, insurance funds and pension funds.

MONEYWISE
ADDRESS: 11 Westferry Circus
London E14 4HE
TELEPHONE: 020 7715 8000
PUBLICATION: Monthly
AVAILABILITY: Leading newsagents
INFORMATION: Good personal finance coverage across the full spectrum of personal finance issues. Strong advice section.

MONEY OBSERVER
ADDRESS: 75 Farringdon Road
London EC1M 3JY
TELEPHONE: 020 7278 2332
PUBLICATION: Monthly
AVAILABILITY: Leading newsagents

INFORMATION: Quality monthly personal finance coverage embracing a mix of news, useful personal finance data and readable features. One of the best of its type and a must read for personal finance junkies.

WHICH?
ADDRESS: PO Box 44
Hertford X SG14 1SH
TELEPHONE: 0800 252 100
PUBLICATION: Monthly
AVAILABILITY: By subscription
INFORMATION: Identifies the best-value-for-money products across all consumer areas – from washing machines through to savings accounts. Analysis is comprehensive, independent and reliable.

BLOOMBERG MONEY
ADDRESS: 7 Air Street
London W1B 5AD
TELEPHONE: 020 7432 6934
PUBLICATION: Monthly
AVAILABILITY: Leading newsagents
INFORMATION: Investment-oriented personal finance magazine with performance tables included for unit trusts and investment trusts. Well-presented money magazine.

YOUR MORTGAGE
ADDRESS: Matching Hat Ltd
Aldwych House
71–91 Aldwych
London WC2B 4HN
TELEPHONE: 020 7404 3123
PUBLICATION: Monthly
AVAILABILITY: Leading newsagents
INFORMATION: Useful magazine for anyone looking to move home or obtain a new mortgage. Full of solid mortgage tips.

YOUR MONEY DIRECT
ADDRESS: Matching Hat Ltd
Aldwych House
71–91 Aldwych
London WC2B 4HN
TELEPHONE: 020 7404 3123
PUBLICATION: Monthly
AVAILABILITY: Leading newsagents
INFORMATION: Basic information on key areas of personal finance. Appeals to people who want to take their own financial decisions rather than go cap in hand to a financial adviser.

WHAT MORTGAGE
ADDRESS: Charterhouse Communications Group
Arnold House
36–41 Holywell Lane
London EC2A 3SF.
TELEPHONE: 020 7827 5454
PUBLICATION: Monthly
AVAILABILITY: Leading newsagents
INFORMATION: Useful magazine for anyone looking to move home or obtain a new mortgage. Includes mortgage comparison tables.

WHAT INVESTMENT
ADDRESS: Charterhouse Communications Group
Arnold House
36–41 Holywell Lane
London EC2A 3SF.
TELEPHONE: 020 7827 5454
PUBLICATION: Monthly
AVAILABILITY: Leading newsagents
INFORMATION: Long-established personal finance magazine. Aimed primarily at private investors with solid coverage of collective investments such as unit trusts and investment trusts. Publication includes performance tables of collective investment funds.

REAL MONEY
ADDRESS: 402 The Fruit & Wool Exchange
Brushfield Street
London E1 6EP
TELEPHONE: 020 7426 0424
PUBLICATION: Monthly
AVAILABILITY: Leading newsagents
INFORMATION: Well-presented all-round personal finance magazine covering everything from investment through to pensions and credit.

INVESTMENT TRUSTS
ADDRESS: Flaxdale Printers
5 Malvern Drive
Woodford Green
Essex IG8 OJR
TELEPHONE: 020 8504 6862
PUBLICATION: Quarterly
AVAILABILITY: Leading newsagents
INFORMATION: Super magazine for anyone interested in learning more about investment trusts. Includes news on the latest developments within the trust world as well as performance tables.

INVESTORS CHRONICLE
ADDRESS: Financial Times Business Ltd
4th Floor
Maple House
149 Tottenham Court Road
London W1T 7LB.
TELEPHONE: 020 7896 2525
PUBLICATION: Weekly
AVAILABILITY: Leading newsagents
INFORMATION: A must for anyone who deals in shares on a regular basis. Contains a useful personal finance section which is heavily investment-oriented.

SHARES
ADDRESS: Thames House
18 Park Street
London SE1 9ER
TELEPHONE: 020 7378 7131
PUBLICATION: Weekly
AVAILABILITY: Leading newsagents
INFORMATION: Another must-buy for active investors. Includes share tips and reports on key company sectors. Very share-oriented with little coverage of collective investments.

Newspapers
FINANCIAL MAIL ON SUNDAY: Produces the country's most comprehensive weekly personal finance coverage as part of the *Mail on Sunday*. Combines a strong campaigning stance with informative articles on all aspects of personal finance. The section is written in plain English and there is good use of illustrations to make articles reader-friendly.

DAILY MAIL: 'Money Mail' is published every Wednesday. Strong campaigning style, backed by informative articles on all aspects of personal finance. The best Wednesday personal finance section.

THE TIMES: *The Times* 'Money' section, published on a Saturday, is as comprehensive a personal finance section as you are going to find. Combines a good mix of educational and investigative personal finance articles.

SUNDAY TIMES: Separate 'Money' section. Takes a strong campaigning stance. Covers most areas of personal finance adequately.

GUARDIAN: Runs a separate 'Jobs and Money' section on a Saturday. The *Guardian*'s money coverage is far better than it was and is now one of the leading Saturday money sections. Good use of best-buy tables.

OBSERVER: The 'Cash' section, which is in tabloid form, offers an intense look at selected personal finance issues. The format is hardly reader-friendly but when a subject is tackled, it is tackled warts and all.

INDEPENDENT: 'Your Money' is published on a Saturday. Weakest of the Saturday sections which reflects a lack of resources. Articles are poorly displayed and too long by far. Poor use of illustrations.

INDEPENDENT ON SUNDAY: The 'Money' section, which forms part of the 'Business' section, is one of the weaker Sunday personal finance editions. It lacks news bite and the articles are too long by half.

DAILY TELEGRAPH: The 'YourMoney' section covers all areas of personal finance. Published on a Saturday, it is never controversial but illustrates key areas of personal finance planning in a reader-friendly fashion.

SUNDAY TELEGRAPH: The 'Money' section is much improved, embracing a mix of hard personal finance news and personal finance features. Unimaginatively illustrated but a better personal finance package than its *Sunday Times* rival.

FINANCIAL TIMES: Its 'Weekend Money' section is comprehensive although wordy and hardly controversial.

DAILY EXPRESS: The 'Money' section, published on a Wednesday, offers a mix of personal finance stories and features. It is a shadow of its 'Money Mail' rival although it can have a harder news edge which may appeal to some.

SUNDAY EXPRESS: Part of the *Financial Express on Sunday*, the personal finance section, 'Your Money', combines a good mix of news and educational articles.

SUN: Ad hoc coverage of personal finance coverage. When it appears, it's good – very case study driven. Written in good old plain English.

NEWS OF THE WORLD: 'Moneyworld' is written in plain English although its breadth of coverage is constrained by the fact that it rarely gets more than a page.

DAILY MIRROR: Published on a Wednesday, 'Mirror Money' offers good personal finance advice. It provides a mix of good educational pieces and exposé articles.

SUNDAY MIRROR: 'SM Money's' personal finance coverage is limited by the fact that it rarely extends above one page. As a result, it lacks the breadth of coverage offered by most of its Sunday rivals.

Websites

www.thisismoney.co.uk

INFORMATION: Its personal finance coverage is unrivalled. It has an exhaustive data bank comprising material on specific personal finance areas – everything from mortgages to pensions. It also provides summaries of the best articles published in the personal finance sections of *Financial Mail on Sunday* and the *Daily Mail*. Best buys, unit trust details and personal finance news are all covered by the website.

www.ft.com

INFORMATION: The personal finance site is to be found at www.ftyourmoney.com. You can use the site to obtain general personal finance information or to store your own personal finance details.

CHAPTER # 15
Dictionary of Terms

ECONOMY

'Going without something you want
in case you should one day want
something else you probably won't.'

Anthony Hope

PERSONAL finance is riddled with jargon. Most of it is unnecessary, most of it is a smokescreen for high charges and most of it is designed to make something far more complicated than it really is.

The terms used in this book are listed below together with a brief description of their meaning. These details might come in handy when someone is trying to flog you something you really do not need and is trying to hide the truth with a phalanx of personal finance terms – 'personal finance speak'.

Remember: if you don't understand something written in a personal finance sales brochure or you are bamboozled with something a salesperson says to you, beware. Don't buy unless you understand everything. Either seek an explanation or walk away.

ACCIDENTAL DAMAGE: A key element of a good home insurance policy enabling claims to be made when items in the house are broken accidentally. Can be a godsend for families with young children although premiums will reflect the broader cover.

ACCIDENT SOCIETIES: A form of friendly society which pays benefits to members' families after an accident.

ACCRUAL RATE: Rate at which you build up a pension under a final salary pension scheme. An accrual rate of one-sixtieth means you build a pension equivalent to one-sixtieth of your final salary for every year you work.

ACCUMULATION UNITS: Issued to unit trust investors who do not want to take an income from their investment.

ACTIVITIES OF DAILY LIVING: These are used in some forms of insurance such as long-term-care insurance to test your eligibility to make a claim. Failure to carry out a preset number of such activities – washing, eating, dressing, going to the toilet unaided – will trigger a claim on the policy.

ADDITIONAL VOLUNTARY CONTRIBUTION: A way of supplementing your contributions into a company pension scheme. If you are a member of a company pension scheme, ask for details of the AVC arrangements which are provided via your employer.

AFFINITY CARDS: Credit cards linked to a charity or a particular group such as a cricket team or football team. You still pay interest on uncleared balances but any spending on your card will result in a small donation being made to the affinity group.

ALTERNATIVE INVESTMENT MARKET: Junior UK stock market. Don't invest in companies or funds based on this market unless you have nerves of steel.

ANNUAL TRAVEL INSURANCE: Covers you all year round – good value for regular travellers.

ANNUITY: A product which provides you with a lifetime income. Usually associated with a pension where the proceeds of a pension are used to purchase an annuity.

ANY OCCUPATION: A definition used by a few (thankfully) insurance companies to determine a policyholder's eligibility to make a claim. If you are unable to pursue any occupation, then the policy will pay out benefit. Such a loose definition ensures any claim you make will not be accepted.

ANY SUITABLE OCCUPATION: A definition used by some insurance companies to determine a policyholder's eligibility to make a claim. If you are unable to carry out a job suitable to your level of experience and training, then the policy will pay out benefit.

APPROPRIATE PERSONAL PENSION: An alternative to a State Earnings Related Pension Scheme.

APR (ANNUAL PERCENTAGE RATE): Total annual charge for credit expressed as a percentage.

ARRANGEMENT FEE: A charge levied by most lenders when you take out a home loan.

ASSIGNMENT: Where an endowment policy is linked to a mortgage. Many lenders asked for policies to be assigned to ensure the endowment was actually used to repay the loans they had granted.

AUTHORISED OVERDRAFT: When the bank has allowed you to put your account in the red. Note: an authorised overdraft does not come cheaply – you will still have to pay steep fees for the privilege.

BABY BONDS: Term used to describe tax-free friendly society investment plans which can be taken out by children. The plans provide tax-free returns.

BANKING CODE: A voluntary code adhered to by the banks which in theory ensures customers are treated fairly. Unfortunately, in practice, the code is much abused.

BANK STATEMENT: Printed confirmation of the transactions – receipts and payments – which have gone through your bank account. These are usually issued on a monthly basis.

BASE RATE TRACKER MORTGAGE: A home loan where the interest rate falls and rises by the same level as base rates. A form of a standard variable rate mortgage but with an in-built guarantee that the rate will move in line with base rates.

BASIC RATE OF TAX: Tax rate which most people have to bear.

BASIC STATE PENSION: Used to describe the pension which most people are eligible for, provided they have paid enough National Insurance contributions throughout their working lives.

BENEFICIARIES: Those who benefit from the wishes of a will being carried out.

BID PRICE: Price at which you sell units in a unit trust.

BLIND PERSON'S ALLOWANCE: State allowance available for people who are registered blind.

BLUE-CHIP SHARES: A term used to describe the shares of the country's biggest companies. Blue-chip does not guarantee stock market performance.

BOAT INSURANCE: A must for boat owners.

BOUNCED CHEQUE: A payment that your bank refuses to honour, maybe because you do not have sufficient funds in your account.

BR1: Form you complete which will pave the way for payment of your state pension.

BR19: Form that enables you to get a forecast of your likely state pension.

BROKER UNIT TRUST: A unit trust managed by a financial adviser. Typically, the trust is invested in a range of unit trusts. Approach with extreme caution.

BUDGET: Annual event where the government, via the chancellor of exchequer, outlines changes to the taxation system.

BUDGET PRIVATE MEDICAL INSURANCE: Cheap and cheerful private medical insurance cover. Budget plans will cover basic costs of private medical treatment but very little else.

BUILDING SOCIETY: A mutually owned organisation whose prime business is to offer mortgages and savings accounts.

BURIAL SOCIETIES: A form of friendly society which pays benefit on the death of a member or spouse.

BUY TO LET MORTGAGES: Home loans for people who want to buy a house for letting.

CAP AND COLLAR MORTGAGE: A home loan where the interest rate cannot rise above a predetermined figure (the cap) and cannot fall below a certain level (the collar). Provide more certainty than a standard variable rate mortgage where rates can rise and fall at will.

CAPITAL GAINS TAX: Tax you pay on profits arising from the sale of certain assets such as shares.

CAPITAL GAINS TAX ALLOWANCE: Amount of profits you are able to earn on personal assets in a tax year before the taxman takes his bite.

CAPITAL UNITS: A smokescreen for high charges. Red warning lights should start flashing if you have a policy with these types of charges.

CAPPED RATE MORTGAGE: A home loan where the interest rate cannot rise above a predetermined figure.

CARD PAYMENT PROTECTION INSURANCE: Insurance which will ensure payments are made on your credit card bill if you fall ill or are made redundant.

CARPETBAGGER: Someone who puts money in a building society or insurance company (mutual) in search of a future windfall.

CAR PURCHASE PLAN: Way of paying for a new car. Again, you pay via a series of monthly payments. Don't enter into such an arrangement unless you know what you are doing.

CASHBACK MORTGAGE: A home loan where a borrower gets back a lump sum upon completion of the mortgage deal. Such loans can come with big strings attached so beware.

CASH CARD (CASHPOINT OR AUTOMATED TELLER CARD): These enable you to withdraw cash from a hole-in-the-wall. The card can also be used to obtain bank balance details and order a cheque book or statement.

CASH UNIT TRUST: A fund that is invested in deposits and pays a decent rate of interest.

CAT: A form of benchmarking introduced by the government to ensure consumers can buy certain financial products confident in the knowledge they are not going to get a poor deal. Most prevalent on mortgages and Isas. C stands for cost, A stands for accessibility and T stands for terms.

CHARGE CARD: A form of interest-free borrowing. You charge purchases to the card and when you receive your monthly statement, you are required to repay the outstanding balance in full.

CHARITABLE TRUST: A tax-efficient way of donating a sizeable amount to charity.

CHATTELS: Your personal possessions such as furniture.

CHEQUE BOOK: One of the main ways in which you can pay for goods. Comes as part of a bank account although cheques are increasingly being superseded by plastic payment.

CHEQUE GUARANTEE CARD: Guarantees to the vendor that the bank will honour your cheque up to the limit stated on the card – typically £100, £200 or £250. Most retailers will not accept a cheque unless it is supported by a cheque guarantee card.

CHILDREN'S SAVINGS ACCOUNTS: Savings accounts offered by banks and building societies and designed for children. Such accounts usually permit small deposits.

CLASS ONE NATIONAL INSURANCE CONTRIBUITIONS: Paid by the employed.

CLASS TWO NATIONAL INSURANCE CONTRIBUTIONS: Paid by the self-employed.

CLASS THREE NATIONAL INSURANCE CONTRIBUTIONS: Paid on a voluntary basis to boost your final state pension.

CLASS FOUR NATIONAL INSURANCE CONTRIBUTIONS: Paid by the self-employed. Are in effect a tax on your profits.

CLOSED ENDED: A term used to describe an investment vehicle such as an investment trust where the number of shares in issue are fixed.

CLOSED FUND: A pension fund or insurance fund where the company is no longer taking new business. Usually, such funds offer policyholders poor value for money.

CODE OF MORTGAGE LENDING PRACTICE: A voluntary code which most lenders and mortgage advisers adhere to. Code sets down acceptable standards.

CODICIL: An addition made to a will.

COLLECTIVE INVESTMENT: A term used to describe investment funds which pool investors' money and then invest it on their behalf. Unit trusts and investment trusts are collective investments. Sometimes they are known as pooled investments.

COMMISSION: The amount that a financial salesman will earn from selling you a particular policy or savings plan. Commission is now disclosed, which means you can see how much the salesman is going to earn from you prior to you signing on the dotted line. You can also quantify the commission against other charges to be taken from your policy or plan. Commission can also be charged by a stockbroker when buying and selling shares on your behalf.

COMPANY PENSION: Pension provided by your employer. If your employer provides one, look at it seriously. However, don't walk into it with blindfolds on, especially with consumer-friendly stakeholder pensions now available.

COMPREHENSIVE PRIVATE MEDICAL INSURANCE: The deluxe version of private medical insurance. Will cover you against the majority of costs but premiums can be daunting.

COMPULSORY PURCHASE ANNUITIES: Term used to describe an annuity which has to be bought rather than voluntarily acquired. Pension annuities fit into this category – you have to buy an annuity with your pension before the age of 75.

CONTRACTED OUT: Term used to describe someone who has opted out of the State Earnings Related Pension Scheme.

CONTRACT NOTE: Sent out by an investment house confirming the purchase or sale of shares or unit trusts.

CONVERTIBLES: Issued by companies, these pay a regular income. Holders have the right to convert them into ordinary shares at redemption.

CONVERTIBLE TERM ASSURANCE: Life assurance where before the end of the plan's term you can convert it to acquire permanent life cover.

COOLING-OFF PERIOD: A period of time given to you when you first purchase a product when you can change your mind over your decision. It is usually 7 or 14 days. However, for investment products, exercising your right to change your mind during this period can mean you being out of pocket so be careful. Cooling off is designed to stop you being pressurised into making financial decisions which are not in your best financial interests.

CORPORATE BOND: Issued by companies, these bonds pay investors a regular fixed rate of interest. Rates vary according to the issuer of the bond. Often the higher the income paid, the riskier the bond. Bonds can be issued by both UK and overseas companies.

CORPORATE BOND INVESTMENT FUND: A unit trust which invests in a range of corporate bonds. Ideal for people in search of a regular income without jeopardising too much of their capital.

COUPON: The fixed rate of interest paid on a gilt or bond.

CREDIT CARD: A simple but dangerous way of borrowing. You are given a credit limit and your commitment is to pay the minimum monthly repayment demanded.

CREDIT REFERENCE AGENCY: An organisation which keeps details of your credit worthiness. They are often used by organisations which want to check out your suitability for a loan or a new credit card. You can apply for details of the information maintained on yourself by the credit reference agencies.

CREDIT UNION: An increasingly popular way for people – usually bonded by occupation or community – to save and borrow.

CREST: A relatively new way of trading in shares. Your shares are held electronically but you maintain the same rights as if you held the shares directly.

CRITICAL ILLNESS INSURANCE: Insurance which pays you a lump sum on the diagnosis of one of a number of major diseases. Sometimes referred to as dread disease cover.

CURRENT ACCOUNT: Your traditional bank account which provides you with a home for your income and allows you to meet regular bills. Current accounts are improving all the time and can come with a number of gizmos including cheque guarantee cards and debit cards. Some current accounts now pay interest.

CYCLE INSURANCE: Insurance for bicyclists. Cheap but could prove a financial lifeline if you are involved in an accident.

DEBIT CARD: Now offered as part of most bank accounts, this allows you to pay for goods without filling out a cheque. Payment is taken straight from your account – it will not be authorised if you have insufficient funds. Debit cards can also be used to obtain cash, at supermarkets, for example. Again, you will need to have sufficient funds in your account. Often referred to as a payment or switch card.

DECREASING TERM ASSURANCE: Life assurance where the benefit payable on death decreases in stages until it is zero by the end of the policy's term.

DEED OF VARIATION: Used to alter the distribution of assets laid down in a will. Usually used to avoid or reduce inheritance tax.

DEFERRED INTEREST MORTGAGE: A home loan where you pay reduced interest payments but where you agree to make good the underpayments – the underpayments are simply added to your outstanding loan. Should be avoided.

DEFINED CONTRIBUTION BASIS: A pension where the pension fund you accumulate is determined by the contributions you make into the fund.

DEPOSIT ACCOUNT: Savings account offered primarily by a bank or building society which allows you to save without jeopardising your capital.

DETERMINATION: A form from the Inland Revenue giving a best estimate of the tax you owe. You don't particularly want to receive one of these – you are obliged to pay it.

DIGITAL BANKING: Use of the television to conduct your banking arangements.

DILUTION CHARGE: A sales charge which you may incur when you sell an investment fund (an OEIC).

DIRECT DEBIT: A way of making regular payments from a bank account with the minimum of paperwork. Used to pay regular household bills such as gas and electricity as well as the minimum payment on a credit card bill.

DISCOUNT BROKER: A broker who allows you to buy unit trusts at a discount. They do this by not taking the full commission available to them.

DISCOUNTED RATE MORTGAGE: A home loan where the

interest rate is reduced by a fixed amount in the early years. Ideal for first-time buyers although the rates are variable and can rise if interest rates increase generally.

DIVIDEND: Income from a shareholding. Most companies, especially those based in the UK, pay an income twice a year.

E111: A form which provides you with medical cover when abroad. Available from your local post office but remember – it is not a substitute for travel insurance.

EARLY REDEMPTION PENALTIES: High charges you may incur if you transfer a mortgage in the early years.

EARLY RETIREMENT FACTOR: Used by companies to reduce the pension they will pay you if you retire early.

ELECTRONIC PURSE: A card which you load with money prior to going shopping.

EMPLOYEE SHARE SCHEME: Where workers are encouraged to buy shares in their employer's business, usually at a discount to their prevailing price.

ENDOWMENT MORTGAGE: A home loan where a savings plan offered by an insurance company is designed to repay your original sum borrowed at the end of the mortgage term. While you pay premiums into the savings plan, you also pay interest on the loan. Endowment mortgages are not as popular as they were.

ENTERPRISE INVESTMENT SCHEMES: Tax-efficient way of investing in new businesses. High risk, high reward. Don't let the tax tail wag the investment dog.

ESCALATING PENSION ANNUITY: An annuity which increases payments every year, either by a predetermined figure or by inflation.

ESCALATOR BOND: A savings account which pays you a higher rate of fixed interest each year. Such bonds must usually be held for a fixed period.

ETHICAL INVESTMENTS: Shares and unit trusts where the underlying companies adopt an eco-friendly approach towards the environment. An increasingly popular form of investment.

EURO MORTGAGES: Home loans denominated in euros. Most people shouldn't go anywhere near these.

EXCESS: Amount an insurance company will ask you to pay if you make a claim on a policy.

EXECUTION-ONLY STOCKBROKER: Someone who will buy and sell shares on your behalf but will not provide you with any advice.

EXECUTIVE PENSION: A special fast-track pension scheme for senior executives and directors of businesses.

EXECUTORS: People you appoint to carry out your wishes under a will.

FAMILY INCOME BENEFIT: Life assurance which upon death of the policyholder pays out a monthly sum until the end of the policy's term.

FINAL DIVIDEND: Second of two income payments paid by a company to shareholders every financial year.

FINAL SALARY PENSION SCHEME: Company pension scheme where your pension at retirement will be determined primarily by the number of years you have worked for the employer and your final salary upon retirement. Such schemes are becoming rarer by the day.

FIXED-RATE MORTGAGE: A home loan where the interest rate charged on the loan is fixed for a predetermined period. Typical fixed-rate deals will apply for three or five years. Although offering certainty, these loans can prove expensive if interest rates start to fall.

FLEXIBLE MORTGAGES: Mortgages which allow you greater flexibility in the way you make your repayments. Extra payments can be made if you come into a lump sum or alternatively you can take payment holidays.

FREE-STANDING ADDITIONAL VOLUNTARY CONTRI-BUTION: A scheme offered by an insurance company or other financial services provider which enables you to supplement your contributions into a company pension scheme. Beware of charges and always look at the in-house AVC arrangements before plumping for an FSAVC.

FRIENDLY SOCIETY: An organisation which offers members a range of financial products – from savings through to insurance cover.

FRIENDLY SOCIETY TAX-FREE INVESTMENT PLAN: A 10-year savings plan which allows you to build up a tax-free lump sum. Charges can be high so beware.

FRINGE BENEFIT: A benefit provided to you by your employer – a company car, for example, or private medical insurance.

FUNDED UNAPPROVED RETIREMENT BENEFIT SCHEMES: Pension scheme designed for high rollers.

FUND SUPERMARKET: An Internet-based site where you are able

to buy unit trusts and Isas without paying full initial costs. Fidelity and Prudential's Egg are leaders in this area.

GEARING: Process by which investment trusts are able to borrow money in order to increase their exposure to world stock markets. Can result in greater returns for shareholders if stock markets then boom but conversely can work against investors if stock markets subsequently plummet.

GENERALIST INVESTMENT TRUST: A trust which invests across the world's stock markets. Great homes for first-time investors.

GIFT AID: Tax-efficient way of giving money to charity.

GIFTS: Way of giving away your assets to friends and relatives without incurring tax.

GILTS: Bonds issued by the government which pay investors a fixed rate of interest for a predetermined period.

GILT UNIT TRUST: An investment fund which invests in a range of gilts and some bonds.

GOING INTO THE RED: You owe the bank account money rather than vice versa. Going into the red will often bring with it a raft of bank charges.

GOLD CARD: A glorified credit card with a number of add-ons (usually of an insurance nature). Rates can be expensive.

GROSS PAY: Pay before deductions for tax and national insurance.

GROUP PERMANENT HEALTH INSURANCE POLICY: Protection insurance offered by your employer. Premiums tend to be cheaper than if you acquire cover on an individual basis.

GROUP PERSONAL PENSION: A pension scheme offered by an employer where you can choose where your contributions are invested. The pension scheme is operated by an insurance company.

GROUP PRIVATE MEDICAL INSURANCE: Private medical cover arranged through your employer. Premiums tend to be cheaper than if you arrange cover on an individual basis.

GUARANTEED INCOME BONDS: These pay a fixed rate of interest for a fixed time period. Issued by insurance companies, investors get back their original capital at the end of the bond's life.

GUARANTEED PENSIONS ANNUITY: Sold by some insurance companies along with pensions. The pension promises a guaranteed annuity rate at retirement. Usually, very attractive for those who hold them.

HEADROOM CHECK: A check to ensure purchasers of free-standing additional voluntary contribution plans are not over-funding their pension.

HIGHER RATE OF TAX: Highest rate of tax applied to your income.

HIRE PURCHASE: Traditional way of financing a car purchase.

HOME INCOME PLANS: A way for the elderly to release equity from their home while remaining in their home. A lifeline for many elderly people who are equity rich, cash poor.

HOME INSURANCE: Insurance which protects your home and its contents. Home insurance embraces buildings insurance (cover against damage to your home) and contents insurance (cover against the contents of your home).

HOME RESPONSIBILITIES PROTECTION: Scheme designed to ensure non-working mothers get a fair state pension.

HOME REVERSION SCHEME: Way of releasing equity from your home in order to generate an income. Appealing to the elderly.

HOSPITAL CASH PLANS: Plans which provide you with a tax-free sum if you have to have medical or dental treatment. Sold as a cheap and cheerful alternative to expensive private medical insurance.

HYBRID COMPANY PENSION SCHEME: A pension scheme which offers members both final salary and money purchase based pensions.

HYBRID INVESTMENT BOND: A bond which invests in a mix of underlying funds – both profits- and unit-linked.

IMMEDIATE CARE PLANS: Provide immediate funds for long-term care. Through the payment of a lump sum, a fixed income is paid which can then be used to fund long-term care costs.

IMPAIRED LIFE PENSION ANNUITY: An annuity which pays an enhanced annuity in recognition of your shorter life expectancy.

INCOME DRAWDOWN: Process of taking an income from your pension fund without using the fund to buy an annuity. Only use after taking independent financial advice. Sometimes referred to as pension income withdrawal.

INCOME MULTIPLIER: The method by which many mortgage lenders assess the amount of money you are able to borrow. The amount borrowed is linked to a multiple of your gross pay.

INCOME SHARES: Issued by split capital investment trusts. Designed to appeal to income seekers.

INCOME TAX: Tax that you pay on your income – both earned and unearned. You can't escape it.

INCOME UNITS: Issued to unit trust investors who want to receive income from their investment.

INCREASING TERM ASSURANCE: Life cover which increases the older you get. The idea is to ensure the sum assured rises to match the ravages of inflation.

INDEPENDENT FINANCIAL ADVISER: An adviser who will shop around the marketplace in search of the best financial deal for you. An adviser's ambit will cover everything from life insurance through to investments and pensions.

INDEPENDENT MORTGAGE ADVISER: An adviser who will shop around the marketplace in search of the best mortgage deal for you.

INDEXATION ALLOWANCE: Used in calculating your liability to capital gains tax.

INDEX-LINKED GILTS: Gilts where returns – both capital and income – are increased in line with inflation.

INDEX TRACKING UNIT TRUST: A unit trust whose objective is to match the performance of a designated stock market such as the FTSE 100 index or the FTSE All-Share index.

INHERITANCE TAX: Tax that is paid on assets you leave when you die.

INHERITANCE TAX THRESHOLD: Amount at which inheritance tax starts to kick in.

INSTANT ACCESS SAVINGS ACCOUNT: A savings vehicle which allows you to withdraw money without penalty. Your capital is not at risk.

INTEREST-ONLY MORTGAGE: Home loan where monthly payments pay the interest on the loan. At the end of the mortgage term, you then repay the capital borrowed as a lump sum, usually from the proceeds of a savings vehicle such as an endowment.

INTERIM DIVIDEND: First of two income payments paid by a company to shareholders every financial year.

INTERNAL TAXATION: Tax paid within a fund on your behalf. Applies to investment bonds.

INTERNET BANKING: Bank accounts where customers do most of their transactions via the net.

INTESTACY LAWS: Rules which kick in when you die without a will. Golden rule is: don't die without making a will.

INVESTMENT BOND: An investment scheme offered by most insurance companies which allows you to make lump-sum investments.

INVESTMENT CLUB: Where friends club together and pool contributions to invest in shares as a group. A popular and fun way of investing in the stock market.

INVESTMENT-LINKED PENSION ANNUITY: Lifetime income where the level of income is dependent upon the investment performance of the underlying units.

INVESTMENT TRUSTS: An investment fund which pools investors' money and uses it to invest in the shares of a broad spread of companies.

INVESTMENT TRUST SAVINGS AND INVESTMENT PLAN: A scheme operated by the managers of an investment trust which enables private investors to buy and sell shares cheaply. Such schemes allow you to buy shares on a one-off or regular basis.

INVESTMENT TRUST WARRANTS: Issued by investment trust companies, usually at launch. Allow you to buy shares in the trust at a set price on a fixed date in the future. High-risk investments – for brave hearts only.

IRREDEEMABLES: Gilts which have no fixed redemption date.

ISA (INDIVIDUAL SAVINGS ACCOUNT): A savings vehicle which enables you to save up to £7,000 per tax year free from the clutches of the taxman. Money can be saved in investment funds, cash and insurance although there are restrictions on how much can be invested in each asset class.

JOINT BANK ACCOUNT: An account run by two people – usually married couples. Either person can make withdrawals and write out cheques. Both people are jointly owners of the money in the account – they are also jointly responsible for the debts.

JOINT LIFE PENSION ANNUITY: An annuity which pays a full or reduced pension to your spouse if you die.

KEY FEATURES DOCUMENT: A document you receive when you buy a life, pensions or investment product. It will spell out all the key details of the product you are buying including the impact of charges on likely returns. Although not particularly reader-friendly, it is essential you scrutinise this document.

KEY MAN INSURANCE: Insurance to protect small businesses against the loss of a key worker (usually a director) as a result of illness.

KINK TEST: Can be used in calculating your liability to capital gains tax.

LEVEL TERM INSURANCE: Life insurance which pays out the same benefit throughout a policy's term.

LIFE INSURANCE: A policy which will pay out if the insured person dies.

LIMITED BENEFIT PERMANENT HEALTH INSURANCE: Protection insurance which will only pay benefit for a maximum pre-defined period. Premiums are cheaper to reflect the lower extent of cover.

LOCAL AUTHORITY BONDS: Bonds issued by local authorities. These pay a fixed rate of interest and are for a fixed term.

LONG-DATED GILTS: Gilts with more than 15 years to redemption.

LONG-TERM-CARE INSURANCE: Insurance against the possibility of requiring long-term care.

LOTTERY WINNINGS: Tax-free!

LOW-START ENDOWMENT: Mortgage repayment vehicle where premiums in early years are low. They then start increasing. Can cause holders a nasty payment shock.

MANAGED FUNDS: Offered by insurance companies and provide investors with exposure to a broad spread of assets.

MARKET VALUE ADJUSTER: A penalty which may be applied by an insurance company to the value of your savings plan when you come to encash it.

MARRIED COUPLE'S ALLOWANCE: An allowance paid by the state to couples where one spouse was aged at least 65 on April 5, 2000.

MAXI ISA: A tax-free investment plan which allows you to invest up to £7,000 per tax year. Most maxi Isas allow you to put your entire £7,000 in equities or collective investments such as unit trusts and investment trusts.

MAXIMUM COVER PLANS: Usually whole-of-life plans where most of your premiums are used to purchase life cover with the balance used to invest.

MEDICAL HISTORY DECLARATION: One of two ways in which cover is offered for private medical insurance or income replacement insurance. Here you declare your medical history and the insurer will offer you cover on this basis. Failure to include past medical problems could invalidate any future claim.

MEDIUM-DATED GILTS: Gilts with between 5 and 15 years until redemption.

MINI ISA: A tax-free savings scheme. Mini Isas come in three shapes – cash Isas, insurance Isas and equity Isas. The maximum investment limit per tax year is £3,000, £1,000 and £3,000 respectively.

MINIMUM COVER PLANS: Usually whole-of-life plans where most of your premiums are invested with the balance used to purchase minimum life cover.

MINIMUM INCOME GUARANTEE: A government scheme designed to ensure all pensioners are in receipt of an adequate income to live on.

MONEY PURCHASE COMPANY PENSION SCHEME: Most popular form of company pension scheme now operated. Your pension is determined primarily by the investment performance of the pension fund assets.

MORATORIA: One of two ways in which cover is offered for private medical insurance or income replacement insurance. Here cover is offered straight away but you will not be covered for any pre-existing condition. Policies written on this basis are simple to arrange but can disappoint later on.

MORTGAGE: The main method by which people are able to fund the purchase of a home. They are effectively long-term home loans.

MORTGAGE ARREARS: When you fall behind with your scheduled mortgage payments. Arrears should be avoided at all cost but can be inevitable as a result of unexpected redundancy, or long-term illness. Speak to your lender straight away if mortgage arrears are likely.

MORTGAGE INDEMNITY GUARANTEE (MIG): A charge applied by some lenders when you take out a loan which represents a big chunk of the property's value. The charge provides you with nothing. Some lenders no longer insist on it.

MORTGAGE PAYMENT PROTECTION INSURANCE: Provides financial protection for homeowners who become unemployed, ill or are unable to work. Often referred to as accident, sickness and unemployment insurance. Payments will cover your mortgage payments.

MUTUAL: An organisation owned by its members. Building societies are mutuals as are many friendly societies and insurance companies. Mutual does not necessarily mean your interests will come first in the pecking order – just ask members of Equitable Life.

NATIONAL INSURANCE: Another form of tax which most people in work have to pay.

NATIONAL SAVINGS: The government-backed savings institution which offers a broad array of savings products.

NATIONAL SAVINGS CAPITAL BOND: A five-year fixed-rate investment.

NATIONAL SAVINGS CHILDREN'S BONUS BOND: A tax-free savings bond for children. Rates are fixed for five years at a time.

NATIONAL SAVINGS FIRST OPTION BOND: A one-year savings bond paying a fixed rate of interest.

NATIONAL SAVINGS FIXED-INTEREST SAVINGS CERTI-FICATES: Tax-free investment offering fixed returns over five years.

NATIONAL SAVINGS INCOME BOND: A bond paying a monthly income which is variable.

NATIONAL SAVINGS INDEX-LINKED SAVINGS CERTI-FICATES: Tax-free investment offering returns linked to inflation over five years.

NATIONAL SAVINGS INVESTMENT ACCOUNT: Thirty-day-notice account which pays a variable rate of interest.

NATIONAL SAVINGS ORDINARY ACCOUNT: Instant-access account paying a variable rate of interest.

NATIONAL SAVINGS PENSIONER'S BOND: A bond paying a fixed rate of monthly income for five years.

NATIONAL SAVINGS PREMIUM BOND: A tax-free investment which provides you with the opportunity to win up to £1 million in prizes.

NET PAY: Take home pay – pay after deductions have been made for tax and National Insurance.

NET RELEVANT EARNINGS: Basis for determining the amount of money you can contribute towards a personal pension.

NEW-FOR-OLD INSURANCE: Home insurance policies which will meet the full cost of replacing items if they are stolen or destroyed.

NO-CLAIMS DISCOUNT: A reduction in premiums to reflect the fact that you have not made a claim on your policy for a pre-defined period. Normally applies to motor insurance but can also be used on other forms of insurance such as private medical insurance.

NO-CLAIMS PROTECTION COVER: A way of protecting your no-claims bonus on your motor insurance.

NOMINAL VALUE: Value attached to shares issued by a company. Don't be distracted by it, it's the market value that counts.

NOMINEE ACCOUNT: Becoming the established way for people to hold shares in companies. Benefits are primarily for the brokers who can cut down on administration. If you hold shares in a nominee account, it might mean you losing out on any company perks on offer plus ready access to company information such as report and accounts.

NON-CONTRIBUTORY COMPANY PENSION SCHEME: Where you do not have to make contributions – all the contributions are made by your employer. Such schemes are now few and far between.

NORMAL RETIREMENT AGE: Age at which your company will typically start paying you your pension.

NOTICE SAVINGS ACCOUNT: A savings account which allows you to withdraw money subject to a predetermined notice period. Your capital is not at risk.

OCCUPATIONAL PENSION SCHEME: A pension scheme operated by your employer. In most instances, both you and your employer will make contributions into the pension fund on your behalf.

OFFER FOR SALE: Term used to describe an issue of shares by a company at an agreed price.

OFFER PRICE: Price at which you buy units in a unit trust.

OFFSHORE SAVINGS ACCOUNTS: Savings accounts offered by banks and building societies but based in places such as Guernsey and Jersey. This allows for interest to be paid gross although interest is still taxable.

OPEN-ENDED: Used to describe unit trusts where the number of units in issue varies according to supply and demand.

OPEN-ENDED INVESTMENT COMPANY (OEIC): Modern version of a unit trust.

OPEN MARKET OPTION: Right to shop around for a best-value pension annuity when you decide to turn your pension fund into a lifetime income.

ORPHAN ASSETS: Surplus funds held by insurance companies. Some insurance companies are now part distributing these assets.

OVER 80S PENSION: State pension payable to the over 80s.

OWN OCCUPATION: A definition used by many insurance companies to determine whether you are eligible to make a claim under their policy. If you are unable to pursue your occupation, then benefit will be payable.

P2: Your notice of tax coding. Check it because it will determine the tax you pay on a monthly basis.

P11D: A form from your employer detailing the taxable value of any perks you have enjoyed such as a company car or private medical insurance. An important document so keep it safe.

P45: Form you receive from an employer when you leave their employment. Details your tax and income.

P60: A form from your employer which details your income for the tax year and the tax you have paid. It's an important document so keep it in a safe place.

PAID-UP: A policy – pension or savings plan – is said to be paid-up when you stop contributing to it but keep the plan in force. The plan will still attract charges, indeed it may be ravaged by charges so beware.

PARTIAL BENEFIT: Reduced benefit paid by an insurance company if you return to work on a part-time basis after long-term illness. Sometimes known as rehabilitation benefit.

PARTICIPATING PREFERENCE SHARES: Offer investors fixed-interest payments plus the right to a limited share of profits generated by the company.

PAY AS YOU EARN: Way in which most employed people pay tax on a regular basis.

PAYING-IN SLIPS: Come as part of most bank accounts, enabling you to make deposits into your account.

PAYROLL GIFTING: Tax-efficient way of making gifts to charity.

PC BANKING: Use of a computer to do your banking.

PENNY SHARES: Term used to describe shares with a minimal value. Often touted by newsletters as the best share thing since sliced bread – for mugs or hearts of steel only.

PENSION ANNUITY: Used in order to convert your pension fund into a lifetime income.

PENSION MORTGAGE: A home loan where you use the tax-free cash lump sum from a pension in order to clear your loan. Not an ideal way of funding a home loan. It is fraught with danger.

PENSIONS ANNUITY GUARANTEE: An annuity which pays an income for a guaranteed period of time irrespective of whether you die before the end of the period.

PENSIONS EARMARKING: Rules introduced to ensure a former spouse gets a fair pensions deal if they divorce.

PENSIONS EARNINGS CAP: Government limit imposed on the amount that you can put into a pension and the amount you can take out from a pension. Only impacts on high earners. A new cap is set each year.

PENSIONS SPLITTING: Scheme introduced to ensure divorced couples split pension assets fairly upon divorce. Alternative to pensions earmarking.

PENSION TERM ASSURANCE: Term assurance bought through your pension provider. By buying term assurance in this way, you can obtain tax relief on the premiums paid.

PEP (PERSONAL EQUITY PLAN): A tax-free investment plan no longer available to the public although plans can still remain in force. Proceeds from a Pep are tax-free.

PERMANENT HEALTH INSURANCE: Insurance which will pay

you an income in the event of serious illness or disability. Often referred to as income replacement insurance, income protection insurance, long-term disability insurance, disability income insurance or personal disability insurance.

PERSONAL ALLOWANCE: Amount of income you are allowed before you are liable to pay income tax.

PERSONAL CONTRACT HIRE: A way of paying for a car without ever actually owning it.

PERSONAL CONTRACT PURCHASE: A way of buying a car by paying a series of monthly payments. Such schemes can often appear more attractive than they really are so tread carefully.

PERSONAL LOAN: A loan taken out for personal use – to buy a car, for example.

PERSONAL PENSION: Vehicle which allows those without a company pension to save for retirement. Suitable for the self-employed although stakeholder pensions now provide competition.

PET INSURANCE: Cover against vet bills. Can be an inexpensive way of ensuring your vet doesn't spring a nasty financial surprise on you.

PETS (POTENTIALLY EXEMPT TRANSFERS): Gifts that you make to friends or relatives that may incur inheritance tax.

PHASED RETIREMENT: Way of taking an income from your pension fund at retirement without the need to buy a full-blown annuity. Only use after taking independent financial advice.

PIN (PERSONAL IDENTIFICATION NUMBER): The number you have to input into a cash machine before a bank will authorise you to make a cash withdrawal. Try to learn it by heart and if you write it down, do so in a form and a place which will not be obvious to unscrupulous people.

PLACING: Where a company issues shares by 'placing' them with financial institutions.

POLICY FEE: A charge taken by an insurance company for administering your savings plan/pension plan/insurance and savings plan. The fee can be charged in many ways but typically it is charged monthly and is a fixed amount, which can discriminate against small savers.

POSTAL BANKING: Bank accounts where most transactions are carried out on a postal basis.

PREFERENCE SHARES: Shares which pay a regular fixed income.

PRE-FUNDED LONG-TERM-CARE INSURANCE: Insurance which covers you against the future costs of long-term care.

PRESERVED PENSION: Pension fund that you leave with an ex-employer.

PRIVATE MEDICAL INSURANCE: Cover against the costs of private medical treatment for curable, short-term medical conditions.

PRIZE INSURANCE: Cover for organisers of events where a big prize is offered. The insurance covers against someone winning the prize.

PROPERTY FUNDS: Offered by insurance companies. Funds tend to invest in direct property rather than property shares.

PROPORTIONATE BENEFIT: Reduced benefit paid by an insurance company if you return to work (not your own occupation) after long-term illness.

PURCHASED LIFE ANNUITY: Voluntary arrangement whereby you invest a lump sum in order to obtain a regular income.

R40: Tax form you fill in to claim back tax on savings.

R85: Tax form you fill in to receive gross income from your savings.

REBATE-ONLY PENSION: An alternative to the State Earnings Related Pension Scheme.

RECURRING SINGLE PREMIUM: Pension scheme where you can make a series of payments into the plan.

REDEMPTION DATE: Date at which a gilt or bond will pay you your money back. The date is usually predetermined.

REDEMPTION PENALTIES: Penalties levied by lenders if you redeem a mortgage before a specified period. Redemption penalties apply to most new mortgage offers so fully understand them before you sign on the dotted line. If you don't understand them or find it hard to quantify them, ask the lender to spell them out for you in pounds and pence.

REDEMPTION YIELD: Expected annual return from a bond including capital gains and losses.

REGULAR INCOME SAVINGS ACCOUNTS: Savings accounts which pay the holder a regular income, usually monthly.

REGULAR SAVINGS ACCOUNTS: Savings accounts which permit you to save small amounts on a regular basis. Usually, a 'loyalty' bonus is paid after a predetermined period.

REMORTGAGE: When a borrower stays in their home but changes lender in order to get a better loan deal. Remortgaging has made great sense for many people in recent years as they have taken advantage of cut-price deals available to new borrowers.

REMOVALS INSURANCE: Cover against accidents caused by employing a removals firm when moving home. Cover will not break the bank.

RENEWABLE TERM ASSURANCE: Life assurance which allows you to exchange your term assurance for another policy at the end of the term, thereby extending your life cover. You can renew your cover irrespective of your health.

REPAYMENT MORTGAGE (CAPITAL AND INTEREST MORTGAGE): A home loan where your monthly repayments comprise both interest and capital repayment.

REVERSIONARY BONUS: An annual bonus paid by an insurance company on a with-profits policy. The idea is that the bonus cannot be taken away once added although you have to pay your premiums until the end of the policy's term in order for that to be ensured.

RIGHTS ISSUES: Where a company invites shareholders to buy more of its shares.

RUNNING YIELD: Indication of the income that a bond is expected to pay.

SAVE AS YOU EARN SCHEME: Form of employee share scheme where you are encouraged to save in order to buy shares in your employer's business in the future.

SAVINGS BOND: An account usually offered by a bank or building society which offers a fixed rate of interest over a pre-determined time period.

SECTION 32 BUYOUT: A pension arrangement into which you can transfer a pension from an ex-employer's pension scheme.

SECTION 226 RETIREMENT ANNUITIES: Old-style personal pensions. You might still have a plan but you can't take out a new plan. Sometimes referred to as self-employed retirement annuities.

SECURED LOAN: A loan where you offer your home (typically) as security in the event of you not been able to make your loan repayments in the future. Because of the security offered by your home, rates on secured loans tend to be lower than for unsecured loans.

SELF-ASSESSMENT: New tax system. Applies primarily to anyone who is self-employed.

SELF-BUILD MORTGAGE: A mortgage designed for those who want to build their own homes. Some building societies such as Ecology and Norwich & Peterborough specialise in this area.

SELF-INVESTED PERSONAL PENSION: A pension plan which gives you greater freedom over where your money is invested than a conventional personal pension.

SELF-INVESTED UNIT-LINKED PENSION ANNUITY: Where your lifetime income is dependent upon the fortunes of various assets which you select.

SERPS (STATE EARNINGS RELATED PENSION SCHEME): A top-up earnings-related pension in addition to your basic state pension.

SETTLEMENT SYSTEM: Payment system for buying and selling of shares. This requires payment within a set period – 5 or 10 days.

SHARE CERTIFICATE: Paper proof that you own shares in a particular company. Becoming a relic of the past as most companies refuse to issue share certificates.

SHARE EXCHANGE: Schemes usually provided by investment trust and unit trust companies which allow you to exchange shares for a holding in a fund.

SHAREHOLDER PERKS: Discounts, special offers provided to shareholders in return for investing in a particular company. Such perks can be attractive but they shouldn't be the main reason for investing. Also perks cannot be obtained if you invest through a nominee account so beware.

SHARES: Issued by companies in order to raise finance. Most shares are traded on a stock market.

SHORT-DATED GILTS: Gilts with less than five years to redemption.

SICKNESS SOCIETIES: A form of friendly society which pays members benefits if they suffer from long-term illness.

SINGLE LIFE PENSION ANNUITY: An annuity which will pay an income until the holder dies.

SINGLE PREMIUM: Pension scheme set up on a single – one-off – basis.

SINGLE PREMIUM WHOLE-OF-LIFE POLICY: Insurance term for an investment plan. Primarily an investment scheme but also offers life cover.

SMALL SELF-ADMINISTERED SCHEME: A pension arrangement designed for small businesses. Gives small businesses great flexibility over where their money is invested.

SMOKERS PENSIONS ANNUITY: An annuity which pays a higher income to reflect your shorter life expectancy.

SPLIT CAPITAL INVESTMENT TRUSTS: Trusts which issue different classes of shares in order to appeal to different types of investors. Treat with caution.

SPREAD: Difference between the buying and selling prices of a unit trust. Can also apply to the difference between the buying and selling prices for shares and bonds.

SPREADBETTING: A way of betting on the future of individual shares or stock market indices. Not something you should get involved in with your eyes closed.

STAKEHOLDER PENSION: New form of saving for retirement giving many people a first opportunity to save via a pension and many others a fair pensions deal for the first time.

STANDARD PRIVATE MEDICAL INSURANCE: A halfway house form of private medical insurance cover, providing you with cover against most medical costs. Falls between the cheapness and cheerfulness of budget plans and the deluxe comprehensive plans.

STANDARD VARIABLE RATE MORTGAGE: The bog standard mortgage offered by most lenders. Rates are variable and vary according to movements in interest rates in the wider economy. Most people can get a better deal by taking out a different type of mortgage.

STANDING ORDER: A way of making regular payments from your bank account without writing out a new cheque every time. Standing orders are often used to pay regular premiums such as for home insurance or for the funding of a savings scheme.

STAMP DUTY: A government tax on share buying and on the buying of homes. For shares, it is 0.5%; for homes, it ranges from 0% to 4%.

STARTING RATE OF TAX: First rate of tax applied on income above your personal tax allowances. Currently 10%.

STATE INCAPACITY BENEFIT: Payment made by the state to people suffering from long-term illness or disability.

STATEMENT OF ACCOUNT: Issued under the self-assessment tax system and details the amounts of tax you are liable to pay.

STATE PENSION: Pension from the state. It's not an automatic right – it depends upon the number of years you have paid National Insurance contributions.

STATUTORY SICK PAY: Minimum amount which your employer must pay you if you suffer from long-term illness.

STOCKBROKER: Someone who advises on and trades shares.

STOCK MARKET-LINKED BONDS: Bonds which pay an income but where the amount of capital you get back is dependent upon the performance of a particular stock market. Don't touch unless you fully understand the risks involved.

STOCKS: Fixed-interest securities such as gilts and bonds.

STORE CARDS: A credit card offered by a retailer. Rates can be expensive so beware.

SURRENDER: When you get rid of a policy before the end of its term. Surrendering a policy to a life company rarely makes financial sense. Think of alternatives such as selling the policy on the open market, making the policy paid-up or borrowing against the policy.

SWITCHING: Process by which an insurance company allows you to transfer your plan to another fund. Some companies offer free switches.

TAPER RELIEF: Used in calculating your liability to any capital gains tax.

TAPERING RELIEF: Reduces the amount of inheritance tax that might be payable on a gift you make to a relative or friend.

TAX: You can't escape it. It's how the government raises revenue and it comes in all shapes and sizes.

TAXABLE INCOME: Amount of income after personal allowances which the taxman applies tax to.

TAX CREDIT: New way of providing cash or tax reductions. Complex but don't be deterred. Claim them if you are eligible. Tax credit is also a term used to describe the tax charged on dividends before they end up in your hands. Currently set at 10%.

TAX RELIEF: Sums paid out of gross pay which do not attract tax – pensions and donations to charity, for example.

TAX RETURN: Form you complete which is used by you or the taxman to work out your tax bill.

TENANTS IN COMMON: Way to own a home which can prove tax-efficient when it comes to inheritance tax.

TENDER: An issue of shares where you nominate the price you are prepared to pay for the shares.

TERM ASSURANCE: The most straightforward – and cheapest – type of life assurance you can buy. It pays out a lump sum upon your death provided the policy is still in force.

TESSA (TAX-EXEMPT SPECIAL SAVINGS ACCOUNT): A deposit-based tax-free savings account. New accounts can no longer be taken out although contributions can be made to existing plans.

TOP SLICING: Process by which you may be liable to further tax on proceeds from an investment bond. It's complicated.

TRADING AT A DISCOUNT: When the shares of an investment trust do not reflect the value of the trust's underlying assets. Happens when a trust's shares are out of favour – there are more sellers than buyers.

TRADING AT A PREMIUM: When the shares of an investment trust are worth more than the trust's underlying assets. Happens when a trust's shares are popular – more buyers than sellers. Approach such trusts with extreme caution – you could end up paying over the odds for trust shares.

TRANSFER VALUE: Assumed value of your pension if you transfer it to another provider. The transfer value may not equal the actual value so beware.

TRAVEL INSURANCE: Cover against accidents and problems incurred when you are on holiday. Shop around – no two policies are alike.

TRUST: A way of holding assets and reducing tax liabilities.

UNAUTHORISED OVERDRAFT: When you have allowed your bank account to slip into the red without informing the bank first. Unauthorised overdraft charges can be excessive so beware.

UNITISED WITH-PROFITS PLAN: A plan where the units you hold increase in value as bonuses are paid by the insurance company.

UNIT-LINKED POLICY: A savings plan where your money buys units in a particular fund. The value of your investment then rises or falls according to the underlying value of the units.

UNIT-LINKED WHOLE-OF-LIFE POLICIES: Mix of an insurance and savings plan. Jack of all trades, master of none.

UNIT TRUST: An investment fund which allows you to invest in world stock markets, specific stock markets (UK for example) or specific sectors of the stock market (smaller companies, for example).

UNIT TRUST CERTIFICATE: A document confirming your ownership of units in a particular trust. Most investment houses no longer issue certificates.

UNIT TRUST SAVINGS SCHEME: A way of investing in a unit trust on a regular basis. Minimum contributions are usually much lower than for people who want to make a single lump-sum investment.

UNITS: What you acquire when you invest in a unit trust or a unit-linked insurance fund or pension plan. The units then rise or fall in value according to the value of the underlying investments.

UNIVERSAL POLICIES: Jack of all trades protection insurance, offering life cover and other benefits such as critical illness cover, disability benefit. Such policies can be expensive.

UNSECURED LOAN: A loan which you do not provide any security for such as a home.

WAITING PERIOD: The time you must wait before a policy will pay out an eligible claim. Often used on protection insurance such as income replacement insurance. The longer waiting period you are willing to accept, the lower your policy premiums.

WAIVER OF PREMIUM: Insurance which will ensure your premiums are paid if you are unable to work as a result of illness. Usually sold with a pension, thereby ensuring your pension contributions are funded if you suffer from a long-term illness.

WEAR AND TEAR INSURANCE: Home insurance policies which will replace stolen or destroyed items but make a reduction for wear, tear and depreciation.

WHOLE-OF-LIFE POLICIES: Investment-based policies which provide life cover for the whole of your life.

WIDOW'S/WIDOWER'S PENSION: A pension payable to your loved one if you die. Usually a reduced pension.

WILL: Legal document which defines the way your assets will be distributed after your death. You shouldn't be without one.

WINDFALL: A payment you receive as a result of an insurance company or building society deciding to demutualise. Windfalls have been paid by a whole host of demutualising organisations in recent years including the AA, Bradford & Bingley and Scottish Widows.

WITH-PROFITS: A form of 'safe' savings plan offered by most insurance companies. Returns principally come in the form of annual bonuses. However, it is the insurer which decides the level of bonus and in recent years, bonuses have been consistently cut. While a safe home for many, with-profits have come in for justifiable criticism because of their lack of transparency.

WITH-PROFITS INVESTMENT BOND: A lump-sum investment scheme which earns you a series of annual bonuses plus the prospect of a further bonus upon encashment of the bond.

WITH-PROFITS PENSION ANNUITY: Lifetime income where future income payments are dependent upon the performance of the with-profits company.

WITH-PROFITS WHOLE-OF-LIFE POLICIES: Mix of an insurance and savings plan. Jack of all trades, master of none.

ZERO DIVIDEND PREFERENCE SHARES: Issued by split capital investment trusts. Appeal to investors in search of low-risk capital returns.

CHAPTER # 16
Final Word

CONCLUSION

'What you reach when you get tired
of thinking.'

Martin Fischer

I TRUST that you have found something in this book which will make your personal finance lot a more rewarding one.

This book is in its first edition and it is my determination to make it 'the' personal finance book to be read. I accept that there are areas that I have merely touched on when maybe more details should have been provided.

In order for this book to become the best of its kind, I need your input. If you feel there are areas of the book which are too complicated or are not detailed enough, drop me a line. I will then incorporate your thoughts in the next edition. In particular, I would love to hear from readers who have golden personal finance nuggets of their own that they feel warrant coverage in the book.

Good personal finance hunting.

JEFF PRESTRIDGE
FINANCIAL MAIL ON SUNDAY
APRIL 2001

INCOME TAX RETURNS

'The most imaginative fiction being written today.'

Herman Wouk

APPENDIX 1

Indexation factors for capital gains tax (see chapter 6)

Indexation factors

Year	Jan	Feb	Mar	Apr	May	Jun	Jul	Aug	Sep	Oct	Nov	Dec
1982			1.047	1.006	0.992	0.978	0.986	0.985	0.987	0.977	0.967	0.971
1983	0.968	0.960	0.956	0.929	0.921	0.917	0.906	0.898	0.889	0.883	0.876	0.871
1984	0.872	0.865	0.859	0.834	0.828	0.823	0.825	0.808	0.804	0.793	0.788	0.798
1985	0.783	0.769	0.752	0.716	0.708	0.704	0.707	0.703	0.704	0.701	0.695	0.693
1986	0.689	0.683	0.681	0.665	0.662	0.663	0.667	0.662	0.654	0.652	0.638	0.632
1987	0.626	0.620	0.616	0.597	0.596	0.596	0.597	0.593	0.588	0.580	0.573	0.574
1988	0.574	0.568	0.562	0.573	0.531	0.525	0.524	0.507	0.500	0.485	0.478	0.474
1989	0.465	0.454	0.448	0.423	0.414	0.409	0.408	0.404	0.395	0.384	0.372	0.369
1990	0.361	0.353	0.339	0.300	0.288	0.283	0.282	0.269	0.258	0.248	0.251	0.252
1991	0.249	0.242	0.237	0.222	0.218	0.213	0.215	0.213	0.208	0.204	0.199	0.198
1992	0.199	0.193	0.189	0.171	0.167	0.167	0.171	0.171	0.166	0.162	0.164	0.168
1993	0.179	0.171	0.167	0.156	0.152	0.153	0.156	0.151	0.146	0.147	0.148	0.146
1994	0.151	0.144	0.141	0.128	0.124	0.124	0.129	0.124	0.121	0.120	0.119	0.114
1995	0.114	0.107	0.102	0.091	0.087	0.085	0.091	0.085	0.080	0.085	0.085	0.079
1996	0.083	0.078	0.073	0.066	0.063	0.063	0.067	0.062	0.057	0.057	0.057	0.053
1997	0.053	0.049	0.046	0.040	0.036	0.032	0.032	0.026	0.021	0.019	0.019	0.016
1998	0.019	0.014	0.011									

APPENDIX # 2

Taper relief for capital gains tax purposes (see chapter 6)

Non-business assets

Number of complete years asset owned after April 5, 1998	taper * relief	% of gain chargeable
0	0	100
1	0	100
2	0	100
3	5	95
4	10	90
5	15	85
6	20	80
7	25	75
8	30	70
9	35	65
10	40	60

* If you owned the asset before March 17, 1998 you will be given one bonus year of ownership if you sold it after April 5, 1998.

3

Car and car fuel benefits – tax year to April 5, 2002

CAR

1.   The assessable amount is based on the 'price' of the car which is the list price at the time the car was first registered plus the price of extras.

2.   Where the 'price' exceeds £80,000 the 'price' used is restricted to £80,000.

3.   The assessable amount is 35% of the 'price' of the car if it is under 4 years old at the end of the tax year and business mileage is less than 2,500.

4.   The percentage in 3. is reduced to 25% of the 'price' of the car if business mileage exceeds 2,499 but is less than 18,000, and to

15% of the 'price' of the car if business mileage is at least 18,000 miles.

5. For a car which is 4 or more years old at the end of the tax year the percentages under 4. (or 3. if applicable) are reduced by one-quarter.

Car Fuel Benefits (Petrol)

	2001/2002
	£
Up to 1400cc	1,930
1401 – 2000cc	2,460
Over 2000cc	3,620

Car Fuel Benefits (Diesel)

	2001/2002
	£
Up to 2000cc	2,460
Over 2000cc	3,620

APPENDIX 4

Changes to car and car fuel benefits from April 2002

AS announced in the 2000 Budget, from April 6, 2002 the present regime outlined in Appendix 3 will be abolished. A new regime will be introduced aimed at:

- removing any incentive to drive unnecessary extra business miles,
- giving company car drivers and their employers a tax incentive to choose more fuel-efficient cars, and
- encouraging manufacturers to produce cars with lower carbon dioxide emissions.

From April 6, 2002, the company car tax charge will be based on a percentage of the car's price graduated according to the level of the car's carbon dioxide (CO_2) emissions. The charge will be 15% of the car's price for cars emitting 165 grams per kilometre (g/km) CO_2, then rise in 1% steps for every additional 5g/km over 165g/km. The maximum charge will be on 35% of the car's price.

Cars with no CO$_2$ emissions figure

Cars first registered after January 1, 1998 that have no approved CO$_2$ emissions figure, perhaps because they have been imported from outside the European Community (EC), will be assessed on engine size as follows:

Engine Size (cc)	Percentage of car's price charged to tax
0–1400	15%
1401 – 2,000	25%
2001 and more	35%

If the car is one without a cylinder capacity, it will be taxed on 15% of the car's price (if it is a car propelled solely by electricity), and 35% in all other cases (rotary engine cars).

Older cars

It appears that it will not be possible to gain reliable sources of information on fuel emissions for cars manufacturer before January 1, 1998, therefore these cars will be taxed according to their engine size as follows:

Engine Size (cc)	Percentage of car's price charged to tax
0–1400	15%
1401–2,000	22%
2001 and more	32%

In addition

- The existing business mileage discounts will be abolished when the new system starts.
- Age-related discounts will be abolished at the same time.
- Diesel cars will be subjected to a 3% supplement in recognition of their higher emissions of pollutants that

damage local air quality. But this will not take the maximum charge above the current maximum of 35% of the car's price.

As stated above the starting point for calculating the tax payable remains the car's price. The charge will be based on a percentage of that price graduated according to the car's carbon dioxide (CO_2) emissions measured in grams per kilometre (g/km). The exact CO_2 figure will be rounded down to the nearest 5g/km for company car tax purposes.

Cars emitting CO_2 at or below a specified level will be taxed on 15% of the car's price (the usual minimum charge). This qualifying level of CO_2 emissions will gradually be reduced over the first few years of the reform. The level of CO_2 emissions qualifying for the minimum charge will be as follows:

2002–03	165g/km CO_2
2003–04	155g/km CO_2
2004–05	145g/km CO_2

Index